Movies as Politics

NATIONAL UNIVERSITY
LIBRARY   SACRAMENTO

Jonathan Rosenbaum

UNIVERSITY OF CALIFORNIA PRESS
BERKELEY / LOS ANGELES / LONDON

Copyright notices for articles in this volume appear on page 361.

University of California Press
Berkeley and Los Angeles, California

University of California Press
London, England

Copyright © 1997 by The Regents of the University of
California

Library of Congress Cataloging-in-Publication Data
Rosenbaum, Jonathan.
    Movies as politics / Jonathan Rosenbaum.
        p.   cm.
    Includes bibliographical references and index.
    ISBN 0-520-20614-2 (alk. paper).
    ISBN 0-520-20615-0 (pbk. alk. paper)
    1. Motion pictures—Political aspects.   I. Title.
PN195.9.P6R67 1997
791.43'658—dc20   96-9916
                                          CIP

Printed in the United States of America

1 2 3 4 5 6 7 8 9
The paper used in this publication is both acid-free and
totally chlorine-free (TCF). It meets the minimum
requirements of American Standard for Information
Sciences—Permanence of Paper for Printed
Library Materials, ANSI Z39.48-1984 ♾

To Samuel Fuller

Contents

Acknowledgments

For diverse kinds of help on these pieces over the years, I'm especially grateful to Thom Andersen, Raymond Bellour, Cecilia Burokas, Ernest Callenbach, Richard Combs, Richard Corliss, Margaret Davis, Eduardo De Gregorio, Nataša Durovicǒvá, David Ehrenstein, Pamela Falkenberg, Sandy Flitterman-Lewis, Carolyn Fireside, Penelope Houston, Richard T. Jameson, Kitry Krause, Bill Krohn, Michael Lenehan, Lorenzo Mans, Tom Milne, Laura Molzhan, Marco Müller, Richard Peña, John Pym, Bérénice Reynaud, Mehrnaz Saeed-Vafa, Gavin Smith, Alison True, Michael Walsh, and Melinda Ward. For more recent help on this book, I'd like to thank Edward Dimendberg, Bernard Eisenschitz, Tom Gunning, Kent Jones, Adrian Martin, James Naremore, Gilberto Perez, Yuval Taylor, Alan Williams, and the John Simon Guggenheim Memorial Foundation.

How to Live in Air Conditioning

A feeling of having no choice is becoming more and more widespread in American life, and particularly among successful people, who are supposedly free beings. On a concrete plane, the lack of choice is often a depressing reality. In national election years, you are free to choose between Johnson and Goldwater or Johnson and Romney or Reagan, which is the same as choosing between a Chevrolet and a Ford—there is a marginal difference in styling. Just as in American hotel rooms you can decide whether or not to turn on the air conditioner (that is *your* business), but you cannot open the window.

—*Mary McCarthy,* Vietnam, *1967*

I await the end of cinema with optimism.

—*Jean-Luc Godard,* Cahiers du cinéma, *1965*

Thirty years later, both these general sentiments describe an impasse in American life that is vividly reflected in the movies we see and the ways that we see them. If the range of cultural choices apparently available at any given time merits some correlation with the range of political choices, it is also true that Godard's optimistic apocalypse heralds a new scale of values, though we don't yet know enough about these to be able to judge them with any confidence. Whether we condemn or applaud the prospect, a first priority might be a simple evaluation of where we are.

It probably isn't being presumptuous to assume that, in one way or another, as we near the century's end, everyone reading these lines is awaiting the end of *some* kind of cinema, either optimistically or pessimistically. Whatever name or interpretation we give to this climate, we all feel that something is in the process of ending—unless we feel that it has ended already. Something is also in the process of beginning; but whatever we choose to call it, I don't think we can call it cinema in the old sense. The rapid spread of movies on video, the astronomical escalation of movie advertising, the depletion of government support for film preservation or new independent work (never very large to begin with), the return to a system of theater monopolies and the concomitant phasing out of independent exhibition (which allows for such alternative fare as art films and midnight movies)—what amounts, in short, to the junking of an already precarious film culture in the interests of short-term financial gains for big business—suggest a historical period being sealed off, so that the past isn't only another country but a different planet, a different language, a different set of aspirations. Like Mary McCarthy, we can learn this new language well or badly and say all kinds of different things with it, but we can't use it to lead us back to cinema in the old sense (cinema, let us say, that was still on speaking terms with the era of Griffith, Murnau, and Stroheim). That's a window that has been nailed shut, and unless we break through the glass—destroy the institutions and the technology that separate us from the past—we have to get used to living in air conditioning.

■

With only a few modifications, the above was written over a decade ago— first for a lecture at the Rotterdam Film Festival's Market in January 1985, then for an article published in *Sight and Sound* the following summer. The fact that much of what I said then still seems applicable suggests not so much a protracted death rattle for cinema as a certain freezing over of film history itself, at least as it's usually being recounted.

I'm writing now in the fall of 1995, when the recent number one box office hit is SEVEN, a stylish, "metaphysical" serial-killer movie whose designer grimness can be said to carry a certain ideological comfort: if mankind is hopelessly blighted and evil is both omnipresent and triumphant—expressionist notions virtually carried over like dress styles from TAXI DRIVER (1976) and BLADE RUNNER (1982)—then it stands to reason that political change isn't even worth hoping for and that legislation designed to make millionaires richer while increasing the suffering of the homeless is the only "realistic" kind we can contemplate. Yet if we accept this made-to-order postulate, we have to overlook the fact that SEVEN originally had an even grimmer ending than it does now—an ending revised as soon as preview audiences objected. We have to consider, in short, that the ideological demands made of entertainment are no more contradictory or foolish than those made of government or the news in general, and that these are usually based on short-term guesses about what makes us feel good, not long-term investments in what might make us stronger or wiser.

After all, only a few years ago, during the Gulf War, there was another serial-killer movie that helped to create the vogue for SEVEN: THE SILENCE OF THE LAMBS. What seemed horrific to me at the time about the specious claim that this movie was teaching us something important about evil or psychosis or violence was that it was being made just as we were gleefully devastating a country and people already oppressed by a dictator—mainly, it seemed, for the sake of holding a weapons trade fair. So our fascination with one individual, Hannibal Lecter, killing without compunction, may have betrayed a certain unconscious narcissism on our part; in fact, that crazy shrink had nothing on us. Moreover, our censored war news at the time also focused mainly on one demonic individual, Saddam Hussein, and clearly all the corpses we and he were creating were made to seem secondary. This was star politics with a vengeance, and when Anthony Hopkins was eventually handed an Oscar, it was oddly evocative of the standing ovation George Bush received in Congress.

A few months later, TERMINATOR 2: JUDGMENT DAY brought back THE TER-MINATOR's former villain, the Arnold Schwarzenegger robot, this time as a hero—neatly echoing Bush's own reversals of policy (albeit in the opposite direction) toward Saddam in the Gulf and, two years earlier, Noreiga in Panama. In all three cases, the euphoria of watching a mean machine plow through everything in its path—whether this was Panama City, Baghdad, or an American freeway—clearly mattered more than whether the machine happened to be a Good Guy or a Bad Guy.

In all three of the examples offered above, there's an effort to link a recent movie with events that are contemporary with it—signaling one of the several polemical approaches to film and politics taken in this book, one that partially echoes the readings given to certain movies I saw as a child in my 1980 memoir, *Moving Places* (2d ed., 1995). It could be argued, of course, that because neither Thomas Harris's best-selling novel nor Jonathan Demme's movie is in any way inspired by the Gulf War, my juxtaposition of that war with the reception of THE SILENCE OF THE LAMBS simply and arbitrarily imposes my own political program on this material. "Keep your politics out of your reviews," wrote an irritated reader in 1993 (as if he or I had a choice in the matter). "It'll destroy your credibility." But keeping politics out of movie reviews, I'd argue, is precisely what makes it easy to cheer and celebrate such CNN "movies"—or "turkey shoots"—as OPERATION DESERT STORM and WAR IN THE GULF.

■

Indeed, a central issue in this book is how closely our news resembles our so-called entertainment and vice versa; and what sort of relation either sphere bears to reality sometimes turns out to be my main subject. Those who question my description of STAR WARS as "a guiltless celebration of unlimited warfare" may want to consider that my piece was written well before that movie title was used to identify a U.S. military weapons program. It might be argued that this proves nothing apart from Ronald Reagan's fondness for movie references, but my main purpose here and elsewhere in this book is to argue that what is designed to make people feel good at the movies has a profound relation to how and what they think and feel about the world around them.

■

Like my previous collection, *Placing Movies: The Practice of Film Criticism* (1995), this volume contains reviews and essays written since the early 70s, but on this occasion I have sought to place them all within a political context—a context of placing movies politically, which also means describing one particular version of what movies are and can be in the 90s. (Movies as politics also generally means movies as history, including an effort to deal with the present historically.) It entails looking not just at the political implications of many different kinds of films as "statements" and processes in themselves but also at the political aspects of what might be called the challenge of cinema—its aesthetic forms, its narrative tactics, and its patterns of production, promotion, distribution, exhibition, and reception. About two-thirds of the pieces here first appeared in the *Chicago Reader,* and though some have been revised and updated, I've retained local references whenever they seemed relevant, trusting that non-Chicagoans will still be able to follow the drift.

A touchstone throughout my career has been George Orwell's "Politics and the English Language," an essay that draws explicit and useful links between writing style and political thought (or its absence). In my first section, I seek to extend this mode of perception by discussing the political implications of film form as well as film style. To some extent, this approach runs through the remainder of the book; it can even be found in my study of Bresson's LANCELOT DU LAC, where it may seem least apparent. For it is my belief that formal procedures—by shaping and ordering our perceptions, by determining how we engage with art as well as life—are always grounded in political decisions of one kind or another, whether we choose to recognize them or not. Contrary to the debilitating American idea that politics are only a matter of elections (and therefore something to be avoided), accepting or rejecting the status quo when it comes to filmgoing is already a political decision in the most basic way, and deserves to be treated as such. For that matter, honoring film as an art or regarding it basically as a form of light entertainment is very much a political issue—though many would call it just a matter of "taste"— and I suspect that my own bias for the former attitude over the latter lies at the root of what makes many of my other positions controversial to some.

How, indeed, do the roles played by sound and image in relation to one another—an important concern in my piece on LANCELOT—function politically? In several ways, I would argue. Though formalist analysis often avoids this, it seems to me that formal innovation is often a matter of finding ways to discover and articulate new kinds of content, to say things that otherwise couldn't be said, find things that otherwise couldn't be found. This is only speculation, but it seems to me that many of Bresson's hallmarks as a filmmaker—such as his uses of offscreen sounds to replace images and the sense found in all his films of souls in hiding, of buried identities and emotions— might be traceable in part to his nine months (1940–1941) as a POW in a German concentration camp and his subsequent experience of the German occupation of France. I'm thinking not only of his masterpiece about the French resistance, A MAN ESCAPED (1956)—where the sounds of the world outside the hero's prison cell create as well as embody his very notion of freedom—but also of LES DAMES DU BOIS DE BOULOGNE (1945), made during the Occupation itself. Speaking recently to the film historian Bernard Eisenschitz, Jean-Luc Godard provocatively called LES DAMES the "only" film of the French Resistance, and in chapter 3A of his video series HISTOIRE(S) DU CINEMA, he cites Elina Labourdette's penultimate line in the film, "Je lutte," to make a similar point. Such an interpretation can of course be debated, but it seems to me a far more fruitful approach to Bresson's style to see it growing out of a concrete and material historical experience than to treat it as a timeless, transcendent, and ultimately mysterious expression of abstract spirituality.

■

Responding to Theodor Adorno's critique of Stravinsky, Milan Kundera writes in *Testaments Betrayed*:

> What irritates me in Adorno is his short-circuit method that, with a fearsome facility, links works of art to political (sociological) causes, consequences, or meanings; extremely nuanced ideas (Adorno's musicological knowledge is admirable) thereby lead to extremely impoverished conclusions; in fact, given that an era's political tendencies are always reducible to just two opposing tendencies, a work of art necessarily ends up being classified as either progressive or reactionary; and since reaction is evil, the inquisition can start the trial proceedings.*

I don't know if this argument is fair to Adorno (I suspect it may be guilty of the kind of mechanical critique it's decrying), but I'd prefer to think it doesn't apply to any of the essays here, even though the issue of "political correctness" might be raised—indeed, has been raised—in relation to some of them. The novelist Paul Auster, a former acquaintance in Paris in the mid-70s, suggested when I ran into him at a film festival two decades later that PC was the gist of my objection to SMOKE in "The World According to Harvey and Bob," after explaining that he had fought a battle of his own (successful in his case) to prevent Miramax from recutting the film.

The problem with a term like PC is that it's no more neutral than the social realities it's supposed to be grappling with. To my mind, there's a PC of the right—in which conservatives like Clarence Thomas and O. J. Simpson both potentially figure as affirmative action beneficiaries—as well as a PC of the left, and in both cases it generally represents a rejection of real politics for the sake of symbolic politics, a politics of representation in which fantasy "role models" usually serve to obfuscate and avoid real issues. In the cases of SMOKE and THE GLASS SHIELD, where I'm chiefly interested in the processes

---

* Translated from the French by Linda Asher (New York: HarperCollins, 1995), 91.

by which both films got defined as well as judged in the mainstream, THE GLASS SHIELD—which shows its black hero committing perjury against another black man—is surely even more "politically incorrect" than SMOKE. (I'm reminded of the objection I once heard made to Danny Glover at a Chicago screening of Burnett's previous feature, TO SLEEP WITH ANGER, for not playing a suitable "role model" for black children in that film—a remark that provoked his understandable ire.) Indeed, my objection to William Hurt and Harvey Keitel in SMOKE is precisely that they *do* provide fanciful white role models and feel-good PC figureheads rather than characters designed to provoke any deep understanding of the complexity of American race relations.*

■

As a critic, I tend to deal with certain aspects of the mainstream from an outsider's position and, conversely, to look at alternative forms of filmmaking from a mainstream position. In the interests of both acknowledging and challenging the usual ghetto boundaries that inform our reception of films, I have highlighted this dichotomy by placing most of my treatments of well-known and recent Hollywood movies in the middle of the book. In a couple of cases, I've even included non-Hollywood pictures in this section if the notion of a Hollywood actor (Keitel in THE PIANO) or a Hollywood studio (Disney, which owns Miramax, the distributor of SMOKE and THE GLASS SHIELD) remains operative in how a picture is received.

A related dichotomy in our film culture, between the marketplace and academic film study, is the central concern of both of the book review essays included—one on musicals in the first section, the other on two collections of articles in the third section. One can also find an impulse recurring throughout the book to stage certain "shotgun marriages" in relation to specific topics: STAR WARS seen in light of some of the political films of Jean-Luc Godard, French serials by Louis Feuillade and Jacques Rivette, a Gypsy musical seen in relation to Hollywood musicals, the operations of chance in films by Robert Altman and Rob Tregenza, and so on.

Recognizing that some readers are reluctant to read about movies they haven't seen—though also realizing that maintaining silence about unavailable films helps to keep them unavailable—I've placed more emphasis in this volume on movies that are widely known, while hoping that some readers engaged by this sandwich filling will be moved to try my bread slices as well, part of which propose a much wider definition of "the cinema" than the mass media generally allow (including even two videos in "Alternate Histories," although paradoxically both of these are concerned with cinema). An earlier

---

*For a devastating critique and wholly convincing analysis of such characters, see Benjamin De Mott's indispensable *The Trouble with Friendship: Why Americans Can't Think Straight About Race* (New York: Atlantic Monthly Press, 1995).

book of mine * is devoted to surveying various North American and European independent filmmakers; this one revives part of that concern, and even extends it to such non-Hollywood outposts as Asia and Africa, but I have still tried to keep much of this book within hailing distance of more common reference points.

"Alternate Histories"—a subgrouping of five final essays, partially predicated on the notion that the future of cinema depends to some extent on our acquaintance with its past—is devoted specifically to adventures in research, which for me has always comprised a major part of criticism. (This is at once the most tentative and the most utopian section in the book.) Another major part, mainly discernible in more recent pieces, is an effort to use films as a way to speak about other things in our society: racism, xenophobia, targeting, tribalism, feminism, illness, urban social engineering, postmodernism, sexual obsession, and class divisions, among several other topics.

■

Unlike my books *Moving Places* and *Placing Movies, Movies as Politics* has no explicit autobiographical agenda, but readers will see that autobiography frequently plays an important role in my critical methodology; it is even, I would argue, central to its politics. One reason for forcing myself into the picture is quite simply to make the criticism more *usable* by contextualizing my positions and showing where they come from—refusing to resort to hidden agendas, and respecting the reader's right to disagree. Another reason is that I believe movies are potentially important enough to be tested in relation to life, not simply accepted as loose approximations or escapist alternatives— a point made in my considerations of MISSISSIPPI BURNING, SAFE, CRUMB, and BLOOD IN THE FACE, among other pieces.

The reviews and essays included here were written between 1972 and 1995, and some readers may conclude that the pieces that come closest to being formalist, such as those on Bresson and Altman, were written toward the beginning of this period, when I was still living in Europe (Paris and London) and arguably had fewer overt political ties to my immediate surroundings. One of the most interesting political lessons I learned from my years abroad (1969–1977), however, was that sensitivity to formal issues doesn't necessarily entail an avoidance of political issues. To put it bluntly, most of the critics I knew in Paris and London who were sophisticated about formal issues were communists, most often party members, while many of their stateside leftist counterparts were more likely to be philistines about such matters. Adapting some of the formal perceptions of European leftists to

---

* Happily, *Film: The Front Line 1983* (along with David Ehrenstein's subsequent 1984 volume in the same series) is still in print and can be ordered directly from Arden Press, P.O. Box 418, Denver, CO 80201 (phone, 303-697-6766) for $10.95; postage is free on prepaid orders.

Anglo-American idioms has probably always been an important part of my contribution as a critic; see, for instance, my remarks in this book about DO THE RIGHT THING, PLAYTIME, LATCHO DROM, SAFE, OUT 1, and the films of Mike Leigh and Cy Endfield.

■

Are there times when one's aesthetic responses and one's politics are in conflict? Certainly, and some of the reviews in this book—notably those of SCHINDLER'S LIST, REDS, PULP FICTION, LA MAMAM ET LA PUTAIN, and SOLARIS—are devoted in part to trying to pinpoint and clarify those conflicts. Hardly anyone can claim to be reducible to his or her political positions at all times, especially at the movies, but the moments when conflicts or contradictions arise usually prove to be highly instructive. Part of my ambition in these essays is to create a mode of inquiry in which honesty about such matters becomes both possible and desirable.

Case in point: Writing about Michael Wadleigh's WOODSTOCK in 1970, I decided that the movie was really the counterculture's equivalent to Leni Riefenstahl's TRIUMPH OF THE WILL, and mentioned this conceit in print several times afterward. Although I liked the film, it seemed worth tweaking some of the things I liked about it: its epic shape and canvas, its teeming crowds, its awestruck euphoria, its adoring low-angles of charismatic performers, plus the fact that it was a film record of an event planned in part for the purpose of making a movie. My point was mainly aesthetic, but I wanted the ideological ramifications to give the reader some pause. Then, after noticing, when WOODSTOCK was rereleased in 1994, that many of my colleagues were making the same comparison, I started to wonder if for some of them the similarity was more ideological than aesthetic—especially when they compared WOODSTOCK unfavorably with GIMME SHELTER, a film I've always disliked politically *and* aesthetically for its self-serving "critique" of the counterculture. A comparison that for me in the 70s and 80s was an ironic form of praise was used by others in the 90s as a straight putdown.

How political was WOODSTOCK in 1970? When I saw it at the Cannes film festival, Wadleigh dedicated the film to the four students killed by National Guardsmen at Kent State only five days earlier; when the screening was over, he stood by the exit doors and passed out black armbands. I took one myself, but two days later some boutiques in Cannes started selling similar armbands. What had seemed political on Saturday had become a sort of marketing device by Monday; it was a key early lesson for me in movies as politics. And the next twenty-five years provided an education outlined in this book.

—J.R.
December 1995

Part One

The Politics of Form

Language, Representation, Narrative

Say the Right Thing
(DO THE RIGHT THING)

It's readily apparent by now that Spike Lee's DO THE RIGHT THING is something of a Rorschach test as well as an ideological litmus test, and not only for critics. It's hard to think of another movie from the past several years that has elicited as much heated debate about what it says and what it means, and it's heartening as well as significant that the picture stirring up all this talk is not a standard Hollywood feature. Because the arguments that are currently being waged about the film are in many ways as important as the film itself, and a lot more important than the issues being raised by other current releases, it seems worth looking at them again in closer detail. Ultimately most of these questions have something to do with language and the way we're accustomed to talking about certain things—race relations and violence as well as movies in general.

We all tend to assume that no matter how imprecise or impure our language may be, it still enables us to tell the truth if we use it carefully. Yet the discourse surrounding DO THE RIGHT THING suggests that at times this assumption may be overly optimistic—that in fact our everyday language has become encrusted with so many assumptions that it may now be inadequate for describing or explaining what is right in front of us.

Consider, just for starters, the use of the word "violence" in connection with Lee's film. Some people have argued that the movie espouses violence, celebrates violence, treats violence as inevitable, or shows violence as therapeutic. (At one of the first local preview screenings of the movie, in Hyde Park, a paddy wagon was parked in front of the theater before the movie even started.) All these statements refer to instances of violence that occur toward the end of the movie, but none of them appears to be referring to all of these instances, which include the smashing of a radio with a baseball bat by the pizza parlor proprietor, Sal (Danny Aiello); a fight between Sal and the owner of the radio, Radio Raheem (Bill Nunn); the killing of Radio Raheem by white policemen who arrive on the scene to break up the fight; the throwing of a garbage can through the front window of the pizzeria by Mookie (Spike Lee), a black delivery boy who works for Sal; the subsequent looting and burning of the pizzeria by several nonwhites in the neighborhood; and the putting out of the fire by firemen, who knock down some people with the force of the water hoses. To make this list complete, one might also include the incident that sets off all the subsequent violent events: Radio Raheem entering the pizzeria after it's officially closed for the day with his ghetto blaster turned up to full volume, accompanied by two angry blacks who have previously been turned away from Sal's establishment for making disturbances—Buggin' Out (Giancarlo Esposito) and Smiley (Roger Guenveur Smith).

No one appears to be arguing that the movie treats *all* of these events positively, so there must be an underlying assumption that not all of these events are equally violent. The "real" violence, according to this discourse, turns out to be the destruction of white property (the throwing of the garbage can, the looting, and the burning)—not the creation of a disturbance (the blasting of the boom box), the destruction of black property (the smashing of the boom box), the fight between the two characters (Sal and Radio Raheem), or the destruction of a human life (the killing of Radio Raheem).

I don't think that the people making these arguments automatically or necessarily assume that a pizzeria is worth more than a human life, but I do think that our everyday use of the word "violence" tends to foster such an impression. There are times when our language becomes so overloaded with ideological assumptions that, however we use certain terms, they wind up speaking more than we do.

■

Stepping outside the immediate context of the film for a minute, consider the appropriateness of terms like "black" and "white"—terms that we've somehow managed to arrive at by default rather than through any sharpening precision in our use of language. The evidence that our senses give us is that so-called white people aren't white at all, but varying gradations of brown and pink, while most so-called black people in the United States are varying gradations of brown and tan. Thus the skin tones in question aren't nearly as oppositional as the words that we use make them out to be. (It could be argued that capitalizing "black" only increases the confusion by further validating the concept behind the term as opposed to the visual reality.) A major reason that "Negro" ceased to be an acceptable word during the 60s was the belief that it was a "white" word and concept; unfortunately, "black" is a term that makes sense in a racial context only in relation to "white," and if "white" is itself a questionable term, "black" or "Black" only compounds the muddle. (Consider also the consequences of this metaphysical mischief when one adds to the discussion Hispanics and Orientals, who are commonly regarded as neither white nor black, and Native Americans, who are arbitrarily designated in our mythology as red.)

I'm not arguing that we should go back to terms like "Negroes" and "Caucasians," or that an arcane term like "colored people" is any better than "black" (it's often been pointed out that "whites" are "colored," too). The point is that we've reached an impasse in the language, and it ensures a certain amount of metaphysical and ideological confusion regardless of what we say.

■

So far I've been speaking exclusively of verbal language. When it comes to the conventions of film language and what's known as the cinematic apparatus as a whole—the institution that regulates the production, distribution, exhibition, consumption, and discussion of movies—we may be in even deeper trouble, because the movie-related conventions that we take for granted aren't nearly as self-evident.

To start with one very general example of this, consider the way that most TV critics talk about movies. If the movies released this year were ten times better than they actually are, *or* if they were ten times worse, the discourse of these critics would be more or less the same, because the critics' functions in relation to this output would be identical. A major effect of this kind of reviewing is to keep the movie market flowing and to make the offerings of every given week seem important—a process that usually entails forgetting that last week's offerings were made to seem equally important. The critics' mission is not to educate us about the movies but to guide us toward some and warn us off others. Movies are either worth seeing or not worth seeing, and every week there are a couple of each.

Another example, this one more to the point: Many critics have commented that the expression "do the right thing" means something different to every character in Spike Lee's movie, but not very many have agreed about whether the movie itself presents its own version of what "the right thing" is or might be. Many people believe that Mookie's throwing of a garbage can through the pizzeria window is Spike Lee's version of "the right thing," but they arrive at this belief through a passive acceptance of certain movie conventions.

Spike Lee plays Mookie himself, and even though everyone knows that

Lee doesn't deliver pizza for a living there's an understandable impulse to interpret his role as that of the hero or protagonist, according to the usual conventions governing writer-directors who double as actors (Woody Allen, for instance). In addition, there's a temptation to interpret the filmmaker's presence in the role metaphorically and autobiographically; for example, Mookie works for a white boss, and one could argue that Lee depends on "white"-run studios for the distribution of his movies (even though he insists on retaining "final cut," which gives Lee an autonomy that Mookie lacks). An even more basic assumption is that all commercial movies have heroes and villains and therefore take relatively unambiguous stands about what's "the right thing" and what's "the wrong thing" in any given conflict.

But what if DO THE RIGHT THING doesn't have any heroes or villains? What if it doesn't propose any particular action as being the right thing? What if, in fact, it postulates—as I believe it does—that given the divisions that already exist in the social situation the film depicts, it's not even possible for any character to "do the right thing" in relation to every other character? If the language that we speak is such that it can only express relative truths rather than absolute truths, it isn't difficult to extrapolate from this that the cinematic apparatus that we take for granted is similarly tainted.

■

Even some of the most intelligent commentary about the movie suffers from certain built-in assumptions about it, which stem from unacknowledged assumptions about movies in general. Terrence Rafferty's review in the July 24 issue of *The New Yorker,* for example, which manages to avoid or refute much of the nonsense that has been circulating about the film elsewhere, still falls into the trap of imputing certain motives to Spike Lee that exist outside the film's own frame of reference.

"Raheem certainly doesn't deserve his fate," Rafferty argues, "but without [Sal's] inflammatory racial epithet"—Sal calls Raheem a "nigger" at the peak of his rage—"Lee would have a tough time convincing any audience that Sal deserves his." Rafferty is assuming here that Lee *wants* to convince the audience that Sal "deserves" to have his pizzeria burn down—an inflammatory accusation whose truth seems less than self-evident to me.

Rafferty continues with a string of rhetorical questions:

Does Lee really believe that . . . any white person, pushed hard enough, will betray his contempt for blacks? Does he believe, for that matter, the tired notion that anger brings out people's *true* feelings? And does he also think that lashing out at Sal because he's white and owns a business and is therefore a representative of the racist structure of the American economy is a legitimate image of "fighting the power"? If you can buy all these axioms smuggled in from outside the lively and particular world this movie creates, then DO THE RIGHT THING is the great movie that so many reviewers have claimed it is. But if you think—as I do—that not every individual is a racist, that angry words are no more revealing than any other kind, and that trashing a small business is a woefully imprecise image of fighting the power, then you have to conclude that Spike Lee has taken a wild shot and missed the target.

This sounds like impeccable reasoning, *if* one accepts the either/or premise and believes that Lee is smuggling these dubious axioms into his movie. But in fact the axioms and the smuggling both belong exclusively to Rafferty. The movie shows certain events happening and certain steps leading up to them; these events include one supposedly levelheaded pizzeria owner blowing his cool and a group of angry blacks trashing his establishment. At no point does the movie either show or argue any of the three axioms cited by Rafferty; at most, one might intuit that some of the film's angry black characters associate their trashing of the pizzeria with "fighting the power," but there's nothing in the film that suggests that they're right about this; nor does the film say that Sal is exposing his "true feelings" or that Sal is the equivalent of "any white person." Indeed, the movie takes great pains to show that the characters who tend to talk the most about "fighting the power" in less hysterical situations—Radio Raheem, Buggin' Out, and Smiley—are relatively myopic and misguided, and are seen as such by their neighbors; it also takes pains to establish Sal as a complex, multifaceted character who can't easily be reduced to platitudes.

Rafferty claims that one must accept questionable axioms to find DO THE RIGHT THING a great movie. I would argue, on the contrary, that the film's distinction largely rests on its freedom from such axioms—a freedom that is part and parcel of Lee's pluralistic view of all his characters. This view simultaneously implies that every character has his or her reasons and that none of them is simply and unequivocally right. To seize upon any of these characters or reasons and to privilege them over the others is to return us to the paradigm of cowboys and Indians, heroes and villains. We've lived with this either/or grid for so long, it's probably inevitable that some spectators will apply it even on that rare occasion, such as this one, when a filmmaker has the courage and insight to do without it.

In place of either/or, Lee gives us both/and—epitomized by the two quotations that close the movie from Martin Luther King, Jr. (condemning violence), and from Malcolm X (describing situations when self-defense may be necessary). Some people have argued that Lee's refusal to choose between these statements proves that he's confused, but this argument only demonstrates how reductive either/or thinking usually turns out to be. The film's closing image is a photograph of King and Malcolm in friendly accord, not in opposition, and if the past of the civil rights movement teaches us anything at all about its future, then surely this future has a sizable stake in the legacies of both men. To view those legacies as complementary rather than oppositional is part of what Spike Lee's project is all about.

■

Let's look at Lee's pluralism at the point when it becomes most radical—when the character who is the closest thing in the movie to a villain (without actually being a villain) is placed in a position where the audience is most likely to agree with him. The character in question is Sal's son Pino (John Turturro), an unabashed racist who despises working in a mainly black neighborhood, which he refers to as "Planet of the Apes." ("I'm sick of niggers. . . . I don't like being around them; they're animals.") The moment in question is at the height of the pizzeria trashing, when the rioters are tearing Sal's establishment to shreds and raiding the cash register in a manic frenzy (certainly a far cry from anything one might call a heroic image). At this point the film cuts to a shot of Sal with his two sons watching from outside; Sal is screaming, "That's my place! That's my fucking place!" Then there's a cut to Pino watching the orgy of destruction with disgust and saying, "Fuckin' niggers."

It's easy enough to interpret this shot as the stock response of a mainly one-note character. But if one were to assume the vantage point of Pino and then select a single instant in the movie when his viewpoint came closest to being emotionally vindicated, or at least partially illustrated, for most people in the audience this would conceivably be the precise instant that Lee has chosen. For about two seconds, Pino is allotted the privilege—a relative privilege, not an absolute one—of saying the right thing.

■

Just as Pino is the closest thing in the movie to a villain, Mookie is the closest thing to a hero. He occupies the space and the relative prominence in the film that would normally be accorded to a hero, but in spite of his overall charisma, his actions and attitudes are far from heroic. As Lee himself remarked to Patrick McGavin and myself in an interview earlier this summer, "He wants to have a little bit of money in his pocket [and] do as little work as possible." (Some viewers have complained that few of the characters in the movie are shown working, apart from the cops, the Korean grocers, and the workers at the pizzeria; these viewers seem to have overlooked the fact that the film takes place on a Saturday.) Mookie's sister, Jade (Joie Lee), who helps to support him, and his Latino girlfriend, Tina (Rosie Perez), who feels neglected by him, both deride him constantly through the film for not living up to his responsibilities, which include concern and care for his infant son, Hector.

Mookie's two major interests appear to be money and baseball; and while he is the only character in the film who serves as a link between the black and white people in the neighborhood, no one in the movie seems to regard him as a role model—with the partial exception of Vito (Richard Edson), Sal's younger son, a relatively sweet-tempered but not especially strong character who regards Mookie somewhat as an older brother in preference to Pino (which further intensifies Pino's racial enmity). In comparison to his sister, Mookie seems utterly lacking in ambition, and although most of the people on the block seem to like him—Sal says that he regards him as a son, and both Da Mayor (Ossie Davis) and Mother Sister (Ruby Dee) show a parental concern for him—no one apart from Vito can be said to look up to him, and there's certainly no hint that Vito's support extends to Mookie's eventual act of violence.

The only decisive moment in the film when Mookie appears to act on behalf of the local residents rather than in his own private interests—discounting the interests of Sal and his sons and the local policemen, none of whom lives in the neighborhood—is when he sparks the riot by throwing the garbage can. But while Mookie clearly sets off the violence that follows, he doesn't participate in it, and there's no indication that he revels in the destruction either (which means the loss of his own job); near the end of the sequence, he can be seen sitting with his sister on the curb in front of the charred ruins, looking disconsolate rather than triumphant about what's happened. Nor can it be said that he is suddenly made into a hero by his one violent act; when Mookie is seen with Sal the following day haggling about money, there is nothing to suggest that he has grown or been changed by the experience of the previous night—his behavior is exactly the same as it was before the riot.

■

The two most insightful remarks I've encountered so far about DO THE RIGHT THING haven't appeared in print; they've come from phone conversations with two friends and fellow critics who happen to be, respectively, the Los Angeles and New York correspondents for *Cahiers du Cinéma,* Bill Krohn and Bérénice Reynaud. Krohn views the film itself as a conflict between discourses, an approach that he traces back to Jean-Luc Godard in films of the 60s like LA CHINOISE and *1 + 1* (the latter known in the United States as SYMPATHY FOR THE DEVIL), films that were similarly misunderstood twenty years ago because people assumed that the violent discourses they contained—from French Maoists in LA CHINOISE and from black radicals in *1 + 1*—were necessarily and unambiguously the views of Godard, rather than simply discourses that he was provocatively juxtaposing with other discourses. (Whether Lee has been directly influenced by Godard is a secondary issue, but it's worth noting that two unorthodox uses of editing in Lee's film are distinctly Godardian: Mookie's initial greeting of Tina with a kiss is shown twice in succession, and there's a similar doubling of the action, from two separate angles, when the garbage can goes through the pizzeria window.)

Bérénice Reynaud believes that the basic conflicts in the film are ethical rather than psychological—particularly the conflict experienced by Mookie that leads to his throwing of the garbage can. The shot that precedes this action is probably the most widely misunderstood in the film; people who think that Mookie's action seems to come out of nowhere may be thinking this because they're misreading what's happening in the shot. Immediately after the police cars leave the scene, carrying away Buggin' Out (who is visibly clubbed by a policeman as the car drives away) and the dead body of Radio Raheem, the camera pans slowly from right to left past a crowd of onlookers in front of Sal's pizzeria. The people in the street are horrified and enraged by what's just happened, and most of them—in fact, all of them who are speaking—are addressing Mookie, who is standing offscreen, in front of the pizzeria with Sal and his two sons.

In part because of the unrealistic and highly stylized nature of the shot—each character delivers a pithy comment in turn as the camera moves past him, rather like the TV interview with combat soldiers in FULL METAL JACKET—it's possible to misread the shot as a group of angry blacks who are simply addressing the camera. To be perfectly honest, I misread the shot in this way myself the first time I saw the film, although what the characters are saying is clearly addressed to Mookie: "Mookie, they killed him!" "It's murder!" and so on. The police are no longer around, and implicitly these characters are all asking Mookie what he's doing standing with the only white people in sight. Ethically speaking, they're all asking Mookie to do the right thing, and he responds accordingly.

But according to what has already been established in the film, there is no absolute or absolutely correct choice available to Mookie; whatever move he makes will at best be "right" for some of the film's characters and wrong for some of the others. He has been forced, in short, into an either/or position that falsely divides the world into heroes and villains—the world, in short, that most moviegoers seem to prefer.

If the audience members cannot think or feel their way into Mookie's position, and can't experience the challenge of those taunts about whom Mookie stands with, then Mookie's act of violence will seem rhetorical and contrived—an act that the film is imposing on the situation from outside to make a polemical point. But for any spectator who agrees to identify with Mookie and his ethical crisis, the moment assumes a certain tragedy—not a tragic inevitability, because Mookie could simply quit his job at this point rather than pick up the garbage can, but a tragic ethical impasse.

It's been reported that a major reason why DO THE RIGHT THING failed to win any prizes at the last Cannes film festival was the objection of Wim Wenders, the president of the jury, that Mookie didn't behave more like a hero. Wenders's implied critique is that Lee should have made Mookie into a role model, superior to every other character in the film—a character who would exalt the either/or principle, which would imply, in turn, that the world is as simple a place as most movies pretend that it is, where simple and unambiguous choices are possible. The world of Rambo, in short—a world that is, curiously enough, not normally accused of fostering and encouraging violence to the degree that Lee's film has been.

Ironically, it is the moment at which Mookie throws the garbage can that he comes closest to functioning as a Rambolike hero—and closest to demonstrating how false and reductive the notion of such simpleminded heroism can be in a world as cluttered, splintered, and confused as ours. If role models are needed, Martin Luther King, Jr., and Malcolm X seem much better choices—not to mention Mister Señor Love Daddy (Sam Jackson), the local disc jockey whose patter periodically serves as narration; his most important message on a very hot day is for all of the characters to cool off.

—Chicago *Reader,* August 4, 1989

Interruption as Style

Buñuel's THE DISCREET CHARM
OF THE BOURGEOISIE

REPORTER: Who are your
favorite characters in the movie?
BUÑUEL: The cockroaches.

—from an interview in Newsweek

"Once upon a time . . ." begins UN CHIEN ANDALOU, in mockery of a narrative form that it seeks to obliterate, and from this title onward, Buñuel's cinema largely comprises a search for an alternative form to contain his passions. After dispensing with plot entirely in UN CHIEN ANDALOU, L'AGE D'OR, and LAS HURDES, his first three films, and remaining inactive as a director for the next fifteen years (1932–1947), Buñuel has been wrestling ever since with the problem of reconciling his surrealistic and anarchistic reflexes to the logic of story lines. How does a sworn enemy of the bourgeoisie keep his identity while devoting himself to bourgeois forms in a bourgeois industry? Either by subverting these forms or by trying to adjust them to his own purposes; and much of the tension in Buñuel's work has come from the play between these two possibilities.

Buñuel can always tell a tale when he wants to, but the better part of his brilliance lies elsewhere. One never finds in his work that grace and economy of narration, that sheer pleasure in exposition, which informs the opening sequences of GREED, LA RÈGLE DU JEU, THE MAGNIFICENT AMBERSONS, REAR WINDOW, SANSHO DAYU, and AU HASARD, BALTHAZAR. On the contrary, Buñuel's usual impulse is to interrupt a narrative line whenever he can find an adequate excuse for doing so—a joke, ironic detail, or startling juxtaposition that deflects the plot's energies in another direction. A typical "Buñuel touch"—the "Last Supper" pose assumed by the beggars in VIRIDIANA—has only a parenthetical relation to the action, however significant it may be thematically. And lengthier intrusions, like the dream sequence in LOS OLVIDADOS, tend to detach themselves from their surroundings as independent interludes, anecdotes, or parables. For the greater part of his career, Buñuel's genius has mainly expressed itself in marginal notations and insertions. To my knowledge, his only previous attempt at an open narrative structure since 1932 has been LA VOIE LACTÉE—a picaresque religious (and antireligious) pageant, much indebted to Godard's WEEKEND, which came uncomfortably close to being all notations and no text, like a string of Sunday school jokes.

If LE CHARME DISCRET DE LA BOURGEOISIE registers as the funniest Buñuel film since L'AGE D'OR, probably the most relaxed *and* controlled film he has ever made, and arguably the first contemporary, global masterpiece to have come from France in the 70s, this is chiefly because he has arrived at a form that covers his full range, permits him to say anything—a form that literally and figuratively lets him get away with murder. One cannot exactly call his new work a bolt from the blue. But its remarkable achievement is to weld together an assortment of his favorite themes, images, and parlor tricks into a discourse that is essentially new. Luring us into the deceptive charms of narrative as well as those of his characters, he undermines the stability of both attractions by turning interruption into the basis of his art, keeping us aloft on the sheer exuberance of his amusement.

Seven years ago, Noël Burch observed that in LE JOURNAL D'UNE FEMME DE CHAMBRE, Buñuel had at last discovered Form—a taste and talent for plastic composition and a "musical" sense of the durations of shots and the "articulations between sequences"; more generally, "a rigorous compartmentalisation of the sequences, each of which follows its own carefully worked out, autonomous curve."* BELLE DE JOUR reconfirmed this discovery, but LE CHARME DISCRET announces still another step forward: at the age of seventy-two, Buñuel has finally achieved Style.

■

Six friends—three men and three women—want to have a meal together, but something keeps going wrong. Four of them arrive at the Sénéchals' country house for dinner, and are told by Mme Sénéchal that they've come a day early; repairing to a local restaurant, they discover that the manager has just died, his corpse laid out in an adjoining room—how can they eat *there*?—so they plan a future lunch date. But each successive engagement is torpedoed: either M. and Mme Sénéchal (Jean-Pierre Cassel and Stéphane Audran) are

* "Two Cinemas," *Moviegoer*, 3 (Summer 1966).

too busy making love to greet their guests, or the cavalry suddenly shows up at dinnertime between maneuvers, or the police raid the premises and arrest everyone. Don Raphael Acosta (Fernando Rey), Ambassador of Miranda—a mythical, campy South American republic resembling several countries, particularly Spain—arranges a secret rendezvous in his flat with Mme Thévenot (Delphine Seyrig), but M. Thévenot (Paul Frankeur) turns up at an inopportune moment. The three ladies—Mmes Sénéchal and Thévenot and the latter's younger sister, Florence (Bulle Ogier)—meet for tea, and the waiter regretfully announces that the kitchen is out of tea, coffee, alcohol, and everything else they try to order. Still other attempted get-togethers and disasters turn out to be dreams, or dreams of dreams. At one dinner party, the guests find themselves sitting on a stage before a restive audience, prompted with lines; another ends with Don Raphael, after a political quarrel, shooting his host; still another concludes with an unidentified group of men breaking in and machine-gunning the lot of them.

At three separate points in the film, including the final sequence, we see all six characters walking wordlessly down a road, somewhere between an unstated starting place and an equally mysterious destination—an image suggesting the continuation both of their class and of the picaresque narrative tradition that propels them forward. Yet if the previous paragraph reads like a plot summary, it is deceptive. The nature and extent of Buñuel's interruptions guarantee the virtual absence of continuous plot. But we remain transfixed as though we were watching one: the sustained charm and glamour of the six characters fool us, much as they fool themselves. Their myths, behavior, and appearance—a seductive, illusory surface—carry us (and them) through the film with a sense of unbroken continuity and logic, a consistency that the rest of the universe and nature itself seem to rail against helplessly. Despite every attempt at annihilation, the myths of the bourgeoisie and of conventional narrative survive and prevail, a certainty that Buñuel reconciles himself to by regarding it as the funniest thing in the world.

Interruptions, of course, are a central fact about modern life; as I write this in a friend's apartment, the phone has been ringing about once every two paragraphs. Using this sort of comic annoyance as a structural tool, Buñuel can shoot as many arrows as he wants into our complacencies about narrative, the characters' complacencies about themselves. He exercises this principle of disruption in a multitude of ways, in matters large and small: in the opening scene at the Sénéchals' house, Florence's dopey, indifferent, comic-strip face drifts irrelevantly into the foreground of a shot while other characters chatter about something else behind her, and similar displacements of emphasis abound everywhere.

Take the last attempted dinner. It begins with a red herring that leads us to suspect poisoning ("I prepared the soup with herbs from the garden"); the conversation is broken off for a cruel exchange with the maid about her age and broken engagement; and while M. Sénéchal demonstrates the correct method of carving lamb, Florence stubbornly insists on pursuing her deadpan astrological profile of Don Raphael. After the gang breaks in to shoot them all, our sense of their total demise—a Godardian image of overlapping corpses—is interrupted when we realize that Don Raphael has hidden under the dinner table, and is reaching for a piece of lamb. Still crouching under the table, he bites savagely into the meat—a comic-terrifying reminder of the dream in LOS OLVIDADOS—and is finished off by a final blast of gunfire. Lest we suppose that this is the last possible interruption, we next see Don Raphael waking up from his nightmare. He gets out of bed, goes into the kitchen, and opens the refrigerator to take out a plate of veal.

■

Every dream and interpolated story in the film carries some threat, knowledge, or certainty of death—the central fact that all six characters ignore, and their charm and elegance seek to camouflage. Ghosts of murder victims and other phantoms of guilt parade through these inserted tales, but the discreet style of the bourgeoisie, boxing them in dreams and dinner anecdotes, holds them forever in check. To some extent, Buñuel shares this discretion in his failure to allude to his native Spain even once in the dialogue, although the pomp and brutality of the Franco regime are frequently evoked. (The recurrent gag of a siren, jet plane, or another disturbance covering up a political declaration—a device familiar from Godard's MADE IN USA—acknowledges this sort of suppression.) But the secret of Buñuel's achieved style is balance, and for that he must lean more on irony—an expedient tactic of the bourgeoisie—than on the aggressions of the rebel classes; when he sought imbalance in L'AGE D'OR, the revolutionary forces had the upper edge. An essential part of his method is to pitch the dialogue and acting somewhere between naturalism and parody, so that no gag is merely a gag, and each commonplace line or gesture becomes a potential gag. Absurdity and elegance, charm and hypocrisy become indistinguishably fused.

Another form of resolution is hinted at in the treatment of a secondary character, Monsignor Dufour (Julien Bertheau), a bishop who is hired by the Sénéchals as a gardener ("You've heard of worker-priests? There are worker-bishops too!"), and figures as clergy-in-residence at many of the abortive dinner parties. Late in the film, he is brought to the bed of an impoverished dying man—a gardener himself—by an old woman who asserts that she's hated Jesus Christ since she was a little girl, and promises to tell him why when she returns from delivering carrots. Dufour then proceeds to attend to the dying gardener, who confesses to having poisoned the bishop's wealthy parents when Dufour was a child. Dufour kindly and dutifully gives him absolution, then lifts up a nearby rifle and shoots the man through the skull. Thus Buñuel appears to arrive at the conclusion that Catholicism, far from being the natural opponent of Surrealism, is the ultimate expression of it; and it seems strangely appropriate that after this scene both the bishop and the old woman with her promised explanation are abruptly dropped from the film, as though they've suddenly canceled each other out.

■

Writing in 1962, Andrew Sarris remarked that Buñuel's "camera has always viewed his characters from a middle distance, too close for cosmic groupings and too far away for self-identification." The singular achievement of Buñuel's crystallized style is to allow both these viewpoints to function—to let us keep our distance from the characters while repeatedly recognizing our own behavior in them. Cryptic throwaway lines, illogically repeated motifs, and displacements in space and time give the film some of the abstractness of MARIENBAD, yet the richness of concretely observed social behavior is often comparable to that in LA RÈGLE DU JEU. A similar mixture was potentially at work in THE EXTERMINATING ANGEL—the obvious companion film to LE CHARME DISCRET, with its guests unable to leave a room *after* finishing dinner. But despite a brilliant script, the uneven execution left too much of the conception unrealized.

Undoubtedly a great deal of credit for the dialogue of LE CHARME DISCRET should go to Jean-Claude Carrière, who has worked on the scripts of all Buñuel's French films since LE JOURNAL D'UNE FEMME DE CHAMBRE: the precise banality of the small talk has a withering accuracy. Even more impressive is the way that Buñuel and Carrière have managed to weave in enough contemporary phenomena to make the film as up-to-date—and as surrealistic, in its crazy-quilt juxtapositions—as the latest global newspaper: Vietnam, Mao, women's lib, various forms of political corruption, and international drug trafficking are all touched upon in witty and apt allusions. Fernando Rey unloading smuggled heroin from his diplomatic pouch is a hip reference to THE FRENCH CONNECTION, and much of the rest of the film works as a parody of icons and stances in modern cinema.

Florence's neuroticism—as evidenced by her loathing of cellos and her "Euclid complex"—lampoons Ogier's role in L'AMOUR FOU; Audran's stiff elegance and country house hark back to LA FEMME INFIDÈLE; while Seyrig's frozen, irrelevant smiles on every occasion are a comic variation of her ambiguous MARIENBAD expressions. And as I've already suggested, Godard has become a crucial reference point in late Buñuel—not only in the parodies and allusions but also in the use of an open form to accommodate these and other intrusions, the tendency to keep shifting the center of attention.

A few years ago, Godard remarked of BELLE DE JOUR that Buñuel seemed to be playing the cinema the way Bach played the organ. The happy news of LE CHARME DISCRET is that while most of the serious French cinema at present—Godard included—seems to be hard at work performing painful duties, the Old Master is still playing—effortlessly, freely, without fluffing a note.

—Sight and Sound, Winter 1972–1973

Polanski and the American Experiment (BITTER MOON)

Fairly late in WHAT? (1973), Roman Polanksi's least seen and least critically approved feature—an absurdist, misogynist, yet oddly affectionate 'Scope comedy filmed in the seaside villa of its producer, Carlo Ponti—the bimbo American heroine (Sydne Rome), an Alice set loose in a decadent wonderland belonging to a dying millionaire named Noblart, wanders for the second time into a living room where she encounters a middle-aged. Englishman. Once again this Noblart employee bemoans his arthritis, cracks his knuckles, and then sits down at a piano to play the treble part of a Mozart sonata for four hands. Immediately recognizing the piece, she joins him, performing the bass part. After a rose petal drops from the bowl of flowers on the piano onto the keyboard, which also happened before, the wide-eyed heroine has an epiphany.

"It's so strange—this keeps happening to me more and more often. You know that strange feeling that all this has happened before?"
"You mean déja vu?"
"No—not exactly."
"Yes—that odd feeling that the moment we're living now we've already lived before."
"Sort of. But in this case it's not just a feeling. This really *has* happened before."

"Not in exactly the same way, though."

"Yes, exactly: your knuckles—Mozart—the rose petal."

"It wasn't the same, I tell you. You can't bathe twice in the same river because it's never the same river—nor the same bather."

Sometime between my first viewing of Polanski's BITTER MOON at the Toronto film festival last September and my second, late last month, WHAT? became available on letterboxed video at Facets Multimedia, and I had another look at it. (Before this, it had only been available in an atrociously recut and shortened version, marketed as a porn item called DIARY OF FORBIDDEN DREAMS.) Though the much less ambitious WHAT? is lighter in tone and accomplishes a good deal less than BITTER MOON, it is still a crucial precedent, not only for its highly personal musings and self-reflections and its frank depictions of kinky sex but also for the distinctive way it treats these matters formally, using an intricate rhyming structure in which everything of importance seems to happen twice—though "not exactly." There are even textual connections between the movies: at the end of WHAT? the heroine, departing on a truckful of pigs in a rainstorm, yells out to her lover (a pimp played by Marcello Mastroianni) that she may be headed next for Istanbul—which is precisely where two of the major characters in BITTER MOON, traveling on a luxury liner, are headed; and BITTER MOON also ends with a rainstorm. (On the other hand, the thematic variations in WHAT? are basically formal whereas those in BITTER MOON are primarily emotional.)

Moreover, WHAT? received the same sort of apoplectic critical rejection in some quarters as BITTER MOON has, no doubt for related reasons. Back in 1973, the *International Herald-Tribune* reviewer was so beside himself that he even got the title wrong and reviewed WHAT? as WHY? And in the *New Republic* last month, Stanley Kauffmann, reviewing three recent Hugh Grant films, referred to BITTER MOON as "swill," ranking it far below FOUR WEDDINGS AND A FUNERAL and SIRENS.

Different strokes for different folks. Personally I find BITTER MOON riveting and energizing as few other recent movies have been, but I can guarantee you won't emerge from it with any songs in your heart or any cares and worries lifted; in fact, it's blacker and in some ways bleaker than any Polanski movie to date. It's also probably his best movie since CHINATOWN (1974), made only four years before he fled the United States.

Although Polanski regular Gérard Brach worked with him on the scripts of both WHAT? and BITTER MOON, the latter film has two other writing credits as well, and is based on a French novel of the same title by Pascal Bruckner, which I haven't read. Perhaps just as pertinent is what happened to Polanski between the two films. After pleading guilty to having sex with a thirteen-year-old girl and submitting to six weeks of "psychiatric evaluation" in a California state prison—and fearing an extended sentence, since the press was having a field day with his case—he escaped to Europe, where he's lived ever since. None of his three subsequent movies—TESS (1979), PIRATES (1986), and FRANTIC (1988)—has had a fraction of the success of his two Hollywood hits, ROSEMARY'S BABY (1968) and CHINATOWN. In the late 80s he married Emmanuelle Seigner, a French actress roughly half his age, the leading lady in both FRANTIC and BITTER MOON; about a year ago they had their first child, a daughter. (His former wife, Sharon Tate, was pregnant when slain in the brutal 1969 Charles Manson murders.)

In short, you might say Polanski has certain things to feel hopeful as well as bitter about: he may have a reputation as a pervert and be unable to return to the United States, but he has also remarried and recently become a father. All these things are clearly inscribed in BITTER MOON, a film that seems virtually driven by a desire to settle his various accounts—entailing an autocritique that's as ruthless and scathing as any committed to film, a portrait of Polanski's own macho perversity calculated to produce shudders. With its American, English, and French characters representing the three cultures he has known since he left Poland, it's probably his most personal and emotionally complex movie to date.

■

The brilliantly designed structure of BITTER MOON is above all novelistic, with particular reference to the nineteenth-century novel (TESS, one should recall, is an adaptation of Thomas Hardy's *Tess of the D'Urbervilles*). This tale-within-a-tale is set onboard a ship, which suggests Joseph Conrad, and told to a rather square and inhibited English Eurobond salesman named Nigel Dobson (Hugh Grant), who suggests Lockwood in *Wuthering Heights*. This framing device is central to the film's meaning; formally, we get a taste of it even before the story begins, behind the opening credits: the camera moves back slowly from a view of the passing sea until a porthole gradually enters the frame and encloses the picture; then the camera moves forward again, past the porthole, and finally pans left to a young English couple standing on deck, Nigel and his wife, Fiona (Kristin Scott-Thomas).

Celebrating their seventh anniversary, Nigel and Fiona are headed for Istanbul, and plan to fly to Bombay from there; clearly the idea behind the trip is to rejuvenate their marriage, although an Indian acquaintance onboard (Victor Bannerjee), a widower traveling with his little girl, gently mocks Nigel's notion of India as a place to find "inner serenity." Later he remarks, "Children are a better form of marital therapy than any trip to India." (The way third world exoticism is enlisted to spice up sex, marital and otherwise, is a subtle but telling theme throughout the movie.)

When Fiona excuses herself to go to the ladies room, the camera remains on deck with Nigel—establishing at the outset that his is the controlling viewpoint in the framing story. Fiona fails to return, so Nigel goes looking for her and discovers that she's helping a young French woman named Mimi (Seigner) who has apparently fainted. That night, after Fiona retires early to their cabin, Nigel finds Mimi in more glamorous attire in the bar, dancing alone to "Fever." After she briefly flirts with him, then sarcastically rebuffs him as she leaves, pronouncing him dull, he encounters her husband, a wild-eyed American named Oscar (Peter Coyote) seated in a wheelchair on deck. Immediately picking up on Nigel's attraction to Mimi, Oscar says, "Beware of her—she's a walking mantrap," then adds, indicating the wheelchair, "Look what she did to me." Getting Nigel to help him back to his cabin, which he explains is separate from Mimi's, Oscar invites him in, baiting him with his curiosity about Mimi; handing him a drink, he proceeds to tell the first of what will be four lengthy chapters in the movie's tale-within-a-tale—the whole story of his relationship with Mimi in Paris.

■

Oscar, a failed, unpublished novelist living in Paris on a trust fund, expresses himself throughout in an ornate purple prose that is one of the movie's most useful and ambiguous narrative devices. It's often so purple as to seem bad writing, hence easy to dismiss (and tempting to hoot at); but it also fully expresses the reckless, romantic intensity of a bored sensualist who's willing to delve into passions that Nigel—the squirming, voyeuristic surrogate for our own puritanical inhibitions—can scarcely even think about. This uncertainty about Oscar's prose style extends to the story he's telling: Is it simple pornography or a cautionary moral tale, a turn-on or a turnoff, or something between the two? Nigel himself isn't sure, and Oscar needles him about this in the same way that Polanski needles us, gleefully and sadistically poking holes in his/our hypocrisies. Compounding our uncertainties are Oscar's problematic reliability as a narrator (which Mimi throws into question) and the fact that we can't always be sure if the flashbacks we're watching are exclusively Oscar's account of events or Nigel's imagining of them.

Each time we return to the events onboard, in between Oscar's chapters, the situation between Nigel and Fiona shifts correspondingly, as Nigel becomes more and more attracted to Mimi. So it's clear early on that Oscar's tale isn't an idle amusement; it's a narrative with immense consequences, and part of the film's power as storytelling is to convey this sense of urgency. You might say that, like musicians, Oscar and Polanski are playing on our uneasy curiosity, and the piece they're playing is a four-part symphony in sonata form, complete with theme and variations. (Readers who don't want any plot points given away are urged to check out here.)

■

The first movement details the birth of passion and the first flush of love between Oscar and Mimi—an erotic romance involving a chance meeting on a bus, Oscar's efforts to find Mimi again, a second meeting, and a first date at a plush Thai restaurant, culminating in lovemaking at dawn in front of his fireplace. (If the heroine's sexual escapades in WHAT? recall the old *Playboy* comic strip "Little Annie Fannie," this scene is virtually "The Playboy Philosophy" made flesh, conspicuous consumption and all: a carefully prepared but ignored breakfast tray is as important as the fireplace.) Mimi promptly moves in, and what follows are a few sexual games but not much more; the first hint of the darkness to come occurs only near the end, when Mimi begs Oscar to let her shave him with his straight razor and accidentally nicks him (a moment that recalls a scene between Lionel Stander and Françoise Dorleac in Polanski's 1966 black comedy CUL-DE-SAC).

The second movement begins when Oscar describes a kinky turn in his relationship with Mimi: on a skiing vacation, she began urinating on the TV set in their hotel room, and he suddenly felt moved to lie under her and drink her urine. His description—we don't see the scene—is a fair sample not only of his overripe prose but also of the third world trappings that seem increasingly necessary to their affair, already signaled by the Thai restaurant and Mimi's candlelit performance of "exotic" dancing in the first movement. "I experienced the orgasm of a lifetime," Oscar says to Nigel. "It was like a white-hot blade piercing me through and through. This was my Nile, my Ganges, my Jordan, my fountain of youth, my second baptism." "Look," Nigel says, "I think I'm probably as broad-minded as the next man, but obviously there are limits." "Stop twittering, Nigel. I'm sharing a revelation with you, dammit. I'm trying to expand your sexual horizons." This leads into a proper flashback of other kinky sexual games (with Oscar's straight razor employed in one as a prop) and the couple's first crisis, when each provokes sexual jealousy in the other at a bar, followed by more sexual games, which now yield diminishing returns. (Furnished with a recording of barnyard noises and a pig mask, Oscar comically deflates one fantasy by talking, implying that sexual fantasies can be undone by words. Yet it's Oscar's words that increase Nigel's attraction to Mimi; and between the third and fourth movements Mimi notes to Nigel of Oscar, "I leave the words to him. It's all he has left.")

In the third movement—ironically narrated while Oscar lies on his bed and Nigel sits in Oscar's wheelchair—things get decidedly uglier. Oscar describes the decline of his sexual interest in Mimi, followed by fights, recriminations, and Mimi leaving, then coming back and begging him to let her stay on any terms. The infidelity, mental cruelty, and other, escalating forms of humiliation her return unleashes in Oscar are truly harrowing, and the thematic variations that dominate this movement are mainly deeroticized, ghoulish replays of previous events. At a breakfast in the first movement, Mimi splashes milk on her breasts for Oscar to lap up; the scene's comic-orgasmic climax is toast springing out of a toaster. At a breakfast in *this* section, Oscar is disgusted when Mimi drinks milk directly from the bottle, and the "comic" orgasmic climax of another scene occurs when Oscar, being serviced by a prostitute, winds up choking her poodle. Finally, after Mimi becomes pregnant and Oscar forces her to abort the child, he proposes a vacation for the two of them in Martinique, then sadistically leaves her alone on the plane just before it takes off. (This is where we discover the source of the film's title: "I could picture her looking out the window at that beautiful moon—the same one I could see, but it didn't look the same to her. . . . To her it must have been poison. To me, sweet as a peach.")

The final movement, which I won't recount in detail, occurs years later, when Mimi returns to Paris and takes her revenge on Oscar: paralyzed from the waist down, he comes fully under her sadistic control.

■

Where do we, as spectators, stand in relation to all this? Though I can't vouch for the responses of women—this is essentially a tale told by one man to another, albeit one in which the two women register much more sympathetically than the two men—my guess is that male and female viewers alike stand in many places in succession, none of them entirely comfortable, most of them pretty unsettling. And of course the shipboard machinations that surround these four movements, holding them in place and sometimes altering their meanings, offer another tense form of narrative striptease, mocking Nigel's responses and our own while contributing a mordant counterpoint to the serial flashbacks. (At the climactic New Year's Eve party on the ship, the increasingly cadaverous Oscar sports a fez—a final third world reference in this account of the Ugly American abroad, exercising his much-vaunted freedom.)

As sexual games turn into games played for keeps and the abuser becomes the abused, every repeated event becomes the infernal rhyme of its predecessor: Mimi kicking over Oscar in his chair as part of a playful sexual charade becomes Mimi viciously kicking Oscar in his wheelchair across the same room. Each lover winding up in a hospital bed becomes the occasion for the hatching of further macabre cruelties. Whether we take BITTER MOON as camp comedy or serious horror story, as pornography or cautionary moral tale, we're implicitly rejecting half the experience the movie offers to go looking for solace in the other half, which we aren't likely to find. What we have to settle for, finally, is Polanski's dry, scary, and ultimately confessional commentary on the perils of the American experiment itself, the so-called freedom of the individual played out in psychosexual terms and staged with French and English participants—a French-English coproduction whose ideal spectators are troubled Americans, and uneasy, childless lovers.

—Chicago *Reader, April 4, 1994*

Utopian Space and Urban Encounters

Like all of the very great comics, before making us laugh,
Tati creates a universe. A world arranges itself around his
character, crystallizes like a supersaturated solution
around a grain of salt. Certainly the character created by
Tati is funny, but almost as an accessory, and in any case
always relative to the universe. He can be personally
absent from the most comical gags, for M. Hulot is only
the metaphysical incarnation of a disorder that is
perpetuated long after his passing.

It is regrettable that André Bazin's seminal essay on Jacques Tati ("M. Hulot et le temps," 1953) has been omitted from both volumes of *What Is Cinema?* in English; regrettable, too, that Bazin didn't live to see Tati's masterpiece. To some degree, PLAYTIME can be regarded as an embodiment and extension of Bazin's most cherished ideas about deep focus, long takes, and the "democratic" freedoms that these techniques offer to the spectator.

It could be argued, of course, that Tati has offered his audience too much freedom, and overestimated the capacities of several spectators—one reason, perhaps, why almost six years were to pass between the film's Paris opening in late 1967 and its American release. "An absolute masterpiece of a confounding and vertiginous beauty," Jean-André Fiéschi reported in *Cahiers du cinéma* shortly after it premiered. "Never, perhaps, has a film placed so much confidence in the intelligence and *activity* of the spectator: the challenge was too great to find a commensurate response." Quite simply, the richness of PLAYTIME is not available to anyone on a single viewing, especially on video. At best, one can discover that this richness is present; at worst, the viewer can become so bored by what he doesn't see that he fails to notice that a radical change in the language of cinema is being proposed. (Something comparable happened to many critics when 2001: A SPACE ODYSSEY opened in the United

States less than four months later.) The film can seem funny or unfunny, empty or full, lively or dull, beautiful or ugly in one viewing, but it cannot come across in its entirety. As Noël Burch observed in *Theory of Film Practice,* Tati's film is "the first in the history of cinema that not only must be seen several times, but also must be viewed from several different distances from the screen. In its form, it is probably the first truly 'open' film."

A group of female American tourists wander through a studio-built Paris of interchangeable steel and glass buildings; Barbara, the youngest member of the group, searches for the "real" Paris. Meanwhile, M. Hulot wanders through the same buildings, mainly in search of a M. Giffard, occasionally crossing the paths of the Americans and various other groups. Midway through the film, Hulot finds Giffard, reencounters an old army friend, and joins all the other characters at the premature opening of an expensive restaurant; as the awkwardly designed establishment gradually falls to pieces, everyone gets acquainted. In the morning, Hulot buys a going-away present for Barbara,* which she opens on the bus ride back to Orly airport: a plastic bouquet of lilies of the valley that closely resembles the streetlamp on the autoroute.

Jacques Rivette has remarked that "PLAYTIME is a revolutionary film, in spite of Tati; the film has completely effaced the creator"—an idea also expressed by Tati himself when I interviewed him around the same time, in late 1972: "PLAYTIME is nobody," he said, specifically distinguishing his film from FELLINI SATYRICON and FELLINI'S ROMA. But how, exactly, is it revolutionary?

In conventional film narrative, there is always a clearly defined separation between "subject" and "background." A character moves through a setting, and our attention is focused on the "action," what the character does; when this setting figures in the action, it becomes a part of the subject. But in PLAYTIME, where every character has the status of an extra, every scene is filmed in long shot, and the surrounding decor is continually relevant to the action, the subject of a typical shot is *everything that appears on the screen.* Many shots, particularly in the restaurant sequence, become open forums where several potential points of interest compete independently for our attention. Whatever we choose to ignore automatically becomes "background," but this arranging of priorities is often no more than a reflection of our own preferences, i.e., which movie we want to see this time around. If we sit tight and wait for gags to come, we won't find very many. But if we let our eyes roam, wander, and gambol about the screen, scanning the totality of the action and translating our gaze into a playful dance, we'll discover multiple relationships between

---

* After we both saw PLAYTIME for the first time in 70-millimeter at New York's Walter Reade Theater in September 1994, Dave Kehr pointed out a touching detail that neither of us had ever noticed over countless screenings in 35- and 16-millimeter prints: near the exit of the shop where he is to buy her going-away present, Hulot briefly notices, with a barely discernible look of regret, that she's wearing a wedding or engagement ring. [1995]

people, people and objects, live moments and dead moments, real gags and potential gags that are hysterically funny: a geometric vaudeville. Viewed individually, details might be dull or interesting; seen together, they become cosmically funny—comic in a philosophical sense.

This vision is not merely revealed in the film, but formulated as a philosophical-aesthetic proposition. Indirectly, through a series of minor events, Hulot proposes this concept to Barbara. This lesson has a lot to do with human, accidental curves breaking the monotony of regimented straight lines.

The opening of the film is oppressively linear in terms of the actions displayed. The initial gag, delineated in the second and third shots, is the sharp left turn taken by two nuns in the passageway of an anonymous building (which we subsequently discover is Orly); and all the various movements of the tourists being led around are equally rigid and unswerving.

Perhaps the first beautiful moment in PLAYTIME occurs when Hulot does an involuntary dance turn on the slippery floor of a waiting room, when the tip of his umbrella momentarily fails to anchor him. This little slide, which lasts only a second or two, is virtually the only instance of physical grace that Tati allows himself as an actor in the entire film: the entire legacy of his music hall experience is alluded to and dispensed with in a single fleeting gesture. (The extraordinary contrast between Tati's directorial ambitions and his modesty as an actor is central to his ideas about comedy; in this respect, the larger role played by Hulot in TRAFIC is a conscious regression, undoubtedly dictated by commercial necessities.)

Later in the film, at a ghastly gadget exhibition, Barbara turns around— shifting her gaze in an arc away from the architecture's linear dictates—to notice a "gag" (a mishap involving Hulot, a German salesman, and the latter's bent spectacles) that makes her laugh. And in the restaurant, which theoretically collapses and comes to life because of the architect's failure to take precise measurements, the regimented lines of movement increasingly turn into a whirlpool of dance curves. At the same time, to maintain any "global" sense of the action as we search out various details, it is virtually essential that we curve the trajectory of our gaze; if our eyes attempt to traverse the screen in straight lines, we simply miss too much. (Significantly, a neon arrow that is straight at one end and curved at the other flashes over the restaurant's entrance, and is the basis for several gags.) Pursuing the action in straight lines, we become victimized, imprisoned by the architecture, much in the way that Giffard, rushing directly toward one of the characters resembling Hulot (the film has several) in an early sequence, runs smack into a glass door. An alternative method of looking is Tati's "message."

In the restaurant, the apparent conflicts between separate points of interest become resolved when we realize that all the wandering strands are bound up in the same fabric, and *every* detail on the screen is privileged in relation to the whole, which gradually assumes the shape of a turning circle. This concept culminates in a climactic "circus" vision of city traffic as an endlessly turning carousel, with all the surrounding action serving to complete rather than deviate from the commanding image. The raising and lowering of cars in an adjacent garage suggest the vertical movements of merry-go-round horses, and the horizontal procession of pedestrians forms a living frame around this festive circle of life. An observation post swings exhilaratingly into view, and, as night illogically but irresistibly overtakes the city a second time, the rule of poetry becomes absolute.

—*Film Comment,* May–June 1973;
revised October 1995

His Mistress's Voice

Considering all the oppositions that inform the work of Chantal Akerman—such as painting versus narrative, France versus Belgium, being Jewish versus being French *and* Belgian, and the commercial versus the experimental—it's only logical that both the plot and the title of NIGHT AND DAY, one of her best features to date, should reflect the same pattern. The situation it refers to is so simple that it's hard to describe without making it sound singsongy: Julie (Guilaine Londez) and Jack (Thomas Langmann), an infatuated young couple from the provinces who've recently come to Paris, live in a small flat near Boulevard Sebastopol. During the day they make love; at night Jack drives a taxi and Julie walks the summer streets, singing happily to herself. One night they meet Joseph (François Negret), another isolated newcomer to Paris, who drives Jack's cab during the day. Jack heads for his shift; Julie goes walking with Joseph, and they quickly fall in love. From then on, Julie becomes a round-the-clock lover, sleeping with each driver as he gets off work; Joseph knows about Jack but not vice versa, and Julie refuses to choose between them. (She eventually arrives at what might be called the ultimate feminist solution.)

Insomnia has long been a basic element of Akerman's nocturnal poetics—especially in LES RENDEZ-VOUS D'ANNA, TOUTE UNE NUIT, and THE MAN

WITH A SUITCASE. But until now Akerman's take on it has seemed troubled and neurotic. Her magically luminous nighttime exteriors and claustrophobic interiors, like those of her painterly influences, the Belgian surrealists Paul Delvaux and René Magritte as well as Edward Hopper, glower with abnormal degrees of presence.

In NIGHT AND DAY, by contrast, insomnia seems a kind of precondition for utopian romance—a sentiment expressed at the very outset by Jack and Julie as they lie together in bed: "Are you sleeping?" "No. Are you?" "No." "You and I never sleep." "Never when we are together." "We like movement better." "Yes, it's true." "When I sleep, I don't live." "Neither do I." "Right now, I prefer living." "So do I."

A little later—after an offscreen female narrator tells us that "they lived casually, had no friends, and didn't know anyone in Paris"—their dialogue resumes: "Maybe we should meet people." "Next year." "And get a telephone?" "Next year."

And finally, after they make love, this closing exchange: "You must sleep, Jack. You'll have an accident." "Next year."

The musical comedy-like rhythms of their dialogue are far from accidental. Roughly speaking, NIGHT AND DAY is Akerman's third and most successful attempt at capturing the feel of a musical—after LES ANNÉES 80 (1983), an inspired feature-length trailer for one, and GOLDEN EIGHTIES (aka WINDOW SHOPPING, 1986), a charming if somewhat disappointing fulfillment of the earlier prospectus. This one succeeds in part because it's less literal in this endeavor than its two predecessors.

A ravishingly beautiful moment immediately follows the above dialogue: Julie starts to sing wordlessly along with the lush strings on the sound track—sometimes in unison, sometimes complementing or augmenting the musical backdrop. After she and Jack walk downstairs to go their separate ways—he to his taxi, she on her nightly tour of the city—she begins to sing out loud to the same tune, this time without accompaniment, a kind of celebration of her life as we've come to understand it: "During the day, he tells me about his night, and at night I wander across Paris. . . . We don't have a child; it isn't really the right time. . . . I always get home before him. I wait for the day and erase the night. It's summer in Paris, the time for abandonment, when days are the longest. . . . We don't have a phone, but we don't know anyone anyway." Sometimes we see her singing while she walks and sometimes we merely hear her offscreen, but the movement of her walk and the movement of the melodic line both proceed continuously in a stream of unbroken poetry.

Not all of NIGHT AND DAY proceeds like a musical. Indeed, the sheer exuberance of the first reel or so isn't really sustained over the film's ninety minutes. At the same time, it would be shortsighted to assume that capturing the spirit of musicals represents the sum of Akerman's ambitions here. To try to understand better all that NIGHT AND DAY achieves, both in relation to Akerman's earlier work and on its own terms, it would help to return to the four separate yet connected oppositions already mentioned.

■

Painting versus narrative. "Carl Dreyer's basic problem as an artist," wrote the late Robert Warshow in 1948, reflecting on Dreyer's DAY OF WRATH, "is one that seems almost inevitably to confront the self-conscious creator of 'art' films: the conflict between a love for the purely visual and the tendencies of a medium that is not only visual but also dramatic." This is the problem addressed in one way or another by each of Akerman's features to date, beginning with her painterly, silent, nonnarrative first feature, HOTEL MONTEREY (1972), made when she was only twenty-two, and her narrative and relatively unpainterly sound feature JE, TU, IL, ELLE, made two years later.

Her 1975 masterpiece JEANNE DIELMAN, 23 QUAI DE COMMERCE, 1080 BRUXELLES was her first major attempt to combine and somehow reconcile the visual with the dramatic, and the features that follow represent different attempts at synthesis. NEWS FROM HOME (1977), for instance, is essentially a nonnarrative study of Manhattan exteriors accompanied by Akerman reading letters she received from her mother while she was in New York, material that inevitably introduces narrative elements. LES RENDEZ-VOUS D'ANNA (1978), THE MAN WITH A SUITCASE (1984), and GOLDEN EIGHTIES are all unabashed story films, but the first two make use of some of the claustrophobic painterly elements in HOTEL MONTEREY (chiefly the discomfort of solitary individuals in rooms), while the third, set almost entirely inside a shopping mall, defines narrative as an interlocking series of mini-plots.

TOUTE UNE NUIT (1982) is also made up of multiple mini-plots, but other than occurring over a single night most of them don't interlock, and the overall effect is more painterly than narrative; the same is true to an even more radical extent of HISTOIRES D'AMÉRIQUE (1989), which stages the recounting over one night of numerous Jewish jokes in and around a Brooklyn park. LES ANNÉES 80, a documentary about Akerman auditioning and rehearsing actresses for GOLDEN EIGHTIES, regards these actresses in part as painterly subjects or models, and incorporates narrative only in the sense that it charts the development of certain songs and performances.

In broad terms, the polarity between painting and narrative is one between persistence and development. A painting exists in space, a narrative in time; persisting is what a painting does in time, and developing is what a narrative does in space. Consequently, insofar as Akerman's films resemble paintings, character and plot development is always something of a problem, and insofar as they impose narratives, the persistence of people and places without any development is also something of a problem.

In the past, camera movements in Akerman's work have tended to be both functional (pans following the movements of actors) and minimal, with the consequence that most of her compositions are static and therefore painterly. In NIGHT AND DAY, camera movements have become copious and descriptive as well as functional; that is, they not only follow, accompany, or precede Julie when she walks down the streets of Paris or from room to room in her flat but also lyrically traverse the bodies of her and her lovers when she's in bed with them. One might say, in other words, that they follow or impose narratives on the people and the places, her painterly subjects.

France versus Belgium. Akerman was born in Brussels in 1950, and Belgium remains an important setting in many of her works, including SAUTE MA VILLE (her first short, made in 1968), JEANNE DIELMAN, LES RENDEZ-VOUS D'ANNA, and TOUTE UNE NUIT. The relatively staid and repressive quality of Belgian culture—including the bourgeois aspects of Belgian surrealism as exemplified by painters like Delvaux and Magritte—has a great deal to do with what these films are about as well as what they're like, which is why they're so much creepier than Akerman's other works. Their decorous sense of the everyday calls to mind what the English writer and broadcaster George Melly once said about Magritte: "He is a secret agent, his object is to bring into disrepute the whole apparatus of bourgeois reality. Like all saboteurs, he avoids detection by dressing and behaving like everybody else."

Magritte's *Man with Newspaper* (1927–1928) tells me something about the customary disquiet of Akerman's world. In it, four panels, two on top and two on the bottom, show the same corner of a sitting room, with one difference: in the first panel a man is seated at the table by the window reading a newspaper, and in the other three panels, neither the man nor the newspaper is in evidence. A narrative is implied between the first and second panel—the disappearance of the man and the newspaper—without being confirmed, and we're left with the eerie fact of three identical "empty" rooms. Similarly, many of Akerman's settings suggest absence even more than presence.

NIGHT AND DAY, like many of Akerman's recent films, is a French-Belgian coproduction, but it has less of this creepy quality than any of her films I've seen to date. There's some evidence that France has been a liberating force in her work, sexually as well as stylistically. Figuratively, at least, one might say that for the first time in her work, there are no empty rooms.

Being Jewish versus being French and Belgian. Akerman is the daughter of Polish Jews who survived the Nazi camps, and this background plays significant roles in NEWS FROM HOME, LES RENDEZ-VOUS D'ANNA, and HISTOIRES D'AMÉRIQUE. Though Thomas Langmann, the actor who plays Jack, played the Jewish leading character in a non-Akerman feature, LES ANNÉES SANDWICHES, 1988), and Guilaine Londez (Julie) has a physiognomy that suggests she might be Jewish, Jewishness appears to have no thematic relevance in NIGHT AND DAY, and to all appearances seems as unimportant here as Akerman's Belgian background. Significantly, however, NIGHT AND DAY immediately follows HISTOIRES D'AMÉRIQUES, which is the most explicitly Jewish and, quite possibly, the least commercially successful of all her features to date. (Its critical reception at the Berlin film festival in 1989 was generally hostile, and it appears to have had few screenings since then.)

The commercial versus the experimental. Throughout her career, Akerman has been commercially ambitious at the same time that she has shown the marked influence of experimental and mainly nonnarrative filmmakers such as Michael Snow, Stan Brakhage, and Jonas Mekas. In JE, TU, IL, ELLE she took her first major steps toward commercial features, introducing sex as well as narrative into her universe while implicating herself personally by playing the lead character. In JEANNE DIELMAN, for the first time, she cast a movie star (and great actress, the late Delphine Seyrig) in the lead role, and in RENDEZ-VOUS D'ANNA she moved closer to articulating a conventional story line. LES ANNÉES 80 and GOLDEN EIGHTIES, by virtue of their charismatic casts and songs, clearly represent further attempts to woo and seduce audiences.

NIGHT AND DAY doesn't qualify exactly as Akerman's first love story— GOLDEN EIGHTIES is full of love stories—but it is probably her first love story that audiences can easily identify with. Similarly, it is certainly not her first feminist film, but possibly the first that could be described as commercial. (The ads, not inappropriately, refer to it as "a postfeminist romance.")

■

One might conclude that Akerman has made a big step with NIGHT AND DAY toward making a conventional narrative feature. But the painterly persistence remains throughout the film; Jack and Joseph's physical resemblance, the repetitions of various camera movements and angles, the similarities of Julie and Joseph's various hotel rooms, and the recurrence of some Paris locales (such as place de Chatelet and rue de Rivoli) are all manifestations of this. And these rhyme effects have thematic as well as stylistic consequences. (Julie's nightly routines become increasingly ritualistic, and the two male lovers seem interchangeable.) On the other hand, it might be argued that these rhyme effects are ultimately less painterly or narrative than they are musical; if the film's music gradually decreases in importance, and disappears entirely in the final sequence, one might argue that the film's rhythms have by this time been taken over by certain visual refrains. (Throughout the film, the feeling of summer nights in Paris is so palpable that one can almost taste it, and this delicious taste may be the film's loveliest achievement in painterly persistence.)

It might be argued that narrative development—which includes character development—remains something of a problem, even if Akerman's attempts to solve this problem are pretty ingenious. Toward the end of the film, Julie and Jack decide to knock out a wall in their flat, largely as a means of rejuvenating their own relationship. The physical change in their apartment leads them to throw a party—a major change in their relationship. Julie, we're told by the offscreen narrator, subsequently undergoes an even more important change, but the fact that we're told about this change rather than shown it indicates to what extent narrative development eludes Akerman—at least formally and dramatically, if not thematically.

This offscreen narrator, which I've neglected so far, is in fact an integral part of the film. Her all-knowing and somewhat personal commentaries on the action may remind us, along with the names Jack and Joseph, of François Truffaut's JULES AND JIM, a classic—and classically romantic—French New Wave depiction of a ménage à trois as well as of a free-spirited woman who makes all the significant moves and calls all the shots. But the offscreen narrator of JULES AND JIM is a man, not a woman—a conventionally patriarchal voice-of-God narrator who ultimately articulates the male viewpoint that JULES AND JIM embodies, merging the viewpoint of Truffaut with that of Henri-Pierre Roché, on whose autobiographical novel the film is based. It's a voice whose narrative authority we're meant to accept without question.

Simply because of this patriarchal convention, it's hard to hear the woman narrator of NIGHT AND DAY without asking—even if only momentarily—who this woman is. Once we ask this question, however, the answer becomes clear: she is the woman Julie will become. And the story she tells is the story of how Julie becomes that narrator.

—Chicago *Reader,* March 26, 1993

Seen and Unseen Encounters

Kieslowski's RED

A film of mystical correspondences, RED triumphantly concludes and summa-rizes Krzysztof Kieslowski's "Three Colors" trilogy by contriving to tell us three stories about three separate characters all at once; yet it does this with such effortless musical grace that we may not even be aware of it at first. Two of the characters, both of them students, are neighbors in Geneva who never meet—a model named Valentine (Irene Jacob) and a law student named Au-guste (Jean-Pierre Lorit)—and the third is a retired judge (Jean-Louis Trintig-nant) who lives in a Geneva suburb and whom Valentine meets quite by chance, when she accidentally runs over his German shepherd.

Eventually we discover that Auguste and the retired judge are younger and older versions of the same man (neither of *them* meets, either). Another set of correspondences is provided when, in separate scenes, Valentine and the judge are able to divine important facts about each other: he correctly guesses that she has a younger brother driven to drug addiction by the discovery that his mother's husband is not his real father; she correctly guesses that he was once betrayed by someone he loved—which also happens to Auguste during the course of the film.

With so many different instances of chance, telepathy, and prophecy in RED, one's credulity is constantly being challenged, but not to the point where the film itself ever threatens to crumble. The coexistence of the real and the everyday, on the one hand, and the mysterious and the miraculous, on the other, is one of the movie's givens, and much of what is beautiful in Kieslowski's style stems from its moment-by-moment charting of that charmed coexistence as he cuts or pans or tracks or cranes between his three characters, interweaving and dovetailing their separate lives and daily movements.

What emerges is not a "realistic" world in any ordinary sense, yet it is a fully and densely realized one, and one that has more insight into the world we all live in than conventional Hollywood wish fulfillments, which are no less fanciful in their details. Even the recurring uses of the color red—which seems to be found rather than planted in the various Geneva locations—impress us less as fantasy or invention than as one person's way of seeing the world, alert to all the feelings and conditions that are generally associated with that color in human interactions: passion, jealousy, pain, injury, fear, embarrassment, love.

Perhaps one reason why we can accept the strange congruences of Kieslowski's world even when our rational responses reject them is that the city of Geneva itself and its customary channels of communication and connection help to bring them about. Streets, cars, windows, posters, newspapers, radios, TVs, and, most of all, telephones become the vehicles of these casual conjunctions and gorgeous everyday miracles, which suggest that these channels *could* bring all of us together in ways that we never suspected, even if they usually don't. Valentine has a jealous boyfriend living in England, and Auguste's girlfriend in her flat operates a telephone weather report service periodically used by the judge. All five of these characters constantly rely on telephones as conduits out of their isolation, even if they more often only confirm their loneliness. The remarkable opening sequence traces the phone lines between Valentine and her boyfriend across the English channel, red wires and all. It's the first of Kieslowski's many dry and mordant Polish jokes: at the end of this epic journey, the call hits a busy signal.

When the judge is brought to court after confessing to a crime, Valentine learns about it in the newspaper, and when Valentine makes an appearance at a fashion show, the judge learns about it the same way. Even if Valentine and Auguste never meet, their apartment windows repeatedly frame each other's activities in the streets below. The huge poster advertising chewing gum that we see Valentine posing for is eventually unfurled on a busy intersection; soon afterward, she returns to her flat and finds the lock to the front door jammed with chewing gum, most likely as a result of this poster. It is a car accident that causes Valentine to come into contact with the judge, and it is a busy intersection where Auguste drops his law books while crossing the street; one book falls open to a page that contains the answer to a key question on the law exam he is about to take, a chance occurrence that also happened to the judge many years before.

In the November–December (1994) *Film Comment,* Dave Kehr—in the best critical account of "Three Colors" that I've read, pointedly titled "To Save the World"—compares this complex juxtaposition to the cutting between different stories and historical periods in D. W. Griffith's INTOLERANCE, seeing it mainly in terms of parallel editing. Yet if one concentrates instead on spatial proximities—the proximities between Valentine and Auguste on the same street or in the same neighborhood, or even the proximities between Valentine and the judge, conversing and interacting in their three pivotal scenes together—one may also be reminded of Jacques Tati's PLAYTIME. But neither reference point, which concentrates, respectively, on temporal and spatial continuities, comes close to fully accounting for the intricate web of interconnectedness and the poem of rhyming destinies that Kieslowski finds between three lonely urban individuals, a vision that is at once ecstatic and despairing, tragic and utopian.

This universe of interconnectedness is bounded at one end by total obliviousness (Valentine and Auguste are strangers to each other in the same neighborhood) and at the other by obsessive, gloating attention: the judge spends much of his time listening to his neighbors' phone calls. When Valentine's horrified discovery of his snooping persuades him to blow his cover, making the neighbors aware of his eavesdropping, many retaliate by throwing rocks through his window. Between that obliviousness and that obsessive attention loom utopian possibilities of communal urban life as well as the essential and debilitating isolation of all these people, and Kieslowski plays on these dialectical registers as if on a master keyboard; the subject of his music is nothing less than human possibility in the contemporary world.

■

Apart from a few obvious exceptions, masterpieces take a while to impose themselves and be recognized as masterpieces. People often prefer to forget this, but excitement about the first features of Godard, Truffaut, and Resnais in the late 50s and early 60s was not universally shared, nor were their meanings fully apparent the first time around, even to critics. A lot of proselytizing, discussion, and debate had to take place before they began to take on the status of classics. The same process took place with Bergman, Antonioni, and Fellini; long before these and other filmmakers became canonized and then vulgarized by imitation in American movies (by directors ranging from Woody Allen to Bob Fosse to Paul Mazursky) they were still regarded as controversial and problematic artists, and in some respects they remain so even today—which is why the most recent works of all three, all made many years ago, have yet to be released in this country. (Bergman's FANNY AND ALEXANDER is a six-hour film made for Swedish TV, and the version shown in the United States is 105 minutes shorter than the original; Antonioni's IDENTIFICATION OF A WOMAN and Fellini's THE VOICE OF THE MOON have never been released here in any form.) Nowadays most critics, lulled by the outsized studio ad campaigns and eager for the currency that comes with instant recognition, tend to be much lazier than they used to be about grappling with more difficult and innovative pictures, and many go out of their way to avoid them entirely. Many of the most important new names in international cinema are missing from the just-published third edition of David Thomson's *A Biographical Dictionary of the Cinema,* and the same is partially true for the posthumously completed second edition of Ephraim Katz's *Film Encyclopedia,* thereby ratifying the relative inertia of critics happy to stick mainly or exclusively with Hollywood merchandise.

Even after three viewings, RED remains an exquisitely mysterious object to me—an experience that has grown in beauty and density each time I've seen it, without ever convincing me for a minute that I've perceived all of its meanings and riches. The same could be said for "Three Colors" as a whole, which has been playing in Chicago in installments since last winter. I'd say WHITE seems the weakest of the three and BLUE the second best, but this comes from seeing them as separate movies; it's possible that after seeing all three in sequence, I might view all of them somewhat differently.

Another school of thought, and one that's a great deal more prevalent, says that movies should blow their wad—put up or shut up—the first time around, even (or especially) if you're a film critic. If this school of thought has a dean, it would be Pauline Kael, and if it has a curriculum, the required movie of the moment would surely be PULP FICTION. Kael, of course, retired four years ago, but that doesn't mean that her gospel of instant response and unretractable opinion isn't fully in force in today's marketplace; given the planned obsolescence of our culture as a whole, and the preference for light entertainment over any other aesthetic activity, it could hardly be otherwise. In fact, if you turn to the testimony of David Denby, one of Kael's oldest disciples, writing recently in *New York,* you might conclude that Kieslowski—"an artificer, perhaps, but not an artist"—isn't fit to polish Quentin Tarantino's boots:

> With RED, Kieslowski has completed the trilogy that began earlier with BLUE and WHITE, and it would be wonderful to announce that the three films amounted to a major work. (They've been hailed as such in Europe and in some quarters in America.) Unfortunately, it's not so; and, if I'm not mistaken, there's an element of dismay and put-on lurking in the praise. One senses an illusion close to cracking—the dissolution of a set of assumptions that animates a half-dozen film festivals a year. The truth is, the European cinema has lost its authority. It's not that there aren't good films every year. Of course there are (and there may be other good ones we don't see). But great films are not being made—not the way they were each year in the 50s and 60s—and much of what we see here of French, German, Italian, and Eastern European movies seems feeble or imitative or cultured in a trancelike way that means little to us. A nihilistic pop masterpiece like PULP FICTION blows away European movies even faster than it

does most American movies. For good or ill, American movies are eating the world market, and until new economic conditions emerge for the film business on the Continent, we may have to do without major European directors.

Given such sentiments, it's small wonder that Kieslowski recently announced his retirement from filmmaking.* Assuming that it's possible to distinguish between economics and aesthetics in the above directive (a frequent problem in writing of this kind), Denby's authority here rests on a form of telepathy and prophecy that goes well beyond Kieslowski's. Like Kael before him, Denby is notorious for avoiding film festivals (making it impossible to determine which half-dozen he could be thinking of), so his conclusion that "great films are not being made" necessarily rests on a faith in the critical acumen of U.S. distributors bordering on religious—not to mention an implied reverence for European cinema in the early 50s that I for one would like to see him justify. Of course he's perfectly entitled to regard "Three Colors" as a failure; what I object to is his presumption of expertise regarding world cinema in general.

In fact, Denby's entire paragraph reeks of the kind of unearned (albeit confident) authority that legislates our entire film culture at the moment. The way he can write that Kieslowski's trilogy has been hailed as a major work "in Europe and in some quarters in America" automatically implies that Europe is unified and uniform in praising "Three Colors" whereas America is not—the sort of assumption one can make only if one doesn't go to the trouble of checking the facts. A few French critics, for instance, scornfully speak about Kieslowski's "cinema of Esperanto." Moreover, Denby's divvying up of "the world market" between America and Europe excludes the rest of the world as immaterial when it might be argued that a key difference between contemporary film culture and that of the 50s and 60s is the emergence of major filmmakers in Africa, the Middle East, and the Chinese-speaking world—not "major" in the sense of Tarantino or Spielberg but "major" in at least the same ballpark as Ozu, Mizoguchi, or Satyajit Ray—and major inroads made by Chinese commercial films in the world market as well. And is "cultured in a trancelike way" supposed to refer only to RED and not to PULP FICTION? Kieslowski has Valentine tell her boyfriend on the phone how much she liked DEAD POETS SOCIETY. Is this pop reference "blown away" by the equally adoring references to McDonald's Quarter Pounders in PULP FICTION?

The words in Denby's paragraph that most reflect Kael's influence are the first-person plural pronouns—the royal "we" and "us" in the phrases "that means little to us" and "we may have to do without major European directors." Both support a fundamental cleavage between foreigners and Ameri-

---

*The unexpected death of Kieslowski from heart surgery in March 1996 suggested that this retreat may have been motivated in part by his poor health, although he had already provisionally begun work again, on a second trilogy. (June 1996)

cans, creating an imaginary rift between foreign and American sensibilities that not even personal pronouns can cross. Perhaps foreigners who regard PULP FICTION as "their" movie—not to the exclusion of Americans, but in concert with them—are provisionally tolerated in this form of tribalism. But Americans who feel the same way about RED (and I'm far from being the only one) become automatically and irrevocably excluded from the discussion; the very notion of a *shared* tradition or experience between Americans and non-Americans is deemed inadmissible by definition, unless a popular American export happens to be at stake. In more ways than one, the xenophobic underpinnings of cold war rhetoric live on (even if multicorporate property rights now commonly take the place of politics), and the growing consequences of this enforced isolation are not pretty to contemplate. If anything or anyone has "lost its authority," this is the part of the critical establishment that continues to pass judgment on films it hasn't seen—unless what Denby means by authority is something that comes out of a cash register or sprays bullets.

■

Born in Warsaw in 1941, Kieslowski is nine years younger than Godard and seven years younger than Truffaut would be if he were alive, but he still can be regarded as a member of their generation, for better and for worse. Though he has described himself as not very religious, and though his main collaborator, Krzysztof Piesiewicz, who has cowritten every Kieslowski film for the past ten years, describes himself as Christian rather than Catholic, the thematic treatment of fate and the worshipful attitude toward young women as Madonna figures in Kieslowski's films both reflect the preoccupations of a Catholic sensibility that can also be traced through the films of Godard and Truffaut (among other French New Wave filmmakers) as well as those of Rossellini and Hitchcock, two of their key mentors.

In this respect, at least, his films are old-fashioned, and RED is no exception. Valentine is viewed throughout in idealistic and sexist terms, as Denby (among others) has pointed out, and the same could be said of Juliette Binoche in BLUE and Julie Delphy in WHITE (though in the latter case, the idealization is complicated by betrayal and treachery, as it often is in Godard's early features). All these women are treated as mythical and transcendental figures, though in some respects the major male characters are mythologized as well—the dead composer-husband in BLUE, the Chaplinesque fall guy (Zbigniew Zamachowski) in WHITE, the retired judge as a caustic, embittered seer in RED. As powerfully and beautifully embodied by Trintignant, this last character may represent the weightiest mythological presence in any Kieslowski film to date.

On the other hand, Kieslowski's sardonic and absurdist Polish wit infuses his films with a kind of harsh irony that is quite distinct from anything found in the French New Wave. As suggested earlier, RED abounds in poker-faced

Polish jokes, from the scene of the German shepherd escaping from Valentine into a church service to Valentine hitting the jackpot in a slot machine in her neighborhood café, which leads a bystander to comment that it's a sign of bad luck. Much later, the row of winning red cherries gets framed in the foreground of a shot while one of the characters passes outside the café in the background, not so much a joke as a reminder of the earlier one. Like so much of Kieslowski's style and vision, his wit tends to be more interrogative than declarative, which may cause some difficulties for viewers accustomed to Hollywood platitudes. The kind of cinema more interested in posing questions than in answering them—the cinema of Stroheim, Preminger, Rossellini, Cassavetes, Rivette, and Kieslowski, among others—is always bound to encounter resistance from viewers who go to movies in search of certainties, and who often settle for half-truths or outright lies as a consequence. To interrogate the world is to inaugurate a search that continues after the movie's over, implying a lack of closure that most commercial movies shun like the plague.

The difficulties of judging, of loving, of trusting are central to the lives of all the leading characters in "Three Colors," and if the burnt-out case of the judge comes to stand in some ways for all of them, this is largely because, like the heroine of BLUE and the hero of WHITE, his identity is chiefly formed by a life already lived—and shattered. Whether or not he has experienced a genuine resurrection by the end of RED remains an open question, but there is little doubt that he has glimpsed the possibility of one, much as Julie (Binoche) and Karol (Zamachowski) have before him. Throughout "Three Colors," Kieslowski's style has been devoted to discovering, exploring, and allowing us to glimpse this possibility. Judging by RED, the more we allow ourselves to experience his style, the more hopeful that possibility becomes.

—Chicago *Reader,* December 16, 1994

Chance and Control

Altman and the Spirit of Improvisation (CALIFORNIA SPLIT)

> Unless it is claimed that a pianist's hands move
> haphazardly up and down the keyboard—and no one
> would be willing to claim this seriously—it must be
> admitted that there exists a guiding thought, conscious or
> subconscious, behind the succession of organized sound
> patterns. . . . Of course, it does happen, and not too
> infrequently, that an instrumentalist's fingers "recite"
> a lesson they have learned; but in such cases
> there is no reason to talk about creation.
>
> —*André Hodeir*, Jazz: Its Evolution and Essence

> I can never think and play at the same time.
> It's emotionally impossible.
>
> —*Lennie Tristano, circa 1962*

Even before the title sequence starts, over the familiar Columbia Pictures logo, CALIFORNIA SPLIT has already begun to chatter. A steady rush of talk—telegraphed, overheard, sometimes barely audible—spills into the opening scenes like a scatter of loose change from a slot machine, meeting and eluding our grasp in imitation of a strictly chance operation. Admittedly the overall odds of the game are somewhat fixed: the movie has a script (by Joseph Walsh), two box office favorites (Elliott Gould and George Segal), and hard Hollywood money behind it. But the improvisatory spirit is unmistakable, if only because an alert audience is obliged to ad lib in order to keep up, feeling its way through a conjunction of foreground and background elements, and compelled to shift its attention as often as the characters.

At first glance a throwback to the rambling antics of M∗A∗S∗H, Robert Altman's new film in fact offers a substantially different experience. While the former film affected to play on the audibility range of its dialogue, it never really let the spectator miss a significant line. MCCABE AND MRS. MILLER, on the other hand, actually broached the idea of a spectator mingling with a plot—discovering it in his or her own way, in his or her own time—rather than simply following it. Altman's conception of character was altered in the process; the notion of collective effort in M∗A∗S∗H became overlaid with irony in MCCABE (where the successful building of a town was offset by the two lost figures who ran it) and virtually atomized in the broken encounters of isolated cranks in THE LONG GOODBYE. Much of this fragmentation and discontinuity persists in CALIFORNIA SPLIT: even if the sense of a common bond between the gambler heroes is practically all that keeps its putative narrative going, it is ostensibly determined and then severed by the arbitrary whims of chance, and continually interwoven with the jabbering world of compulsive night people around them.

For the first time in Altman, there is no moral judgment of the behavior occurring within this absurdist framework: the respective introverted and extroverted styles of Segal and Gould are presented in their own terms, as they play against each other, and interpretations are left to the viewer's discretion. The interest of these styles is based on a kind of existential suspense common to jazz and bullfighting, where identity/authenticity is prodded, tested, and revealed by outside pressures requiring some sort of accommodation— whether it's winning, losing, betting, being robbed, seduced (an extraordinary scene between Gwen Welles and Segal), interrupted (as, in the same scene, by Ann Prentiss), or otherwise challenged.

Altman's establishment of this climate largely derives from the chance encounters staged by his sound tracks through the intervention of an "independent" text, achieving some of its jazziest effects here through Phyllis Shotwell's raunchy delivery of (mainly) offscreen tunes. In the second scene at the local casino, a song begins loudly over the poker players in long shot, recedes to a murmur overtaken by these viewers in medium shot, then regains volume with a close-up of Segal—playing with an audience's diverse routes into a scene. The lyrics usually have only the broadest relation to the action, but sometimes they draw closer in witty surprises: "I'm goin' to Kansas City" is heard over the trip to Reno, and after the heroes arrive, Shotwell's and Gould's wholly independent raps suddenly converge on the word "nobody." Gould's verbal cadenzas embody this spirit throughout, for Charlie is an aggressive loudmouth forced to justify his vulgarity with inventiveness and virtuosity, whereas Segal plays, as it were, a sort of inner-fire Miles Davis to Gould's Charlie Parker. A similar contrast is afforded by the respective "hard" and "soft" styles of Prentiss and Welles, each as remarkable as the other.

After the more simplistic formal conjunctions of THIEVES LIKE US—Altman's touching demonstration that he can pursue a linear plot as such when he wants to—the life of the latest film is motored by a series of gambles taken for their own sake. Perhaps the most notable carryovers are the scenes of awkward domesticity: the polyphonic dinners of THIEVES LIKE US are matched by Charlie and Bill's wonderful breakfast of Froot Loops, Lucky Charms, and beer. The mottled lighting schemes of bars and gambling dens exploit the notion of competing centers of attention, and what might first appear as a loose construction of gags is in fact a packed surface composed of many constantly shifting parts.

Broadly speaking, as in the work of Jean Renoir, one witnesses the inscription of the experience of making a film onto the illusionist experience of watching one. Bridging the sense of play and chance that determines the conditions of both experiences, this essential "bifocal" vision guarantees some elements of documentary behind every fiction, a distinguishable counterline intertwined around each thread in a plot. In short, the charges already brought against CALIFORNIA SPLIT for formlessness suggests a grammatical problem more than a real one: its triumphant achievement—and Altman's—is to change form from a noun into a verb.

> —Adapted from a review in *Monthly Film Bulletin,* no. 491 (December 1974), with elements borrowed from "Improvisations and Interactions in Altmanville," *Sight and Sound,* Spring 1975 and a review of books by or about Jean Renoir (*Film Comment,* May–June 1976)

Lies of the Mind
(TALKING TO STRANGERS)

> Let us consider this waiter in the café. His movement is
> quick and forward, a little too precise, a little too rapid.
> He comes toward the patrons with a step a little too
> quick. He bends forward a little too eagerly; his voice, his
> eyes express an interest a little too solicitous for the order
> of the customer. . . . All his behavior seems to us a game.
> He applies himself to chaining his movements as if they
> were mechanisms, the one regulating the other; his
> gestures and even his voice seem to be mechanisms; he
> gives himself the quickness and pitiless rapidity of things.
> He is playing, he is amusing himself. But what is
> he playing? We need not watch long before we can
> explain it: he is playing at *being* a waiter in a café.
>
> —*Jean-Paul Sartre,* Being and Nothingness

As it happens, Sartre's waiter makes his guest appearance in the midst of a discussion about "patterns of bad faith." Let's assume, for our present purposes, that we're all playing at being philosophers in relation to a particular pattern of bad faith ("a lie to oneself") known as the movies, specifically, the activity of watching movies. Movies, in the everyday sense of the term, are staged fictions, and the everyday activity of watching movies entails lying to oneself in order to participate in these fictions.

To say that watching a movie is a form of bad faith is not necessarily to condemn that activity, either morally or philosophically. The presumption that movies are an art implies that they entail telling a lie to oneself that ultimately leads to a form of truth; and on some level, if we're sophisticated adult spectators, we always know that there's a lie involved in the experience. We know, for example, that we're watching twenty-four frames per second rather than a continuous, ongoing event, and that Orson Welles and Charles Foster Kane are not one and the same person, even if we agree to accept these fictions (among others) for a couple of hours. Yet by participating in this form of knowing and not-knowing, we share in some of the "bad faith" of role-playing pursued by the movie and the actors. Just as Sartre's waiter plays at being a waiter and Welles plays at being Kane, we play at being spectators—to our advantage and our peril.

Part of the presumption of Rob Tregenza's TALKING TO STRANGERS (which is showing this weekend at the Film Center) is that when strangers meet, they immediately and automatically fall into a kind of role-playing, a form of lying. But one of the many radical differences between this movie and most others is that it doesn't establish any privileged source of truth about its characters' identities in order to allow us to measure the extent of their lying. We see what these characters do, but we remain strangers to who and what they are, just as they remain strangers to one another. When we see a priest in a confessional (Henry Strozier), we know that he is a priest, but all we know about how he relates to being a priest is what he says and does; the rest of his identity remains inaccessible to us.

If one of the earmarks of a groundbreaking work is its capacity to confound and/or challenge existing categories and assumptions, Tregenza's first feature qualifies on several counts. Frankly and audaciously "experimental"—in the original rather than the generic sense of that term—it is shot in wide-screen 35 millimeter and direct Dolby sound, implicitly inviting us to experience it as a movie in a theater, not as a film in an austere screening space. Financed and photographed by the writer-director himself, a Baltimore resident who raised the money by making TV commercials, it combines the rigors of elaborate preplanning with the bold risk-taking of an aleatory event.

The movie consists of nine ten-minute takes, each of which features elaborately choreographed camera movements and an intricately calculated mise en scène; and though all of these sequences were carefully rehearsed, Tregenza insisted on shooting each of them only once. His basic rule was that each sequence would consist of ten minutes of uncut film (all that would fit in the camera), and the one time he encountered a technical difficulty (during the first 90 seconds of a scene mainly set inside a potter's studio) he used only the remaining footage, so this particular shot runs for only 8½ minutes. This adoption of a virtual one-to-one shooting ratio is central rather than incidental to the film's premise. Like the 35-millimeter film and the stereo sound recorded direct, it aims to maximize a sense of performance and presence and involve us fully in the contours of an *event* rather than oblige us to regard its idealized representation as we would in a Hollywood movie. All nine shots feature the same young man, Jesse (Ken Gruz); he is alone in the first and last shots and confronting one or more other people—talking to strangers—in the intervening seven; because of the present-tense quality of the shooting, the sense of confrontation is just as strong between the audience and the screen as it is between Jesse and the various people he encounters. The movie itself, in other words, is "talking to strangers" with the same uncertainty, ambiguity, disequilibrium, and suspense that are generated between Jesse and the other characters.

Equally important to the movie's premise, and in striking contrast to the eight one-reel takes that make up Hitchcock's ROPE (1948), is that Tregenza's nine shots are nonsequential and discontinuous. The placement of the first and last shots, when Jesse is alone—walking for several blocks through the busy streets of downtown Baltimore in the first and spray-painting an entire interior white in the last—was predetermined, but the order of the other seven was dictated by chance operations. This means that while each shot has a distinct narrative exposition regarding character as well as the scene's unfolding space, and each "tells a story," the movie as a whole is a string of isolated episodes that doesn't tell a single story.

The result of these procedures isn't a puzzle, but it does engage the spectator in a kind of game. The overall project of TALKING TO STRANGERS is existential—the game of defining and interpreting the reality of an event while it's unfolding without the safety net (i.e., focus or frame) of a narrator, character's viewpoint, or authorial voice. And to play this game, the spectator has to play a creative and participatory role and supply his or her own interpretive safety net, a "reading" of the events. This is not a game that can be won, but rather a dance of shifting accommodations and hypotheses—a bit like some of the challenges and invitations offered by life—that can be performed either well or badly. Since virtually all of the characters in TALKING TO STRANGERS, Jesse in particular, perform this dance badly, the stakes are increased, challenging us to understand the events better than they do.

One way to interpret this challenge is to regard Tregenza's movie as a kind of shaggy dog comedy, as Barbara Scharres suggestively does in her notes on the film in the November *Film Center Gazette*: "Jesse, a would-be writer, wanders the urban landscape like a particularly obnoxious graduate student in search of the experiences that will inspire his art. Meet one of the all-time screen jerks—impossible to like, yet thoroughly fascinating, appallingly funny, and finally pathetic in the impermeable self-centered denseness with which he encounters the world." While this is plausible as an after-the-fact impression of the film, it can only function intermittently while we're watching it, because the film can only suggest without confirming some of the hypotheses that make this reading possible.

Indeed, part of the trickiness of Tregenza's game is that Jesse's identity—as well as our relation to it—seems to shift from one sequence to the next. In the first, we follow his restless movement over several city blocks, including his nearly boarding three separate buses. In the second, a theatrical, pontificating regular at a soup kitchen—a character known as the General (Marvin Hunter)—engages Jesse in conversation and asks him what he does. After facetiously replying that he's a brain surgeon, Jesse says that he's a writer, and the General immediately leaps to the conclusion (which Scharres shares) that he's at the soup kitchen in search of material—a notion that makes the General so angry he calls Jesse a "spy" and indignantly gets a friend to eject him from the place. But Jesse insists that he's there because he's hungry, and in this scene, at least, we have no firm basis for doubting his word.

In the third sequence, shot on a riverbank, Jesse has a camera and a car, and claims to a stranger who pesters him (Dennis Jordan) that he's scouting locations for a fashion magazine; in the fourth, he's seeing a loan officer (Caron Tate) in a bank about paying back a college loan. But in later sequences, he describes himself variously as someone who's never been to college, as someone who's only passing through town and doesn't live there, and as a local waiter; and in a sequence on a taxi boat, where he appears to be either drunk or stoned *and* unemployed, he seems to be as presumptuous about labeling some fellow passengers as the General was about labeling him in the soup kitchen. In short, though we can easily conclude from the movie as a whole that Jesse is a compulsive bullshit artist, we can never fully determine which identities are real and which are assumed (including whether he's a real or would-be writer); and most of the other characters are comparably unfixed.

Needless to say, this makes it difficult to identify with any of the people in the movie, and I must admit that TALKING TO STRANGERS is a movie for viewers who are more likely to identify with a film's maker than with any of its characters. This may help to explain why this picture—which was enthusiastically and perceptively praised by both Dave Kehr in the *Chicago Tribune* and John Powers in the *L.A. Weekly* when it was shown at the Berlin Film Festival last winter—has been systematically rejected by every American film festival and distributor and every New York screening venue it has been submitted to. Luckily, it turned up at the Toronto Festival of Festivals in September, where I was able to see it twice, and it has subsequently been shown in Baltimore and Los Angeles, but as far as I know, this has so far represented the sum of its screenings in North America prior to its arrival in Chicago.*

It is clearly a movie that divides audiences, and one should add that Tregenza's decision to make it in 35 millimeter and stereo automatically excludes it from certain alternative venues that it might have otherwise had. But the importance of this utopian gesture in relation to the ghetto classification of most experimental films—Tregenza's insistence on making a *movie*—can't be overestimated.

A "masterpiece" is generally the work of a master, but the mastery of TALK-ING TO STRANGERS can't be broken down into the usual Oscar categories. Tregenza's cinematography is masterful by even the most conventional standards, though his dialogue and direction of actors simply are not. But what do we mean by "masterful" dialogue and acting? What we usually mean, I think, is dialogue and acting that are eloquent, witty, lucid, and believable, and that collectively "say something" in terms of a given reality.

---

*It was belatedly released on letterboxed video in November 1995 on Tregenza's own label after he started his own distribution company, Cinema Parallel, in the 90s, and it has also had brief theatrical runs in New York and Los Angeles since this article was written (1996).

This movie, however, is not interested in "saying something" apart from what the camera and microphones capture. It is interested in *doing* something, and any statement that arises from this act has to come from the spectator, contemplating a reality that is not so much given as jointly constructed, by the movie and spectator working together—just as the various strangers in the movie are working together to create any reality (or lack of same) that they happen to share.

What this means in practical terms is that the acting styles are often divergent and that the dialogue, which has fleeting moments of elegance, wit, and lucidity, seldom exists in a context where these moments are qualities that are shared by any two or more characters on-screen. The two most remarkable and action-packed sequences, which are set in a bank and on a bus, are both in fact terrifying in the degree to which they exhibit strong emotions and attitudes that are *un*shared, portraying an unsettling view of America as an extended lunatic fringe.

In the bank, a woman working as a loan officer is driven to a nervous collapse by the competing and overlapping demands of an irate customer, a bank manager, and her husband or lover, who repeatedly calls her on the phone. (For once, Jesse figures here as the sanest active character—another customer who becomes a bemused but sympathetic spectator.) The scene's overall thrust is realistic, but there's a brief moment or two in the timing of Caron Tate's otherwise believable performance as the loan officer—when she becomes hysterical and throws the phone receiver down—that registers as false. (We eventually learn from her dialogue that she's recently had an abortion, but that's all we find out about her background.) The contrived moment in her performance—assuming we all identify it as such—complicates the scene's tension by making us aware of the actress as actress, but in no respect does it detract from the scene's power and our own uneasy relation to it; it merely adds another level of uncertainty to our response.

The scene on the bus, the most complex and disturbing in the movie, begins as a conversation between Jesse and a middle-aged woman from Pennsylvania who has just boarded without the correct change, which Jesse supplies. Suddenly, a female punk named Trigger (Linda Chambers) enters the bus through the rear door and pulls out a gun. She's followed by her boyfriend, Slick (Richard Foster), and three other raucous males, who proceed to beat the driver unconscious, take over the wheel, and drag the middle-aged woman to the back of the bus and rape her in turn. The gang rape is glimpsed only peripherally and periodically at the edge of the screen while the camera focuses on Slick forcibly engaging Jesse in a kind of mock-Platonic dialogue about society, morality, and violence, with interjections from Trigger, who is meanwhile reading a book about astronomy.

Slick's nihilistic, quasi-intellectual discourse, which includes allusions to Freud and a proposal to force Jesse to participate in the gang rape, and is briefly interrupted by his cutting Jesse's shoulder with his knife, is eventually taken over by Trigger. Slick suggests that she participate in the rape as well and then moves to the back of the bus. She questions Jesse about homosexuality and then delivers a monologue about a hypothetical situation in which Jesse might rape a woman without witness or fear of reprisal. Jesse replies, "I'd require her to love me first," and Trigger calls him a "dinosaur." Slick then returns and tries to get Trigger to join in the rape; she shoots Slick in the belly, asks Slick and Jesse in turn at gunpoint whether they love her (Slick says yes, Jesse no), and the scene ends with another, offscreen gunshot.

The acting of this sequence is virtually flawless, as are the cinematography and direction (if one excepts the slight miscalculation in timing that prohibits our view of the final gunshot). The Dostoyevskian extravagance of the dialogue, on the other hand, though central to the scene's brilliance and horror, is so out of keeping with the relative verisimilitude of the rest of the film that it pushes Tregenza's philosophical and phenomenological project to its limits. So much happens within the space of ten minutes—even more than I've recounted here—we may feel afterward that we've just lived through an entire feature, in contrast to the minimal amount of incident in many other sequences.

A veritable anthology of Sartrean bad faith, social slights, and egocentric misapprehensions, TALKING TO STRANGERS repeatedly implicates the viewer in its awkward, fractured encounters by emphasizing the rawness and potential wildness of every event—an anything-can-happen feeling that is akin to some of the best jazz improvisations. Much as jazz presupposes a freedom to make mistakes, this movie assumes a fallibility in human interactions that has its comic as well as tragic side, for the hapless spectators as well as for the people on-screen.

Rather like Tati's PLAYTIME—the supreme "open" narrative work in movies that treats viewers and characters alike as distracted tourists—TALKING TO STRANGERS both offers and addresses itself to a gaggle of pontificators, theorists, and con artists who all play at constructing reality and themselves, at the same time and in the same gestures. (In this respect, it's also like Rivette's massive "board game" OUT 1, explored elsewhere in this book.) While Tregenza's sense of play is decidedly less sunny than Tati's, its feeling of adventure still calls to mind Charlie Parker's parting words to the father of existentialism when the two of them met in 1949: "I'm very glad to have met you, Mr. Sartre. I like your playing very much."

—Chicago *Reader,* November 4, 1988;
revised December 1995

Classification and Genre:
Musical Ghettos

If you haven't already heard of LATCHO DROM—an exuberant and stirring Gypsy musical, filmed in CinemaScope and stereophonic sound in eight countries on three separate continents—you shouldn't be surprised. Although the movie has been slowly wending its way across the planet for the past couple of years and picking up plenty of enthusiasts en route, it has at least three commercial strikes against it, any one of which would probably suffice to keep it out of the mainstream. The first two of these are the words "Gypsy" and "musical"; the third is the fact that it qualifies as neither documentary nor fiction, thereby confounding critics and other packagers everywhere.

These "problems," I hasten to add, are what make the picture pleasurable, thrilling, and important; but media hype to the contrary, sales pitches and audience enlightenment aren't always on the same wavelength. Though this movie is so powerful you virtually have to force yourself not to dance during long stretches of it, that fact doesn't translate easily into a thirty-second prime time spot or a review in a national magazine (though CNN did devote a four-minute feature to LATCHO DROM some time ago). Released in this country by a small company in Maine aptly called Shadow Distribution, it's been making the rounds like a faint rumor, generally without the assistance of our national drumbeaters; so when people stumble upon it, it carries all the excitement of a buried treasure.

Maybe one should cite as a fourth liability the foreign title, difficult for some to remember; it means "safe journey" in Romany, the Gypsy tongue. U.S. distributors have recently balked at such "difficult" titles as PRET À POR-TER and THE MADNESS OF KING GEORGE III (the latter, I'm told, because it sounds like a sequel—a drawback that will presumably keep Shakespeare's *Richard II* and *Richard III* off future marquees as well), changing them to READY TO WEAR and THE MADNESS OF KING GEORGE. An actual Gypsy phrase must sound as esoteric to them as something in Sanskrit. But this obstacle is minuscule compared to the other three.

■

Culture as we know it nowadays is most often defined, either implicitly or explicitly, in nationalistic terms. (We're apt to think of American culture as culture plain and simple, an implicit national imprint.) But Gypsy culture has no country, so we're stuck for labels. Technically LATCHO DROM is a French film—written and directed by an Algerian-born French citizen named Tony Gatlif, who has seven previous features under his belt, one of them Spanish. But existentially and aesthetically, LATCHO DROM is a Gypsy film—a film about Gypsies made by a Gypsy—which means it has no nationality at all. (Not having seen Gatlif's earlier features, I can't characterize them in this way, though the titles of the second and third, CANTA GITANO and CORRE GI-TANO, suggest Gypsy subjects.) And insofar as Gypsy experience falls between the cracks, a Gypsy movie is bound to do the same.

According to the *Encyclopedia Britannica,* a Gypsy is "any member of a dark Caucasoid people originating in northern India but living in modern times worldwide, principally in Europe. Most Gypsies speak Romany, a language closely related to the modern Indo-European languages of northern India, as well as the major languages of the country in which they live. It is generally agreed that Gypsy groups left India in repeated migrations and that they were in Persia by the 11th century, in southeastern Europe by the beginning of the 14th, and in western Europe by the 15th century." Broadly speaking, this last sentence provides a geographic synopsis of LATCHO DROM, which begins in northern India (Rajasthan) and proceeds though Egypt, Turkey, Romania, Hungary, Slovakia, France, and Spain. In each country, we find Gypsies making music, and often dancing.

But this bald description doesn't begin to do justice to the film's force and subtlety, both as filmmaking and as epic narrative. Sometimes we see music and dancing emerge out of everyday work (as in India); sometimes we see Gypsies observing other performers appreciatively (as in Egypt) and then translating these music and dance idioms into their own. In a Turkish restaurant and in a rural Hungarian train station we see them performing joyously for others, and in a Romanian village and in diverse locations in France we see them playing no less infectiously for themselves. In each country we find a different kind of Gypsy music and dancing, inflected in each case by the surrounding culture: the section in France culminates in a kind of jazz identified with Django Reinhardt; the Spanish finale begins with flamenco.

The *Britannica* also states: "All nomadic Gypsies migrate at least seasonally along patterned routes that ignore national boundaries." This conveys the temporal side of the film's structure, which begins in the summer and proceeds through the following three seasons. Though the film is uncluttered by dates or narration (apart from a brief passage at the very beginning), it gracefully unfolds within three simultaneous time frames: the past thousand years (tracing the Gypsy migrations from India to western Europe), the span of a single year, and ninety-nine minutes—that is, the length of the film itself. In the process it manages to convey a wealth of information about Gypsy history and current life without any didacticism. Apart from a few song lyrics and phrases of dialogue given minimal subtitles, it tends to do without words, relying mainly on images, music, and gestures—universal languages that, like Gypsy culture itself, traverse continents and centuries.

Emotionally, the movie conveys an intense, exuberant feeling of belonging that seems intimately tied to the alienation and persecution of Gypsies— though here it's nearly always the joy that's emphasized, not the suffering. The only exceptions that come to mind are pointed and brief. When the camera pans past a barbed-wire fence against a snow-covered field in Slovakia, then encounters an elderly Gypsy woman singing about Auschwitz, a tattooed number visible on her forearm, we may be reminded that nearly half a million Gypsies—an estimated one-fourth to one-sixth of their total numbers today— were exterminated in the Nazi death camps. And when we later see Gypsies being expelled from an abandoned building in a Spanish city, and the doors and windows of the building bricked over to keep them out, we're alerted to the external forces that keep Gypsies nomadic. (This scene leads into a climactic, soulful one in which a woman on top of a barren hill overlooking the city sings a lyric Gatlif himself wrote: "Some evenings, like many other evenings, I find myself envying the respect that you give your dog.") We're reminded at times of the persecution of other peoples, such as blacks, Jews, and homosexuals, and of the emotionally rich cultures that have resulted.

But chiefly the movie is celebratory, even ecstatic, about Gypsy experience. As Gatlif says,

> I wanted to make a film that the Roms [Gypsies] could be proud of, a film that wouldn't make a sideshow of their misery. I wanted to write a song of praise to this people I love. . . . I felt that if people really got to know Gypsies, they would lose their age-old prejudices: child kidnappers, chicken thieves. . . . Who cares about chickens anyway?

Some Gypsy friends from Paris and I wanted to buy 3,000 chickens with my author's royalties, put them in two semi-trailers and set them loose at dawn on the Champs-Elysées, handing out flyers saying: "The Gypsies give you back your chickens!" But we chickened out at the thought of the poor firemen who would have to run around rounding up 3,000 chickens!

■

Generically speaking, LATCHO DROM is a musical. But as we all know, the musical is dead—which means that this movie can't possibly exist. Why do we know that the musical is dead? Because the Hollywood propaganda machine has told us so, repeatedly. Now that the multinationals are in effect licensed to rewrite and regulate our film history, movie genres are restricted to the genres American studios feel equipped to make and promote, and everything else gets pushed off the sidewalk.

The industry wisdom is that the only kind of movie with singing and dancing that people will currently spend money to see is a cartoon feature. The reasons offered for this peculiar state of affairs vary. In his preface to *They Went Thataway,* a recent critical anthology devoted to movie genres, Richard T. Jameson explains why he has omitted musicals and included film noir and gangster films, westerns, comedies, romance, horror, science fiction, war films, women's films, literary adaptations, sequels, and remakes—even "the director as genre" and "the star as genre." Musicals, he says, have "all but vanished from the modern scene": the musical "has been run off by the rock-concert movie and the music video and, perhaps even more decisively, made redundant by the wall-to-wall song accompaniment of nonmusical films."

This is suggestive speculation, but it ignores the fact that successful stage musicals are still produced. And when you stop to consider that each of the last few Disney animated features has topped every one of its predecessors at the box office, it's even possible to conclude that audiences are starved for the kind of lift that only musicals can provide. One might argue further that the only reason Hollywood filmmakers aren't making other kinds of musicals is that they're no longer artistically or temperamentally equipped to do so—at least according to the studio executives who would OK such projects.

So much for traditional Hollywood musicals, and what other kind is there? Here again our implicit nationalistic bias comes into play: we equate Hollywood with conventional Hollywood, conventional Hollywood with America, and America with everything else in the world, as the current execrable PBS miniseries "American Cinema" seems to do. But if we stretch the "musical" genre to include nonconcert movies that feature musical performances and/or dancing, we get, for starters, ROUND MIDNIGHT, BIRD, MO' BETTER BLUES, HAIRSPRAY, EARTH GIRLS ARE EASY, THE FABULOUS BAKER BOYS, POSTCARDS FROM THE EDGE, BOB ROBERTS, LIFE STINKS, THE THING CALLED LOVE, IMMOR-

TAL BELOVED, and even PULP FICTION—all of them commercial Hollywood products.

Outside that category are three recent masterpieces indebted in many ways to the aesthetics and emotional dynamics of Hollywood musicals: Terence Davies's DISTANT VOICES, STILL LIVES, and THE LONG DAY CLOSES and Chantal Akerman's NIGHT AND DAY. There's the strange and beautiful last feature of Jacques Demy, THREE SEATS FOR THE 26TH, and Raul Ruiz's mesmerizing dance spectacle MAMMAME (both undistributed in this country). A couple of recent Mark Rappaport videos, POSTCARDS and EXTERIOR NIGHT, make exciting use of ballads, one of them brand-new. Then there are diverse classical music musicals like TOUS LES MATINS DU MONDE, THE PIANO, UN COEUR EN HIVER, THE ACCOMPANIST, and best of all THE SECOND HEIMAT. In short, you might say the musical is alive and well, though thanks to the ruling business discourse, it's in hiding. Only the conventional Hollywood musical is in eclipse.

In LATCHO DROM Gatlif appropriates what might be termed the stylistic architecture of older Hollywood musicals as purposefully as the Gypsy performers appropriate "national" music and dance, proving that the same sort of elation can be achieved without pit orchestras or soundstages. When the drudgery of everyday work is turned into music and dance, as in the opening sequence here, we could be watching the beginning of the classic 1932 musical LOVE ME TONIGHT. And when the camera cranes up from two elderly instrumentalists into the treetops, the exhilaration is worthy of the Arthur Freed unit at MGM. For a Gypsy caravan moving through a French village at dawn, Gatlif puts together a montage of barking dogs that's as musical as many of the numbers.

The only other attempt at a large-scale Gypsy musical that I'm aware of—Nicholas Ray's HOT BLOOD (1956)—pales in comparison to this one, at least when it comes to authenticity: Cornell Wilde and Jane Russell play the lead Gypsies. Still, HOT BLOOD isn't quite the debacle most accounts would have you believe. Bernard Eisenschitz in his recent invaluable Ray biography offers an interesting defense of its giddy stylistics as well as its "gaiety and energy." Better yet, maybe someone can be persuaded to screen a decent 'Scope print so we can judge for ourselves. It proves, along with LATCHO DROM, that the stylization of the Hollywood musical and the color and vibrancy of Gypsy life can find common ground.

■

Another important cross-reference to LATCHO DROM is Jacques Tati's last feature, PARADE. The comparison may seem far-fetched because PARADE—a circus film—isn't really a musical, doesn't feature Gypsies, and is mainly shot on video rather than on film. Yet in many crucial respects its formal procedures are the same, pointing to a radical social and political position on the meaning of spectacle. This position is anti-Hollywood and antielitist in roughly equal measure, constituting a kind of populism that rejects the usual hierarchies of class, race, and gender (as well as genre) without ever becoming esoteric or less than entertaining. In fact both movies appropriate certain aspects of popular entertainment—the circus for Tati, the musical for Gatlif—in order to redirect their energies.

Strictly speaking, LATCHO DROM qualifies as neither documentary nor fiction; it freely mixes both modes in a manner reminiscent of PARADE. Even more significant, both films break down the usual distinctions between performers and spectators; in every scene, being a member of the audience in the film means being an active participant in the unfolding spectacle, and by the same token, every performer becomes an audience member for other performers. Moreover, the democratic privilege of performing is extended to every age and both genders; young and old, male and female are equally involved in the festivities, and everyone is able to become the "star" at one point or another. In both movies young children play pivotal roles as guides, witnesses, pupils, and performers. Equally striking in both movies is the use of bricolage—the appropriation of impersonal objects for personal use that enables ordinary people to reshape and reclaim their environments: the fiddling geezer in LATCHO DROM who produces uncanny tonalities out of a loose violin string is the blood brother of the PARADE performers who juggle paintbrushes.*

Finally, and most radically, the points at which a number or sequence begins or ends in both films are usually almost impossible to determine. (A good example of this in recorded music is the album *Miles Ahead,* the first collaboration between Miles Davis and Gil Evans.) To define Gatlif's mastery, one merely has to look at his remarkable and subtle transitions, which bridge countries, sequences, and sometimes the segments within a sequence—transitions that closely correspond to Tati's own segues between onstage and offstage space and to his creative obfuscations of when a specific "act" or activity starts and stops. These subtle transitions subvert our usual notions of spectacle, tied to the stylization of most musicals, in which passing from "life" to the heightened reality of a particular musical number is emphasized rather than glossed over. But in this movie, as in PARADE, every event has a heightened reality that never ceases to be life. Both films create an impression of unbroken poetic continuity—a continuity between life and performance that sweeps the spectator along. In the case of LATCHO DROM that continuity traverses centuries and seasons as well as continents, becoming a function of nature as well as human endurance. Check it out.

—Chicago *Reader,* February 10, 1995

*For more particulars on the radicalism of PARADE, see my article on the film in *Foreign Affairs,* edited by Kathy Schulz Huffhines (San Francisco: Mercury House, 1991), 231–237.

Four Books on the Hollywood Musical

THE HOLLYWOOD MUSICAL,
by Clive Hirschhorn. New York: Crown.

HOLLYWOOD MUSICALS,
by Ted Sennett. New York: Harry N. Abrams.

THE HOLLYWOOD MUSICAL,
by Ethan Mordden. New York: St. Martin's Press.

GENRE: THE MUSICAL,
edited by Rick Altman. London & Boston:
Routledge & Kegan Paul
(BFI Readers in Film Studies).

If the musical has nearly been vanquished as a popular form by the increasing subdivision of its audience into separate classes, age groups, and ethnic interests, these four books on the subject which nostalgically chart its heyday are similarly compartmentalized and exclusive. It seems inevitable that each of these four elegant receptacles for the most libidinal of American movie genres should address a different portion of our psyches: after all, if our society and minds are splintered, why shouldn't our integral genres be as well?

The glib marketing strategies that aim each book at a somewhat different audience create the odd social effect of four high-rises, each constructed inside a separate ghetto—although the attractive coffee table books of Clive Hirschhorn and Ted Sennett might also be regarded with some justice as adjacent towers on somewhere like Sutton Place. The former—by describing in detail 1,344 musicals (a longish paragraph devoted to each) that are listed year by year, then cross-indexed by titles, songs, performers, composers, lyricists, and other creative personnel—is an indispensable reference tool, and, as far as I know, the best of its kind. The latter is of interest chiefly for its beautifully reproduced stills and frame enlargements, many of them in full color—making this book the only pure luxury item in the bunch. Sennett's critical-survey text, while serviceable and pleasant enough, can't really compete with the dazzling illustrations, which can only be gaped at or mooned over. (Beneath a big color image of the climax of Carmen Miranda's "The Lady in the Tutti-Frutti Hat" number in the 1943 THE GANG'S ALL HERE—with the star wedged under an expanding thirty-foot cascade of bananas and flanked on each side by an army of gigantic, Magritte-like strawberries—is a caption that can only rationalize delirium with production anecdotes, amusing yet secondary.)

It's hard to think of two better books about the musical than Ethan Mordden's and Rick Altman's; why, then, are they so completely at loggerheads with one another? Mordden's fund of facts about the musical is encyclopedic, vast, intelligent, and usually on display like an Afghan hound; he doesn't mind letting you know that he knows such things as how they say "supercalifragilisticexpialidocious" in the German-dubbed versions of MARY POPPINS. Much more important, a sensitivity for and technical grasp of the *music* in musicals virtually place him in a class by himself. His overall command of information is awesome, yet on a stylistic level of aspiration he often seems to aim at the consistency of chatter rather than of sustained thought—a journalistic trait shared at times by writers such as Stephen Harvey and Vito Russo, predicated on the assumption that, existentially speaking, nothing is important enough to be extended beyond the boundaries of a wisecrack or pithy paragraph. "A string of pearls without a string" is how Eisenstein once described the great Russian formalist Viktor Shklovsky, but a single page of Mordden is often little more than a sack of brightly colored jelly beans: "Lawrence Tibbett invaded a song, John Boles comforted it. Chevalier attended it as if it were a party in his honor."

At its best, in the short run, this is like the celebrated form of one-shot skeet-shooting practiced by writers like James Agee and Arlene Croce in their reviews and essays. At its worst, particularly over the long haul, it can trivialize its own claims for seriousness with its virtual enslavement to a bantering tone that places everything on the same level of nonimportance. ("How is HALLELUJAH patronizing? True, it doesn't show us any white oppressors. But you can't have everything." Apparently you can't in prose, either.) The culmination of both strains in Mordden's writing can be found in the Ethan Mordden Hall of Fame and Disrepute that comes at the end, after a useful discography and bibliography—a jokey, self-indulgent, and campier version of Andrew Sarris's Pantheon exercises that offers us such gold-plated prizes as "Most Daring Studio" (Paramount), "Least Faithful Adaptation from Broadway" (the 1938 SALLY, IRENE AND MARY), "Best Editing" (ALL THAT JAZZ), "Best Argument from the Right" (THE WIZARD OF OZ), and "Fernando Lamas Award for Best Male Singer Born in Argentina Who Appeared in FOUR JILLS AND A JEEP" (Dick Haymes).

If Mordden singles out THE BAND WAGON as the "Worst Celebrated Film," his short paragraph on the film in the main text begins to explain why:

A back-stager without the slightest taste of the theatre, it was fashioned by Minnelli, Comden and Green, all stage veterans who should know better, using Schwartz and Dietz standards. The score is great and "The Girl Hunt Ballet," a Mickey Spillane takeoff for Astaire and Cyd Charisse, amusing. But the story is tired, the attempted burlesque of "serious" musicals rude, Oscar Levant atrocious, and Jack Buchanan as uncharming as when he marred MONTE CARLO back in 1930.

But apart from telling us why Ethan Mordden doesn't like THE BAND WAGON—which may or may not be meaningful in a separate context—the actual information or insight conveyed in such a summary is surprisingly meager.

Among the references to THE BAND WAGON in the index to the Altman anthology are some insightful remarks about the film by Thomas Elsaesser (in a first-rate 1970 postauteurist study of Minnelli drawn from the *Brighton Film Review*), a passing but pointed observation by Alain Masson about the film's functional uses of nonrealism (in the midst of a brilliant, perverse, and semi-persuasive defense of George Sidney translated from *Positif*), some brief reflections on the validation of entertainment versus art from Robin Wood in *Film Comment,* and some detailed psychoanalytical annotations from Dennis Giles in *Movie*. There's also a fascinating and original argument by Alan Williams, written expressly for this volume, about the functions of sound recording in the illusionism of musicals, with Fred Astaire's delivery of the film's opening number used as a central example; Jane Feuer, in a *Quarterly Review of Film Studies* article, uses the film to illustrate myths about entertainment (involving spontaneity, integration, and the audience) that crop up in self-reflective musicals; and Martin Sutton, in another original essay, reflects on the movie's narrative patterns involving isolation (e.g., "By Myself," Astaire's opening number) and group acceptance (e.g., "That's Entertainment").

"That's *entertainment?*" I can hear some of my anti-intellectual, musical-buff colleagues skeptically declaring, on being faced with the diverse investigations of the Altman anthology. All I can say is, *I* was entertained much of the time—believing, as I firmly do, that entertainment and enlightenment are ideally (if often deviously) interconnected. (As bathtub reading, I would argue that the Mordden and Altman score about equally.) As Alan Williams notes, "Some of the *pleasure* given by musical numbers might actually be something closer to *pseudo-bliss,* since the effect, so subtle as to pass generally unperceived, is an implicit loss of coherence of the sustained spectator." One could almost say that the critical prose of Mordden, Croce, and Kael also implies a loss of coherence through its absence of sustained theory or argument; in this respect, it seems that the musical and this kind of prose are both predicated on the puritanical assumption that pleasure and intelligence (or analysis) are incompatible bedfellows.

Consequently, in the world of these latter writers, the diverse achievements of the authors of the Altman anthology don't even deserve to be dismissed; instead they are systematically ignored. Thus it seems only logical that in a recent roundup review in *The New Yorker,* Arlene Croce decried the relative absence of intelligent writing about the musical—rightly pointing to the Mordden as a prize catch—while steadfastly refusing to acknowledge the existence of the Altman book, or any related academic endeavors. It may not be irrelevant to add that Altman's book takes a swipe at Croce in turn, in its generally useful bibliography by Jane Feuer, when it refers to her classic book on Astaire and Rogers as "a witty and elegant though superficial analysis." (Alas, the respective professional armor of the journalist and the academic is stronger in both these cases than any sense of allegiance to the unaffiliated reader looking for a good intelligent text on a subject. Croce and Feuer are both witty writers, as it happens, who happen to be answerable to what amounts to rival cults.)

The best so far of the BFI Readers in Film Studies, *Genre: The Musical* is full of interesting ideas about its subject, and fully deserves a place on my shelf right next to Mordden's book. Especially helpful are the remarks by Williams and Feuer about the manner in which musicals, to paraphrase Rick Altman, mobilize radical techniques for conservative purposes. When Richard Dyer remarks, in one of the best essays, that entertainment presents what utopia feels like rather than how it would be organized, he's merely touching on the existence of a social and ideological structure that most journalists would rather adopt (or adapt) than acknowledge, analyze, or contest. Characteristic of this mode is Mordden's show-bizzy gloss on W. Franklyn Moshier's *The Alice Faye Book* in his own bibliography:

> Faye and her films are basic to the musical both historically and today on television, and serious students should put some time in here. A good start: turn to page 98 for a still of what Moshier captions as the "distinctive Faye pose." Try striking this pose yourself, if possible in one of Faye's costumes. How do you feel?

If Mordden's bibliography and Feuer's went out on a blind date, it is difficult to imagine all the comic complications that might ensue. Set those collisions and accommodations to music, and you might even have a hit on your hands. In the meantime, within the mutually exclusive environments fostered by these four books, there is plenty of value to be found in each one. It all depends on what you're looking for, how you feel, and who you are.

—*Film Quarterly* 35, no. 4 (Summer 1982)

Part Two

Entertainment as Oppression

The Hollywood Apparatus

Entertainment as Oppression

1. The conviction that our world is being run and destroyed by scoundrels or lunatics, combined with a feeling of helplessness about any possibility of changing this, can be found in at least three of the most popular recent American movies—a mainstream fantasy-adventure (BATMAN), an art house picture (CRIMES AND MISDEMEANORS), and a radical leftist documentary (ROGER & ME). Oddly enough, the implication of the responses to these films is that if they were any less pessimistic and defeatist, they'd also be less entertaining.

Wittingly or not, all three movies derive much of their entertainment value from a form of cruelty and black humor that largely depends on a frustrated nerd hero—Bruce Wayne/Batman (Michael Keaton) in BATMAN, a "serious" unsuccessful documentary filmmaker named Cliff Stern (Woody Allen) in CRIMES AND MISDEMEANORS, and the director Michael Moore himself in ROGER & ME—who is less a target of ridicule than a conduit by which ridicule can be deflected onto other victims or stooges. All three movies also have a powerful amoral villain who elicits uneasy envy and/or admiration: Jack Nicholson's Jack Napier/Joker in BATMAN, Alan Alda's TV producer in CRIMES AND MISDEMEANORS, and Roger Smith, the dry and elusive chairman of General Motors, in ROGER & ME.

Some of the cruelty can be felt in the unusually loud laughter in cinemas that greets the Joker's "artistic" murders and media crimes, the account by Cliff Stern's sister of her humiliation by a sexual pervert whom she met through a classified ad (and Stern's horrified responses, which are telegraphed to the audience as gag lines), and the eviction of unemployed workers from their homes in Flint, Michigan, on Christmas Eve.

The *Chicago Tribune*'s Dave Kehr has pointedly referred to ROGER & ME as the first feel-good atrocity film, but the same sort of pleasure and delight can be found in savoring the infested universe of BATMAN, characterized by the battles between a neurotic and a psychotic in a postapocalyptic Gotham City, and CRIMES AND MISDEMEANORS, where crime pays, philosophers with faith in love commit suicide, and nice guys finish last.

The entertainment quotient of these films is in fact so similar that it may be misleading to give them the genre labels I've selected. One might equally call BATMAN an expensive art film, CRIMES AND MISDEMEANORS a tragicomic soap opera, and ROGER & ME a sour sitcom: many of the former divisions separating the mainstream from any kind of counterculture are effectively wiped out by this new sort of be-all and end-all movie. We seem to be transfixed by a single movie culture now, and it's a chilling one to contemplate.

Ironically, BATMAN is the only one of the three to own up to its own perversity—the fact that one winds up preferring the creativity and vitality of Jack/Joker, a virtual blood brother to Alex in A CLOCKWORK ORANGE, to the humorless, iconographic rigidity of Bruce/Batman, who turns out to be as charismatic as J. Edgar Hoover—although it happens to be the only one of the three in which the forces of "good" triumph. The other two postulate a contemporary moral crisis in the way that we live and think, but without investing the victims of this crisis—the murdered mistress (Angelica Huston) of an ophthalmologist in CRIMES AND MISDEMEANORS, the unemployed and evicted ex-auto workers in ROGER & ME—with the roundness and humanity that would make them something more than abstractions. If anyone appeals to the audience's heart, it is the actors/filmmakers Allen and Moore, ineffectual sad sacks who serve as witnesses and spokespeople for the audience's self-satisfied despair.

The fact that Michael Moore's vantage point is strictly that of the disaffiliated working class while Allen's is no less strictly that of the comfortable white bourgeoisie certainly deserves mention, as does the fact that both films, unlike BATMAN, launch attacks on the ruthlessness of the rich (and, in Moore's case, a particularly stinging one). But when it comes to audience responses, upper-middle-class viewers feel rewarded and enlightened rather than challenged or threatened by CRIMES AND MISDEMEANORS, which attacks self-interest without being able to see beyond it, and yuppie viewers find little trouble laughing at their counterparts in ROGER & ME.

The polemical aspects of these films may not be entirely neutralized by their success as entertainments. There is something irreducible about the anger in ROGER & ME—to my mind the most serious and most entertaining film of the lot—which no amount of laughter can wash away. But these polemics are nevertheless mitigated and complicated by spectators who find the very notion of moral bankruptcy enjoyable.

2. A front-page story in the August 24, 1988, *Variety* began, "Last week's Republican National Convention garnered the worst network ratings of any convention in TV history." The story went on to report that the summer's political conventions significantly boosted video rentals by 30 to 57 percent. Should we interpret this as an opting for entertainment over news coverage or as a preference for one kind of entertainment over another? Do we read it as a sign of desperate cynicism or healthy liberation? And if the latter, was it liberation only from the routine network shows that the conventions were preempting? By normal standards, it degrades a political convention—but validates a movie—to regard it simply as entertainment. But with show biz equally operative and pertinent in both spheres, we do ourselves a disservice by making these hard distinctions.

As American movies and political candidates get progressively worse, the talent for marketing them steadily increases. Yet on the whole, the promotion of movies has been more successful than the promotion of politicians. In its current state-of-the-art phase, the former consists not only of luring people into theaters but also of convincing them afterward that the experience was worthwhile. This has been facilitated over the past several years by the media's willingness to furnish "big" releases with unprecedented free advertising to bolster the studio's own lavish campaigns.

Major cable channels that profess to be commercial-free now routinely run free trailers or diverse promotional features for the same pictures, and most popular newspapers and magazines follow suit. Very occasionally an attempt is made to follow the procedures of honest journalism rather than simple promotion. But in effect all the bought and unbought media attention yields the same result: the ironclad certainty that only a few titles, the same ones being pushed through almost every channel at once, can impinge on one's consciousness at any given moment. Thus the ordinary spectator, who innocently assumes that there is no essential difference between publicity and criticism, usually turns out to be correct.

The final arbiter in this process, after all, is not the critic but the weekly box office charts, which have gone beyond their original (debatable) function as popularity polls and are now more like weather reports. The "canny" reviewer is often the one most adept at predicting the weather. Some of the movies being promoted like this turn out to be boosting other products as well: BACK TO THE FUTURE PART II, which can already be regarded as a commercial for its predecessor—at least until it reaches its climax, which is a trailer for PART III—is also roomy enough to accommodate numerous other product plugs; and when it is released on video, one would not be surprised to find it preceded by more ads and/or trailers. Given the success of that picture and BATMAN, with its own warehouse of ancillary products, it's beginning to seem that whatever sells most sells best.

3. It may be a partial legacy of the Puritan work ethic that making money is never regarded in our society as any sort of escape. So little, in fact, is it currently considered a form of escape that virtually every other activity that fills our lives—eating, reading, thinking, sleeping, going to the bathroom, having sex, exercising, watching TV, talking to friends or relatives, going to movies, getting drunk or stoned—*is* considered a form of escape, an escape from making money and whatever that entails.

One obvious reason why entertainment is treated more respectfully in our culture than art is because it has more to do with making money—that is, making money for somebody else in most cases. The general view of this phenomenon is even a bit tautological: if a movie makes a lot of money, it *has to be* entertaining. And because participation in the moneymaking process is seen as a serious, responsible communal activity, even if one participates only as a consumer, the Puritan work ethic has somehow gotten turned around in our minds to form a kind of imperative about entertainment: it is our *duty* to be entertained and thereby contribute to the moneymaking process. (Moviegoing may be a minor form of escape from making money, but it's an excusable one if the movie is a box office hit, which means that at least someone is making money from it, thanks to our participation.) Art, by contrast, is seen as a kind of rarefied luxury—unless it also happens to bring in large sums of money, in which case it can at least aspire to the seriousness of entertainment.

Consider the controversies in recent years about federal arts funding. Many U.S. liberals now, happily ignoring what most of the rest of the world thinks (or knows, based on experience) about this subject, believe that federally funded art of any kind is a mistake—even, potentially, a form of "enslavement." Ask them what they think about federally funded business (which can and often does mean federally funded entertainment), and chances are they'll either scratch their heads or argue that, contrary to federally funded art, it's a form of "freedom" (never mind who's being freed or enslaved in such transactions). But it's clear that we'll never have a National Endowment for Business only because we'll never need one; federal assistance to business is already so all-pervasive that such an agency would be redundant. By contrast, any federal funding of art today apart from, say, military marching bands (which commands more of federal arts funding than everything else combined) automatically becomes dangerous by virtue of the fact that it valorizes art over business (i.e., entertainment).

4. Entertainment is often defined in our minds by what it isn't. "The life of Jesus isn't entertainment," read one of the placards in front of Chicago's Biograph Theater protesting THE LAST TEMPTATION OF CHRIST. Another placard read, "God doesn't like this movie." Does that mean that God wasn't entertained by it?

5. Perhaps the division set up between entertainment and art is misleading. There was a time, after all, in the English-speaking world, when "art films" were associated mainly with foreign-language pictures. The revolution in taste brought about by Andrew Sarris in the United States and by *Movie* in Britain argued that directors such as Hawks and Hitchcock were every bit as artistic as Bergman and Fellini, and that automatically associating art with subtitles was a form of snobbery.

By the time this new taste took hold on the level of film production and promotion, it was less beneficial to the old-style auteurs, who had got their way artistically chiefly through subterfuge, than it was to the new generation of "movie brats," Bogdanovich, Coppola, De Palma, Scorsese, and Spielberg, who were suddenly bestowed with the honors and credentials of authorship and artistry that had largely been denied their predecessors. Ironically, most were praised less for their originality than for the degrees to which they emulated their American masters, much as Allen and Cimino were applauded for their appropriations of Bergman and Visconti.

This confusion between art and entertainment involves questions of content as well as style. Significantly, Roger Ebert recently selected both MISSISSIPPI BURNING and DO THE RIGHT THING as two of the ten best movies released in the 80s, implicitly giving the same sort of value to a studio picture with stars that postulates the FBI (represented by two white stars) as the progressive spearhead of the civil rights movement and an independent production that accords the same position to Martin Luther King, Jr., and Malcolm X (while pointedly making use of no heroes in its plot). The same leveling takes place when one considers the press treatment of Spielberg's THE COLOR PURPLE and EMPIRE OF THE SUN, both regarded as "art films" and hence somehow more comparable to PASSION or SHOAH than to SONG OF THE SOUTH, THE LONGEST DAY, or E.T.

Some readers may feel I'm exaggerating the turnaround, but consider the evidence. In the summer of 1989, at a seminar on American independent cinema held in Lisbon, Richard Peña, Jon Jost, and I were asked by several Portuguese participants why Spielberg wasn't regarded as an American independent. A look at what was then playing in Lisbon—exclusively American and English movies, apart from AU REVOIR LES ENFANTS and WOMEN ON THE VERGE OF A NERVOUS BREAKDOWN, with no Portuguese films in sight—helped to explain how such a question could be asked.

6. Some healthy confusion about what constitutes art was aroused by the U.S. release of Terence Davies's remarkable DISTANT VOICES, STILL LIVES (1988). Most art films scare away large audiences by their intellectual content or their exotic subject matter, but this masterpiece has neither. It was probably the relative absence of plot—the ne plus ultra of commercial filmmaking—that deprived the movie of the larger audience it could and should have had, even if this absence permits a wholeness and an intensity to every moment that is inaccessible to most narrative filmmaking.*

The fact that domestic violence and emotional pain form part of this intensity led some critics to confuse the part with the whole and conclude that the film was a "downer"; even worse, some evoked the specter of pretension and *rigor artis* (Agee's phrase). These responses overlooked the fact that an extraordinary amount of the film was devoted to people *enjoying* themselves, above all by singing in communal get-togethers.

We all go to movies for pleasure, and it appears that more people have been going to movies lately than ever before; but how often do we see the people *in* these movies enjoying themselves? The sheer pleasure shown by the women (and occasionally the men) while they're performing songs throughout Davies's film makes these moments into exquisite, sustained epiphanies—stretches of unabashed delight totally unlike the kinds of enjoyment that we can find in recent commercial movies. I'm not just thinking of Batman's melancholia or Indiana Jones's frustration. I'm also thinking of the catalogs of physical and emotional punishment meted out to characters in nearly all the movies I saw during the same summer that Davies's film played in Chicago, including THE ABYSS, DEAD POETS SOCIETY, THE KARATE KID PART III, LETHAL WEAPON 2, LOCK UP, A NIGHTMARE ON ELM STREET 5, SCENES FROM THE CLASS STRUGGLE IN BEVERLY HILLS, TURNER & HOOCH, UNCLE BUCK, WEEKEND AT BERNIE'S, AND WHEN HARRY MET SALLY . . .

I'm not trying to deny that the characters in Davies's film suffer a great deal as well. But given the hype about how much "fun" the aforementioned Hollywood features were supposed to be—and the bias in this culture that "art films" like DISTANT VOICES, STILL LIVES are supposed to be dreary yet vaguely edifying experiences, rather like castor oil—it's amazing how little real and sustained pleasure there is in the former movies, and how much we're allowed to see and share with Davies's people (how much, in fact, we're able to luxuri-

---

*As in Davies's subsequent THE LONG DAY CLOSES (1992), the structure and movement of thought itself are what compose the "action," but it is not the kind of thought that can be translated into prose; it thinks in sounds and images. The difficulties for criticism in handling this sort of expression are manifold; in the case of THE LONG DAY CLOSES, part of the problem may have stemmed from critics having already squandered most of the apt terms on Hollywood thrillers and the like. After one read and heard in numerous places that RESERVOIR DOGS, CLIFFHANGER, and IN THE LINE OF FIRE were all about "redemption," how much sense did it make to say that THE LONG DAY CLOSES was about redemption as well? [1995]

ate in their fleeting yet ecstatic happiness). The sheer physicality and empowerment of their songs, their laughter, their smiles, and even on occasion their tears make one feel grateful to be alive; by contrast, even some of the more exciting moments in INDIANA JONES AND THE LAST CRUSADE and BATMAN make one feel like an invalid on sedation getting jolts of electroshock.

7. The French are fond of using the word "pleasure" a little bit like the way we use the word "entertainment." One advantage to "pleasure" is that it implies commitment rather than distraction, and doesn't create an implied pejorative distinction between art (serious) and entertainment (nonserious). When entertainment is defined as a form of relaxation, or at least closely associated with that experience, the implication is that an absence of excitement or passionate feeling is as important to the experience as an absence of thought. (Ronald Reagan, by this criterion, is entertainment, not art.)

What is the stereotypical desire of the hardworking capitalist who comes home from a long day at work carving up his or her neighbors and wants a little peace and quiet? To unwind, relax, take it easy; take a bath, read the paper, see a show. To forget the world and the bloodbath one's left behind and divert one's attention to something else.

The problem is, all of us, even the bloodthirstiest capitalists, cheat on this premise. People don't stand in line to see movies like WHO FRAMED ROGER RABBIT, A FISH CALLED WANDA, DIE HARD, or BATMAN with the intention of being put to sleep by them. One thing these four hits have in common is that they're frenetic; their action is defined by catastrophes, and they're populated largely by manic types. To call them utopian may not be wholly inaccurate, but it doesn't get us very far in describing what it's like on an immediate level to watch them. *Almost* going to hell in a handbasket is what most of the characters in these movies seem to be doing. Are narrow escapes from oblivion and destruction the only form of utopia available to us—perhaps because we're too jaded to believe in any others?

8. Would it be acceptable to assert that I happen to find SHOAH, a 503-minute nonfiction investigation into the Holocaust, "entertaining"? I certainly don't mean to imply that it isn't full of pain and sorrow. And it certainly compels one to think; as a complex statement that stages a dialectical encounter between existentialism and Judaism, the present and the past, it obliges us to reflect on the Holocaust in a way that many of us have never done before.

But it's only the use of "entertainment" in our vocabulary as a puritanical censoring device that arbitrarily isolates the experience of an art film like SHOAH from the experience of being entertained at the movies. After all, SHOAH is a more concentrated, extended, and serious version of what we're asked to think about in a "pure" movie such as JUDGMENT AT NUREMBERG. Why should the fact that Claude Lanzmann performs this task infinitely better than Stanley Kramer—without the benefit of Judy Garland or the ultimate certification of Oscars—deprive us of the validating term "entertainment"?

9. THE BEST YEARS OF OUR LIVES (1946) is a good example of how the postwar 40s dealt with the challenge of bearing witness to a social reality and entertaining an audience at the same time. The mesh of strategies isn't a perfect fit, and much of the film trails off into mystifications about what happens to armless veterans, but at least the 40s audience was willing to accept the results as a "movie" and a "film" at the same. In the case of George Romero's MONKEY SHINES, the mass audience got scared away from one of the purest movie entertainments of that year (1988) because the hero is a quadriplegic, and quadriplegics by (puritanical mis-) definition are incompatible with entertainment—unlike heroes who have two broken legs, like James Stewart in REAR WINDOW. It sounds crazy and it certainly becomes self-defeating, but the very word "quadriplegic" makes MONKEY SHINES sound like a film rather than a movie to people who haven't seen it. Even quadriplegics themselves aren't amused, to judge from reports of a protest by quadriplegics against the movie's trailer in Los Angeles—which suggests that practically everyone seems to agree a priori that quadriplegics and movies don't mix. Consequently, one of the year's most effective entertainments gets treated like a leper.

10. On the other hand, an alleged "film" like WINGS OF DESIRE is chock-full of old-fashioned movie pleasures, from ethereal flights over Berlin to Peter Falk's gutbucket voice and husky charisma, and audiences don't seem to mind at all. The movie doesn't even ask us to think very much (indeed, by the final scenes it seems to ask us to stop thinking entirely)—less, say, than THE LAST EMPEROR, another good example of crossover between film and movie that doesn't scare an audience away. But the best cover of all for a filmmaker who wants to do something adventurous and "filmic" is to hide behind a foolproof package and formula, as director Renny Harlin does in A NIGHTMARE ON ELM STREET 4. As long as there's no apparent threat that anything "serious" is being attempted, a filmmaker is free to do anything at all—in this case, put together a film that is little more than a nonnarrative string of dreams.

11. Once upon a time, a turkey was a bad film and a bomb was a film that lost money. Even as recently as 1985, when Harry and Michael Medved's *Son of Golden Turkey Awards* appeared, calling a movie a turkey was still a matter of taste and opinion (as it was in 1980, when the Medved brothers cited both IVAN THE TERRIBLE and LAST YEAR AT MARIENBAD as two of "the fifty worst movies of all time"). But by late 1989, a press release from James Monaco's Baseline ("the entertainment industry's information service") about "the ten

top turkeys of the 80s" suggested that taste and opinion had finally given way to the bottom line, at least where turkeys were concerned.

Estimating budgets, rentals, and losses in separate columns, Baseline listed, in descending order:

1. INCHON
2. THE ADVENTURES OF BARON MUNCHAUSEN
3. ISHTAR
4. HEAVEN'S GATE
5. THE COTTON CLUB
6. PIRATES
7. RAMBO III
8. SANTA CLAUS
9. LION OF THE DESERT
10. EMPIRE OF THE SUN
11. ONCE UPON A TIME IN AMERICA

To give some sense of the overall range, no. 1 lost $44 million, while no. 11 lost $27.5 million—at least if Baseline's arithmetic (which equates eleven turkeys with ten) is reliable.

What conclusions, if any, are we to draw from this? Out of the seven that I've seen, three (nos. 2, 3, and 11) are among my favorite films of the 80s, and I know critics who would include nos. 4, 5, and 10 on their own lists. None of these comes close to qualifying as the worst movies of the decade, although I suspect that is exactly how some Baseline subscribers will interpret the list (the same ones, in fact, who equate bombs with turkeys).

Reflecting on the widespread critical disapproval of nos. 2 and 3, I believe it could be argued that the expectation that they would lose a fortune had a lot to do with their repudiation. It's rather as if many critics chose to identify with investors rather than with characters or filmmakers. Elaine May, in particular, seemed to get lost in much of the negative hyperbole surrounding ISHTAR, so that almost no one saw fit to relate it to her three previous features. The configuration made by all four is strikingly coherent: two films about betrayed marriages, A NEW LEAF and THE HEARTBREAK KID, followed by two films about betrayed friendships, MIKEY AND NICKY and ISHTAR, the first and last of the four concluding with reconciliations.

12. Entertainment usually implies that only one part of the brain is being used. Secretly, I suspect, all of us would rather be enraptured than diverted, and shaken up rather than soothed; but supposedly, goes the received wisdom, there's something "safer" about mild diversion—even if it eventually becomes a bludgeoning form of oppression. Imagine drowning in a sea of Perry Comos

and you've got the 50s and its taste for tranquilizers down to a tee. Or think of Ronald Reagan, who wouldn't be caught dead in a film and has managed to catch us all, dead as doornails, at the movies. But to reduce our possibilities to a distorted series of either/or propositions, which producers, distributors, exhibitors, reviewers, and audiences seem to be doing in increasing numbers—art *or* entertainment, entertainment *or* edification, film *or* movie, artistic (hit) *or* economic (turkey)—is to limit our capacities to experience any of them.

—Derived from articles in Chicago *Reader,*
September 23, 1988, and *Sight and Sound,*
Spring 1990

> Who is correct? Are we becoming better off
> or worse off? Where are we heading?
> It depends on whom you mean by "we."
>
> —*Robert B. Reich,* The Work of Nations

"Men never *get* this movie," a woman says to her friend in Nora Ephron's
SLEEPLESS IN SEATTLE, referring to Leo McCarey's 1957 AN AFFAIR TO RE-
MEMBER, with Cary Grant and Deborah Kerr, which is showing on TV. In fact,
we're told this again and again. Another woman tearfully describes the last
scene of AN AFFAIR TO REMEMBER to the hero, who remarks, "That's a chick's
movie." To clinch the point, female characters in this romantic comedy are
repeatedly shown watching this movie and sobbing (as if the TV stations in
Seattle and Baltimore, where most of the action takes place, showed little
else), and men are never seen watching it at all. And just in case we're left
with any doubts about the matter, the reviewer of SLEEPLESS IN SEATTLE in
Variety assures us that AN AFFAIR TO REMEMBER's "squishy romantic elements
appeal to women more than men."

This is utter nonsense. Since the time of the movie's first release, when I
was fourteen, I've seen this movie countless times, and I'm incapable of getting through it without crying. I have plenty of male friends who love it too—
more of them, as it happens, than female friends. In fact, when I went to see
the movie with a highly emotional English girlfriend in Paris twenty years
ago, I was in tears at the end and her eyes were completely dry; she thought
it was a hoot.

Moreover, during the movie's initial release, you could still see AN AFFAIR TO REMEMBER in CinemaScope—as you could at the Chicago Film Festival's CinemaScope retrospective a couple of years back, and as you probably still can in Paris today. In SLEEPLESS IN SEATTLE you can catch only "scanned" clips of it on various TV sets, with about a third of the image removed from both sides of the frame. Some marketing executives decided many years ago that we all preferred to see films that way on TV, without the benefit of McCarey's exquisitely composed and measured framing; they assumed it was better to eliminate a third of the image than to use a letterboxed format. Properly speaking, a better title for the movie as it now appears in SLEEPLESS IN SEATTLE would be AN AFFAIR TO REMEMBER PIECEMEAL.

There are two kinds of misjudgment (and abridgment) going on here—demographic and aesthetic—and they seem to go together, because they're both dictated by unreflecting and ahistorical marketplace thinking. This kind of thinking now determines many of the ways we experience movies; it tells us what we're supposed to like and implies that we're not being cooperative—not behaving like happy campers—if we happen to disagree.

It's probable, of course, that producers and marketing "experts" at 20th Century-Fox back in 1957 decided, long before Nora Ephron, that AN AFFAIR TO REMEMBER was to some extent a woman's picture. But even if they did, it's important to bear in mind that a division of labor still existed then between creative people and salespeople: regardless of what the producers thought and regardless of what the ads said, McCarey could still turn out a movie that could make someone like me cry. Today, when demographic thinking exerts a much greater influence on screenwriting and directing, as I'm sure it did on SLEEPLESS IN SEATTLE, the chance of someone like me being reduced to tears is much lower. And if I wanted to explain why I wept at McCarey's movie in Paris twenty years ago while my former girlfriend laughed, I wouldn't try to delve into what was wrong with me or with her; I'd try instead to discuss what was right about AN AFFAIR TO REMEMBER—irrespective of what marketing executives thought then or now.

■

Targeting has been part of our cultural life for some time, but it has become so prominent over the past few years that I think it's making a mess of the way we live and think and relate to one another. When businesses treat us demographically, as simple parts of vast marketing units, we eventually start thinking of ourselves in the same way—with the frequent result that whatever confounds, contradicts, or challenges these calculations gets factored out of art, communication, and even what we regard as our own identities. (Either these elements are eliminated at the outset or, if they're left in, we're encouraged not to notice them.) And when marketing executives start molding not only our tastes but our own self-definitions, it's time to start wondering who is serving whom and why.

It would be wrong, I think, to place all the blame for this state of affairs on the film industry. Out in the "real" world, where competing interest groups clamor for "politically correct" representations of their identities and concerns, what these identities and concerns actually consist of is often reduced and oversimplified for practical reasons. Just as some men cry at so-called women's pictures, some women may feel that their political interests can be represented by men, even if it isn't always politically efficacious to say so. Unfortunately, what gets said is assumed to be what "women want." The same thing applies, of course, to whites who feel that blacks can represent them (or the reverse). As one woman writer pointed out to me recently—to cite one of the many disparate casualties of PC discourse—it's becoming very hard nowadays to even think of criticizing mothers or motherhood.

Consequently, whenever we hear about "women's" interests, "black" interests, or "gay" interests—and we hear about them much more than we hear about "men's" interests, "white" interests, or "straight" interests only because the latter are already firmly entrenched—we're usually asked to assume that these are homogeneous, coherent entities. The assumption behind these shorthand formulas, which are becoming increasingly institutionalized throughout our culture, seems to be that all women, all blacks, and all gays have the same interests, just as all men, all whites, and all straights are presumed to have the same interests. (For the record, Ephron indirectly mocks this notion in SLEEP-LESS IN SEATTLE when she has a male character describe how he cried during the last scene of THE DIRTY DOZEN—perhaps the only display of wit in the entire movie.)

However these assumptions may (or may not) apply to legislation or short-term business investments, they often play havoc with how we perceive ourselves as human beings. After all, no one is *ever* any one of these categories to the exclusion of all others. And whatever's left out of these calculations simply isn't being addressed.

All these impoverished definitions of who we are wind up operating as negative or oppositional descriptions, sometimes even in spite of the intentions of whoever utters them. Regardless of what Robert B. Reich means in his book *The Work of Nations,* it's entirely possible to conclude from his arguments, given the divisions currently built into our discourse, that we should be ecstatically happy about our future in the world economy if we're well educated, despairing to the point of suicidal if we're not; and I guess if we're unlucky enough to be homeless, we're probably not reading his book anyway. Demographically speaking, this gives us three scintillating choices of how to feel about ourselves in relation to the present global economy: selfish, defeated, or off the graph entirely.

Once upon a time, in a galaxy far, far away, movies were supposed to be for everyone—made that way and seen that way—and were therefore social events that involved a diversified community. Some of this universality was undoubtedly mythical, but another part was surely real—and accounts for the continuing appeal of such certified popular classics as KING KONG, GONE WITH THE WIND, THE WIZARD OF OZ, and CASABLANCA, not to mention AN AFFAIR TO REMEMBER. But movies today, even when they cite such models as exemplary, almost invariably intensify the distances between us instead of speaking to our common situation. They are designed to splinter and isolate us from one another, not draw us together. Apparently someone figured out that more money could be made that way.

■

A playwright friend of mine says there are two ways you can look at plays or movies—as windows or as mirrors—and for some time now, at least since the early Reagan years, mirrors have been the only thing we're supposed to want. This has a direct bearing on the way films get programmed, exhibited, and promoted, and has an even more insidious effect on the way they're conceived and made—or not made in many more cases. It affects the independent sector every bit as much as the mainstream, perhaps even more: how else to explain the relatively recent growth of film festivals devoted to films by and about women, blacks, and gays—films whose feminism, blackness, or gayness is automatically assumed to supersede their other qualities? The fact that these mirrors are mainly supposed to be mainly flattering limits the options of filmmakers and audiences even further. (Sometimes, to be sure, the same movie can function as both window and mirror—MENACE II SOCIETY presumably serves as both a window for middle-class audiences looking at ghetto horrors and as a mirror for certain blacks in ghettos. But in this case it might be argued that both audiences are insulted to some extent by the degrees of sensationalism and violence thought necessary to engage their interest in this subject. And in WHAT'S LOVE GOT TO DO WITH IT, another combined window and mirror, everybody gets to look at wife beating, but no one gets to see Tina Turner relating sexually to a white man.)

We're all being repeatedly assured—not least by the discourse about "correct" representations that surrounds us—that, regardless of who we are, we all go to movies chiefly in search of role models, positive images of ourselves. (Feminists who might object to my formulation, pointing out that misogyny is given unbridled play in contemporary movies, should consider that they may be considered demographically less important than misogynists.) According to this rule, I should be on the lookout for movies that project positive images of straight, middle-aged, southern-born male Jews—though the only recent example that springs to mind, DRIVING MISS DAISY, makes me more than slightly ill. Clearly I'm being irresponsible by not living up to my demographic duties, but I'm not inclined to feel apologetic. The truth is, I prefer windows to mirrors.

I admit that the reasons for this may be partly generational, partly circumstantial. Growing up Jewish in a southern town during the 50s undoubtedly made me—along with my playwright friend, who grew up as a French Protestant during the same period in Cuba—something of a xenophile, with a desire to project myself into cultures, ethnicities, and lifestyles other than my own. The common and defeatist supposition that most Americans are xenophobic by nature rather than because of their culture and education is so seldom challenged that any deviations from this profile tend to be rejected before they're even considered.

My own belief, for whatever it's worth, is that the reliance of recent movies on tried-and-true xenophobia or tribal self-glorification—which often amounts to right and left variations on the same narrow marketthink—is largely predicated on an absence of imagination, courage, inclination to develop fresh markets, or ability to understand what audiences are open to. These absences may not matter to multinationals that couldn't care less about where their money's coming from, but they're depressing to just about anyone who cares about movies.

In terms of short-term gains, the logic of these companies' lack of concern may seem impeccable, but the tendency of this policy to waste genres and cycles as well as sensibilities recalls the scorched-earth policy of Reaganomics: use up whatever resources you have now and don't worry about next year's crop. If you believe the industry analysts, there's simply no way out of this sterile recycling of old ideas and compulsive remakes and sequels; so much for the alleged freedom of open minds and markets.

If we accept this prognosis, there's no point in going to movies any longer—not if we're looking for fanciful windows like AN AFFAIR TO REMEMBER instead of flattering mirrors like SLEEPLESS IN SEATTLE. This is not to say I don't believe in identifying with characters in movies, or even with movies inside of other movies. (If Ephron's film showed she had even a clue as to why McCarey's movie makes anyone cry, her elaborate exercise in piety might have seemed worth it.) But the fact that I find it easier to empathize with the dinosaurs in JURASSIC PARK than with any of the human beings probably stems from the fact that, as far as the movie's calculations about my profile as a viewer are concerned, I'm as much of a clone as any of them. Like those Disneyfied prehistoric animals—alternately stuffed toys and predatory beasts—I'm waiting for all the high-tech computer systems in the control station to shut down so I can run free for a spell, even if that means causing some damage. I want to be liberated from the itinerary this theme park ride has mapped out for me. It assumes that I'll be delighted to see greedy ersatz characters get their just desserts and accept the movie's moralism about tampering with nature for profit—which I'm expected to associate only with the designated villains, not with Spielberg and company.

■

More than anything else, what has destroyed the possibility of good or even coherent studio pictures getting made in recent years has been test-marketing previews. It's inconceivable that a movie like CITIZEN KANE could have survived previews, and the same could be said of any movie that steps off the beaten path and can't be absorbed without a moment's reflection. Though previewing movies makes sense in determining how to publicize them, previewing them to determine how to *make* them seems more a form of hysteria than a form of business or art—yet most industry reporters treat test marketing as if it were a hallowed, proven science rather than a high-tech form of fortune-telling. (Remember, these are the soothsayers who reported that THE WAR OF THE ROSES would flop.) I recently learned that it was thanks to this practice that Joe Dante's THE 'BURBS wound up with a stupid ending that contradicts the clever preceding premises and that Dante disapproves of. The movie flopped anyway, so everyone lost out—a turn of events I'd wager happens much more often than most studio executives would care to admit. Perhaps irrationally, I'm still hankering after the volcano climax that once ended SLIVER (which, after the strong opening weekend the targeters were aiming for, has been deservedly plummeting at the box office), if only because it implied a form of dementia much more entertaining than what replaced it after the test previews. For all the satisfaction of Sharon Stone's closing line in the release version—"Get a life!"—one is still prompted to bark back at the screen, "Get a movie!" *

Obviously, desperate, last-minute second-guessing of this kind is more likely to produce gibberish than anything promised by the ads. Because very few spectators, including those at test previews, are prone to analyze or think much about what they're watching on the spot, putting their collective twitches into the auteur's seat makes about as much sense as sculpting our foreign policy around the public's gut reactions to TV news reports, a procedure that can reduce countries instead of mere movies to rubble. (People are at their most reactionary when they're least prone to be thinking, something marketing experts bank on.) This strategy doesn't allow for second thoughts— the sort of response that might come an hour or a day after leaving the theater—or for fidelity to the sort of long-range educated strategies or reasoned deliberations that might have preceded the market tests. Everything is tossed out for the sake of that opening weekend, with the often empty assurance that

---

* If any proof were needed that the process of previewing is largely a joke, a story in the December 17, 1993, *Wall Street Journal*, headlined "Film Flam Movie-Research Kingpin Is Accused By Former Employees of Selling Manipulated Data," offers plenty of confirmation. While Joseph Farrell of National Research Group Inc., the firm handling most Hollywood test marketing, denied all such accusations, the story reports that about two dozen former employees "ranging from hourly workers to senior officials," and including mostly people who left the firm voluntarily, claim that the research data are sometimes doctored to conform to what paying clients ask for. All the examples given in the story involve boosting a movie's score, as with TEEN WOLF, L.A. STORY, and THE GODFATHER, PART III. But one can well imagine the reverse happening when certain studios perversely want certain good films to fail, e.g., most recently and blatantly, Paramount and Peter Bogdanovich's THE THING CALLED LOVE, and Warner Brothers and Abel Ferrara's THE BODY SNATCHERS. [From a review of I'LL DO ANYTHING in the *Chicago Reader*, February 18, 1994]

restoring the "original director's cut" (whatever that is) on laserdisc will make everything all right again. (Too bad we can't do the same thing with Baghdad.)

■

I've seen three movies recently in which an arrogant male chauvinist character plays a central role—a crime writer (Tom Berenger) in SLIVER, an upper-class gigolo (Don Johnson) in GUILTY AS SIN, and an art critic (Robin Renucci) in a French film from 1985 by Jean-Charles Tacchella, STAIRWAY C. All three movies threaten to show us a sympathetic female character who's sexually attracted to the male chauvinist. Not surprisingly, the French movie meets this challenge head-on, without flinching, whereas the two American movies devise various excuses for backing away from it—in both cases to their detriment as thrillers exploring certain moral tensions. (STAIRWAY C, I should hasten to add, isn't a thriller, and its implications are quite different.) We all know women who are turned on by male chauvinists, but the chances of encountering this phenomenon in a "major studio release" are lessened by the offense it would likely bring to certain members of the audience (myself, no doubt, included).

This example of studios making decisions about a movie's content based on "political correctness" is a minor one—the everyday sort of simplification that's currently expected from movie mirrors. A more grotesque example of the same tendency can be found in the determination of CLIFFHANGER to cast blacks and women in positive as well as negative roles and as victims as well as nonvictims, despite the fact that the movie's modus operandi throughout is to treat its audience as a callous mob howling for blood. This places women and blacks in politically correct roles at the same time that it allows misogynists and racists to satisfy their blood lust: democracy at work. Thanks to careful targeting, neither xenophobes nor tribal narcissists should have any cause for complaint; it's only all the rest of us—a negligible pack of humanists, xenophiles, and various others missing from the charts—who've been left out in the cold.

—Chicago *Reader,* June 18, 1993

Spielberg's Gentiles (SCHINDLER'S LIST)

> The ideological structures of Spielberg's films "hail" the spectator into a world of the obvious that affirms the viewer's presence (even while dissolving it), affirms that what the viewer has always believed or hoped is (obviously) right and accessible, and assures the viewer excitement and comfort in the process. The films offer nothing new beyond their spectacle, nothing the viewer does not already want, does not immediately accept. That is their conservative power, and it has spread throughout the cinema of the 80s.
>
> —*Robert Phillip Kolker,*
> A Cinema of Loneliness *(1988)*

Confessions are in order. From DUEL to JURASSIC PARK, there are few Steven Spielberg movies I admire, and none I fully respect—though I respond to a good many of them as obediently as any well-oiled automaton. My first look at CLOSE ENCOUNTERS OF THE THIRD KIND actually brought tears to my eyes. I can't say that on reflection I felt much pride in this response, though the experience of becoming a boy again in relation to the imagined parental benevolence of the cosmos—which also happens with Ray Bradbury's best early tales about Mars—may be morally preferable to feeding on the murderous xenophobia of STAR WARS, released the same year (1977); at worst one winds up feeling silly rather than dirty afterward. But the long-term gains from either patriarchal vision are questionable. And once Spielberg joined the Lucas camp with the Indiana Jones cycle—combining the ruthless efficiency of JAWS with the colonialist fervor of STAR WARS—my misgivings about the power of his work only escalated. If the euphoria Orson Welles conveys about filmmaking in CITIZEN KANE can be summed up in the line, "I think it would be fun to run a newspaper," the euphoria Spielberg conveys about filmmaking in RAIDERS OF THE LOST ARK, expressed in its most effective action moment, could just as aptly be summed up by the thought, "I think it would be fun to shoot an Arab." Indeed, though Spielberg has not yet given us a BEAVIS AND BUTT-

HEAD IN THE PERSIAN GULF, I have every expectation that if or when such a movie comes along, the imprimatur of his divine inspiration will be stamped onto every frame.

Perhaps due to my many years of living abroad and not eating the proper number of hamburgers, the suburban spirituality of E.T. left me relatively untouched. I was more impressed by the virtuosity of 1941, a picture whose honest mean-spiritedness and teenage irreverence—both partially the contribution of cowriter Robert Zemeckis—struck me as closer to Spielberg's soul, if not to his moneymaking skills. By contrast, THE COLOR PURPLE and EMPIRE OF THE SUN were both grotesque Oscar bids—strained subliterary attempts to make reparations for the genocidal glee of the Indiana Jones romps by expensively dry cleaning the work of distinguished authors—and I had every expectation that SCHINDLER'S LIST would complete Spielberg's dubious trilogy of good intentions.

Up to a point, these expectations have been fulfilled. But candor compels me to admit that SCHINDLER'S LIST not only made me blubber helplessly both times I saw it, once before and once after reading Thomas Keneally's fascinating nonfiction novel; it has also, in spite of some misgivings, won my gratitude and respect.

A small but significant part of my reaction can probably be traced to personal factors: as the grandson of Polish Jews, I am one of those who might have been saved (or not saved) from the gas ovens by Oskar Schindler if my father's father hadn't immigrated to the states when he was eight. My grandfather, a self-made businessman, also resembled the non-Jewish Oskar Schindler in certain respects; he was a hedonistic bon vivant whose successful business tactics, including bribery when it seemed necessary, filled him with such guilt that he became a leading philanthropist in the same community where he made his fortune.

But though these facts undoubtedly color my experience of SCHINDLER'S LIST, they don't account for why I think it qualifies as Spielberg's best film, as well as the first one really worth quarreling with. Just for starters, I can think of four reasons to praise it:

(1) The beauty and density of Janusz Kaminski's black-and-white cinematography, ranging from exquisite high-contrast night scenes to richly textured deep-focus long shots to grayish handheld "documentary"-style footage. It far surpasses the look of any other new American feature I've seen this year and reminds me once again how the idiotic commercial requirement of color in Hollywood movies—usually blamed on the tastes of brain-dead teenage viewers (who don't know any better) rather than on gutless producers and other movie executives (who should)—steadily deprives us of both visual pleasure and verisimilitude. I know that "life is in color" is supposed to shoot down every argument on behalf of the verisimilitude of black and white, but the fact remains that the colors in the life *I* know have scant relation to the colors I

usually see in commercial movies; and the failure (both artistic and technical) of most directors and cinematographers to control color meaningfully has turned good contemporary black-and-white cinematography into even more of an aesthetic luxury. Alas, Spielberg's expressed justification for using it— "Virtually everything I've seen on the Holocaust is in black and white"—is the lamest excuse I can think of, denying any motive beyond an obeisance to dubious popular clichés about the past versus the present. But fortunately Kaminski's work shows us countless better reasons for what he and Spielberg have done.

(2) Spielberg's power as a storyteller. The film runs for 185 minutes, and none of it drags or stalls. Very little of it fragments into show-offy set pieces or sequences destined for *Premiere* magazine's "Shot By Shot" feature, the standard bane of this sort of Oscar-mongering. The most important exception to this is a fancy montage sequence intercutting a Jewish wedding in a labor camp, the camp director harassing and then beating his Jewish maid in his wine cellar, and Schindler cavorting at a nightclub—a sequence that is on all counts the worst thing in the film. Otherwise, the script credited to Steven Zaillian (most recently the writer-director of the first-rate SEARCHING FOR BOBBY FISCHER) is generally a model of exposition and pacing. If it leads to certain questions about the ideological implications of Spielberg's method— implications already suggested in the above quotation by Robert Philip Kolker—it can't be faulted for its craft.

(3) The performances. Liam Neeson as Oskar Schindler and Ben Kingsley as Itzhak Stern, Schindler's Jewish accountant and right-hand man, are both indelible portraits, and as good as any work I've seen from either actor. I'm somewhat less happy with the characterization of Amon Goeth, the camp director, but the performance of British stage actor Ralph Fiennes in the part is good (in fact, I suspect Fiennes may wind up with the most prizes). And the work of countless other actors, mainly Eastern Europeans, is no less accomplished.

(4) The film's success at conveying some of the enormity of the Holocaust, as well as some of its banal details, in a fully accessible manner, at a time when much of our collective memory and understanding of it is rapidly slipping away. Much of the time it accomplishes this less through graphic portrayals than through direct appeals to our imaginations. Another film that took on this task and performed it more responsibly and comprehensibly—if less accessibly—is Claude Lanzmann's SHOAH (1985). But SHOAH is a documentary and explicitly a Jewish film, and with an eight-hour running time to boot it clearly can't address as wide an audience. Despite both the subject matter and the fact that Spielberg himself is Jewish, SCHINDLER'S LIST is anything but a Jewish film. Indeed, as I hope to show, even Jews who see this film are implicitly transformed by the narrative structure into Gentile viewers.

■

Although the book is technically a novel, Keneally's author's note states, "I have attempted . . . to avoid all fiction, since fiction would debase the record, and to distinguish between reality and the myths which are likely to attach themselves to a man of [Oskar Schindler's] stature." Though the same claim can't be made for the film—Spielberg's desire to dramatize clearly exceeds Keneally's need to fictionalize—it's worth stressing that with a few notable exceptions everything in the film can be traced in some form back to the book, which is itself based on detailed research, including interviews with more than two dozen participants in (and witnesses to) the events described. Thus many of the film's oddest departures—such as the use of color to highlight the red overcoat of a little girl in an otherwise black-and-white crowd during the evacuation of the Krakow ghetto—find their basis in Keneally's narrative even when the reason for them has been obscured or elided.

Oskar Schindler—born in 1908 in Moravia, a province in the Austrian empire that later became part of Czechoslovakia, and raised as a Catholic—was a Nazi war profiteer who earned most of his wealth by employing Jews in a enamel cookware factory in Krakow, Poland. He hired his workers in 1939, shortly after the beginning of the German occupation, when Jews from all over Poland were already being forcibly relocated to the Krakow ghetto.

A well-dressed partygoer and womanizer who excelled in bribery and black-market deals, Schindler hired the Jewish accountant Itzhak Stern to help run his plant and later managed to set up a second plant on the grounds of a forced labor camp near Krakow after his Jewish workers were relocated there. Then, when the camp was about to be shut down, with all its residents slated for extermination in Auschwitz, he wound up saving the lives of more than 1,100 Jews by effectively buying them from Nazi officials and shipping them to an ersatz munitions plant in his hometown, where he protected and supported them until the end of the war, spending the remainder of his fortune in the process. After the war his various business enterprises were all failures, and he was sustained until his death in 1974 by some of the Jews he saved, who called themselves *Schindlerjuden,* or Schindler's Jews. At his own request, he was buried in Jerusalem; though the film, which concludes with a color documentary sequence at his grave site, neglects to say so, his final resting place is in a Catholic cemetery.

■

Spielberg's film—which functions in part as a fanciful and idealistic self-portrait—is patriarchal to the core, even when this means tampering with some of the facts. While it's true that Schindler resumed living with his long-estranged wife, Emilie, when he established his mock munitions plant in

Moravia, the film shows him pledging sexual loyalty to her—during a church service, no less—just after he arrives there. In the book there is every indication that his sexual carousing continued as before, which makes for a more intriguing story that the script chooses to ignore; two of the Schindlerjuden told Keneally about finding Schindler one day skinny-dipping with a voluptuous blond SS woman in a water tank inside the factory.

Emilie's tireless efforts in helping the Schindlerjuden in Moravia—which Keneally attributes to her strong religious convictions as well as her loyalty to her relatively unreligious husband—also get short shrift in the movie. As Spielberg recounts the story, this is Schindler's show all the way, with only poker-faced Stern posited as a worthy crony and accomplice. The extraordinary tale of collective resistance told in Pierre Sauvage's 1989 documentary WEAPONS OF THE SPIRIT—about the five thousand inhabitants of Le Chambon, France, most of them Huguenots, who managed to shelter five thousand Jews during the Nazi occupation, only twenty miles from Vichy—is in some ways even more remarkable than Schindler's unselfish feat, because many more people were involved in the effort, Christians and Jews alike. But Spielberg's interest is generally in lone, charismatic father figures like E.T. and Schindler. If the term "Schindler's Jews" irresistibly calls to mind the telethon catchphrase "Jerry's kids," the notion of single male parent is equally operative in both cases; and in this case, the single male parent is Gentile. One might add that to the same degree that the saved Jews became "Oskar's kids," we, as viewers, become Steven's.

Another omission relates to the final compiling of the list of Jews Schindler is to take out of Poland with him. In the film, this is accomplished exclusively by Schindler and Stern; in reality, a personnel clerk named Marcel Goldberg—a character who's present only in passing in the film—put the finishing touches on the list, accepting diamonds as bribes from some families in exchange for their inclusion and excluding others when they couldn't cough up the necessary loot. Keneally plausibly absolves Schindler—who was busy at the time pulling strings elsewhere—from any direct blame in this matter, but it's symptomatic of the movie's tactics to omit such disturbing details to avoid the resulting moral complications. In the final analysis, Spielberg wants to show Schindler's goodness as the ultimate defense of capitalism, just as Nazism and the Holocaust itself are viewed as the ultimate perversions of capitalism—horrors requiring only a Schindler to set things right again. Including Goldberg on Schindler's side of the fence would only confuse this mythology.

A more general difference between the book and the film relates to our understanding of Schindler's personality. In the book he remains a genuine enigma—the sum of sometimes conflicting and often speculative accounts of the people who knew him. Spielberg, whose sense of drama won't tolerate such uncertainty, sees this strictly as a conversion story—a Nazi meanie who becomes a saint—even though the implied conversion occurs offscreen. It's an easier story to tell, but ultimately less interesting and less believable than what actually happened. (Not all of Keneally's most hair-raising anecdotes are in the movie; I hope that many people who like the movie will be led to the book by it, as I was.)

The character of Amon Goeth, the Nazi director of the forced labor camp and the main villain in book and movie alike, is likewise simplified—played by Fiennes as a classically foppish German decadent with Caligula-like flourishes. Though Spielberg takes much of this character's monstrous behavior, such as his shooting of Jews arbitrarily or for minor offenses, straight from the book, he chooses to minimize Goeth's growing obesity. And while he takes the trouble of flashing forward to show him being hung in 1946, he omits entirely an unforgettable scene from the book in which Goeth, now lean and diabetic, having been imprisoned and then released by the Nazis for his aberrant behavior, visits Schindler's factory in Moravia a defeated man.

Keeping Goeth slim and glamorous seems central to Spielberg's overall narrative strategy. The point isn't merely to make his villain more theatrical (as it is when, in one of the film's corniest conceits, he has another Nazi officer playing Mozart on a piano in a ghetto flat while his colleagues are busy machine-gunning Jews flushed out of hiding). The main idea is to assist us in identifying with Nazis—not with their cruelty, which we're supposed to recoil from, but with their privileged vantage point, their glamorous power and preeminence (Goeth is not unlike a studio head). Schindler himself, as Goeth's friend and confidant, the saintly businessman who even manages to dream up a scheme for curbing Goeth's murderous impulses, serves as the expedient emissary of this process (not unlike a film director). Thanks to him we have the vicarious thrill of attending Nazi parties and enjoying the lush revelry in Nazi nightclubs (both rendered in some of the film's silkiest, most gorgeous high-contrast black-and-white images), looking down at the Jewish prisoners from the balcony of Goeth's château (perched on a hill high above the camp), savoring the luxury of Schindler's new Krakow flat (freshly evacuated by a once-wealthy Jewish family forced to move into a ghetto hovel), and so on.

On a few special occasions, the film also asks us to identify with the Jewish victims—again as Gentile viewers, using Schindler's humane sympathy as our guide. On these occasions the shots generally become newsreel-gray and handheld, and the language we hear often switches from English to less familiar (if more authentic) gutteral European tongues, increasing our terror with both a sense of actuality and a sense of the unknown. But more often we're asked to sit with Schindler or Goeth in the catbird seat. That's why, when Goeth sadistically flirts with, interrogates, and finally beats his abused Jewish maid (Embeth Davidtz) in the wine cellar where she usually hides from him, during the montage sequence already described, Spielberg takes care to show us Davidtz's nipples through the slip she's wearing—to ask us as Gentile males to share Goeth's unresolved sexual attraction to her.

■

It might be inferred from the above that I'm only denouncing Spielberg's tactics. But the fact remains that if he weren't this ruthless or this efficient I wouldn't have wept at the end of SCHINDLER'S LIST both times I saw it. And as tempting as it is to ridicule Spielberg's reasons for making it—which probably include a narcissistically far-fetched identification with Schindler, and may even, for all I know, incorporate George Bush's evocation of a "kinder, gentler" America—it would be stupid to deny that art often grows out of just such contradictions.

It's virtually axiomatic that to make a big-budget commercial movie with a moral purpose behind it these days, something immoral in the viewer has to be not only assumed but addressed—and maybe even cultivated. The forthcoming PHILADELPHIA, about a gay lawyer, is essentially addressed to homophobes. Likewise, SCHINDLER'S LIST assumes a desire to identify with the class in power; it can only tell us what it has to say about Schindler by turning us into Schindler—which also means turning us into a Nazi.

For all Spielberg's efforts to account for Schindler's actions by describing his growth as a religious conversion, the mystery of the man and what he managed to do stubbornly remains. And when Schindler weeps for not having been able to do more—a scene that this movie has the brass to invent out of whole cloth—I'm ready to weep with him.

—Chicago *Reader*, December 17, 1993

The Solitary Pleasures of STAR WARS

"A long time ago in a galaxy far, far away . . ." reads the opening title, over vast interstellar reaches of wide-screen space. "I've seen the future and it works!" declares a happy teenager on his way out of the movie to a TV reporter in Los Angeles—oddly parroting what Lincoln Steffens said about Russia over fifty years ago, before Ford Motors gave the slogan a second lease on life. "Another galaxy, another time," begins the novel's prologue more noncommittally, carefully hedging all bets. But confusion between past and future, however useful to the tactics of George Lucas's STAR WARS, seems almost secondary to the overriding insistence that whenever this giddy space opera is taking place, it can't possibly be anywhere quite so disagreeable as the present.

"Rather than do some angry, socially relevant film," Lucas has said, "I realized there was another relevance that is even more important—dreams and fantasies, getting children to believe there is more to life than garbage and killing and all that real stuff like stealing hubcaps—that you could still sit and dream about exotic lands and strange creatures." Although garbage and killing are anything but absent from STAR WARS, and stealing hubcaps is around in spirit if not in letter, Lucas's aspiration is easy enough to comprehend, even after the social interests of his THX 1138 and AMERICAN GRAFFITI. The

disconcerting thing for a good many critics about his latest box office mono-
lith is that it doesn't seem to *mean* anything other than what it unabashedly is:
a well-crafted, dehumanized update of FLASH GORDON with better production
values, no ironic overtones, and a battery of special effects.

Consider the plot, which any well-behaved computer fed with the right
amount of pulp could probably regurgitate: Luke Skywalker (Mark Hamill),
farm youth living with uncle and aunt on the remote planet Tatooine, son of a
vanquished Jedi warrior of the Old Republic—an order overturned by the evil
Galactic Empire, headed by former Jedi warrior Darth Vader and the malignant Grand Moff Tarkin (Peter Cushing)—accidentally intercepts part of a
sound-and-image message sent by beautiful princess Leia Organa (Carrie
Fisher), a rebel senator from planet Alderaan held captive by the Empire, to
Ben "Obi-Wan" Kenobi (Alec Guinness), legendary Jedi warrior now living
as an outlaw in the Tatooine mountains. . . .

Following the squat robot who carries the message—R2-D2, who is usually
accompanied by C-3PO, a tall vocal sidekick that mumbles like an English
butler—Luke meets Kenobi, who bequeaths him his father's light saber and,
after uncle and aunt are promptly killed in an Empire raid, enlists his aid in
Leia's rescue. Meanwhile, he trains the youth in the mystical powers of the
Force, a spiritual order that bestows extrasensory talents. Hiring the hardened
mercenary Han Solo (Harrison Ford) and his nonhuman servant Chewbacca
in the grubby Mos Eisley Spaceport to pilot them, Luke and Kenobi set off
on a string of adventures, during which the latter is killed in a duel with Vader
and Leia is freed. Luke then accompanies the rebel freedom fighters in an
offensive against Death Star, the Empire's seemingly impregnable battle station, and single-handedly succeeds in blowing it to attractively bubbly, spar-
kling, and satisfying smithereens.

All this is very clean and bloodless. Vader crunches a few audible bones;
aunt and uncle are burned to black cinders in homage to THE SEARCHERS;
Kenobi executes a smooth forearm amputation with his saber in the Mos Eisley saloon, and meets his own saber death by vanishing into thin air, to be
absorbed within the Force; the rest is mainly fireworks and pinball machines.
The smirking idealism of Luke, the sullen cynicism of Han, the shrewish
irritability of Leia, the growls and whines of Chewbacca, the fussy chattering
of C-3PO, and the electronic chirping of R2-D2 are all set up as "cute" objects
of delighted audience ridicule. Hamill, Ford, and Fisher are made to look like
surfers at an s-f masquerade ball; Cushing, the only visibly human villain,
comes off as a rather improbable blend of Ming the Merciless and Jean-Luc
Godard, in physiognomy as well as emotional tone. And apart from the stead-
fast Alec Guinness, who is respectfully allowed to assume a vaguer and more
benign flatness as archetypal father figure, nearly everyone else is a monster,
whether lovable (domestic) or disgusting (threatening), with the borderline
between human and nonhuman often indistinguishable. (The gibbering, scav-

enging Jawas on Tattooine are a striking case in point: brown-robed and black-gloved, their only visible features are firefly eyes.)

The deliberate silliness of all this—like the intricate silliness that has always been part of Disney's stock-in-trade—leaves the audience free to react from a safe voyeuristic distance, enjoying "pure" sensations that are unencumbered by any moral or emotional investments. Indeed, the cursory treatment of "romantic interest" (with Leia still prevaricating at the end between both male leads via bored winks) leaves the way open for a very different sort of titillation. In the exhilarating space battles, with their odorless ecstasies of annihilation, and the various space-gun skirmishes, with their fancy dismemberings and eliminations, this essentially becomes an occasion for sexual release devoid of any partner. Like the remote-control TV channel selectors that children love to play with, and the mechanical shooting games found in arcades, STAR WARS offers solitary, narcissistic pleasures more than communal or romantic myths to keep its audience cheering.

Admittedly, Westerns, samurai sagas, Arthurian legends, Disney bestiaries, DeMille spectaculars, and World War II epics have been borrowed from as liberally as earlier s-f. The climactic Death Star attack is modeled directly after a compilation of air battle clips from over fifty war films, and even the final procession of Luke, Han, and Chewbacca down a long aisle to receive their medals has been identified by Arthur Lubow as a conscious "restaging of the march of Hitler, Himmler and Lutze to the Nuremberg monument" in TRIUMPH OF THE WILL. But the point of this approach is to make all the myths it plunders equally trivial and "usable" as nostalgic plot fodder, even if most of the emotions are absent. One would probably have to go back to the 40s, as Lucas did, to find such a guiltless celebration of unlimited warfare, but one needs to escape history entirely in order to set up oppositions of good and bad—reflected in black-and-white patternings of costume and decor—as unambiguous. On the level of racial ideology, this knowing mindlessness is even shrewder. While the original 1936 FLASH GORDON serial could allude to the "Yellow Peril" directly through Ming the Merciless without any sort of embarrassment, the styling of the Jawas as stingy Jewish merchants—"Munchkin Shylocks," in Richard Corliss's apt phrase—is much more oblique and subtle; one might even have to see the relationship of "Jawa" to the Hebrew "Yaweh" in order to catch the clue.

Following the fashion set by 2001 in some aspects of its design—robots programmed to be more "personable" than any of the actors, in-depth trajectories of slablike missiles entering the lower foreground of shots and sliding away diagonally (including the three long paragraphs preceding the action)—STAR WARS postulates itself as the anti-2001 in nearly every other respect, and not only because fantasy is systematically substituted for technology. If Kubrick's central subject was intelligence, Lucas's is predicated on blind instinct: Luke's initiation into the Force, like the spectator's into the film, is basically a matter of surrendering to conditioned reflexes and letting the cosmic mise en scène take over. And where 2001's sense of spectacle was contemplative, STAR WARS' is near-Pavlovian in its careful measurements of give-and-take, making it impossible on a practical level to isolate many of the special effects from the editing.

Working on the assumption that the enchantment of any creature, landscape, gadget, or set decreases in ratio to the length of time it's on the screen— a withholding premise already evident in the Krel episodes of FORBIDDEN PLANET and the brief, last-minute glimpses of a perishing city in THIS ISLAND EARTH—the movie is constructed like a teasing comic strip storyboard. Nothing incidental or scenic is allowed to retard the rapidly paced narrative, but is merely packed along en route (like the twin moons of Tatooine, or the binoculars Luke uses while scouting for R2-D2). A rare exception is made for diverse beasties in the inventive Mos Eisley Western saloon sequence, where spectacle momentarily triumphs over event.

Less imaginative in its otherworldly architecture than THE 5000 FINGERS OF DR. T—an all but forgotten Stanley Kramer production of the 50s, which, unlike STAR WARS, incorporated an escape from an unbearable present in its plot—Lucas's smorgasbord of styles is often more a matter of quantity than quality, as in the dense profusion of red laser beams that periodically streak across the screen. An effort is made, however, to make some of the locations (the scrapheap inside the Jawas' Sandcrawler, Mos Eisley, Han's pirate starship) untidy enough to seem lived in. Sound, including the nearly continuous music, serves the elliptical pacing throughout: intimations of Tarkin's imminent torture of Leia are limited to a brief shot of a syringe and the loud sliding shut of a door; the beast that pulls Luke down into the slimy muck of a shrinking garbage bin is more heard than seen; and the whistling sounds of the attacking rebel starships work a lot better as drama than as science.

For a film so devoid of any dialectic, one is tempted to speculate what its absolute antithesis might be. Would the recent films of Grand Moff Godard— low-budget, experimental, pleasurable to the mind rather than to the reflexes—be far off the mark? Yet if any parallel can be found between the film world and Lucas's Manichaean universe, it is the blitzkrieg of media fanfare celebrating STAR WARS and its countless spinoff industries—not the trifling efforts to get Godard's films seen or acknowledged anywhere—that corresponds to the Empire's efforts to snuff out every form of resistance. And the consortium that is currently contriving to inundate everyone's mind with a few profitable monoliths and assign the rebel forces of cinema to cheerful oblivion is not merely a group of big business men, but a movement composed of critics, editors, and media programmers and broadcasters—all of whom collaborate with other consumers in making STAR WARS (which is already threatening to topple JAWS as the all-time moneymaker) more than a simple movie, but an appreciable dent in the landscape.

What has any of this to do with esoteric items like NUMÉRO DEUX and ICI ET AILLEURS, whose more fragile transactions might as well be occurring on another planet? Simply the fact that both are concerned with advancing knowledge in the here and now, and this is generally taken to be such a distasteful activity that even defenders of such films generally feel compelled to describe their experiences as ones of necessary "unpleasure." The mere title of an earlier Godard film, LE GAI SAVOIR, already sounds anachronistic within the present climate. Who but a sick person, runs the implied argument, could take pleasure in a documentary shot of Palestinian soldiers in ICI ET AILLEURS, followed by a title saying that "Nearly all these actors are dead"? Better to take a calculated step backward in knowledge, sever communal and historical ties, hoot at heroes and villains alike, blow up invisible, imaginary enemies from a safe video distance, and enjoy it all as good, clean, healthy fun— marking time until the next real opportunities for automatic, xenophobic destruction arrive. This is the "relevance" of STAR WARS that a Lucas finds "more important"; and several million filmgoers are heartily agreeing.

—*Sight and Sound,* Autumn 1977

Jack Reed's Christmas Puppy

Reflections on REDS

On the Unreliability of Memory

> Men make their own history, but they do not make it just as they please; they do not make it under circumstances chosen by themselves, but under circumstances directly encountered, given and transmitted from the past.
>
> —*Karl Marx,* The Eighteenth Brumaire

"Was it 1913 or '17?" wonders the first ancient voice, male and faltering, after a burst of vigorous ragtime has faded out, before the opening credits have left the screen. "I can't remember now—I'm beginning to forget all the people I used to know." "Do I remember Louise Bryant?" asks the voice of another male oldster. "Why, of course; I couldn't forget her if I tried." A third witness of that period, female, appears on the right of the screen against a black background, lit like a Richard Avedon portrait. "I can't tell you," she replies to an unheard question. "I might sort of scratch my memory, but not at the moment . . . you know, things go and come back again."

At once the conscience and the Greek chorus of REDS, the thirty-two "witnesses" who prattle and reminisce about the real characters and events—John Reed, Louise Bryant, Eugene O'Neill, Emma Goldman, World War I, the Russian Revolution—are immediately perceived as human, charming, and indispensable; without them, the film and its achievement could not even begin to exist. Like the gaggle of gossiping locals who occupy the foreground of several pivotal shots in Orson Welles's THE MAGNIFICENT AMBERSONS, they embody the sense of community and popular wisdom that the film defines itself in relation to—the multifaceted oral history that paradoxically buries the characters at the same time that it keeps them alive for us.

Yet from the outset, the fallibility of these survivors is stressed as much as their reliability. Later on, they will contradict one another (on matters as disparate as John Reed's talent as a poet and U.S. involvement in World War I), get names wrong and exhibit other confusions, refuse to speak or speculate on certain matters ("I'm not a purveyor of neighborhood gossip, nossir, that's not my job"); but here they are already bearing witness to their shortcomings—sometimes knowingly, sometimes not. One witness worries about the correct Greenwich Village location: "It was Christopher Street, and I was thinking about another street down there instead. . . . Sometimes I have lapses like that." Another virtually places political affiliation in the realm of irrelevance: "I've forgotten all about it. *Were* there socialists? I guess there must have been, but I don't think they were of any importance—I don't remember them at all." Still another shrugs off the importance of romantic entanglements: "I know that Jack went around with Mabel Dodge, and then went around with another gal, and then went around with Louise Bryant. . . . It never impinged on my own personal life: I like baseball."

It is within such parameters that Warren Beatty situates his own history and audience, his own appeals to us. And while it might enhance our pleasure in some cases if each of the witnesses were identified when he or she is speaking—so that we would all know, for instance, that the codger commenting about sexual attitudes in the 1910s is Henry Miller, the one in a World War I outfit singing "Over There" is George Jessel, and the fellow who good-naturedly mutters "I urged the deportation of all alien Commonists [*sic*]" is Hamilton Fish—the absence of their names during their appearances can be justified strategically and aesthetically. Surely the fact that some participants are well known (Rebecca West, Will Durant) while others are not (acquaintances of Reed and Bryant in Portland) is less important than the democratic equality their anonymity grants them: they are here *dialectically,* as real contemporaries of the fictionalized characters, not as stars. And the fact that the rest of the movie already tends to keep us busy spotting the historical names—whether these are Floyd Dell or Aleksandr Kerensky (played, apparently, by a relative, Oleg Kerensky, who doubles as a witness), Max Eastman or Leon Trotsky—suggests that name tags here would create a cluttered effect.

In one of the several graceful rhyme effects established by Beatty between the United States and Russia in the fictive, "Hollywood" parts of the film, the question of John Reed's "credentials" allowing him to speak at a political rally comes up twice: at an American Socialist party meeting in 1916, when he espouses war resistance (and is told he has no credentials, being a mere journalist), and at a revolutionary assembly the following year in Petrograd, when he expresses the solidarity of American workers (and is told that he *needs* no credentials, that everyone present has them). The essential fact about all the witnesses is that, in the final analysis, they have no credentials beyond what we see and hear of them—which proves to be more than enough. For all their individual memory lapses, their proximity in time to the people and events depicted in REDS—which camera and microphone suffice to reveal—gives them an authenticity to which the remainder of the film can't pretend to aspire.

Collectively, they assume the role of the film's narrator, the guiding consciousness and authorial voice that traditionally needs no name in third-person narrative. At the same time, they foreground the issue of their unreliability as individual commentators, creating a dispersed texture that is quite different from the unilateral continuity and supposed truth of, say, Welles's impersonal third-person narration in AMBERSONS. Critics, of course, can be forgetful, too; when Pauline Kael argues, "In technique, REDS is the least radical, the least innovative epic you can imagine," she can't be remembering the witnesses, or Beatty's use of them.

On the Unreliability of Hollywood

"Paramount Has Made a Communist Propaganda Epic" trumpeted the headline to an outraged editorial in *Barron's* (December 14, 1981), but not many other critical commentaries to date appear to share this worry. Even Ronald Reagan, after attending a presidential screening with Beatty and Diane Keaton, reportedly said something to the effect that the film shows up the communists for what they are. Between his response and the *Barron's* editorial looms the whole knotty problem of accepting the premise of the "revolutionary" blockbuster even theoretically. (Given the sources of financing—including a novel arrangement with Barclays' Mercantile Industrial Finance Ltd, inspired by British tax law, whereby the film was sold prior to release and then leased back—as well as anticipated revenues, it's difficult to conceive of an investment that knowingly betrays those interests.) The curious notion that Hollywood or its European counterparts could produce a truly and unequivocally progressive spectacle—what one might call the RED BALLOON fallacy, recalling the title of Serge Toubiana's review of 1900 in *Cahiers du cinéma*—continues to be as much a facet of Hollywood myth and its policy of containment as it is a popular utopian leftist dream.

The utopian idealism of John Reed himself, however, was in many ways compatible with such a dream. According to his biographer, Robert A. Rosenstone, the Paterson Pageant organized by Reed for the IWW silk strike, held at

Madison Square Garden in 1913, two years before the action of REDS begins, "diverted attention from the central issues," namely, "hours and wages," and the long-range overall effect it had on the strike was disastrous. (In fairness to Reed, it might be said that he learned from such blunders, and grew substantially in political maturity afterward.) So, too, one might protest that Beatty drains the real politics out of Reed's life—the issues of class and revolution—for the sake of their traditional Hollywood replacements, romance and spectacle.

According to this argument, the radical lifestyles of Reed and Bryant are either diluted beyond recognition (by such things as severely limiting the degree of promiscuity practiced by both) or subsumed into sentimental Norman Rockwell magazine covers of cozy domesticity in New York, Provincetown, and Croton. Thus the gift-wrapped puppy given by Jack to Louise under one of the film's many Christmas trees undermines their rhetoric about free love as effectively as the adorable Russian tot briefly encountered by Louise in the hospital during the final scene, wistfully standing in for the child they never got around to having. Both are characteristic emblems of the narcissism projected by Hollywood stars like Beatty and Keaton. Significantly, Jack Nicholson as Eugene O'Neill—in what might well be his best *and* most delicately shaded performance since EASY RIDER—establishes himself more sharply as an erotic presence than either of the leads. He shares this quality, moreover, with Jerzy Kosinski as Grigory Zinoviev, whose role in the film also challenges the Reed-Bryant relationship, but from the left rather than the "apolitical" right.

Central to the Hollywood cosmetics job performed on history is the treatment of Louise Bryant and the performance of Diane Keaton—separate but related issues in the film's overall strategies. Regarding the former, Beatty's use of Bryant as the principal identification figure—a partial equivalent to the semifaceless reporter Thompson in CITIZEN KANE, following in the wake of a mysterious, heroic myth (Reed) and pulling the audience along with her as she goes—severely limits the character as a representation of the real Louise Bryant.* Regarding the latter, it is worth noting the widespread dissatisfaction with Keaton in REDS that is currently being expressed, at least in the United States. In a Washington, D.C., cinema, during Bryant's (fictional) trek across Finland in search of Reed, a skeptical spectator reportedly sang out "La-dee-da," Keaton's tagline as Annie Hall, to loud laughter and applause—suggesting part of the nature of the problem.

One might compare this response to the disaffection of the public with the character of the film director played by Jean-Pierre Léaud in LAST TANGO IN PARIS. In both cases, a formerly indulged romantic icon—New Wave adoles-

---

* According to Laura Cottingham ("What REDS Won't Tell You About Louise Bryant," *Soho News,* December 22, 1981), Bryant was somewhat more substantial as an independent thinker and journalist than the movie suggests. A recently reprinted excerpt from her 1918 book *Six Red Months in Russia* seems to bear this out.

cent cinéphile, flighty and eccentric star—becomes stale, loses conviction and glamour. And the superimposed hints of Keaton's characters in ANNIE HALL, INTERIORS, and MANHATTAN, whether willed or not, saddles Bryant with the contemporary tics of a Woody Allen heroine, making the character less than ideal as a credible leftist model. As Veronica Geng has aptly noted, "The movement in her face reflects a mind that's a garden of second thoughts; as soon as she asserts something, she takes it back," so that her "outbursts in REDS are prime artifacts of feminist confusion."

Such problems are perhaps only to be expected in a Hollywood framework whose invitations for identification are largely predicated on the necessity of describing the late 1910s in terms of the late 1960s (and afterward). And the collapse of these periods into one another is no doubt responsible for the relatively short shrift paid to such matters as class difference: as important as this was in Reed's life and development, it finds few correspondences in the student revolts of the 60s, which were essentially a middle-class phenomenon. (The fact of Reed's upper-class and Harvard background clearly played a role in his charisma, but although Upton Sinclair once irritated him by referring to him as "the playboy of the social revolution," closer study of his career reveals him to be anything but a dilettante. In "A Taste of Justice" [1913], a brief but powerful story included in the collection *Adventures of a Young Man,* he describes with shocking candor the privilege he enjoys as a celebrity in relation to a prostitute facing a charge in a Manhattan night court.)

On the Importance of John Reed

> As soon as the winter of the armoury show was over Mabel Dodge came back to Europe and brought with her what Jacques Emile-Blanche called her collection des jeunes gens assortis, a mixed assortment of young men. In the lot were Carl Van Vechten, Robert Jones and John Reed. . . . I remember the evening they all came. Picasso was there too. He looked at John Reed critically and said, le genre de Braque mais beaucoup moins rigolo, Braque's kind but much less diverting. I remember also that Reed told me about his trip through Spain. He told me he had seen many strange sights there, that he had seen witches chased through the streets of Salamanca. As I had been spending months in Spain and he only weeks I neither liked his stories nor believed them.
>
> —*Gertrude Stein,* The Autobiography of Alice B. Toklas

> Reed was a westerner and words meant what they said.
> The war was a blast that blew out all the Diogenes lanterns;
> the good men began to gang up to call for machine guns. Jack
> Reed was the last of the great race of war correspondents who

ducked under censorships and risked their skins for a story.

Jack Reed was the best American writer of his time, if anybody wanted to know about the war they could have read about it in the articles he wrote

about the German front,

the Serbian retreat,

Saloniki;

behind the lines in the tottering empire of the Czar,

dodging the secret police,

jail in Cholm.

—John Dos Passos, "Playboy" (in 1919)

As I look back on it all, it seems to me that the most important thing to know about the war is how the different peoples live; their environment, tradition, and the revealing things they do and say. In time of peace, many human qualities are covered up which come to the surface in a sharp crisis; but on the other hand, much of personal and racial quality is submerged in time of great public stress. And in this book [illustrator Boardman] Robinson and I have simply tried to give our impressions of human beings as we found them.

—John Reed, The War in Eastern Europe *(1916)*

Considering how far John Reed actively sought to become a legend during his own lifetime, it hardly seems surprising that so many accounts of him— including the first two cited above, written at almost precisely the same time half a century ago, in 1932—differ so strikingly. As the first of the novelistic journalists—a breed of macho adventurer that would later include Hemingway and Mailer (both, as it happens, third-rate poets like Reed when it came to affecting Kipling-style doggerel) as well as Orwell—Reed still serves to embody the active, committed reporter in opposition to the armchair analyst. If memory serves, it is just this image that informs Paul Leduc's Mexican film REED: MÉXICO INSURGENTE (1969), shot documentary-style in sepia, which concludes with a freeze-frame of Reed breaking a shop window to steal a camera; it is certainly the spirit that underlies Reed's own *Ten Days That Shook the World.*

By insisting throughout on the fusion of the personal with the political, REDS postulates as a fundamental aspect of its seductive appeal that spectators perform something of the same synthesis, within the terms of their own psychological, sexual, and political chemistries—forging their own personal links and private bridges between the recent 1960s and the remote 1910s, with the elderly witnesses officiating like partial and informal guides in these subtle and delicate transactions. As suggested above, Beatty's singular stroke of brilliance in using these mediators is to create a form of dialectics, a kind of dialectical play of historical analysis, which to a limited (if invaluable) degree authenticates and objectifies two otherwise debatable positions: the forgetful personal account and the nostalgic Hollywood myth. Thus two forms of sentimentality and unreliability complement and challenge one another, across a canvas comprising five years and six locations (less than a sixth of Reed's life), in the separate titled panels of the movie: Portland, 1915; Croton-on-Hudson, 1916; Paris, 1917; New York, 1918; Chicago, 1919; Petrograd, 1920. From their conjunction and juxtaposition comes a certain kind of honesty, a modest yet workable access to truth.

The occasional use of overlapping voices on the sound track (mainly Beatty's or Keaton's) serves to remind one how much of the film's narrative structure and use of incidental detail is based on principles of overlap between documentary and fiction, between sex or art and politics. The period song "I Don't Want to Play in Your Yard"—as relevant to personal borders as one wants to make it—is first sung by a male witness, then taken up by the orchestra on the sound track before being resumed by Louise, singing it to O'Neill and others in Provincetown (in Jack's absence, shortly after her affair with Eugene has begun), where it takes on a decidedly sexual resonance. Conversely, the performance of the "Internationale" by a Russian chorus just before the film's intermission, when Reed and Bryant's encounter with the Russian Revolution is unmistakably linked to their orgasmic sexual reunion in Petrograd, is followed, just after the interval, by one of the female witnesses singing the same song in English.

By the same token, two emblematic objects spanning separate scenes are O'Neill's unopened love letter to Bryant, pressed between pages of *Leaves of Grass,* and Reed's unfinished poem on the back of an IWW flyer—each reflecting the untidy, giddy overlays of energetic, incomplete lives caught up in external events. Many of the masterful early scenes seem constructed around comparable notions of superimposed layers involving sound and image: Emma Goldman (superbly played by Maureen Stapleton) introduced from Louise's viewpoint as a chattering offscreen voice entering Reed's Village flat; an argument in the same place on a rainy afternoon (all mottled patterns and flickering shadows in Vittorio Storaro's beautifully textured tones); a skillful evocation of a Bohemian community in Provincetown executed in simple, consecutive strokes effectively blended together, like some of the atmospheric mixes of vacation-time impressions that open SUNRISE. A montage of Greenwich Village social gatherings at which Louise comically strives to establish her own credentials directly evokes, for that matter, the speeded-up account of Charles Foster Kane's first marriage, with its own use of overlapping breakfasts. But if KANE is recalled at many junctures throughout REDS, it is worth noting the political difference that KANE views journalism more from the vantage point of management than from that of labor.

If REDS reaches a political conclusion of any sort, this may be the recognition that certain events, like certain lives, invariably get lost in (or devoured by) history, but collective struggle and romantic love are not necessarily strange bedfellows. One of the more striking rhyme effects has Reed angrily declaring, "You don't rewrite what I write"—initially to a New York editor (Gene Hackman), later to Kosinski's Zinoviev. And the climactic framing rhyme of Jack proposing to Louise that they go to New York together—first from Portland in 1915, shortly after they've met; then from Petrograd in 1920—raises the question each time of what they are to go as. Lovers or comrades? The film's efforts to collapse these categories into one are as idealistic and courageous, in a way, as Reed and Bryant were themselves, as touching and as serious and as foolhardy.

As the witnesses once again take over the narrative reins, continuing behind the final credits, a synthesis of old and new commentaries paradoxically leaves us with the same doubts and yet with firmer commitments, stronger beliefs. "I've forgotten all about it. *Were* there socialists?" ". . . I don't remember his exact words, but the meaning was that great things are ahead, worth living and worth dying for. He himself said that."

—*Sight and Sound,* Spring 1982

A Perversion of the Past
(MISSISSIPPI BURNING)

This whole country is full of lies.

—*Nina Simone, "Mississippi Goddam"*

The time in my youth when I was most physically afraid was a period of six weeks during the summer of 1961, when I was eighteen. I was attending an interracial, coed camp at Highlander Folk School in Monteagle, Tennessee—the place where the Montgomery bus boycott, the proper beginning of the civil rights movement, was planned by Martin Luther King, Jr., and Rosa Parks in the mid-50s. As a white native of Alabama, I had never before experienced the everyday dangers faced by southern blacks, much less those faced by activists who participated in Freedom Rides and similar demonstrations. But that summer, my coed camp was beset by people armed with rocks and guns.

I believe that we were the first group of people who ever sang an old hymn called "We Shall Overcome" as a civil rights anthem, thanks to the efforts of the camp's musical director, Guy Carawan. But the songs, powerful as they were, weren't the main thing that kept us together; it was the fear of dying. When a local white cracker turned up on the grounds and fired a shotgun at campers who were swimming in the lake; or, on a drive back from Chattanooga, when a group of kids threw bricks and bottles at our cars; or when a midnight raid by several carloads of local rednecks who were ready to beat us up (or worse) was called off only because of a rainstorm, the question that always came up was whom we could turn to in a pinch for protection.

The answer was no one. Certainly not the local police or the FBI, as I quickly learned from the more experienced campers and counselors; the most we could expect from them was that they'd look the other way—or laugh in our faces. (I had already been warned by several white friends in Alabama that the FBI considered Highlander a Communist training school, which meant that if I went there I'd never be able to get a job in government—or so they claimed.) In fact, the best that one could hope for in a tight situation in the Deep South was the presence of a *New York Times* reporter, and this was only because a white racist was less likely to bash in your skull if he thought it might get written up in a big Yankee paper.

Three summers after my stay at Highlander, three activists working to register black voters were killed by the Ku Klux Klan. With the complicity of a local sheriff and deputy, James Chaney, who was black, and Andrew Goodman and Michael Schwerner, who were white, were murdered in Neshoba County, Mississippi. Luckily, I was safe at home that summer; but my uncle, Arthur Lelyveld, a rabbi from Cleveland involved in the civil rights struggle, was bashed in the head with a piece of heavy pipe in Hattiesburg, Mississippi, a month later; and he delivered Goodman's funeral eulogy two months after that, when the bodies were finally found by the FBI. (His son Joseph—a *New York Times* reporter, as it happens—wound up interviewing former deputy Cecil Ray Price, who participated in the cover-ups, in 1977.) My own limited civil rights activities in Tennessee and Alabama never took me to Mississippi, an even more fearful place.

Given this background, it would be foolish to claim that I can approach MISSISSIPPI BURNING, which deals with those three killings, impartially. But it would be equally foolish to claim that the movie elicits impartiality from anyone, or that impartiality of any kind informs its contents. It is, after all, a movie by Alan Parker, a stylish English director who got his start in TV commercials, and whose most popular features (MIDNIGHT EXPRESS, FAME, SHOOT THE MOON, PINK FLOYD—THE WALL, and ANGEL HEART) all reek of advertising's overheated style, where, regardless of truth or meaning, anything goes if it produces the desired hyped-up effect.

It's emblematic of the entire approach of Parker and screenwriter Chris Gerolmo that the movie focuses almost exclusively on the investigation of the murders by two FBI agents, fictional characters named Ward (Willem Dafoe) and Anderson (Gene Hackman), and that they're the only good guys in sight. Much of the drama, in fact, concentrates on the conflict between them: prim, moralistic, and zealous Ward, who antagonizes the local white community, and loose, ambling Anderson, who prefers to mingle with the locals, objecting that Ward's blunt methods might attract the northern press. Both are represented as moral spokesmen without a trace of prejudice—unlike every other white person in town—although the movie clearly favors Anderson's methods over Ward's. Broadly speaking, their positions might be called federal (Ward) and local (Anderson) ways of handling civil rights problems in the South, although needless to say the blacks themselves are given no voice at all in the debate; they're essentially treated like children, and emotionally speaking Ward and Anderson are the parents who have to decide what's best for them.

For most of its history, including the 60s, the FBI has been a racist organization. This isn't simply a matter of hearsay or folk wisdom; it's amply demonstrated in such places as I. F. Stone's 1961 article, "The Negro, the FBI and Police Brutality," James Farmer's *Lay Bare the Heart,* and any Martin Luther King, Jr., biography you care to pick. (The protracted persecution of King by J. Edgar Hoover is now part of the public record.) It's even come to light recently, when a black FBI agent brought charges of racial harassment against his colleagues. In 1964, of course, there was no such thing as a black FBI agent anywhere in the United States.

Unfortunately, the central narrative premise of MISSISSIPPI BURNING sets up the FBI as the sole heroic defender of the victims of southern racism in 1964, which is more than a little disgusting. Embracing the premise unconditionally—unless one counts a single fleeting remark from a redneck to a journalist, that "J. Edgar Hoover said Martin Luther King was a Communist," which the film neither confirms nor privileges—the film tampers more than a little with historical facts: It subverts the history of the civil rights movement itself.

It's true that the FBI did conduct a detailed and extensive investigation, file name "Mississippi Burning," in the summer of 1964, before the bodies of Chaney, Goodman, and Schwerner were finally found under more than ten tons of earth. But a look at the context of this investigation, which the movie can't be bothered with, tells us a lot more. Two of the three missing civil rights workers came from well-to-do white families. After the 1963 assassination of John F. Kennedy, the FBI's prestige was conceivably at an all-time low; Lyndon Johnson had signed the 1964 Civil Rights Act into law on the same day that Hoover finally announced his intention to open an FBI office in Jackson, Mississippi; and apparently Johnson had to twist Hoover's arm in the bargain. (As I. F. Stone wrote in 1961, "Mr. Hoover has made it clear that the FBI acts in civil rights cases only because ordered to.")

"1964 . . . Not Forgotten" is the final message of the movie—the words appear on the chipped, defaced tombstone of one of the slain activists—but it's hard to forget something that isn't known in the first place, much less remembered. The movie purports to re-create the past and to tell us what it meant, but the ignorance of MISSISSIPPI BURNING is so studied that it only can be accounted for as a bulwark *against* knowledge, a denial of history for the sake of striking a glib and simple and easily digestible attitude against injustice.

It's not enough to counter that any Hollywood movie entails a certain amount of distortion. When Phil Karlson brought his actors and camera crew to Alabama in the 50s to shoot his low-budget "exploitation" docudrama

THE PHENIX CITY STORY (1955), which dealt with crime and racism in a similarly corrupt and terrorized community, he showed an attentiveness to the sound and look of his milieu, and the facts of his story, that even his own taste for lurid melodrama didn't falsify. Although it's shot on location in Mississippi and Alabama, MISSISSIPPI BURNING doesn't try for even a fraction of the same authenticity; an undistorted depiction couldn't be further from its agenda. Parker's MIDNIGHT EXPRESS contrived to horrify audiences with the experience of an American teenager in a Turkish prison, while blithely ignoring what happened to Turks in the same place. MISSISSIPPI BURNING shows a comparable indifference to the inhabitants and everyday life of its small southern town.

The film's two major characters are fictional, but both are analogous to real agents who worked on "Mississippi Burning" in 1964. Anderson is partially based on John Proctor, an agent from Alabama who worked in the North before he was assigned to Meridian, Mississippi, and who was friendly with two of the conspirators, Sheriff Lawrence Rainey and Deputy Cecil Ray Price. But the differences between the real agent and character are glaring. In the film, Anderson is a Mississippian who has worked both in the North and as a sheriff in Mississippi; he is untarnished by his friendly relations with the murderous villains. Joseph Sullivan—Proctor's superior, and the partial model for Ward (Dafoe)—hailed from the Midwest. In their recent book *We Are Not Afraid: The Story of Goodman, Schwerner, and Chaney and the Civil Rights Campaign for Mississippi,* Seth Cagin and Philip Dray describe him as follows: "A rugged six-two and known for his thoroughness and efficiency, Sullivan was the very personification of the qualities that epitomized the public image of Hoover's FBI."

Given the script that they have to work with, Dafoe and Hackman can't be blamed if their characters come across as dedicated liberals surrounded by evil rednecks. The only exception to this polarity is the deputy's wife (Frances McDormand), with whom Anderson flirts until she reveals the location of the activists' bodies. (In real life, the location of the bodies was found by bribing an undisclosed Neshoba citizen with $30,000.) But properly speaking, Ward, Anderson, and the deputy's wife are the only figures with any density in the plot. The nameless murder victims, seen only in the opening sequence, are never allowed to exist as characters, and the local blacks—noble, suffering icons without any depth or personality—hardly fare better.

In fact, Ward and Anderson are practically the only people in the movie, apart from a barber or two, who are ever shown working. Their ninety-eight co-workers are mainly shown shuffling papers; the sheriff (Gailard Sartain), deputy, and other local racists seem to devote their hours exclusively to holding Klan or White Citizens' Council meetings, firebombing black homes and churches, and beating up blacks. (Even more improbably, despite placing the local blacks throughout the film in small, ramshackle, easy-to-burn houses and churches, Parker sets a black funeral near the end in a palatial sanctuary that's the film's biggest and most expensive interior—a good example of his preference for splashy effect over logic or continuity.)

I wouldn't expect a docudrama of this sort to deal with the literal truth. Even Parker admits in his production notes that "Our film cannot be the definitive film of the black Civil Rights struggle. Our heroes are still white. And in truth, the film would probably never have been made if they weren't. This is a reflection of our society, not the Film Industry." But Parker has stuck so exclusively to his white heroes that he has drained all complexity out of everyone else, blacks and racists alike, and he even passes over many real-life details that would have made his simple melodramatic approach stronger.

Cagin and Dray cite five local whites in Philadelphia, Mississippi, who stood against the community's conspiracy of silence, "all of whom were threatened and ostracized" and none of whom seems to bear any resemblance to the deputy's wife in the movie. Apparently, Parker and Gerolmo don't want to complicate their scenario with such people, or any other southern whites who showed courage, such as James W. Silver (whose remarkable and chilling *Mississippi: The Closed Society* was published the same year) or William Bradford Huie, a journalist who compared the race murders in Mississippi and Alabama with those of Auschwitz. They could have gotten a lot of mileage out of Buford Pusey, one of the local white dissidents, who joined the Mississippi NAACP in 1946 at age twenty-one because he thought that black World War veterans had a right to vote, challenged the local newspaper editor (who repeatedly called him a Communist) to a duel in the late 50s, and as a consequence was himself denied the right to vote. (He also proved to be one of the few locals who assisted the FBI.)

Alternatively, if Parker and Gerolmo didn't want to deal with local eccentrics—which would have complicated their premise that the community consisted entirely of ignorant, bigoted, and interchangeable poor white trash—they could have dealt with certain aspects of the FBI investigation that are even more horrifying than anything they show. To cite Cagin and Dray again: "To the horror and disgust of southern blacks and movement people, several black corpses were found in Mississippi by authorities searching for Goodman, Schwerner, and Chaney. They were the routine victims of the Mississippi police/Klan juggernaut—found and identified this particular summer only as an unintended consequence of the national attention drawn to the state."

But fires are more photogenic than decomposing corpses. Since more than twenty black churches were firebombed in Mississippi that summer, MISSISSIPPI BURNING opts for an endless spectacle of fires and beatings instead, taking care not to individuate too many of the black victims for fear of alienating "our society" (as opposed to the "Film Industry"). And what about the civil rights movement? What about the visits of King, James Farmer, John Lewis, Dick Gregory, relatives of the slain victims, and countless others to that part of Mississippi while the investigations were taking place? The movie can't begin to acknowledge any of these people as presences or voices, because, in terms of its own deranged emotional-ideological agenda, the FBI *is* the civil rights movement.

Parker's basic procedure is to stage as many dramatic confrontations as possible—between Ward and Anderson, between either or both of them and the townspeople, between the Klan and the blacks, or between an imaginary black FBI agent (Badja Djola) and the racist mayor (R. Lee Ermey)—without regard for the basic historical facts. One of the first confrontations between Ward and Anderson occurs when they enter a luncheonette and Ward insists on joining the black men seated at a segregated counter (all of whom fearfully refuse to speak to him) despite Anderson's objections that this will cause an unnecessary commotion.

In order to stage such a scene, the filmmakers had to ignore the fact that, thanks to Jim Crow laws, no such seating arrangement was possible in Mississippi in 1964, even after the signing of the civil rights bill. Blacks were simply not allowed as customers in white restaurants; at best they could order take-out food from the back of some establishments, waiting outside near the kitchen. The film's indifference to the truth of the situation is indicative of where its real interest lies: with the good or evil intentions of whites, not with the everyday experiences of blacks.

But the movie's distortions go even further than that. Seth Cagin's article about the film in the December *Vogue* suggests that the movie's defamation (through neglect) of the civil rights movement is matched by its cockeyed distortion of the FBI's methods. An honest depiction might have pointed out, for instance, that their infiltration of the Klan was facilitated by agents who were themselves southern segregationists. But Parker's integrationist FBI, which even includes a couple of black agents whimsically known as Bird and Monk, opts instead for abduction and threats of violence (which, Cagin argues, fits directly into the Klan's cherished paranoid fantasies about the FBI).

This leads to one of the movie's most ludicrous scenes, when agent Monk, initially garbed in a Klan outfit, abducts the mayor to extract information. Threatening him with a razor, Monk proceeds to tell the (true) story of Judge Edward Aaron (called Homer Wilkes in the film), a black man selected at random, who was castrated with a razor by a white Alabama Klansman in 1957. That the movie occasionally makes use of actual historical occurrences—such as the horrifying crime against Aaron—can't really excuse its compulsion to use them to erect its own lurid fantasy scenarios.

I believe it was James Agee who remarked that some of the best art can grow out of moral simplification. It's a point that has some merit, but I would defy anyone who knows or cares about the civil rights struggle in any way to find much merit or art in the pile-driver simplifications of MISSISSIPPI BURNING or the feast for the self-righteous that they make possible. Ward makes a fancy speech (written by Parker himself) near the end of the movie, after the mayor has hanged himself (another clumsy invention), that argues that even though he wasn't a member of the Klan and didn't participate in the killings, the mayor is guilty—"maybe we all are"—because he stood by and allowed the murders and cover-ups to happen.

If Ward has a point, it's one that could also be made about this movie. The extravagant praise that's already been heaped on it by several national critics is apparently motivated by the sentiment that *any* treatment of the subject that is unsympathetic to the Klan has got to be an important step forward for mankind, regardless of how much obfuscation is perpetrated. Or perhaps some of these critics are too far removed from the historical facts to realize just how far the movie's distortions go.

But whether or not they realize what they're endorsing, critics and other spectators who celebrate this perversion of the past, this racism posing as humanism, this murder and cover-up of the historical record, this insult to the memory and legacy of Chaney, Goodman, and Schwerner, are as guilty in a way as Parker and Gerolmo, because they stand by and allow it to happen. Or maybe, better yet, we're all guilty—a nifty little formula that lets everyone off the hook.

—Chicago *Reader,* December 16, 1988

Circle of Pain

The Cinema of Nicholas Ray

Surfacing in Cannes in the worst of conditions—not quite finished, unsubtitled, shrieking with technical problems of all kinds, and dropped into the lap of an exhausted press fighting to stay awake through the fifteenth and final afternoon of the festival—Nicholas Ray's WE CAN'T GO HOME AGAIN may have actually hurried a few critics back to their homes; but it probably shook a few heads loose in the process. Clearly it wasn't the sort of experience anyone was likely to come to terms with, much less assimilate, in such an unfavorable setting, although the demands it makes on an audience would be pretty strenuous under any circumstances.

Created in collaboration with Ray's film class at the State University of New York at Binghamton, and featuring Ray and his students, the film attempts to do at least five separate things at once: (1) describe the conditions and ramifications of the filmmaking itself, from observations at the editing table to all sorts of peripheral factors (e.g., a female student becoming a part-time prostitute in order to raise money for the film); (2) explore the political alienation experienced by many young Americans in the late 60s and early 70s; (3) demystify Ray's image as a Hollywood director, in relation to both his film class and his audience; (4) implicate the private lives and personalities of Ray and his students in all of the preceding; and (5) integrate these concerns in a radical form that permits an audience to view them in several aspects at once. Thus, for the better part of two hours, six separate images are projected on the screen together, juxtaposing super-8 and 16-millimeter footage against a 35-millimeter backdrop (with the aid of a videotape synthesizer) in one crowded fresco.

Quite simply, it is a Faustian attempt to do the impossible: as Ray indicated at his press conference, an effort to make "what in our minds is a *Guernica*" out of such tools as a "broken-down Bolex," "a Mitchell that cost $25 out of Navy surplus," and a lot of impatient maverick energy. The hysteria underlining most of the film is reflected in the title Ray originally gave to the project, THE GUN UNDER MY PILLOW; the level of aspiration can be seen in the fact that it is announced as the first part of a trilogy.

At its "best"—an excruciating sequence in close-up where a student savagely hacks off his beard—it arrives at some very potent psychodrama. At its "worst," it becomes an uneven struggle toward coherence landing in chaos, like some orgy of collective action-painting that leaves a classroom in a state of carnage. The theme of autodestruction in one form or another is fairly constant. Ray himself is seen undergoing at least two symbolic deaths: one as Santa Claus, knocked into the air by a hit-and-run driver (his costume lyrically cascading to the pavement in gracefully cut slow motion); another in his own person, near the film's end, when after preparing his suicide and then changing his mind (like Pierrot le fou), he accidentally hangs himself while attempting to remove the rope. His parting message to his students: "Take care of each other—all the rest is vanity—and let the rest of us swing"—a form of self-abasement that Ray believes appropriate to his generation, described at his press conference as "more guilty of betrayal than any other generation in history."

WE CAN'T GO HOME AGAIN is certainly cinema at the end of its tether; like the fatal test of courage in REBEL WITHOUT A CAUSE, a "blind run" up to and maybe even over the edge of a cliff. But the autobiographical involvement is not exactly new to Ray's work: there's a troubled novelist named Nick in BORN TO BE BAD and a sympathetic policeman named Ray in REBEL; Ray acted the part of the American ambassador in 55 DAYS AT PEKING, and a gallery of partial stand-ins can be found in many of his other works. Self-accusal in the first-person plural is nothing new either: the original title that Ray wanted for THEY LIVE BY NIGHT—the name of the Edward Anderson novel it was based on—was THIEVES LIKE US.

■

Before the credits of THEY LIVE BY NIGHT appear, we see the two major characters, Bowie (Farley Granger) and Keechie (Cathy O'Donnell) kissing, while a subtitle introduces them in consecutive phrases, parsed out like the lines of a folk ballad: "This boy . . ." "and this girl . . ." "were never properly introduced to the world we live in . . ." Then behind the credits is shown a speeding car contaning four men, filmed from the changing perspectives of a helicopter following its progress. As the credits end, we return to ground level in time to see and hear a tire blow out; the car swerves over and jerks to a stop. The driver, who has been carrying three escaped convicts (Chicamaw: Howard da Silva; T-Dub: J. C. Flippen; and Bowie), is forced out of the car and—outside the camera's range—beaten: the sound of the first fist blow coincides with a cut to Bowie's response as he watches the violence. Then we return to the helicopter's viewpoint, which gradually descends as the convicts flee across an open field, approaching and passing a giant billboard.

The extraordinary beginning of Ray's first movie prefigures not only the remainder of the film but also most of the major impulses in his subsequent work. A romantic vision of the Couple is immediately juxtaposed with anarchic movement erupting into violence; desperate action is treated as a spectacular form of choreography. Each element is intensely articulated, yet "distanced" into a sort of abstraction: the spatial-emotional continuity of the first shot set in relief by the underlining verbal montage that "explains" it, the speeding car turned into creeping insect by the deterministic overhead angles that circumscribe its apparent freedom, and the violence displaced by the cut to Bowie, bringing us full circle back to the romantic hero already condemned in the opening shot—a circle of pain defining the limits of Ray's universe. And the exhilarating plasticity of the flight across the field, pivoted around the imposing billboard, fastens all three characters to the pop iconography of a society that surrounds and ultimately crushes them, the social recognition that molds their identities and makes them "real" at the same time that it signs their death warrants. (When Chicamaw later reads about their escape in the newspaper, he remarks to Bowie, "You're in luck, kid. You're travelin' with real people . . .")

The second sequence begins with Bowie looking through the holes in a garden lattice like a caged animal while Keechie drives up in a car. A series of guarded exchanges initiates the defensive dialogues that invariably take place between Ray's couples before they strike a balance—a compromise between duel and duet that recurs with variations in the celebrated kitchen scenes of IN A LONELY PLACE (Humphrey Bogart straightening out a grapefruit knife while he talks to Gloria Grahame) and JOHNNY GUITAR (Sterling Hayden asking Joan Crawford to tell him lies, which she does in cadenced, balladlike refrains), and comparable first encounters in ON DANGEROUS GROUND, REBEL WITHOUT A CAUSE, HOT BLOOD, BITTER VICTORY, and PARTY GIRL. As their mutual suspicions begin to cool and Bowie gets into the car, the sound of a passing train is faintly heard, a prefiguration of the much louder one that we hear just before Bowie is shot in the final scene. And after Bowie sits down next to Keechie, there is a cut to a shot framing them from the back of the car, where we see them through another mesh pattern, caged together at the very instant that they visually "compose" a couple.

To etch out a framework of romantic futility and then to dive into it without restraint is very characteristic of Ray. If we add to this tendency a strong empathy for adolescents, a particular flair for color and CinemaScope, a visibly recurrent (but perpetually unfulfilled) desire to film a musical, a social conscience seeking to bear witness to the major problems of its time, and a taste for anarchic violence that alternately obscures, complicates, and helps to illuminate these issues—culminating in grandiose fables, parables, and pedagogical "lessons" followed by a total break with commercial filmmaking, and the gradual creation of a new aesthetic based on an increased degree of political engagement and a new emphasis on collective authorship—we have arrived at a description of not only Ray's career, but a considerable portion of Godard's.

Obviously one shouldn't push these parallels too far: the "lessons" of WEEKEND and LE GAI SAVOIR are not the same as those in THE SAVAGE INNOCENTS (although all three films perform radical assaults on many concepts central to Western culture); and if the alienating aspects of WE CAN'T GO HOME AGAIN recall some of those in VENT D'EST and VLADIMIR ET ROSA, this is not to say that they are structurally or ideologically equivalent. But when we consider that Ray attracted more sustained enthusiasm among Godard and his colleagues at *Cahiers du cinéma* than any other American director in the 50s, and was subsequently mentioned more often than any other director in Godard's films, it becomes clear that many of these relationships are far from coincidental.

One suspects that what Ray represented for many of the younger *Cahiers* critics was the triumph of a very personal, autobiographical cinema forged into the studio styles of RKO, Republic, Paramount, Warners, Columbia, Fox, and MGM; a restless exploratory nature that tended to regard each project as an existential adventure and a foray of research into the background of a given topic (police brutality, rodeo people, juvenile delinquency, Gypsies, Chicago gangsters, Eskimos); a loner mentality epitomized in a line from JOHNNY GUITAR ("I'm a stranger here myself"); a florid romantic imagination, dramatic intensity, and visual bravado that could make THE LUSTY MEN evidence of an obsession for abstraction equal to Bresson's (Rivette), JOHNNY GUITAR the Beauty and the Beast of Westerns (Truffaut), REBEL WITHOUT A CAUSE and BIGGER THAN LIFE modern evocations of Greek tragedy (Rohmer), and BITTER VICTORY "the most Goethian of films" (Godard).

■

Unlike Godard, Ray cannot be considered a major stylistic innovator, at least not yet: it is much too soon to determine whether the use of multiple images in WE CAN'T GO HOME AGAIN will bear any fruit. (Tati's PLAYTIME, which utilizes multiple focal points within single images, was released six years ago, and its innovations have not yet made any visible impact on other directors.) But it is equally evident that in his choice of subjects as well as his treatments of them, Ray has frequently been ten years or more ahead of his time: consider his handling of youth culture in REBEL WITHOUT A CAUSE (1955), drugs in BIGGER THAN LIFE (1956), ecology in WIND ACROSS THE EVERGLADES (1958), and anthropology in THE SAVAGE INNOCENTS (1959–1960). From this point of view, KING OF KINGS (1961) is Ray's JESUS CHRIST SUPERSTAR, not only for its somewhat pop (and pop art) treatment of the Gospels avant la lettre, but more specifically because the flaming red garments and rebellious stances of its Jesus (Jeffrey Hunter) take us right back to James Dean in his zipper jacket. (As though to remind us of this icon—currently on display in Henri Langlois's Cinema Museum—Ray is seen wearing a near-replica in WE CAN'T GO HOME AGAIN.)

Paradoxically, it is the pop imagery of REBEL WITHOUT A CAUSE that makes the film now appear somewhat dated in relation to EAST OF EDEN (1954), a quasi-anachronistic work less bound to the zeitgeist of any particular period. But it has dated interestingly. If the manners and moods of mid-1950s teenagers are captured with a comic book flourish and heightened lyricism that seems slightly surreal now, this enables us to see only that much more of the mythology of that time and culture. Yet for all the concreteness of its observations, it is probably, after BITTER VICTORY, the most schematic and abstract of Ray's films. Jim (James Dean), Judy (Natalie Wood), Plato (Sal Mineo), and Buzz (Corey Allen) are carefully differentiated in their backgrounds in order to suggest a sociological cross section, but at the same time they represent variations of the same dilemmas, and can even be called different facets of a single personality.

The first shot introduces us to Jim; the second and third link him to Judy and Plato in the police station, each counterpart unobtrusively providing a compositional "balance" within the CinemaScope frame. Later, in a moving scene on the edge of a precipice, Jim and Buzz suddenly become equals and friends before competing in a "Chickie-run" where the latter plunges to his death; Jim promptly assumes Buzz's role as Judy's boyfriend, and we realize that Buzz's death could just as easily have been Jim's, just as Plato's subsequent madness and death could also have been Jim's—indeed, the appearance and stances of Dean and Mineo recall separate aspects of Farley Granger in THEY LIVE BY NIGHT. In another sense, Jim's anger and imperiousness matches his mother's: the two are linked in an extraordinary subjective shot (later echoed in HOT BLOOD and WIND ACROSS THE EVERGLADES) involving a 360° camera tilt when he sees her upside down, then right-side-up, descending a stairway; and he later assumes his father's role when he forms a nuclear family with Judy and Plato in a deserted mansion.

This semimystical sense of equality between individuals is central to Ray's work. The discovery of a moral equivalence between the supposedly antithetical natures of the antagonist heroes in BITTER VICTORY and WIND ACROSS THE EVERGLADES provides the dramatic climax of both films; in KING OF KINGS, the treatment of the Sermon on the Mount as a series of personal exchanges reflects the same preoccupation. Between Ray's couples, we usually find a set of precise antitheses and balances. In PARTY GIRL, the hero (Robert Taylor) is lame and the heroine (Cyd Charisse) is a dancer; each is a "prostitute"—he as a gangster's lawyer, she as a party girl—who reforms with the help of the other. In ON DANGEROUS GROUND, Ida Lupino's literal blindness balances—and helps to overcome—Robert Ryan's emotional blindness, and his uncontrolled sadism is similarly altered by the psychosis of Lupino's brother. It is worth remarking, however, that with the possible exceptions of Gloria Grahame in IN A LONELY PLACE and Chana Eden in WIND ACROSS THE EVERGLADES—both highly original and unjustly neglected performances—Ray's heroines seldom seem to have much identity apart from their relationships to men; in BIGGER THAN LIFE, the difficulty of Lou Avery (Barbara Rush) in acting contrary to her husband's crazed demands is one of the tragic levers in the plot.

Aside from its system of character equations, REBEL abounds in other abstract elements: the cramming of all the action into one improbable twenty-four-hour period; the link between the global annihilation in "a burst of gas and fire" enacted in the planetarium, where the astronomer announces that "the earth will not be missed," and the explosion of Buzz's car at the end of the "Chickie-run" (and the implicit fact that Buzz is subsequently not missed very much either); the arrival of Plato at Dawson High, with a sharp cut from the loud backfire of his motor scooter (horizontal) to the raising of the American flag (vertical); the curious recapitulation of references to animals (the toy monkey in the first shot and Jim's joke when handing Judy her compact: "You wanna see a monkey?"; the epithet "chicken" and Jim's reply in the deserted house to Plato's "Who's there?"—"Nobody, just us chickens!"; Jim mooing at a reference to Taurus in the planetarium, then being taunted in the knife fight with Buzz like a torero's bull); the "musical" stylization of the slow buildup to the knife fight outside the planetarium, with the actors posed and choreographed around Jim's car in a way that suggests a superior version of WEST SIDE STORY.

Ray's occasional tendency to gravitate toward the style of musicals—a function of his colors, his somewhat theatrical manner of lighting sets, a penchant for viewing physical movement as spectacle, and a use of folk ballads (real or implied) along with other musical interludes—can be seen more distinctly in PARTY GIRL, or in the opening scene at Vienna's saloon in JOHNNY GUITAR, when Johnny introduces himself with a strum on his guitar and the Dancing Kid reciprocates by grabbing Emma and dancing her across the floor. But Ray's furthest step in this direction remains HOT BLOOD, an unevenly realized film that springs to vibrant life in all its "musical" sequences: Cornell Wilde's defiant dance when he is refused employment as a dancing teacher (sarcastically flaunting the Gypsy stereotype that has been assigned to him), his "whip dance" with Jane Russell, and the Gypsies' triumphant song that celebrates their marriage and later reconciliation.

■

Considering the stylistic traits touched on so far—from romanticism to anarchistic violence, pop imagery to "cosmic" abstraction, symmetry to choreography—we have clearly arrived at a complex of themes, procedures, and attitudes that could legitimately be called larger than life, an impulse that manifests itself in details as fleeting as the word "God" scrawled on the bark of a tree in JOHNNY GUITAR, or as central as Richard Burton's dismissal of tenth-century Berber ruins in BITTER VICTORY as "too modern for me." It is a vision suggesting and requiring a large canvas—something closer to the all-encompassing breadth of the planetarium in REBEL WITHOUT A CAUSE than the confines of a television screen smaller than life, where most of Ray's films are condemned to seek recognition today.*

Limitless aspiration combined with profound alienation is the condition suffered by the hero of BIGGER THAN LIFE, Ray's most powerful film; and if his rendering of this anguish occupies a special place in his work, this is largely because it succeeds in attacking the roots of this condition rather than remaining on the level of its various symptoms. IN A LONELY PLACE, containing many elements of an autocritique, is an earlier foray into a similar form of investigation: set in an extremely deglamorized Hollywood, it deals with the uncontrolled violence of a scriptwriter (Humphrey Bogart) and its tragic consequences, his gradual alienation from everyone he feels closest to. BIGGER THAN LIFE, which concerns the effects of cortisone on a schoolteacher (James Mason) who has contracted a painful, incurable inflammation of the arteries—an objective correlative, perhaps, for Ray's own vision?—is obviously less "personal" in any autobiographical sense, but its implications are more universal. Its real subject is not the drug itself but what it reveals about Ed Avery; and beyond that, what Ed Avery reveals about the society he inhabits and—to a greater and lesser extent—emulates.

BIGGER THAN LIFE is a profoundly upsetting exposure of middle-class aspirations because it virtually defines madness—Avery's drug-induced psychosis—as taking these values seriously. Each emblem of the American Dream implicitly honored by Avery in the opening scenes (his ideals about education, his respect for class and social status, his desire for his son "to improve himself") is systematically turned on its head, converted from dream to night-

---

* Even more unfortunate is the perishability of 20th Century-Fox's Deluxe Color, which guarantees the virtual extinction of BIGGER THAN LIFE and THE TRUE STORY OF JESSE JAMES as integral works. It is no small irony that Republic's low-budget Trucolor in JOHNNY GUITAR survives intact today, while Fox's color films of the same period are gradually deteriorating into a ghastly corpselike pink as the other colors irrevocably drain away.

mare, by becoming only more explicit in his behavior. The dramatic function of his incurable disease and his taking of cortisone, carrying the respective promises of death and superlife, is to act on the slick magazine ads that he and his family try to inhabit in much the same way that the doctor's X-ray of his torso illuminates his terminal condition: an appearance of normality is subverted before our eyes, bit by bit, until it achieves the Gothic dimensions of a horror story that has always existed beneath the surface of his life.

Returning to school after his release from the hospital, Ed tells his wife Lou that he feels "ten feet tall," and a grotesque low-angle shot of him as he turns toward the school building echoes and parodies this notion; but as he walks away from the camera, his body becomes progressively dwarfed by the building—which, for all its apparent mediocrity, is a lot taller than ten feet. Similarly, a scene where Ed, playing the big shot, forces Lou to purchase gaudy clothes they can't afford, undermines the Hollywood images that inspire such a gesture to the point where they become loathsome—deranged and obscene. And Ed's monomaniacal concern for his son's "improvement," a direct consequence of his unadmitted despair, reaches its apex when, after hearing a church sermon, he decides to "sacrifice" his son to his ideals by killing him with a pair of scissors. When Lou reminds him that God told Abraham to spare Isaac, he can only reply with the reductio ad absurdum of his outsized egotism: "God was wrong."

A general sense that, insofar as He exists at all, "God was wrong," infuses the world of Ray's films, from the nervous instability of his compositions to the unrelieved torment of his heroes. In a rare and unprecedented moment of rebellion against Ed's demands, Lou slams the door of a medicine cabinet and the mirror cracks. Ed sees himself fragmented and duplicated in the broken surface—a crowd of images alienated from one another that gives the lie to his fantasy that he maintains a consistent, logical, and continuous identity.

∎

If Ed Avery's madness is implicitly the madness of America and Hollywood, perhaps the radical approach of WE CAN'T GO HOME AGAIN, coming seventeen years later, is to offer a structural equivalent to Lou's rebellious gesture. Splintering their image into several independent variants of the same thing that refuse to cohere, Ray and his students seem to be implying that the state of America has become similarly fragmented and discontinuous. We can't go home again because "home" is no longer a single place and "we" are no longer one:

> Things fall apart; the centre cannot hold;
> Mere anarchy is loosed upon the world,
> The blood-dimmed tide is loosed, and everywhere
> The ceremony of innocence is drowned;

The best lack all conviction, while the worst
Are full of passionate intensity.
                    (Yeats, *The Second Coming*)

Within such a context of alienation, it is pointless and more than a little premature to talk about success or failure. Over a decade after his departure from commercial filmmaking, Ray has returned to a public forum to officiate at the conception of a very rough beast.

—*Sight and Sound*, Autumn 1973

Vietnam, the Theme Park
(HEARTS OF DARKNESS: A FILMMAKER'S APOCALYPSE)

A little over a decade ago in an English film magazine I made a rather foolish prediction: "Perhaps by the 90s a sufficient time gap will have elapsed to allow [American] filmmakers to approach the subject of Vietnam in a more detached, balanced, and analytical manner." Cockeyed optimist that I was, I reasoned that some historical distance would allow certain blank spots in our knowledge and understanding of Vietnam to be filled—not doused in amber and framed in gold while remaining blank spots. I took to heart Ernest Hemingway's famous declaration in a *Paris Review* interview: "If a writer omits something because he does not know it then there is a hole in the story." I reasoned that the gaping holes in our Vietnam cover story would finally reduce that protective garment to tatters and finally permit some light to shine through.

Little did I know that these holes themselves would come to be defined as points of illumination—a bit like George Bush's "thousand points of light"— and would decorate our consciousness like Christmas trees. As Exhibit A I offer HEARTS OF DARKNESS: A FILMMAKER'S APOCALYPSE, directed by Fax Bahr, George Hickenlooper, and Eleanor Coppola, a compulsively watchable, fairly entertaining, and superficially informative documentary about the making of Francis Coppola's APOCALYPSE NOW (1979); it premiered on cable late last year, wound up on a few critics' "ten best" lists, and is currently showing at the Fine Arts. A great deal of the film is drawn from location footage originally shot by Coppola's wife, Eleanor, as well as from some tape recordings of private conversations with her husband during the same period. This material is buttressed with recent interviews of many participants and observers—among them, Francis and Eleanor Coppola; writer John Milius; actors Martin Sheen, Robert Duvall, Sam Bottoms, Larry Fishburne, and Dennis Hopper; producers Tom Sternberg and Fred Roos; production designer Dean Tavoularis; and George Lucas, who was originally set to direct the picture around 1969 before the project was shelved for lack of interest from the major studios.

Like much of Coppola's best work—THE CONVERSATION, the GODFATHER trilogy—APOCALYPSE NOW teeters on the edge of greatness, and perhaps it wouldn't teeter at all if greatness weren't so palpably what it was lusting after. To my mind it functions best as a series of superbly realized set pieces bracketed by a certain amount of pretentious guff, some of which might be traced back to Joseph Conrad's novella *Heart of Darkness,* the movie's point of departure. ("Is anything," asked the critic F. R. Leavis, "added to the oppressive mysteriousness of the Congo by such sentences as: 'It was the stillness of an implacable force brooding over an inscrutable intention—'?") But much of the guff, I'd wager, stems from the fact that Coppola never quite worked out what he wanted to say, a fact he often acknowledged at the time and for which there's plenty of evidence in HEARTS OF DARKNESS. Indeed, Coppola's continuing doubt and verbal self-laceration—at one point he calls the film "The Idiodyssey"—are a major part of the saga being celebrated here: the Passion of the Artist writ large, made to seem far more important than the mere suffering and deaths of a few hundred thousand nameless and faceless peasants (and American soldiers) across the South China Sea.

My point is that this documentary only compounds and intensifies a refusal to deal with Vietnam that existed in embryo even in Coppola's film. The only chance APOCALYPSE NOW had to succeed commercially was if it pleased everyone—hawks, doves, and everyone in between. Somehow it achieved that, not merely confirming everyone's prejudices about the war simultaneously but also convincing members of each faction that it was speaking only to them. At the time the journalist Deirdre English compared APOCALYPSE NOW to the unabashedly racist THE DEER HUNTER, pointing out that each film "takes a fabricated act of Vietnamese terror"—the ultrasadistic Russian roulette game of THE DEER HUNTER, the hacking off of inoculated children's arms (recounted in a climactic monologue by Marlon Brando) in APOCALYPSE—"and elevates it to become the central metaphor of the war." Both fabrications undoubtedly grew out of tall tales told by returning American soldiers—I assume they're fabrications because I've yet to see any documentary evidence of either—and they play a central ideological role in both films by furnishing a myth and metaphor to plug up a gaping hole in our understanding of what that war and that country were all about.

The opening lines of HEARTS OF DARKNESS, spoken by Francis Coppola at the 1979 Cannes film festival, are characteristic of the overall thrust of the documentary and of the rhetoric surrounding APOCALYPSE NOW from its inception: "My film is not a movie. My film is not about Vietnam. It *is* Vietnam. It's what it was really like—it was crazy. And the way we made it was very much like the way the Americans were in Vietnam. We were in the jungle, there were too many of us, we had access to too much money, too much equipment, and little by little we went insane."

Coppola's movie is a nice late-70s liberal statement about U.S. involvement in Vietnam and the excess it entailed—and I don't intend "nice" or "late 70s liberal" to be condescending. For all its failings and shortcomings, APOCALYPSE NOW was probably the best big-budget, big-statement American movie blockbuster about the Vietnam War that we had in the 70s, and it's questionable whether we've seen much improvement in this subgenre since. PLATOON clearly is more authentic and FULL METAL JACKET at its best moments may conjure up more profound ideas about warfare, but neither film comes close to the total experience of spaced-out insanity and sensory overload that Coppola's Cannes statement suggests and that his movie amply furnishes.

But consider what Coppola actually says: his movie *is* Vietnam, and by "Vietnam" he means "us," not "them"; Americans, not Vietnamese. Milius put together his hawkish script out of his own imagination and tales told him by returning soldiers; he himself had no firsthand experience. Coppola had no such experience either, though he viewed U.S. involvement more skeptically. He shot the entire film in the Philippines, selected for its reputed topographical similarity to Vietnam. Only after all the footage was shot did he hire Michael Herr—the author of a first-rate book of reportage about Americans fighting in Vietnam, *Dispatches*—to write the film's very effective offscreen commentary, delivered by the hero, Willard (Sheen).

Curiously, though Herr is the only creative member of the APOCALYPSE NOW team who had firsthand knowledge of Vietnam, he isn't interviewed or even mentioned in HEARTS OF DARKNESS. Of course, Herr's view of the war is considerably to the left of Milius's "Conan the Barbarian" outlook. (Usually when we see Milius in this film, he's chortling with enjoyment over his favorite instances of macho piggishness, including a favorable humorous comparison of Coppola with Hitler and himself with Gerd von Rundstedt.) Political views are not supposed to matter, however, because the facts of the war are seen as piffling next to the glorious spectacle of an American director shooting a movie in Southeast Asia. As a press release puts it, "HEARTS OF DARKNESS is an examination of Francis Coppola—a director who, at the height of his political and creative powers, placed himself, his family, and his crew in a set of dangerous circumstances to discover the truths in Conrad's story and inside himself." Or as his wife puts it at one point, "He'd gone to the threshold of his sanity . . . or something."

Whatever that "something" is, Vietnam isn't within light-years of it, though it's supposed to be the subject of the film—sort of. When Eleanor Coppola arrives in the Philippines with her three children in March 1976, she approvingly quotes her daughter's remark: "It looks like the Disneyland jungle tour." In the first year, deals are made with Ferdinand Marcos for a fleet of helicopters (some of them later called away in the middle of a take to fight a civil war in the south), six hundred or so natives are hired at a dollar a day to build a temple set, typhoons and monsoons destroy the sets, the lead actor is replaced (Sheen for Harvey Keitel) after a week's shooting, and Sheen's major heart attack causes further delays. More than a year after her arrival, Eleanor Coppola films a local Philippine ritual that involves drinking, dancing, and the slaughter of pigs and chickens; profoundly moved, she drags her husband to the next ceremony, the slaughter of a caribou. The caribou is then eaten at a festival, and as a gesture of respect the mayor gives Francis Coppola the "best part," the heart. Much later, when Coppola is shooting the final scene of APOCALYPSE NOW, he shows the sacrificial killing of a caribou at the same time that Willard emerges from the primordial slime of the river to keep his date with destiny and murder Kurtz (Brando), the mad officer he's been ordered to "terminate with extreme prejudice."

What, you may ask, does any of this have to do with Vietnam? Of course, the Philippines and Vietnam are both in Southeast Asia. But let's suppose that North Vietnam had invaded the United States in the midst of a civil war. How would we feel if a Vietnamese filmmaker proceeded to Mexico to make a film about our war, and wound up shooting a bullfight he happened to visit as a potent example of the activities of typical U.S. savages? And what if he then declared to the press, "My film is not about the United States. It *is* the United States. It's what it was really like . . . it was crazy"?

"What it was really like" means, of course, what it was like for Americans in Vietnam—Herr's subject in *Dispatches*—not what it was like for the Vietnamese. And the main poetic insight of APOCALYPSE NOW—which borrows more than just a page or two from Herr—is that, for Americans at least, Vietnam was just like a movie. In HEARTS OF DARKNESS, Coppola remarks at one point, "A film director is one of the last dictatorial posts left in a world getting more and more democratic." Clearly Coppola is likening himself to Kurtz, and similar comments crop up frequently in the documentary—as well they should, because above all else APOCALYPSE NOW is a movie about being a movie director. The key sequence, the one everyone remembers, is Lieutenant Colonel Kilgore (Duvall) of the Ninth Air Cavalry attacking a Vietcong beachhead with Wagner blaring from the helicopters and soldiers surfing ecstatically behind the boats. (The character of Kilgore, modeled mainly on George C. Scott's General Buck Turgidson in DR. STRANGELOVE, offers a comic preview of Kurtz.) We don't need HEARTS OF DARKNESS to tell us that Kilgore's "achievement" in this attack parallels Coppola's achievement in setting up and executing the sequence.

To my mind, Willard functions best as first-person narrator and observer, and Kurtz functions best as his and our narrative destination (we encounter him only toward the end of the story, as we do in the Conrad novella). As characters they're both pompous, boring macho types who seem to spend much of their time shadowboxing, quoting T. S. Eliot, or sucking on pieces of exotic fruit. (Another inspiration for APOCALYPSE NOW may be Werner Herzog's AGUIRRE: THE WRATH OF GOD, which links the fanaticism of a mad conquistador with that of the film director. But in Herzog's film we don't have to wait for the madman to make a grand entrance; he's there and raving from the beginning.) The true meaning of Conrad's story comes from what the narrator encounters on his trip down the river en route to Kurtz, and the same could be said for Coppola's movie; these encounters are like clues to a mystery, but they're much more suggestive and interesting when they *remain* clues, like the encounter with Kilgore.

■

It's entirely to the credit of HEARTS OF DARKNESS that it traces APOCALYPSE NOW back to Orson Welles's adaptations of Conrad's novella. Welles's first half-hour adaptation for radio, with Ray Collins as Marlow and himself as Kurtz, aired on November 6, 1938, exactly one week after his famous *War of the Worlds* broadcast. In 1939 Welles developed an ambitious screenplay (never produced) that updated the story to make it reflect the rise in totalitarianism in Western Europe—as well as colonialist ventures in the Belgian Congo and elsewhere in Africa—and that was constructed around an extremely daring use of the first-person camera, which took the place of Marlow. Welles's second (and much better) radio adaptation, with Welles playing both Marlow and Kurtz, derived some of its ideas from the screenplay and was broadcast on March 13, 1945. The documentary cites only the first two adaptations and plays several excerpts from Welles's radio narration, but unless my ears were playing tricks on me, these snippets come from both radio shows, not just the first.

The Welles connection is worth bearing in mind, in any case, because APOCALYPSE NOW reeks with his influence: not only the portentous offscreen narration, first-person camera angles, and juicy larger-than-life character acting, but much of the chiaroscuro and other lighting effects of Vittorio Storaro's cinematography. Even the opening shot—a close-up of Willard's face shown upside down—seems a direct steal of the opening shots from two Welles films, OTHELLO and THE TRIAL. It's also worth pointing out that if Welles's screenplay had been filmed, it would almost certainly have had a much more pointed contemporary relevance than Coppola's version of the story.

It's also to the credit of HEARTS OF DARKNESS that in most of the clips from APOCALYPSE NOW the original 'Scope format is preserved rather than cut down to the usual video-screen ratio. Moreover, many of the participants interviewed in the film show a sophisticated awareness of the ambiguity of their enterprise. (We're told a lot about the massive drug consumption; Frederic Forrest remarks at one point, "We felt like we really weren't there," and Sam Bottoms admits to using pot, LSD, speed, and alcohol between as well as during various takes. Indeed, the communal high may have been the crew and cast's closest spiritual link to the American soldiers in Vietnam, and this registers all the way through the picture.)

Missing from this production story are the scenes shot with Harvey Keitel as Willard, as well as the voice tracks of the heated script conferences between Coppola and Brando, some of which we briefly see. (We do, however, see Brando blow a couple of takes, in one case by announcing he's just swallowed a bug.) But the biggest absence in HEARTS OF DARKNESS is not Vietnam itself, but the shadow of any awareness that it's missing. Like Willard and Coppola, we're still journeying into ourselves—and still coming up with the same old nonanswers. In effect, we've been triumphantly brought to the same level of understanding experienced by Coppola's daughter when she observed: "It looks like the Disneyland jungle tour."

—Chicago *Reader,* January 24, 1992

Given how sexy and volatile it is, it's no surprise at all that THE PIANO is a hit. It's also no surprise, given the strong-arm tactics of Miramax and the hype of some reviewers, that a certain critical backlash is already setting in, as evidenced by a lucid and considered dissent by Stuart Klawans in the *Nation* and a rather lazy dismissal by Stanley Kauffmann in the *New Republic.* People like myself who are passionate fans of Jane Campion's previous work may be somewhat churlish that many other people are finding their way to her work only after it has become juiced up, simplified, and mainstreamed—like the people who bypassed the dreamy finesse of ERASERHEAD on their way to the relative crudeness of BLUE VELVET. It's certainly regrettable that people who weren't interested in seeing Campion's 1989 film SWEETIE until after they saw THE PIANO now have to contend with a lousy video transfer that doesn't begin to do justice to Campion's colors and compositions.

Technically speaking, THE PIANO is Campion's second feature; AN ANGEL AT MY TABLE (1990) was a three-part TV miniseries that was shown theatrically only after it won several prizes at film festivals. The distinction seems important because the relatively conventional and naturalistic style of the miniseries, in terms of acting as well as filmmaking, was clearly designed for the small screen (as was 2 FRIENDS, a 1985 TV feature, and AFTER HOURS, a half-hour short about sexual harassment she made in 1991), and blowing it up deprived it of some of its intimacy. The film also suffered in temporal terms: it presents the early life of New Zealand writer Janet Frame in three separate stages, with three separate actresses playing her, and was designed to be seen on separate occasions, with time for reflection in between. (The same episodic design can be found in Krzysztof Kieslowski's DECALOGUE—still, scandalously, unseen here apart from a few festivals.)

Both of Campion's theatrical features are bold expressionist works about female sexual desire that make free and idiosyncratic use of central metaphors—though here their similarities end, and it will be interesting to see whether Campion's next feature, an adaptation of Henry James's *The Portrait of a Lady*, bears any relationship at all to this pattern. In SWEETIE, the principal drama is between two antagonistic sisters—one of them sexually repressed and neurotic, the other uninhibited and psychotic—and the central metaphor is trees. Though a couple of trees actually figure in the plot, Campion mainly uses trees as a poetic organizing image in the consciousness of Kay, the neurotic sister, who narrates the film: she sees them in terms of family trees, planted and uprooted lives, unseen depths and giddy elevations, blooming versus dying, and various forms of encroachments and entanglements.

THE PIANO has a narrator as well, but only at the very beginning and the very end of the picture, and the voice in this case is the inner consciousness of the mute heroine. Ada (Holly Hunter), a nineteenth-century Scottish woman with a little girl named Flora (Anna Paquin), informs us at the outset that she hasn't spoken since the age of six—though, she adds, she doesn't consider herself silent because she's able to express herself through her piano playing. We quickly discover that Flora—with whom she converses in sign language (which is often subtitled), and who serves as her main instrument of communication with others—is the only one she readily communicates with.

The reason for her muteness is something we never find out, and that's the first of the film's many structuring absences; another is the identity of Flora's father. Though some reviewers have been calling Ada a widow, the little I can surmise is that the marriage her father (never seen) arranges for her at the beginning of the film to Stewart (Sam Neill), an English settler in the wilds of New Zealand, is her first. She and Flora are shipped off from Europe, and when they arrive with their belongings, on a beach thunderous with waves, Ada's crated piano gets left behind at Stewart's insistence, despite her protests. Not long after their arrival, Flora spins an elaborate yarn for Stewart's Aunt Morag (Kerry Walker) about her parents: how they met ("in Austria, where he conducted the Royal Orchestra"), where they were married (in a forest with fairies and elves, which she then revises into a country church near the Alps), and how Ada lost her voice (a bolt of lightning struck Flora's father and burned him to a crisp when he and Ada were singing in the mountains; this jazzy demise is illustrated by a quick patch of animation—one of many striking images in the film omitted in the published version of the script).

Much later, however, a scene between mother and daughter informs us that Flora was fathered by Ada's teacher (presumably music teacher), whom Ada communicated with telepathically: "I didn't need to speak; I could lay thoughts out in his mind like they were a sheet," read the subtitles. But they didn't get married because "after a while he became frightened and he stopped listening," and after Flora was born "he was sent away." The conclusion of Ada's "explanation"—"I think he's looking for us now all across the world, across the red sea"—sounds about as mythological as the elves, fairies, and lightning bolt in Flora's account.

In short, we wind up learning as little about Flora's father—apart from the fact that he *may* have been connected to Ada's music—as we learn about the cause of her muteness. One reason for this, I think, is that a mythology of origins—the origins of New Zealand as well as the origins of female self-expression and self-realization, both personal origins of Campion herself—is at the roots of THE PIANO, which she has been working on since 1984. Within this mythology, Ada's muteness and her piano are closely interrelated metaphors—and metaphors for irreducible givens, not for subjects meant to be analyzed. In nineteenth-century New Zealand, where female self-expression, like civilization, is postulated as still being on the brink of formation, Ada's muteness is set forth as a kind of inexact metaphor for the repression of women—an oddity and an encumbrance, like her enormous hoopskirts, but still a fact of life. Her piano, which signifies civilized speech, is a personal necessity to Ada but only an oddity and an encumbrance for Stewart (which is why he orders it left behind). Completing this awkward schema are the Maori natives, a chattering Greek chorus of noble and enlightened primitives, and Baines (Harvey Keitel), an American settler and a neighbor of Stewart's, who has "gone native" by getting himself tattooed and learning the local Maori lingo. There are also a few other white locals, such as the Reverend and his sister Nessie (the latter played by Genevieve Lemon, the actress who played Sweetie).

Unlike the half dozen or so major figures in SWEETIE, none of the participants in THE PIANO qualifies as a character in the round, with an implied reality beyond the frame of Campion's story; for all the power of the three central performances, they're merely vehicles for a series of jolting effects and escalating climaxes, providing at best annexes to the central metaphors. (In some ways Stewart can be read as inhibited and voyeuristic Europe, Baines as action-hero America with a trace of Mr. Natural. It's tempting to read even Campion's projected professional future into the fate of Ada, with Stewart as the European art movie and Baines as Hollywood.) When Stewart tells Baines quite late in the film that he's achieved telepathic communication with Ada, presumably as Flora's father once did, and then recites a message from her verbatim, this comes across not as any sort of character development but as a contrived narrative device.

Near the beginning of the story, Baines buys the piano from Stewart (who assumes ownership rights over Ada's property immediately upon her arrival). Baines, who values the piano because he associates it with Ada and values Ada because he associates her with sex, has it transported from the beach to his hut, and then strikes a deal with Ada: he'll swap piano lessons for the piano itself. In fact, these "lessons" consist of erotic favors Ada hesitantly dispenses at Baines's request: letting him crawl under her skirts, finger the hole in her stocking, and ultimately getting them both to strip. It's a barter arrangement that parallels Stewart's attempted deals with the natives (at one point he absurdly offers buttons in exchange for land), but it's much more successful: by the end of the lessons, it has transformed Ada from a repressed being to a fully sexual one.

Their arrangement also bears an unsettling relationship to the deal between cannibalistic serial killer Hannibal Lecter and FBI agent Clarice Starling in THE SILENCE OF THE LAMBS whereby she dispenses intimate revelations about herself in exchange for his insights into the minds of serial killers. In both cases, the intimations of rape and prostitution are overridden (or, more precisely, justified) by the notion of consent; and both THE SILENCE OF THE LAMBS and THE PIANO have been celebrated in some quarters—though not generally the same quarters—as both feminist *and* erotic: politically correct porn.

The position Ada puts herself in also bears some relation to arguments about Madonna "being in control of her own image"—unlike, say, Marilyn Monroe, who comprises part of the image Madonna allegedly controls—and strikes me as being about equally questionable. This isn't to say that men and women shouldn't be allowed to entertain and enjoy sexual fantasies. (Personally I get plenty of kicks out of Campion's film, a stray few out of Madonna's music videos, and none at all out of the Hannibal-Clarice tango, but tastes clearly differ.) But squaring such kicks with an idealist political agenda is difficult—especially if you're going to sweep the issue of male coercion hurriedly under the carpet; the barter arrangements in both THE SILENCE OF THE LAMBS and THE PIANO are proposed and launched by the men, and the women's initial response to them are recoil and resistance. And when Ada's libido finally runs free of male coercion toward the end of the picture, Campion seems far from endorsing the consequences. (It's clear, for one thing, that Ada's independence hurts her relationship with Flora, and before long she's ready to chuck the piano and herself, too.)

To Campion's credit, one can't say that the erotic power and political agenda of THE PIANO are simply unrelated or without mutual relevance—even if her references in interviews to the romanticism of *Wuthering Heights* tend to muddy the waters on this matter. (Arguably this movie comes closer to the neoprimitivism of D. H. Lawrence than to the Gothic romanticism of Emily Brontë.) After Baines ends the "piano lessons" ("I'm giving the piano back to you. The arrangement is making you a whore and me wretched"), she applies what she's learned to her marriage, treating Stewart as a sex object—someone to be touched and caressed who is not supposed to return any caresses. From here on, the fury of Ada's will matches the fury of Campion's will as filmmaker, for better and for worse; it's exciting to watch, but calculated to overwhelm rather than stimulate thought, so that when Ada is finally learning to speak at the end, you aren't really prepared to listen; you're more inclined to sigh with exhausted relief that the picture's finally over.

The metaphorical transformations of speech into music and music into sex—like the literal transformations of both sign language and Maori into English speech and subtitles—only clarify the extent to which this is really a film about *discourse,* including film language itself. When the camera caresses the naked back of Baines as he polishes the piano in his hut, it seems to "polish" him as well; Baines getting under Ada's skirts is roughly equivalent to the camera getting under the boat carrying her piano. When Ada strokes Stewart's body, she seems to be playing him like a piano, and at the film's gruesome climax, even fingers and piano keys—both displaced phallic images—start to become interchangeable. In the course of reminding us that sex is a form of discourse, the film also reminds us that all forms of discourse have political implications. Just what those implications are is still open to debate.

—Chicago *Reader,* December 10, 1993

Hollywood Radical (MALCOLM X)

At the top of 1968, over the vehement protests of my family and my friends, I flew to Hollywood to write the screenplay for THE AUTOBIOGRAPHY OF MALCOLM X. My family and my friends were entirely right; but I was not (since I survived it) entirely wrong. Still, I think that I would rather be horsewhipped, or incarcerated in the forthright bedlam of Bellevue, than repeat the adventure—not, luckily, that I will ever be allowed to repeat it: it is not an adventure which one permits a friend, or brother, to attempt to survive twice. It was a gamble which I knew I might lose, and which I lost—a very bad day at the races: but I learned something.

—*James Baldwin,* The Devil Finds Work *(1976)*

If the complexity that was Malcolm X survives this moment as only a T-shirt or a trademark, then it is no wonder that Clarence Thomas has emerged as the perfect co-optive successor—an heir-transparent, a product with real producers; the new improved apparition of Malcolm, the cleaned-up version of what he could have been with a good strong grandfather figure to set him right. Clarence X gone good.

Clarence Thomas is to Malcolm X what "Unforgettable. The perfume. By Revlon" is to Nat King Cole. A sea change of intriguing dimension, like when Eldridge Cleaver came back from Algeria preaching the good news of free enterprise and started marketing trousers with codpieces and barbecue sauce. Or when Ray Charles proclaimed that, while he sang "America the Beautiful" at the 1988 Republican National Convention, he would have done it for the Democrats "if they had paid me some money. I'm just telling the truth."

—*Patricia J. Williams, in* Malcolm X: In Our Own Image, *edited by Joe Wood (1992)*

Both of these quotations help to show how and why, given what we all have to work with—three decades of mythification and contradictory appropriations; tons of shameless Spike Lee hype and shamefaced white guilt converging in ecstatic interface; miles of media jive and ancillary products devoted to black pride and manhood and inner-city role models—there's no possible way that MALCOLM X could be completely accurate and truthful. Let's be real: the fact that this movie exists at all automatically overwhelms almost anything that might be said about it.

"Malcolm constitutes the quintessential unfinished text," notes Marlon Riggs in *Malcolm X: In Our Own Image,* an excellent recent collection that is cited above. "He is a text that we, as Black people, can finish, that we can write the ending for, that we can give closure to—or reopen—depending on our own psychic and social needs." Considering the diverse passions and biases reflected in the fifteen black contributors to this book, it is easy enough to see what Riggs means, and not at all easy for a white writer like myself to feel like a legitimate voice in this debate.

But the root difficulties of coming to some kind of terms with Malcolm X in 1992 are still plainly shared by everyone. If James Baldwin's lost gamble has improbably mutated into Spike Lee's bluff and triumph, extenuating circumstances and interfering noise prevent us from thinking straight about it: there are simply too many interests to be placated, prejudices to be honored and exercised, heated emotions to be respected, feathers unruffled, industry palms greased. If you genuinely believe that there's no contradiction in making an Oscar-lusting movie with big-studio backing and wanting to tell the unvarnished truth about Malcolm X—if, in other words, Baldwin is wrong and Lee is right—then I can only say that Warners has done an even better job than usual of selling you the Brooklyn Bridge with butter-flavored cholesterol sprayed all over it.

Lee dramatizes the fusion of—and confusion between—business and art better than any other American filmmaker who comes to mind. I certainly don't begrudge him his marketing talent, including selling "Malcolm" products to white kids on Melrose Avenue in LA: he's not doing anything the big corporations wouldn't. When he inherits the talented Denzel Washington as his star from a package previously assembled for director Norman Jewison— an actor who seems too handsome, too dark-skinned, and too elegant for the part—I can sympathize and wish him well. (Larry Fishburne, for one, would almost certainly have been better casting.) Or when Lee calls Warner Brothers a plantation while clamoring for a higher budget and doing everything he can to emulate and imitate JFK, I can both see what he means and appreciate his ability to milk the press, the studio, and the audience at the same time. (He may be no David Lean, but there are times when his show-biz religiosity and his total lack of self-consciousness remind me of Cecil B. DeMille.) I can even understand, if not exactly appreciate, the reasons why he occasionally conflates himself with Malcolm X as a controversial outspoken figure, apparently regarding his life at times as a similar process of getting from one damned press conference to the next.

But when Lee manages his art *by choice* like a boorish and aggressive businessman, with seeming indifference to the aesthetic consequences, I start to have doubts. When he begins his movie with a speech by Malcolm X *and* clips of the Rodney King video *and* shots of an American flag burning down to an X *and* a full serving of Terrence Blanchard's overloaded score, all delivered more or less at once and at full blast, I'm forced to conclude that he doesn't respect any of these ingredients enough to allow them to be heard or seen with close attention—which is another way of saying that he doesn't really respect his audience either. Later in the film, he offers a comparable MTV fruit salad of another Malcolm X speech, shots of Malcolm thinking (as if to remind us briefly of what he won't let us do ourselves), John Coltrane's "Alabama," and archival footage of Martin Luther King, Jr., and police violence during the civil rights movement.

Like someone wearing a belt and suspenders at the same time, Lee doesn't want to leave anything to chance—he avoids silence (the ultimate taboo) in all his films—so the very idea of being able to listen briefly to the beautiful "Alabama" as opposed to being sprayed with it by a fire hose never comes up. One would like to think that Lee would be capable of presenting Malcolm X's various messages without feeling obliged to advertise them, along with the caps and T-shirts.

A postmodernist Brooklyn provincial, Lee tends to lose his bearings whenever he strays very far from the present and his home turf—one reason why DO THE RIGHT THING, which sticks to a single block of Bed-Stuy over one recent summer day, remains his best movie. When he settles on what he knows, both a world and characters come into view, even if they're perceived through a miasma of wallpaper music and endless show-off camera moves. When he doesn't know as much about what he's filming, the empty technique and the salad dressing take over, ejecting us from his material and straight into the Spike mystique, which is strictly business, not art. This is undoubtedly why the first hour or so of MALCOLM X—set mainly during the early 40s in Boston and Harlem, with brief flashbacks to Michigan—probably contains the least reality of any Lee feature to date, although there are plenty of fancy zoot suits and glitzy crane shots to detract from the overall lack of conviction.

To be fair, the movie *does* have a visual plan built around various uses of black and white: check out, among other things, Ernest Dickerson's interesting and inventive uses of blinding sunlight in the opening Roxbury sequence, absolute darkness when Malcolm is in solitary confinement, and the black-and-white stripes of light through a venetian blind when Malcolm confronts Elijah Muhammad about his sexual transgressions. But the possibility of finding or creating any recognizable sort of social reality in Roxbury or Harlem in the 40s, apart from images in other bad movies, seems not only beyond Lee's range but beyond his comprehension or interest.

Consider Roxbury's Roseland Ballroom, where Malcolm Little, then known as "Red," worked for a time as a shoeshine boy, and which takes up about ten pages in the *Autobiography*. This pungent section inspired one of the giddiest flights of fancy in the novel *Gravity's Rainbow*, but it's hard to know how this richly evoked world could have been captured on film, even if Lee had devoted a whole feature to it. Any hope that this world or a shadow of it would make it to the screen was immediately jettisoned once Lee opted for a musical comedy production number in this setting.

It's a move clearly designed to show us only what Lee can do; all it can do for the Roseland or Malcolm X's life at this point is trivialize them and make them more remote, even with a Lionel Hampton look-alike leading the band. So it's irrelevant to note that this sequence improves on the production numbers in SCHOOL DAZE—unless we decide, as some critics apparently have, that Lee's career rather than Malcolm X's life should be the key reference point of this movie.

Fortunately the movie gets much better once its hero lands in prison, and ideas and rhetoric—most of it supplied by the *Autobiography*—fill in some of the cavities in the screen left by the period, settings, and characters. As soon as Malcolm finds a language and a new surname to go with his first pair of glasses, the movie acquires a voice, and even though Lee rarely allows this voice to speak more than sound bites, it still has plenty to say. And toward the end of the film, when Lee arrives at the assassination, he finally achieves some of the filmmaking power that his flashy technique has been striving for, wedded for once to his subject matter.

■

Considering all the gaps, ambiguities, and contradictions that continue to circulate around Malcolm's life and death, it probably shouldn't be too surprising that there are almost as many mysteries surrounding the history of this movie's script. According to Lee in *By Any Means Necessary,* his latest thrown-together movie tie-in book, "[James] Baldwin wrote the first script. At the time he was really drinking heavily, and eventually another writer named Arnold Perl helped him finish it." The way that Lee casually throws in a reference to Baldwin's drinking is characteristically unreflective and ungenerous; I'm not aware that Baldwin, heavy drinker or not, needed collaborators to help "finish" any of the articles or books he wrote over the same period.

Perl, a TV writer, playwright *(The World of Sholem Aleichem),* and occasional screenwriter (COTTON COMES TO HARLEM), was blacklisted during the McCarthy era and died in 1971. According to a friend of his whom I recently spoke to, Perl had already written his own screen adaptation of Malcolm X's autobiography before Baldwin was hired by Columbia Pictures. He subsequently wrote and produced THE DOCUMENTARY OF MALCOLM X, nominated for an Oscar in 1972.

And according to Baldwin in *The Devil Finds Work,* which never mentions Perl by name, "Near the end of my Hollywood sentence, the studio assigned me a 'technical' expert, who was, in fact, to act as my collaborator. . . . Each week, I would deliver two or three scenes, which he would take home, breaking them—translating them—into cinematic language, shot by shot, camera angle by camera angle. This seemed to me a somewhat strangling way to make a film. . . . As the weeks wore on, and my scenes were returned to me, 'translated,' it began to be despairingly clear (to me) that all meaning was being siphoned out of them."

Baldwin then describes a key instance of this—a short scene set in Small's Paradise in Harlem in which Malcolm, still fresh from the country, first meets West Indian Archie, "the numbers man who introduced Malcolm to the rackets." In Baldwin's version, while Malcolm orders a drink at the bar, Archie and his friends, sitting at a nearby table, make jokes about his naïveté while obliquely acknowledging that they all used to be like him themselves; then, after Malcolm stumbles over Archie's shoes, Archie invites him to sit down at his table. In Perl's version, Baldwin reports, Malcolm's stumbling over Archie's shoes precipitated an angry showdown—"a shoot-out from HIGH NOON, with everybody in the bar taking bets as to who will draw first." The studio approved this expansion, and Baldwin, patiently explaining the irrelevance to reality and common sense of such a scene, explains how, after he saw what was being done to his work by both Perl and the studio, he eventually "walked out, taking my original script with me."

That script, entitled *One Day, When I Was Lost,* was published twenty years ago and recently reprinted. Lee never mentions it or any of Baldwin's dissatisfactions with what was done to it in *By Any Means Necessary,* which includes the fourth draft of the script he used, credited to Baldwin, Perl, and himself, in that order. The final movie, which differs from this fourth draft in many respects, credits only Perl and Lee because Baldwin's sister Gloria, the executor of his estate, asked that her brother's name be removed. It's easy to sympathize with her decision; as the scene in Small's Paradise now unfolds, Perl's HIGH NOON showdown is made to look like social realism. A big bully collides with Malcolm at the bar, derides him for not saying "Excuse me," calls him an "old country nigger," knocks off his hat, and adds, "What's you gonna do? Run home to your mama?" Malcolm grabs a whiskey bottle, smashes it to smithereens against the guy's jaw, and says, "Don't you ever in your life say anything against my mama." Then he retrieves his hat from a pretty and adoring woman at the bar, tenderly caresses her cheek, and orders a whiskey. Archie (Delroy Lindo) at his table in the next room is so awed by all this that he quickly contrives to buy Malcolm's drink. It's a quintessential Oscar-movie moment—complete with macho childishness, violent excess, and a comfortable irrelevance to history, setting, and character. If Baldwin's name were still on the picture, he'd undoubtedly be spinning in his grave.

Structured rather like an Alain Resnais film, and therefore anything but Oscar-ready, *One Day, When I Was Lost* is a poetic, personal reading of the *Autobiography* that, as Terrence Rafferty in *The New Yorker* has remarked, "plays beautifully in the reader's mind"—a work that Perl and Lee have successively plundered in order to yield something unpoetic, impersonal, and conventionally commercial. Malcolm's stint in prison, the part of the movie that comes closest to Baldwin's original script, is probably the most didactic stretch in both works, and in the movie it certainly carries some of Baldwin's power (though paradoxically, the most potent *and* poetic part of this section—a meditation on the dictionary definitions of "black" and "white"—is not in Baldwin's version).

Perhaps the most beautiful part of Baldwin's script, its handling of colloquial black speech, is missing from much of both the *Autobiography* and the movie, perhaps for related reasons. As John Edgar Wideman points out in a fascinating essay on the *Autobiography* included in the collection *Malcolm X: In Our Own Image,* which focuses on Alex Haley's scrupulous invisibility as a mediator of Malcolm's voice and narrative, "Haley finesses potential problems by sticking to transparent, colorless dialect." But if Haley's colorless dialect and Baldwin's funky dialect both conjure up living, breathing worlds, Lee's jazzy stylistic flourishes in a void can at best only conjure up rhetorical attitudes—most of them middle-class responses to a working-class hero with a working-class audience.

I don't mean to suggest, however, that Baldwin's original script is flawless as a recounting of Malcolm's life and death. Lee is right to criticize the "last act" of the Perl rewrite (a criticism that applies also to Baldwin's original) for the absence of Elijah Muhammad as a character—still alive when these scripts were written—as well as its neglect of other factors relating to Malcolm's eventual martyrdom, such as possible roles played by the FBI. (On the other hand, casting John Sayles as one of the FBI agents wiretapping Malcolm's phone immediately trivializes this theme for the sake of some nudging film buff gratification—another form of product placement.) Unfortunately, many of the obfuscations that Lee objects to are still central parts of the movie and have apparently been retained because a more truthful version would have led to embarrassing difficulties with Malcolm's family.

For starters, it should be noted that it was Malcolm X's own brothers and sisters in Detroit and Chicago who brought about his conversion to the Nation of Islam when he was in prison, which is made perfectly clear in the *Autobiography.* None of this is alluded to in Baldwin's version, which invents a fellow prisoner and father figure—called Luther in the original script and Baines (Albert Hall) in the movie—and most reviewers and other publicists have been going along with this deception by calling this character a "composite." (It's true that Malcolm's self-education in prison was inspired by a fellow inmate—an "old-time burglar" he calls "Bimbi," who also tutored him in "some little cellblock swindles"—but it's rather cavalier to assume that any character, much less this one, could represent a combination of "Bimbi" and Malcolm's siblings—and Elijah Muhammad himself in the case of Luther—without some major distortions. And furthermore, the narrative functions performed by Luther/Baines's son Sidney in the movie make the distortions even more elaborate.)

The fact that some of Malcolm's siblings remained Muslims after their brother broke with Elijah Muhammad—and that, according to Marshall Frady's recent article in *The New Yorker,* two of his brothers publicly denounced Malcolm as "a man who was no good" even after his death—raises questions that Lee obviously prefers to avoid. He similarly neglects to follow up on the claim made to him by Yusuf Shah, the former head of the Fruit of Islam, and reported in *By Any Means Necessary* that Malcolm had at different times shown interest in marrying two secretaries whom he much later discovered Elijah Muhammad had impregnated—a situation heavy with Oedipal implications that increases one's sense of familial betrayal.

Thanks to such strategic avoidances, a great deal of the movie's energies seem to be devoted to marshaling offscreen sound bites to play over aerial shots of crowds (in keeping with the DeMille movies Lee emulates) rather than delving too deeply into Malcolm X's psyche or personal life. And when it comes to making any ideological distinctions—such as dealing directly with the reactionary misogyny of certain Muslim teachings, highlighted in Malcolm's intercut parallel dialogues with Betty Shabazz (Angela Bassett) and Elijah Muhammad (Al Freeman, Jr.) and in a prominent banner at one of the rallies ("We Must Protect Our Most Valuable Property—Our Women")—the movie can mainly only hem and haw and look the other way, waiting for Malcolm's next press conference to come into view.

■

The Autobiography of Malcolm X may be the best book ever written about what it means to be black and American—even better than Richard Wright's *Native Son* and *Black Boy* or Baldwin's early essays. For its mercurial intelligence, its value as social and cultural history, its stinging power as critique and indictment, its indelible character sketches, its moral and polemical rage, its dialectical sense of development, its meticulous self-scrutiny as seen through several overlapping identities and self-portraits, and its feeling for atmosphere and detail, it is clearly one of he most valuable of all twentieth-century American autobiographies.

The cheapest paperback edition is $5.95—a buck less than what it costs to see MALCOLM X in Chicago, and $7 less than *By Any Means Necessary*. And the immediate pleasure of reading it will last more than twice the length of the movie.

The possibility that the movie will encourage some people to read the book has to be weighed against the fact that it will provide many others with a perfect excuse not to go anywhere near it, bolstered by the unshakable (if unjustifiable) confidence that, thanks to Spike Lee, they now know what the *Autobiography* consists of, sort of. And even though it cost about a dollar more to purchase this pseudoknowledge than it does to expose ourselves to the genuine experience of the book, we all know which choice the media has already made for us, well in advance.

■

I'm not claiming that *The Autobiography of Malcolm X*, great as it is, is any model of fact checking and truth telling. Sometimes myths and simplifications are necessary tools in political struggles. It makes more sense, for instance, to claim that the civil rights struggle started when a black woman spontaneously refused to relinquish her seat on a bus to a white man in Montgomery, Alabama, than to state that this action was planned well in advance—by Mrs. Rosa Parks and Martin Luther King, Jr., among others—at a meeting held in Monteagle, Tennessee.

Similarly, as various scholars have shown, the *Autobiography*, which certainly had political purposes of its own, is guilty in spots of hyperbole and invention. There are documented reasons to at least question such matters, left unquestioned by Lee, as the nature and extent of Malcolm's early criminal career, whether Malcolm's father's house was really burned by the Klan, and whether years later Malcolm's own house was burned by the Muslims. (The movie is somewhat more open about the degree to which Malcolm may have been complicitous in his own assassination and martyrdom by deliberately avoiding certain security precautions.) Even so, the *Autobiography* is valuable as myth, and one can easily understand Lee's desire to preserve that myth. On the other hand, the political agenda of this movie cannot by any stretch of the imagination be equated with that of the *Autobiography*, much less Baldwin's original script. Let's consider how each of them end. The *Autobiography*, not counting Ossie Davis's eulogy, has two endings. The first comes from Malcolm: "If I can die having brought any light, having exposed any meaningful truth that will help to destroy the racist cancer that is malignant in the body of America—then, all of the credit is due to Allah. Only the mistakes have been mine." The second comes from Alex Haley in his lengthy epilogue: "It still feels to me as if [Malcolm X] has gone into some next chapter, to be written by historians."

The movie—again, not counting Ossie Davis's eulogy, which is heard over archival footage of Malcolm (mixed in with a few matching black-and-white shots of Denzel Washington à la JFK)—also might be said to have two endings, though Lee originally wanted it to have only one, the following text by Malcolm X as recited by Nelson Mandela: "We declare our right on this earth to be a man, to be a human being, to be respected as a human being, in this society, on this earth, in this day, which we intend to bring into existence by any means necessary." Mandela refused to speak the last phrase, so Lee cuts to Malcolm X himself saying it.

On the face of it, Lee's ending might sound more radical than either Malcolm X's or Haley's. But if we consider that *By Any Means Necessary* is also the title of Lee's book about his efforts to get his movie made, the implied equation between the rights of all black people to be considered human beings and the desire of privileged hotshot Lee to make a big-budget movie based on other corny period biopics can only be seen as a business move, not as an ethical or artistic statement worth repeating. To paraphrase Haley, it feels to me that Malcolm X himself has gone into some next chapter, now written by Warner Communications. If Spike Lee, who signs the text, thinks that either he or Malcolm wrote it, he has rocks in his head; radical sound bites or not, most of the heart and guts of this movie was written by Hollywood studios years before he was born. But maybe you have to believe such nonsense if you want to get ahead.

—Chicago *Reader,* December 11, 1992

Why go back to a movie that affected me the first time like a piece of chalk squeaking across a blackboard? Well, for one thing, neither I nor any other reviewer I know of came anywhere close to predicting that ACE VENTURA: PET DETECTIVE would not only find an audience but also sail to the top of the box office charts. How did we all miss the boat? "An appallingly bad movie, a certain candidate for worst of the year," begins Gene Siskel's capsule review in the *Tribune;* it concludes, "Don't ask how this was financed." These were my sentiments exactly at the press screening—a sort of stupefied horror at the manic leers and terminally stupid gags of star and cowriter Jim Carrey, coupled with disbelief that anyone could possibly go for them. But when the movie opened it soon became clear that at least some financiers knew exactly what they were doing. What did they understand that the rest of us grown-ups missed out on?

Turning up for an early show of this PG-13 opus at Webster Place one Friday last month, along with a fair number of others, including many preteen boys, provided me with some clues. For one thing, I saw that being grossed out was part of the game. After all, couldn't it be argued that JURASSIC PARK's two real "money" shots, pitched at more or less the same audience, were (1) a man on a toilet getting devoured by a dinosaur and (2) a gigantic pile of dinosaur shit? And wasn't it part of the appeal to kids of *The Simpsons,* when that show first premiered on TV, that parents were less than happy about Bart? One should consider the possibility that TV has as much to do with tearing families apart as it does with binding them together—and not only because it gives everyone a good excuse not to communicate. It also helps to create distinctly demographic market targets within every home, providing different age groups with different narcissistic models. And since one of the prime products sold on TV is movies, it stands to reason that movies should divide us from one another as well—in terms of class as well as age. From this point of view, "movies for the whole family" like THE WIZARD OF OZ are already becoming relics of our pre-TV past.

Jim Carrey is a recognizable product because ACE VENTURA: PET DETEC-TIVE is a spin-off of a TV show called *In Living Color,* which I haven't seen. The movie differs most noticeably from TV in its raunchy humor, which often goes beyond what one would expect for a preteen audience. Ace Ventura's opening adventure at first seems very much in keeping with standard Saturday matinee farce: Ace retrieves a kidnapped dog by pretending to be a delivery boy, using a cartonful of broken glass and a toy dog resembling the real one. Finally the foiled villain smashes Ventura's car to smithereens with a baseball bat as Ace drives away with the dog. Then come the first intimations of a burlesque show: Ventura goes to collect his reward, which is a blow job (offscreen) from the dog's owner, a woman with bulging breasts. He responds ecstatically by swinging wildly from some unseen ceiling fixture.

After this slam-bang opening, Ventura's arrival home to a veritable Noah's ark of pets in his run-down Miami apartment seemed not at all hyperbolic. The blow job got at least as many laughs from the Webster Place crowd as the attack with the baseball bat, but the relatively sweet and longer sequence about Ventura's hidden menagerie—a fantasy smacking of old-fashioned Disney—was received more coolly. This is hardly surprising given the torrential self-ingratiation of the hotshot hero: his identity as a principled animal lover, however necessary to the overall concept, seems distinctly pasted on.

The movie's main event is tracking down the kidnapped mascot of the Miami Dolphins as well as the team's star quarterback (Dan Marino, playing himself), who also gets kidnapped on the eve of the Super Bowl. Along the way Ace gets romantically matched up with the team's marketing director (Courteney Cox), whom he eventually humps four times in succession while his pets watch (again, to much appreciation from the Webster Place crowd). Among other highlights, Ace catches a bullet between his teeth, grosses everyone out—including his lover-to-be—at a party thrown by a billionaire fish collector (Udo Kier) who may be linked to the kidnapping, and finally exposes a demented transsexual criminal in a xenophobic finale that dimly recalls BE-YOND THE VALLEY OF THE DOLLS in its giddy tastelessness. The bad vibes that accumulate seem part and parcel of the hero's narcissism, and the overall "message" recalls a friend's description of the spirit of Milos Forman's HAIR—"Fuck you, you're not me."

Still, being part of a happy crowd is different from being part of an unhappy one, and even if a second viewing of ACE VENTURA didn't convert me into a fan, at least it gave me a better idea of where some of the battle lines are drawn. I even found myself laughing once, at Carrey's mugging when his character, wearing a tutu over Bermuda shorts, is behaving like a lunatic in order to get himself admitted to an insane asylum. He impersonates a football player running in slow motion, then prepares for an "instant replay" by reversing the whole routine, garbled speech and all—a form of VCR humor I could share.

What also got me thinking about ACE VENTURA were a couple of facts that came up in the recently aired fourth part of a series devoted to Dean Martin and Jerry Lewis on the Disney channel. First, the 1954 Martin and Lewis remake of NOTHING SACRED, LIVING IT UP, made more money than SINGIN' IN THE RAIN, ON THE WATERFRONT, or THE AFRICAN QUEEN. Second, the 1951 SAILOR BEWARE, the duo's third feature and their biggest hit, a black-and-white remake of THE FLEET'S IN, was seen by an estimated eighty million people during its initial run. As someone who's been a passionate Lewis fan since the age of six, when he made his first screen appearance in MY FRIEND IRMA, I've long been fascinated by the hostility toward him expressed by many of my contemporaries in recent years, coupled in some cases with an irrational denial that he was all that popular to begin with. Certain parallels between Lewis and Carrey—leaving aside the issue of their respective talents, they're both aggressive, hyperbolic, and infantile—made me start speculating about how much one's age and the correspondingly different relationship with one's own body tend to affect one's responses to physical comedy. Adolescents, whose bodily changes induce a perpetual feeling of awkwardness, may laugh in recognition at the same gag that to adults serves only as a reminder of their former anguish. (There are differences between Carrey and Lewis, however: Ace projects a smug narcissism closer to Lewis's Buddy Love in THE NUTTY PROFESSOR—a deliberate antihero or villain in some ways resembling Martin and Lewis combined—than to the usually meek Lewis character.)

Such comics as Lewis, Pee-wee Herman, and, much earlier, Charlie Chaplin seem to provoke in us unreasoning love, hatred, or both. Sometimes one emotion succeeds the other. Martin Scorsese in THE KING OF COMEDY included a true incident from Lewis's life, a virtual digest of his career: Lewis's character, a talk show host, is walking down a midtown Manhattan street when an awed fan standing at a pay phone tries to get him to say something to a relative she has on the line. When he politely demurs, she immediately turns on him, blurting out, "You should get cancer."

For Chaplin and Lewis, nearly universal love turned into widespread disaffection; Chaplin was in effect hounded out of the country, then barred from reentry in 1952 by the U.S. attorney general (a move recently defended by good-guy Ronald Reagan). In the more ambiguous cases of Herman and Carrey, the love of children is pitted against the hatred of grown-ups. It's worth adding that puritanical hysteria about Chaplin's and Herman's offscreen behavior had a lot to do with the banishment of both from their privileged places in the media.

■

Jim Carrey resembles Andrew Dice Clay, and Ventura resembles Clay's character Ford Fairlane; so why is it that THE ADVENTURES OF FORD FAIRLANE flopped and ACE VENTURA hasn't? The differences in response may be partly demographic, related to both age and political orientation. Both detectives are depicted as godlike superstuds, but Clay's Fairlane seems to belong to the Rush Limbaugh camp—not exactly a preteen constituency—whereas Carrey's Ventura (who seems to own as vast a collection of unbuttoned Hawaiian shirts as James Woods in SALVADOR) might be said to embody Oliver Stone's idea of a macho progressive. (Imagine Limbaugh as Wyatt Earp in TOMBSTONE: you'd have as big a box office disaster as FORD FAIRLANE.)

I'm not arguing that the mainly young audience of ACE VENTURA is politically minded, at least on any conscious level. But the fact remains that familiar character types on TV—most kids' daily fare—still have plenty of political connotations and meanings in their everyday lives. Ventura, a friend of birds and animals who specializes in bathroom jokes and can't pay the rent, is a misfit and outsider, whereas Fairlane is a spiffy dandy and thus has a closer relationship to the world of adults. Ventura's prime weapon in the corrupt world of grown-ups is the gross-out, for which a good many preteen boys feel a special affinity.

Though I can't claim to share this affinity—at least not when Ventura plays ventriloquist with his own asshole for what feels like an entire reel—I can still recall laughing my head off when I saw my first Luc Moullet movie in my early thirties. The film, Moullet's first, was the 1960 short UN STEACK TROP CUIT (OVERDONE STEAK), and a lot of it consists of the young hero grossing out his older sister with his obnoxious table manners—eating with his fingers, noisily spitting out pieces of food, sucking juice off his plate. When she asks him what time it is, he responds, "At the sound of the third belch, it'll be exactly 7:49," and demonstrates. But one reason I was able to laugh so guiltlessly at these puerile goings-on was the subtext of complicity and affection between the siblings, which gave the whole film a warm and poignant afterglow. The only such moments found in ACE VENTURA—and there are not very many of them—transpire between the pet detective and his birds and animals; other humans are conspicuously absent from this sort of spiritual bonding, and it's not hard to understand why, given Ace's requited self-infatuation. Moullet, who may be the most consistently neglected comic director alive, has made twenty-one more shorts and features since OVERDONE STEAK* but has never made any inroads at all in the U.S. market. Still, it's impossible for me to forget his shining example when I'm confronted with obnoxious comedy in its less humanistic forms.

■

"All right we are two nations," wrote John Dos Passos in *U.S.A.,* a trilogy that came out during the depression. The two nations the novelist had in mind were different social classes. Obviously the same divisions exist today, but access to technology more and more defines the experiences of the two; and *within* each class, generational differences concerning that technology may be becoming just as divisive. Earlier generations were linked primarily by wars and social movements, but a recent movie like REALITY BITES suggests that the members of "Generation X"—a concept manufactured by TV—are linked only by their experience of 70s TV shows. This suggests that if you're in that age group and you weren't watching TV back then, poor sap, you don't belong to any generation at all. Even worse, it suggests that wars and social movements—present and future—may be only TV shows or video games to begin with. (It's easy to imagine that "Generation Y" will be defined by the video games they played, and "Generation Z" by their software programs.) If Andy Warhol's famous utopian remark "In the future everyone will be famous for 15 minutes" sounded pretty fanciful during the 60s, this was largely because of the faith it implied in the media's universality. In the 90s, there's more reason to believe that eventually most people will either live on the so-called information superhighway—permanently plugged into a computer *and* an interactive TV set—or be in prison, which entails only limited use of TV and still more limited use of computers. Within this universe, having no connection with TV or computers will be tantamount to not existing. In contemporary terms, that means being homeless.

Ace Ventura, who might be described as TV's answer to Saint Francis of Assisi, offers shelter to the homeless, which given the world of children's TV can mean only one thing—animals. Animals, after all, are permitted to live without computers or TV sets and still earn our affection because they're our pets. But human beings without computers or TVs implicitly deserve only our scorn—the kind that Ace dishes out in gleeful abundance to fellow slum dwellers as well as billionaires—and punishment, to be provided by our costly crime legislation.

I still don't like this movie.

—Chicago *Reader,* March 4, 1994

---

* In fact, twenty-five by late 1995, the most recent of which is a short documentary filmed in Des Moines.

The World According to Harvey and Bob
(SMOKE, THE GLASS SHIELD)

My dozen favorite films at Cannes this year? Terence Davies's THE NEON
BIBLE (an ecstatic string of epiphanies in 'Scope, set in a perfectly imagined
Georgia in the early 40s); Emir Kusturica's Serbian black comedy epic UN-
DERGROUND; Hou Hsiao-hsien's beautiful if difficult GOOD MEN, GOOD
WOMEN; Jim Jarmusch's transgressive western DEAD MAN; Jafar Panahi's THE
WHITE BALLOON, an Iranian urban comedy about children that unfolds in real
time; Zhang Yimou's SHANGHAI TRIAD, a cross between Sternberg's THE
DEVIL IS A WOMAN—with Gong Li taking the place of Marlene Dietrich—and
BILLY BATHGATE; and Manoel De Oliveira's THE CONVENT (Ruizian metaphys-
ics and theology with John Malkovich and Catherine Deneuve). Then there
were such pleasures on the market as Gianni Amelio's LAMERICA, a mordant
treatment of the collapse of communism in Albania; lively low-budget musicals by Jacques Rivette (HAUT BAS FRAGILE) and Joseph P. Vasquez (MANHAT-
TAN MERINGUEZ); and a memorable period extravaganza by Cheik Oumar
Sissoko from Burkina Faso called GUIMBA. My least favorite festival movie
was THINGS TO DO IN DENVER WHEN YOU'RE DEAD—the latest stupid and
hollow Tarantino spin-off, whose wit ends with its title. The only one of the
bunch you're likely to see soon, of course, is the last. If you want to know
why, ask Harvey and Bob.

The fact is, my opinions and those of thousands of other critics, the festival programmers, and the jury count for less than the opinions of Harvey and Bob Weinstein, head honchos of Miramax, a production company and distributor that currently has something resembling a monopoly on the art-movie market. If my sources are accurate, Miramax is tickled pink about THINGS TO DO IN DENVER, which it produced; has no plans to distribute the Davies film, which it coproduced, in the United States; has picked up the Jarmusch;* and might or might not handle one or two other items listed above. Other pets of theirs have included THE CRYING GAME, THE PIANO, PULP FICTION, QUEEN MARGOT (which they extensively and expensively recut), BULLETS OVER BROADWAY, READY TO WEAR, Kieslowski's trilogy, PRIEST, THE ENGLISHMAN WHO WENT UP A HILL BUT CAME DOWN A MOUNTAIN, the forthcoming KIDS, and both THE GLASS SHIELD and SMOKE—two nearly antithetical takes on contemporary black-white relations, set respectively in Los Angeles and Brooklyn.

What Harvey and Bob think will determine not only whether you'll see the film and whether and how it will be recut or reshot but also how it will be promoted and discussed by the media—including most critics. For THE ENGLISHMAN WHO WENT UP A HILL, Harvey and Bob threw a big party on the Majestic beach the last night of Cannes, right next to a reconstruction of said hill/mountain (perfect for photo ops with Hugh Grant) and blasted the score from several speakers loudly enough to discourage conversation. Accurately gauging the puritanical hysteria of this country, they promoted KIDS, a so-so AIDS fable about heartless, unsafe teen sex, by showing it only once, at midnight, at the Sundance festival in January, setting up an aura of mystery and money that lasted for four breathless months. Sure enough, many who saw it at Sundance† wrote excitedly (and inaccurately) about "kiddie porn" and searing artistic vision, creating expectations that couldn't possibly be met when the film showed in Cannes, underwhelming practically everyone but the hopeful hacks eager to gull the American public all over again. (Keep watching your TV sets, and don't forget to ask Bob Dole what he thinks about it, too. If Dole said he saw an elephant fly, you can bet *Time* would offer a cover story on whether elephants in fact sprout wings.)

You can glean the sort of commercial scheming Miramax does from its presentation of PRIEST: after cutting a lot of the gay sex to secure an R rating, they gave the film its national release on Good Friday. The prominent Catholics who then denounced the picture—many of whom couldn't distinguish

---

* Which it subsequently handled with dismissive contempt after being prevented by Jarmusch from recutting it. [June 1996]

† "A wakeup call to the world," wrote a *New York Times* reviewer, drawing a firm line in the sand and declaring that rice paddy workers everywhere—or at least those with phones—should lay down their hoes and stop evading the problems of white Manhattan teenagers. This may help to explain why the *New York Times* neglects to inform its public that it helps to sponsor the Sundance film festival, so that when it offers its "in-depth" coverage of Sundance every year, it's essentially promoting its own operations.

between Miramax's efforts and those of the filmmakers—played right into their hands. (Despite such noble efforts, the film still performed disappointingly, as has THE ENGLISHMAN WHO WENT UP A HILL and QUEEN MARGOT, demonstrating that the Weinstein brothers aren't always the experts people say they are.)

To give you some idea of what Harvey and Bob think of Charles Burnett's THE GLASS SHIELD, they blocked the film's release for a full year, forced Burnett to substitute a less blunt and despairing ending after some test-marketing, refused to let the original version be shown at a Burnett retrospective in New York, and finally, after sending Burnett on a few interviews, shoved the picture out earlier this month. Thanks to Miramax's handling, this art movie's local bookings have been exclusively at drive-ins and theaters like Ford City and Chestnut Station, until it turned up this week at the Three Penny. For SMOKE, on the other hand, they flew journalists into New York to chat with screenwriter Paul Auster, director Wayne Wang, and actor William Hurt and dispensed numerous other courtesies; if you compare the pressbooks for THE GLASS SHIELD and SMOKE, the differences in care are palpable (the one for THE GLASS SHIELD consistently misspells Elliott Gould's name, for instance).

Of course, some Miramax pictures get treated even worse than THE GLASS SHIELD. I shudder to imagine what Harvey and Bob must think of Abbas Kiarostami's THROUGH THE OLIVE TREES—the first Iranian art feature ever released in this country, and one of my favorite films at Cannes last year. A few months ago Miramax gave it only minimal, last-minute press screenings in New York or Los Angeles and minuscule ads that virtually guaranteed minuscule business, then withdrew it from circulation, which means that it won't show in Chicago at all.* In other words, it's Harvey and Bob—not Roger and Gene, say, or some *New York Times* reviewer—who determine what most of this country will think (or not think) about Iranian cinema, just as it's Harvey and Bob who've defined the genre of THE GLASS SHIELD as "Hollywood cop movie" for most critics. (Not all of them, however: check out Terrence Rafferty's perceptive review in the June 12 issue of *The New Yorker,* which ranks the film alongside Kurosawa's THE BAD SLEEP WELL and Satyajit Ray's THE MIDDLEMAN "as an anatomy of moral corruption.")

People who regard movies as an occasional diversion and nothing else find it perfectly OK for people like Harvey and Bob to serve as their cultural arbiters and commissars, determining when, how, and even if they will be

---

* In fact, it did show at the Film Center in the fall, though Miramax was unwilling to supply a print or video for a press preview even then. Though arguably less strong than Kiarostami's HOMEWORK and CLOSE-UP (both 1990) and LIFE AND NOTHING MORE . . . (1992), all masterpieces that deal with the same fruitful theme—the interactions between filmmakers and ordinary people—THROUGH THE OLIVE TREES still might have offered an ideal introduction to Kiarostami's cosmic view of landscape and his witty sense of character if Miramax had allowed it to. [November 1995]

introduced to the masters of Asian cinema and dictating, for example, the emotional tone of the last scene in THE GLASS SHIELD on the basis of responses from teenagers at a Bronx preview. After all, the willing delegation of critical responsibility to a couple of brassy salesmen is the logical outcome when our culture considers the weekly grosses much more interesting and worthy of close analysis than anything else about a film. The fault, dear Brutus, is not in Miramax but in ourselves, that we are their underlings.

■

It's quite possible that I'd like SMOKE a little more if Harvey and Bob and their cheering sections liked it a little less. True, its central story is a self-congratulatory lie about American race relations—a macho security blanket specifically designed for those who can't bear the art and lucidity of something more complex and threatening like THE GLASS SHIELD. But many of the performances, especially those by Harvey Keitel and Forest Whitaker, are beautifully inflected, and Paul Auster's script, an intricate set of interlocking stories and anecdotes, is clever and graceful. The film created pandemonium at its press conference in Berlin last February, where the international press seemed filled with a kind of blood lust for the next PULP FICTION. (At big film festivals these days, nobody seems to care about good films per se, only about potential blockbusters.) I don't expect SMOKE to become the monster success PULP FICTION was—it doesn't have enough sex or violence or visual style or star power even to try. But there's no question that it speaks to the ideological needs of guilty white liberals; it's small wonder that the movie's source was a Christmas story written by Auster for the op-ed page of the *New York Times*.

It's no surprise, then, that SMOKE is opening in an exclusive run at Pipers Alley rather than at drive-ins, Ford City, or Chestnut Station, venues generally attended by a good many black people. Something tells me that black teenagers aren't going to be thrilled about a movie telling them how fortunate they are to have great white fathers like Hurt and Keitel watching out for them and their interests. For the same reason, I seriously doubt that SMOKE was test-marketed in ghetto theaters, despite the presence of a few black characters. Unlike THE GLASS SHIELD, it's been treated as an art film from the outset, not as a failed Hollywood or TV movie. (Of course, HOOP DREAMS has proved that an art movie can also play successfully at ghetto theaters, but this break-through required the sort of special handling Miramax was too busy to bother with in Burnett's case.)

Divided into five chapters—each named after a separate character, as in a novel—SMOKE gives us a novelist named Paul (Hurt), grieving after the acci-dental street death of his pregnant wife, and a black teenager named Rashid (Harold Perrineau) who lies compulsively and tracks down his long-lost father (Whitaker) but doesn't reveal his own identity. Paul takes him in for a spell; the second father figure is Auggie (Keitel), a cigar store manager in the neighborhood who's a friend of Paul and becomes Rashid's employer. Midway through the film Auggie's former girlfriend Ruby (Stockard Channing) turns up asking for help for her daughter Felicity (Ashley Judd), who's pregnant and addicted to crack, claiming that he's her father. Other key elements in this narrative roundelay are the daily photographs Auggie has been taking in front of his store for the past fourteen years and a paper bag containing $5,000 Rashid stole from other thieves.

Auster is a Beckett-influenced modernist with mystical underpinnings who writes in lean, musical prose, but he took a lamentable turn in his seventh novel, *Leviathan,* by broaching 60s radical politics from a safe, voyeuristic distance—which meant, in effect, not exploring 60s politics at all. He started writing SMOKE immediately after *Leviathan,* and in a way the two projects have identical ideological agendas: to tell the white middle class exactly what it wants to hear about itself in relation to the unmet challenges of the 60s. In keeping with this program, everything SMOKE has to say about crack addicts, black teenagers, errant black fathers, and black toughs is some form of warmed-over Hollywood cliché; but that's OK, folks, because this is an up-scale art movie for thinking people, not Hollywood fodder for the masses. What it *does* have is an idealized view of white tolerance and philanthropy and the kind of philosophical irony about social problems that makes one feel (as only the op-ed page of the *Times* can) that all's right with the world as long as there are a few urbane white people to take care of business and provide pearls of wisdom for everybody else. Director Wang serves all this up with taste, tact, and intelligence—which is a lot more than it deserves—mainly restricting his sense of style to an increasing use of close-ups over the course of the film.

■

Maybe it's the failure of THE GLASS SHIELD to offer any trace of such reassurance that turned Harvey and Bob against it: Burnett's world is bereft of role models white or black. Heroes of both races and villains (mostly white) can still be found, but they're not the sort of heroes easily identified with. The main ones here are both Los Angeles cops: Johnson (Michael Boatman), a black rookie in an otherwise all-white precinct, and Fields (Lori Petty), a Jewish woman who's the precinct's only female. He's ambitious enough to think that one day the station house will be named after him and she's smart enough to know that it will never be, but there's nothing glamorous about either of them, and the only thing that binds them—politically, not romantically—is their mutual exclusion from the force. Furthermore, the Hollywood narrative streamlining that would normally help us identify with them is purposefully subverted virtually from the beginning.

Johnson's first act as a cop is to stop a speeding car, but he drops all charges when the black woman driver flirts with him. Appalled, his white partner chews him out, then stops the same woman again and gives her a ticket. Even though we're made to feel that the white partner is right and Johnson is wrong, the way Johnson is berated is disquieting, suggesting racist attitudes. Immediately we're placed in a quandary that's unthinkable in most Hollywood cop movies—a situation in which we're less than sure about who's "good" and who's "bad." And rather than relax this tension, Burnett reproduces it again and again, in varying degrees and forms, throughout the picture, even after Johnson perjures himself to protect a white officer who may have helped frame an innocent black man. Johnson's burning desire to be accepted by his white colleagues winds up affecting his judgment, and we can't help but be swept up in some of his uncertainties. Based on the true story of John Eddie Johnson, the first black officer in an all-white sheriff's office in Los Angeles County, THE GLASS SHIELD is essentially concerned with the kind of everyday moral dilemmas everyone encounters; as Rafferty cogently puts it, "The truth that informs all the action . . . is simple and profoundly political: you can't know yourself until you know what you're a part of."

In short, what's confusing about THE GLASS SHIELD, Burnett's fourth feature (after KILLER OF SHEEP, MY BROTHER'S WEDDING, and TO SLEEP WITH ANGER) is that it's a police procedural that refuses to play most of the Hollywood games associated with police procedurals: there's no profanity, little violence, not much humor, and just a smattering of action. The film is loaded with plot, however, and if the movie has a serious flaw, it's that a plethora of incidents and procedures sometimes overwhelms the only story that really matters—Johnson's gradual horrified discovery of the way that American power and justice work in a Los Angeles police station, and what this process has done to him and to others. I've seen the film three times now—twice with its original bleak ending, without all the gratuitous closing titles about what happened to the characters—and each time the plot has seemed a bit overloaded just before moving into the powerful, lucid final act.*

Yet THE GLASS SHIELD has a specifically cinematic vision and visual poetry utterly foreign to the strictly literary virtues of SMOKE, and it hurtles along with a distinct narrative style of its own. A beautiful succession of comic book panels behind the opening credits and the following slow-motion sequence in which police academy graduates toss their batons into the air establish a dreamlike drift, illustrating Johnson's fantasies about being a cop. Everything else that follows serves to undermine this drift, but Burnett remains a filmmaker who avoids simple or didactic visual effects. The noirish figures in silhouette that dominate the film's later sections may suggest nightmares, but

---

* By contrast, Burnett's two subsequent films—WHEN IT RAINS, a joyous, twelve-minute jazz parable about community and common 60s roots in Watts, made for French television, and NIGHTJOHN, a powerful feature about antebellum plantation slaves discovering literacy, scripted by Bill Cain and made for the Disney Channel—are both models of compressed storytelling. [June 1996]

they're realistic rather than expressionistic nightmares, the kind we all live in.

Burnett's sense of character is similarly fresh and unpredictable and ambiguous, and his quirky direction of actors keeps all the mysteries of their characters alive and swarming—not only in Michael Boatman's expressive performance as Johnson but also in the pivotal smaller roles played by Ice Cube, Don Harvey, and Elliott Gould. Some critics have apparently expected THE GLASS SHIELD to adopt the convention of Hollywood and TV movies that characters must be instantly readable. But part of what's subversive about Burnett's manner is that despite the profusion of characters here, they're almost never clear-cut. For all the old-boy villainy exuded by such classic Hollywood character actors as Richard Anderson and M. Emmet Walsh as senior officers—Burnett seems to relish capturing their rotting corruption in rogues' gallery close-ups under Rembrandt-like lighting—one never feels he's content to stick with these simplifications: his eccentric, inquiring sensibility keeps getting in the way of the stereotypes, complicating our responses.

And what he does with Lori Petty—both in defining her sexuality and in ruthlessly excluding everything about her that's unrelated to her professional life—is so interesting and so contrary to standard Hollywood practice that this underrated actress is able to grab whole sections of this movie for herself. But given Harvey and Bob's promotion of this picture—and their very different way of handling SMOKE, all of whose female characters are pathetically lame, clichéd, and/or marginalized—I suspect they wouldn't agree. And in the final analysis it's their opinion that counts, not yours or mine or Burnett's.

—Chicago *Reader,* June 16, 1995

Stupidity as Redemption
(FORREST GUMP)

In the opening shot of FORREST GUMP—a movie that might be described as Robert Zemeckis's flag-waving Oscar bid—the camera meticulously follows the drifting, wayward trajectory of a white feather all the way from the heavens to the ground, just beside the muddy tennis shoes of the title hero (Tom Hanks). Forrest Gump, a slow-witted, sweet-tempered, straight-shooting fellow from Alabama with an IQ of 75, is waiting for a bus in a small park in Savannah, Georgia. Picking up the feather and placing it inside a book, he proceeds to recount his life story to various passing strangers; in the film's final shot, over two hours later, we see a breeze carry the same white feather up and away.

These framing shots—a poetic statement about the vicissitudes of chance, how histories are made, unmade, and remade—are meant to say something about a half century of American life, from the 40s to the present; and the tragicomic life of Forrest Gump, a saintly fool, is meant to embody those years. How curious, then, that one irresistibly focuses on the careful, deliberate way Zemeckis has plotted the feather's seemingly arbitrary progress—and on how calculated and contrived Gump's supposedly absurdist story turns out to be. Figuratively, the feather being blown around is us, not Gump or American history. What's blowing it around is a Hollywood wind machine exuding hot air, and what's guiding its trajectory is an invisible wire pulled by a puppet master.

"Of all the forms of genius," Thornton Wilder wrote in *The Woman of Andros* (1930), "goodness has the longest awkward age"; and five years later he made this the epigraph for *Heaven's My Destination,* his novel about another saintly fool. The figure whose moral purity leads to endless comic complications is a staple in many of Frank Capra's best-known movies—and is central to Leo McCarey's underrated GOOD SAM, which can be read as a sort of dialectical response to Capra. In fact it's a tradition in American thought extending well beyond movies: FORREST GUMP has many literary precedents apart from the novel by Winston Grooms (which I haven't read) on which Eric Roth's screenplay is said to be vaguely based. One can trace related fancies in the ironies of Jewish novelists such as Saul Bellow and Bernard Malamud (both of whom undoubtedly influenced Woody Allen's ZELIG, one of FORREST GUMP's more obvious sources) and the whimsy of Kurt Vonnegut, Jr., Joseph Heller, and other "black humor" novelists. Benjy, the literal idiot who narrates the first section of Faulkner's *The Sound and the Fury,* offers an even stronger (if less comic) analogy.

One is tempted to say, with apologies to Wilder, that of all the myths of innocence that have spurred this country on, from George Washington to O. J. Simpson, the myth that innocence *is* goodness (and vice versa) has surely had the longest awkward age; we haven't yet outgrown it. Even Wilder and Faulkner bought into it, and it still dictates not only a good deal of our literature and movies but also much of our foreign policy. From beginning to end, FORREST GUMP plays this myth like a grand organ.

■

I can't say I wasn't moved. The sweetness of Tom Hanks's performance, and Zemeckis's mastery as a storyteller and technical wizard, can't be denied. If the movie were less skilled and effective, I'd have less reason to feel such rage about what it's doing.

Born in the mid-40s, Forrest Gump is raised by a devoted, resourceful single mother (Sally Fields) who runs a boardinghouse in the remote imaginary town of Greenbow, Alabama. Speaking as someone born in a small town in Alabama around the same time, I find little about this town and the surrounding terrain believable (in fact, the Greenbow sections and those set in Vietnam were both filmed in South Carolina). But for Zemeckis's purposes, this is of no importance; it's the mythical South he's aiming for and achieves. Fitted with leg braces by a doctor who declares his back to be "as crooked as a politician," Forrest is an outcast from early childhood on, befriended only by a poor classmate named Jenny (Robin Wright). Sexually abused by her father, she has even more misery to contend with than he does. Jenny, who dreams of being a singer like Joan Baez, becomes by turn a stripper in a

Nashville dive, a flower-child hippie with ties to the Black Panthers and the antiwar movement, and a cokehead; and it's typical of the movie's tacit emotional connections that we're somehow made to feel (rather than think) she's been driven into all these things by the abuse she's suffered. Those connections are also a good example of how this "apolitical" movie takes a stand on such issues as the 60s counterculture. And the reason Zemeckis can get away with this and many related ploys is that Jenny and Forrest's "history" is merely the version of it propounded on and ratified by TV.

Back in Greenbow, before Jenny has all these adventures, she counsels Forrest to run as fast as he can from a gang of bullies; eventually he becomes such a good runner that he gets a football scholarship at the University of Alabama. It's about the same time that George Wallace is trying to block integration there, occasioning one of the many ZELIG-like special effects in which Forrest appears in TV news footage. (Earlier, Forrest is shown innocently "teaching" one of his mother's boarders, Elvis Presley, how to shake his hips before he appears on *The Ed Sullivan Show,* and one of his ancestors, a Ku Klux Klan general, can be glimpsed in a clip from THE BIRTH OF A NATION.) Subsequently Forrest shares the small screen with John F. Kennedy, Lyndon Johnson, Dick Cavett, John Lennon, and Richard Nixon, among others, as he becomes first a football hero, then a war hero, and finally an international Ping-Pong champion.

Apart from their varying effectiveness as gags, these visual stunts, unlike others in the movie, are technically shoddy. The lip movements of the famous people in the original footage have been grotesquely altered—a technique also used in the hideous SPEAKING OF ANIMALS shorts of the 50s, in which zoo animals would turn to the camera and deliver pithy one-liners—and the dubbing in of punch lines by vocal impersonators is imprecise. As part of the film's implicit ideological project, however, these gags are essential. For one thing, they trade on the sound bite and image bite TV concept of history: Forrest exposing the war wound on his buttocks to LBJ alludes directly to LBJ revealing his surgical scar to the public—the only thing about Johnson deemed historically significant here. These stunts also create a sense that history is absurdist and accidental rather than willed: the film ascribes the discovery of the Watergate burglary to Forrest, in essence feeding the couch potato's triumphant sense of one-upmanship, as in much of ZELIG or in INDIANA JONES AND THE LAST CRUSADE when Jones gets Hitler's personal autograph. Finally, these spots create the equally comforting sense that sharing media space puts everyone on the same level: U.S. presidents are "celebrities" just like Cavett and Lennon. In much the same way, sexual abuse and AIDS in this movie become discrete little nuggets of American history, along with various bumper stickers ("Shit happens") and T-shirts ("Have a nice day"), the civil rights movement, the 70s popularity of jogging, familiar pop tunes, and the attempted assassinations of Wallace, Ford, and Reagan. TV, the great leveler, brings them all together, like acts on *The Tonight Show,* and Zemeckis dishes them out accordingly, one bite apiece.

Through it all Forrest remains firmly lodged in our affections because, aside from his unwavering loyalty to his mother and his few friends—Jenny and two Vietnam buddies, Bubba (Mykelti Williamson) and Lieutenant Dan (Gary Sinise)—he literally doesn't know what he's doing. Whatever he becomes a part of—Vietnam, the antiwar movement, Watergate, new-age spiritualism, capitalist success—his sanctity is guaranteed by the fact that he knows how to follow orders, letting others determine his fate. Just like Oliver North, we'll stand on his head if someone in authority tells him to, and we're supposed to love him for it. His lack of guile and volition ("Shit happens") becomes our ultimate safeguard—living proof that good-natured innocence will enable us to survive and even prevail as inert, uncritical spectators of the passing parade. Like Forrest, we may lose most of our loved ones along the way, but after all we still have our TV sets.

■

Not a director previously known for his humanism or his sentimentality, Zemeckis seems to have his cultural roots firmly planted in the iconoclasm of *Mad* comics of the 50s. This spirited, anarchic nastiness can be detected in the script of 1941 (which he coauthored with Bob Gale and John Milius) as well as in the pictures he's directed, including USED CARS, the BACK TO THE FUTURE trilogy, WHO FRAMED ROGER RABBIT, and DEATH BECOMES HER. As a showman who remains adept at scrambling and reprocessing media stereotypes in the *Mad* manner, he's fully capable of wringing yocks out of wartime deaths (as in the gags in FORREST GUMP about Lieutenant Dan's military ancestors croaking) as well as out of civilian mutilations (the hole blown through Goldie Hawn's stomach in DEATH BECOMES HER). In most of FORREST GUMP, I hasten to add, deaths are played for tears rather than laughs—though our awe at the technical stunt of making Sinise appear legless matches our awe at the hole in Hawn's stomach, an awe that may actually supersede any other emotion.

It could be argued that *Mad*-style satire, which was a form of rebellion against the straight-laced repression of the 50s, has become an easy way for both entertainers and viewers to avoid political commitment of any kind. Some of this may apply to FORREST GUMP, but the movie is nowhere near as politically uncommitted as it pretends to be. The style of humor may be indebted to the 50s, but the particular "insights" into the 50s, 60s, and early 70s belong almost exclusively to the late 70s, 80s, and 90s, and smack of the neocon jeering found these days in the pages of publications like the *American Spectator,* a view to which this movie seems very committed indeed.

Consider the evidence: FORREST GUMP depicts Vietnam as a tragedy only for Americans (there's not a single Vietnamese in sight), none of whom exactly "chose" to go: they simply found themselves miraculously transported there (see THE DEER HUNTER and CASUALTIES OF WAR), fighting for incomprehensible reasons. The antiwar movement was a cynical con game spearheaded by pushy women, ranting Black Panthers, and unwashed male hippies who liked to slap their flower-power girlfriends around, giving the lie to their "peace" platform; hallucinogens led straight to hard drugs; and so on. The mutilated war veteran (Lieutenant Dan) is understood strictly in terms of other Hollywood movies—MIDNIGHT COWBOY in one gag, then BORN ON THE 4TH OF JULY more generally—because no other reference points are considered viable. (Maybe that's the reason for a clip from THE BIRTH OF A NATION—because only a famous movie can authenticate the Civil War.)

In the past I think I've overrated Zemeckis for his craft and cunning (WHO FRAMED ROGER RABBIT) and perhaps underrated him for his brutality and misogyny (DEATH BECOMES HER). I've focused here almost exclusively on what strikes me as appalling about FORREST GUMP, but it does have its fair share of attractively composed shots, shimmering landscapes, finely tuned performances, tender moments, funny lines, and sincere emotions built around a touching love story (Forrest and Jenny) developing over several decades. What all these virtues are placed in the service of, however, is monstrous.

It often suits our vanity to say that the wind blows us this way and that way, that life is ineffably absurd and loaded with ironic twists: it's a philosophical escape hatch, freeing us of all responsibility. But FORREST GUMP is actually predicated less on arbitrary fate than on the pleasure of two forms of redemptive innocence. There's the innocence of Forrest Gump toward American life and history: we're asked to be charmed by yet feel superior to his fool's progress. Then there's the innocent nostalgia of our own more "sophisticated" (i.e., jaded) view of American life and history, which is assumed and imposed by the movie—a cornucopia of received media ideas, images, and artifacts—and which we're not supposed to question. Eventually these two levels of innocence—which might be more rudely defined as two levels of stupidity—merge, so that by the film's end, Forrest Gump's innocence is felt to be a higher form of wisdom: our own. It's a classic American myth, the celebration of stupidity as redemption, and the "whims of fate" idea is little more than a smokescreen for the highly orchestrated marketing campaign that puts it across.

—Chicago *Reader*, July 8, 1994

Allusion Profusion
(ED WOOD, PULP FICTION)

[The media] ask those who know nothing to represent the ignorance of the public and, in so doing, to legitimize it.

—*Serge Daney*

If you want a happy ending, that depends, of course, on where you stop your story.

—*Orson Welles*

In *Vamps & Tramps*, Camille Paglia's latest collection of sound bites and press clips, one finds an extended account of her long-term obsession with Susan Sontag, including the following nugget: "She is literally being *passed* by a younger rival, and she's not handling it, I'm afraid, very gracefully. . . . *I* am the Sontag of the 90s, there's no doubt of it."

Her statements recall Wynton Marsalis's compulsive self-positioning as Miles Davis's rival/replacement—especially in the 80s, when Davis was still alive—as well as the repeated assertions reviewers have made over the past several weeks that Quentin Tarantino is Jean-Luc Godard's successor. All three comparisons belittle the talent, intelligence, and historical roles of Sontag, Davis, and Godard, but it's become increasingly apparent in our postmodern age that the logic of such comparisons has little to do with the original artists' accomplishments. They're about something else—an assertion of market value in a market defined by preexisting molds.

When Sontag wrote *Against Interpretation*, Davis recorded *Kind of Blue*, and Godard made BREATHLESS, in the late 50s and early 60s, thereby expanding the possibilities of criticism, jazz, and movies, none of them was the successor to anyone else; for better and for worse, they were creating new molds, not filling old ones. Sontag made popular art, movies in particular, a suitable subject in serious discussions of art, literature, and philosophy, while Godard, apart from popularizing jump cuts, introduced those discussions into movies; Davis introduced scales or modes as a basis for improvisation, which eventually made other kinds of jazz possible, such as certain long works by John Coltrane. Their would-be successors, however, are generally heralded not for their innovations but for their cleverness in recycling old works and attitudes, revitalizing their market value. Within the present economic setup, which also defines our cultural setup, Godard himself couldn't qualify as "the new Godard," even though he continues to be an innovator, because "the new Godard" mainly means the old Godard three decades later.

You won't find any serious discussion of art, literature, or philosophy or any serious technical innovations in Tarantino's PULP FICTION. But you *will* find an allusion to Anna Karina's dance around a pool table in Godard's VIVRE SA VIE and some dandyish dialogue from two hit men that may remind you of Jean-Paul Belmondo in BREATHLESS—dialogue that includes an extended discussion about the difference between McDonald's Quarter Pounders in Amsterdam, Paris, and the United States. If you can't figure out whether this gab (like the debate about Madonna's "Like a Virgin" that opens RESERVOIR DOGS) is supposed to be a satiric put-down or a dumb-ass celebration of American self-absorption, that's undoubtedly because Tarantino's mode of hipness involves straddling both positions. This choice, more economic than moral or aesthetic, invites both yahoos and snobs into the tent on an equal footing; nobody feels left out and everyone feels hip. Much the same sort of double-think in FORREST GUMP and NATURAL BORN KILLERS seems to be contributing to their commercial successes: whatever you think is wrong with the world, these movies are here to tell you you're absolutely right.

■

Films that feed parasitically on earlier films are nothing new; Godard's own early films teemed with such references—though they tended to be critical rather than simple replays, and they always rubbed shoulders with countless other cultural references. Hollywood directors since the 60s influenced by Godard, Truffaut, and Resnais began a process of cinematic citation that has escalated up to the present; sequels and spin-offs are part of the same phenomenon. But until fairly recently such references haven't composed a self-sufficient world of their own. TAXI DRIVER borrowed some of its plot from THE SEARCHERS and some of its stylistic devices from Godard and elsewhere, but aspects of 70s life in Manhattan still managed to leak through.

FORREST GUMP, NATURAL BORN KILLERS, PULP FICTION, and ED WOOD suggest a new stage in this process—a stage in which the world and the media become not so much interactive as interchangeable and indistinguishable, yielding an all-pervasive zone of perpetual disbelief that simultaneously saturates and alienates the viewer, confusing affect with effect, stylistic flourish with story, morality with attitude. To a greater or lesser extent, all these movies imply that life can only be what we already see in the media; and since what we see there is invariably false and concocted, all that ultimately matters is the stylishness and purity of gestures, not what these gestures yield or produce. Symptomatically, all four movies feature dense, irrational protagonists whose gestures and personalities we're asked to admire but whose activities—serving in Vietnam, shrimp boating, Ping-Pong playing, jogging, killing for the fun of it, killing for hire, killing by accident, taking drugs, making terrible movies— are essentially absurd; their lives and fortunes are equally illogical, though often fun and glamorous. All four movies purport to be about transcendence and redemption, but it's only nominally the heroes who are redeemed—they usually wind up no wiser than they were at the outset. More centrally it's the media-saturated viewer whom these charismatic figures are designed to ennoble and justify. For all their kinetic pleasures, these movies offer the comfort of cocoons, richly appointed with the same furnishings we grew up with.

Significantly, the concept of the media-savvy viewer—characterized more by hip attitudes than by concrete information—finds its counterpart among reviewers. Consider *The New Yorker*'s Anthony Lane, who last month built an entire review around the erroneous premise that Boaz Yakin, the director of FRESH, was black. This month, writing about PULP FICTION, he speculates whether it will date as much as "the rolling nudes and long, soporific takes" of Antonioni's RED DESERT, a film that has neither rolling nudes nor long takes. The magazine (and apparently its readers) may be indifferent to such trivia, but they aren't indifferent to Lane's prose style, which depends on references and asides as carefully planted as Tarantino's to convey a fashion-plate surface of knowingness; what's actually known is obviously less important.

PULP FICTION and ED WOOD strike me as being superior to FORREST GUMP and NATURAL BORN KILLERS because they're less pretentious, less self-righteous, and less hypocritical about the redemption and transcendence they have to offer. Their human resources also run somewhat deeper: PULP FICTION has more of a head than the other three, ED WOOD more heart. But all four movies gain their distinction largely by flattering our sense of ourselves as media savants, and all are con games to varying extents because they're predicated simultaneously on our equivalence to the on-screen characters and our innate superiority, since we're able to see through all their absurdities. In the final analysis, these movies have more to say about us than they do about their makers, and not always to our credit.

■

Fourteen years ago, when the Toronto film festival still had a sidebar called "Buried Treasures," selected each year by a guest critic, I was invited to take over that slot. I put together a program called "Bad Movies," intending to play with the ambiguity of the word "bad"—the only thing these films had in common, apart from the fact that I liked them, was that each of them had been pegged with that label at some point: Leo McCarey's AN AFFAIR TO REMEMBER, Jean Grémillon's LUMIÈRE D'ÉTÉ, Elaine May's MIKEY AND NICKY, Kon Ichikawa's AN ACTOR'S REVENGE, James B. Harris's SOME CALL IT LOVING, Delmer Daves's BIRD OF PARADISE, Edward D. Wood's GLEN OR GLENDA?, Fritz Lang's THE TIGER OF ESCHNAPUR and THE INDIAN TOMB, and William Wellman's TRACK OF THE CAT.

This was the theory, at any rate—that all my selections were good movies that had wrongly been considered bad. But in practice, the single smash success of the series was GLEN OR GLENDA?—a film appreciated by the audience only for its badness. And since then, the evidence increasingly provided by movie fanzines—which by now far outnumber "serious" film magazines—is that among film cultists, bad movies are immensely more popular than good ones. Or, to put it in more concrete terms, at that festival the North American premiere of the penultimate, two-part masterwork of Fritz Lang, one of the greatest filmmakers who ever lived, was much less popular than the latest replay of a low-budget exploitation item by an inept amateur. Both films are campy, highly personal, and characterized by endearing technical flaws, but Wood's unintentional hilarity counted for more than Lang's intentional sublimity.

One can see how much this taste has prospered since then by turning to the October issue of *Cinefantastique,* where no fewer than a dozen articles celebrate various aspects of Ed Wood the cult figure and ED WOOD the movie. But it's not as though this relish for badness has any developed definition of goodness behind it. One article heralding the first publication of a nonfiction manuscript by Wood, lovingly reproduced with all its original misspellings, typos, and atrocious grammar, is almost as badly written as the text it's describing:

> *The Hollywood Rat Race* truly comes into its morbid own in Wood's closing chapters on writing. Here, Wood's weirdly touching ineptitude at his own calling reveals itself in almost every dizzying line. Wood on inspiration: " . . . it isn't every morning you get up, sit down with the old pencil and paper and the greatest ideas in the world flow out—more so it is you will sit down and the blank sheet of paper will stare right back at you. An angry something that lays there defying every thought you might have. A white glob starching every urge into a thoughtless plan which means nothing, or little more than nothing."

However inferior Wood may be to his chronicler in matters of grammar, it's hard to deny that he's vastly more expressive.

The cultural and ideological alchemy that has transformed Wood's miserable, abject failure of a career into the cause for affection and celebration that it is today is not a process that ED WOOD cares to examine, though it is central to its meaning. The simplest word for this alchemy is mythmaking—specifically, of the sort in which the mythical "world's worst" somehow taps into the posthumous acclamation of his own life and oeuvre and smiles back at us in mutual recognition.

The historical stumbling block is that a certain alienation from the media— an alienation unknown to Wood and his original audiences—is the sine qua non of our mythic appreciation today, thereby blocking any real sense of what it meant to be Wood or even to see a Wood movie during the 50s. Without any knowledge or even any visible curiosity about this subject, all that director Tim Burton and writers Scott Alexander and Larry Karaszewski can do is build a monument to their and our complex sympathies for Wood from the vantage point of today's alienation and knowingness—not a monument to Wood himself, who remains unknown and unknowable in the very terms of our enjoyment.

A case in point is the movie's climactic premiere of Wood's PLAN 9 FROM OUTER SPACE, which the film sets in the Pantages Theater, one of the largest and most opulent movie houses in Hollywood. Rudolph Grey's *Nightmare of Ecstasy,* the oral history of Wood's life and career that ED WOOD purports to be based on, asserts that the shoestring PLAN 9 never played in Hollywood at all, so I asked Burton at the New York Film Festival why he made this radical change. He replied, with no irony whatsoever, that some portions of the movie take place inside Ed Wood's head, and this is one of them; in other words, he preferred to show us this event as Wood would have imagined it. Of course, this idea would never occur to most viewers—especially those who know little about 1959 or Wood—but even more amazing is that Burton can claim with such confidence that he knows the inside of Ed Wood's head.

ED WOOD doesn't really give us the inside of Wood's head, but it does treat imaginatively a number of Wood movies that retain a certain fascination (although in my mind everything after GLEN OR GLENDA?—Wood's uniquely deranged first feature, a 1953 documentary about transvestites—is relatively esoteric and boring). One of the undeniable pleasures of ED WOOD is its treatment of three features—GLEN OR GLENDA?, BRIDE OF THE MONSTER, and PLAN 9—as holy writ to be lovingly interpreted, imagining how certain scenes were actually shot or, in the wonderful opening sequence, offering a passionate pastiche in Wood's style. We also get speculative, sympathetic re-creations of Wood's freakish milieu, associates, and habits, suggested by various verifiable facts; most impressive of these is Martin Landau's charismatic, ingenious impersonation of Bela Lugosi and the film's warm depiction of his friendship with Wood (Johnny Depp). To be sure, much of this interpretation is as mythic as the rest of the film—nothing here indicates that Lugosi was a devout Catholic not prone to swearing, that he was hampered in his acting by his poor grasp of English, and that he was once a vigorous trade union official back in Hungary. But at least the movie offers us a viable route into imagining the man's pathos at this terminal stage in his career.

But when it comes to Wood himself, the movie can't get beyond a mythic depiction of his glee and determination, or the usual lore about his angora fetish and his oddball entourage. Indeed, all that can be furnished of that lore is a series of signals designed to set off knowing nods among audience aficionados, creating a jaunty boys' club atmosphere that seems largely imposed on the material. Also imposed are a nightmarish audience for the premiere of BRIDE OF THE MONSTER (no doubt occurring inside Wood's mythical head again), in which the hostile patrons are jeering before the movie even comes on, and a mythical encounter with Orson Welles (the worst meets the best) to seal Wood's future immortality. And to spare the viewer the embarrassment of burrowing through the final nineteen years of Wood's life—a grim tale of alcoholism, poverty, trash novels, and porn loops, encapsulated in one of the end titles—the movie chooses to take leave of him in 1959. In short, because the movie is incapable of imagining a precamp context for Wood, it has to import today's audience for his movies—contemptuous at one premiere, reverential at the other—back into the unknowable 50s, along with 90s versions of Welles and Lugosi. In this way Wood's alienation and our own are both validated in the same charmed (and charming) gesture: his doomed innocence becomes our doomed sophistication, and vice versa, and we all go happily to hell together, borne aloft by Burton's warm feeling for outcasts.

■

If the historical past looms as a lost continent to Burton, morality seems to have a comparable remoteness to Tarantino. Perhaps the reason is his well-advertised artistic formation as a video store clerk—a couch-potato savant par excellence—for whom instant-action kicks and their usual antihumanist justifications define the boundaries of any moral universe. "Redemption" in this context invariably requires vats of blood, disposable corpses, and guys doing guy things with other guys (such as producing the vats and corpses). And invariably such redemption is signaled by nudges to the academically attentive: for example, a license plate that says "GRACE" on the back of a redneck's filched chopper. Homoeroticism for heterosexuals is the order of the day, served up with the kind of gusto designed to make little boys squeal with delight.

Like RESERVOIR DOGS before it, PULP FICTION defines transgression and attitude largely through language. Most noticeably, it celebrates racial verbal abuse within an elaborately and strategically muddled PC context. By my count, PULP FICTION employs the word "nigger" at least sixteen times—spoken sometimes by black characters and sometimes by whites, always to great effect. But it does this within a racially complicated narrative framework: black and white hit men (Samuel L. Jackson and John Travolta) work for a black boss (Ving Rhames) who has a white mistress (Uma Thurman); to complicate matters further, Tarantino's own bit character—who says "nigger"

more often and more gratuitously than any other white person in the movie—
is married to a black nurse.

All these narrative elements are possible, if not plausible, reflections of
interactions that might take place in the real world, but Tarantino's point in
using them clearly isn't to say anything about reality but to produce certain
effects. When asked in Cannes why the word "nigger" cropped up so often in
the film, Tarantino replied that he wasn't really sure where it came from, but
then added ingenuously that he liked to think that if the word were repeated
often enough it would lose all its meaning and potency. A poignant prospect:
if such a thing should happen through Tarantino's noble efforts, it might actually put him out of business—unless, of course, he turns to "gook," "spic,"
"wop," "chink," or "kike" to furnish his future screenplays with comparable
spiky, crowd-pleasing effects.

I hasten to add that PULP FICTION is the most thoroughly and consistently
entertaining Hollywood picture I've seen this year, brimming with energy, star
power, humor, and ingenuity. It's only when I start to ponder the giddy moral
vacuum that produces and validates much of its entertainment—and the dearth
of wisdom or vision yielded by these kicks—that my enthusiasm starts to sour.

Like the racial epithets, the treatment of coke and heroin is similarly styled
for kicks while being tricked out with certain checks and balances (shooting
up is fetishized like a perfume ad, snorting leads to an overdose). The same
can be said of Tarantino's cherished theme of anal penetration, which figures
here as mean slang, the central gag in a ponderous Christopher Walken monologue, and a gratuitous rape during an already ridiculous basement sequence,
apparently designed just to show how mean some hillbillies are—only to be
wistfully recalled, like a favorite musical theme, by two sessions with Travolta
on the toilet.

It's true that some of these details, unlike the "nigger" mantra, provide
Tarantino with excuses for his much-applauded and genuinely enjoyable plot
swerves. The point is that all this "liberating," golly-gee narrative promiscuity
is so cynically, nihilistically calculated that it leaves a bad aftertaste. Though
this is another boys' club movie, PULP FICTION has enough generosity, as critic
Godfrey Cheshire points out, to give nearly every one of its characters—including three of its four female characters—a second chance. It also has
enough wit to scramble its interlocking stories, for maximum effect and meaning. But all these tales, including the characters and their second chances,
derive their meaning, their impact, and even their limited truth from other
movies and TV shows. To call this the best that American filmmaking can do
at the moment, as the Cannes jury and most reviewers have been doing, is
another way of saying that American filmmaking can't do much at all—certainly not deal with the world that's right in front of us, as Charles Burnett's
powerful forthcoming THE GLASS SHIELD does. (Shown at many of the same
festivals as PULP FICTION, it's gotten very little attention, perhaps because it

treats racism honestly rather than as an excuse for cheap thrills.) Even the spiritual awakening at the end of PULP FICTION, which Jackson performs beautifully, is a piece of jive avowedly inspired by kung-fu movies. It may make you feel good, but it certainly doesn't leave you any wiser.

On the other hand, Tarantino's flair for unorthodox plot construction, goofy dialogue, and dreamy interludes always keeps the viewer alert. The funny quasi-philosophical dialogues between hit men Jackson and Travolta about such matters as the definition of a TV pilot, the relative intimacy of foot massages, what constitutes a miracle or divine intervention, and the cleanliness of pigs and dogs are like extended musical vamps that playfully retard the action, meanwhile establishing motifs of their own to be developed later; and a visit by Travolta and Thurman to a lush 50s-style hamburger joint that ends with a wonderful patch of dancing not only becomes another gleeful interruption but also allows for more spot-the-reference games.

All this suggests another legitimate parallel with early Godard: the director's determination to cram everything he likes into a movie. But the differences between what Godard likes and what Tarantino likes and why are astronomical; it's like comparing a combined museum, library, film archive, record shop, and department store with a jukebox, a video-rental outlet, and an issue of *TV Guide*. The fact that PULP FICTION is garnering more extravagant raves than BREATHLESS ever did tells you plenty about which kind of cultural references are regarded as more fruitful—namely, the ones we already have and don't wish to expand. If the studios and their many publicists (including reviewers) get their way, we can expect to see a lot more of such references—maybe even on an endless porn loop, which would finally validate the end of Ed Wood's career as well as the beginning.

—Chicago *Reader,* October 21, 1994

Part Three

Issues of Ideology

Alternatives

The Problem with Poetry

Leos Carax

> First come words. No, emotions . . .
>
> —*line overheard in party scene of*
> BOY MEETS GIRL

Introducing André Bazin's *Orson Welles: A Critical View* in the late 70s, François Truffaut registered his opinion that "all the difficulties that Orson Welles has encountered with the box office . . . stem from the fact that he is a film poet. The Hollywood financiers (and, to be fair, the public throughout the world) accept beautiful prose—John Ford, Howard Hawks—or even poetic prose—Hitchcock, Roman Polanski—but have much more difficulty accepting pure poetry, fables, allegories, fairy tales."*

I'm not at all sure about fables and allegories—think of Campion's THE PIANO and Kieslowski's BLUE for two recent examples, neither of which the public seems to have much difficulty in accepting—and the Disney organization churns out fairy tales on a regular basis. But when it comes to poetry, pure and otherwise, I think Truffaut had a point. It explains not only why Welles never made a movie that was a commercial hit when it was first released but also why filmmakers as otherwise dissimilar as F. W. Murnau, Jean Vigo, Jean Cocteau, and even Jacques Tati could never belong entirely and unproblematically to the U.S. mainstream.

The problem isn't merely poetry as a general concept, but French poetry in

---

*Translated by Jonathan Rosenbaum (Los Angeles: Acrobat Books, 1991), 26.

particular. At a panel discussion held at the New York Film Festival in 1966, Pier Paolo Pasolini, propounding his recently formulated concept of the cinema of poetry, noted, "For a literary critic, the distinction between the linguistics of prose and poetry are absolutely clear. Each one of us, just by opening a book without even reading it, understands immediately whether the book is poetry or prose." At this point, Annette Michelson, who was sitting on the same panel, made a one-word comment: "Lautréamont"—because, as she noted later, "Lautréamont represents that point in poetry in the nineteenth century when the distinctions between poetry and prose begin to break down." *

In the world of the American mainstream, where Lautréamont has yet to become a viable concept, prose is still prose, hence marketable, and poetry is still poetry, hence esoteric. Yet regarding that mainstream, an interesting change in thresholds has been taking place over the past few years. With the Reaganite support of movie theater chain monopolies still in full power, the strength of independent exhibition and its alternative options—traditionally, arthouse fare and midnight movies—has been dealt a series of damaging blows. Yet at the same time, in an apparent effort to grind all the remaining Mom and Pop venues into dust, the multinationals have been attempting to broaden their and our definitions of "mainstream," with many interesting results. A few selected examples of what used to be regarded as alternative choices—comprising a menu ranging from *Twin Peaks* to THREE COLORS: BLUE, or from THE PIANO to FAREWELL MY CONCUBINE—have been smeared across public consciousness like lowfat margarine. To coin a verb inspired by the distributor most interested in pursuing this all-or-nothing game, such movies have been Miramaxed—in contrast to all the alternative titles in our midst that never get mentioned in the infotainment universe, receive a minimum of free advertising (including reviews) from all branches of the media, and in general exist in public discourse to the same degree and in roughly the same way that "homeless" people (i.e., those without computers or TV sets) exist as citizens in society.

The myth that "mainstream" invariably reflects some sifting through of popular consensus is predicated on at least three bizarre assumptions: that contemporary cultural choices can operate independently of advertising, both paid and unpaid; that a viable distinction exists in most people's minds between information and advertising; and, most operative of all in the present climate, that the publicist is always—or almost always—right. Yet when push comes to shove, the movies that people hear about are precisely those that publicists feel equipped to hype, and all the others—the films of Leos Carax,

---

*For a more complete account of this exchange, see *Film Culture,* no. 42 (Fall 1966): 97–100.

for instance—are condemned to be regarded as marginal, specialized, *weird.*
To what extent is mainstream status something legitimately recognized by distributors, and to what extent is it something created by promotion, including press coverage? That's a tough question to answer, but the issue of changing thresholds remains a fascinating one. Until fairly recently, films from mainland China were deemed marginal to public interest, while films from Africa continue to be regarded that way. This is not, I would wager, an aesthetic judgment made independently by critics, but an economic one made by distributors, though it is reflected in the discourse of most mainstream critics *as if* it represented their own aesthetic judgment: China's hot, Africa's not. Souleymane Cissé's YEELEN (BRIGHTNESS, 1987) may be one of the supreme masterpieces in film history—vastly more interesting and beautiful than the complete works of either Sydney Pollack or Brian De Palma, in my opinion—but the only way such a movie could get discussed in *The New Yorker* or *Time* or *Newsweek* would be if a major studio did a remake, no matter how stupid or offensive, with a bankable star like Cruise or Hanks taking over the Isiakka Kane part in blackface. The results would probably be slammed in favor of the original (at least by those critics who bothered to see Cissé's masterpiece), but that's probably the only way the *existence* of the original could ever get acknowledged in print—unless, of course, the next Cissé film got Miramaxed, which would automatically change everything. Properly speaking, most reviewers and journalists take their cues nowadays directly from distributors and publicists, and if the pressbook of our hypothetical YEELEN remake mentions the original picture, then, by golly, I guess that Cissé's movie must exist.
Much of the discussion that follows is an inquiry into the matter of why Leos Carax, the best new French director to have come along in years, hasn't yet been Miramaxed, and why, until or unless he does, you probably won't get many chances to see his movies. This isn't to suggest that Carax's three features to date are unreleasable in the United States or that they couldn't acquire substantial audiences here, with or without sympathetic reviews in the *New York Times.* In fact, his first feature, BOY MEETS GIRL, was briefly distributed by Cinecom. And when all three of his features were shown at the New York's Walter Reade Theater late last winter as part of a *Cahiers du cinéma* program, I'm told that about two hundred people had to be turned away at the last screening of THE LOVERS OF PONT-NEUF. But if a deal with a distributor still hasn't been cinched, I suspect this nonetheless has something to do with the different sort of valuation that French and stateside tastemakers place on Carax's gifts and his poetics—comparable in some ways to the respective valuation placed on some of Godard's recent features like NOUVELLE VAGUE (which finally "came out" in this country in video without ever having a theatrical opening). The question, in other words, is whether *Entertainment Tonight* and the *New York Times* are ready for him yet—and if they aren't, why not.

∎

"Anna—do you think there's a love that burns fast, but lasts
forever?"

—Alex, in MAUVAIS SANG

One possible reason why they aren't is that Carax's films are simply too personal to be regarded as impersonal mainstream product—personal to the point
of obsession—and too contemporary to be regarded as something we already
know about, which creates problems for the publicists. All three of his features
star the same lead actor, Denis Lavant, who's roughly the same age and height
as Carax and plays more or less the same character—or variations of the
same character—named Alex, a sort of anarchistic street punk. (All three were
produced by Alain Dahan, who died in early 1992, and all were shot by the
same cinematographer, Jean-Yves Escoffier.) As David Thompson reports in
the September 1992 *Sight and Sound,* Carax's real name is Alexandre Dupont
and "Leos Carax" is an anagram for "Alex Oscar." The point isn't to insist
that Alex is a literal stand-in for Carax but that one feels that Carax's work
teems with coded personal references of various kinds, and these references
tend to be more in the style of, say, Jean Cocteau than they are in the style of
Alfred Hitchcock.

Three self-conscious examples from BAD BLOOD and THE LOVERS OF PONT-
NEUF: both have characters named Hans who partially serve as father surro-
gates to Alex and also dispense drugs; both allude to an offscreen lover of
Juliette Binoche's character who is a doctor named Destouches, the real last
name of French writer (and doctor) Louis-Ferdinand Céline, one of Carax's
favorite writers; and in both films her character rejects Alex for a much older
man. Comparable recurrences are observable between BOY MEETS GIRL and
BAD BLOOD; for example, in both, Alex's best friend is named Thomas—
though played by a different actor—and winds up with Alex's girlfriend. But
Carax's features are every bit as striking for their differences as for their similarities: while Alex has a father (but no mother) in both BOY MEETS GIRL and
BAD BLOOD, he pointedly lacks a background of any kind in PONT-NEUF—in
contrast to the other two leading characters, both homeless, who are clearly
in flight from their pasts.

In various interviews, Carax notes that he embarked on his first short
film—the unfinished LA FILLE REVÉE (1978)—as a teenager in order to cast a
girl he was romantically interested in at the time, and it appears that this
dimension of his work has continued to be operative afterward. The female
lead in his first feature, BOY MEETS GIRL, is Mireille Perrier, whom Carax was
living with at the time; the female lead in the second and third, MAUVAIS SANG
(BAD BLOOD) and LES AMANTS DU PONT-NEUF (THE LOVERS OF PONT-NEUF), is

Juliette Binoche, whom Carax was living with at *those* times—although Perrier also appears in a strange cameo in MAUVAIS SANG as a young mother with a toddler, accompanied by the theme from Chaplin's LIMELIGHT.

Other familiar bits of Carax lore: As a child or young teenager, he went for long periods without speaking (something also true of Alex in MAUVAIS SANG, who is ironically nicknamed "Chatterbox" as a consequence), and during one of these periods, he discovered, at the Cinémathèque Française, the silent cinema, which remains a central source of inspiration in his work. (Among his favorite directors of the silent period are Griffith, Vidor, and Jean Epstein.) His most prominent mentors and role models appear to be Godard and Philippe Garrel—the latter a relatively unknown figure in the United States who is also a "child" of the Cinémathèque, a lover of silent cinema with a taste for eclectic experiment and "pure" emotion, and a director obsessively preoccupied with his own actresses.

Clearly the romance of the couple is at the center of Carax's poetic universe, regardless of whether it figures in a given case as a realized fact or as a Platonic ideal. The first two Carax features largely consist of a discontinuity of separate scenes, uncertain gestures, and fragments of ideas until Alex and the heroine finally get together—boy meets girl—and something more fluid and potent and sustained and even awesome takes hold. This "something" is not really a narrative—Carax isn't much of a storyteller, at least by American standards (though he improves a great deal in this respect in THE LOVERS OF PONT-NEUF)—but, rather, a delirious and lyrical form of nonnarrative consisting of cascading and overlapping poetic conceits, explosions of feeling, and pure sensation. "Story" in a Carax movie up to now has basically been a matter of what becomes necessary to bring a couple together and start these fireworks (figurative or literal), and what ensues in the world as a result of their remaining together or their drifting apart.

Rarely do poetics and libido coexist in movies quite as nakedly and as shamelessly as they do in Carax's, and the anarchic and often amoral implications of this *l'amour fou* are never backed away from: all of Carax's lovers are fully capable of committing murder, and do so if the spirit moves them. The opening event of THE LOVERS OF PONT-NEUF—a car running over Alex's leg as he lies drunkenly stretched out on Paris's Boulevard Sebastapol, which also occasions the heroine's first encounter with him—is subtly but unmistakably brought about by the distracted self-absorption of the lovers in the car, whom we glimpse only elliptically. And for all the tenderness with which the film regards Alex's feelings for Michelle (Juliette Binoche), a slumming middle-class artist who is progressively losing her eyesight, it is also tough and unsentimental about his desire for her to remain both blind and poor, so he can keep her. (If the plot recalls CITY LIGHTS in some particulars, it is Chaplin fully revised and updated by contemporary posthumanism.)

Bringing the couple together is not necessarily an easy matter either. In BOY MEETS GIRL, a veritable eternity has to pass before this happens. In BAD BLOOD, one has to wait for nearly half the movie, and after an extended sequence during which the couple spends an intense if sexless night together, the movie more or less returns to the doldrums (specifically, to relatively shopworn allusions to other thrillers, heist movies, or Godard movies like PIERROT LE FOU and ALPHAVILLE that allude to these genres—or else to freakish variations on these models, like Alex holding *himself* as hostage during the heist when he's surrounded by police, holding a gun to his own head). Happily, in THE LOVERS OF PONT-NEUF, the couple meets right away, which is one of the reasons why this feature represents a quantum leap over the two preceding it.

Another reason for the special status of THE LOVERS OF PONT-NEUF in Carax's work is that it partakes of one of the most potent poetic ideas ever dreamed up for movies—an idea that has particular links with French cinema but that can also be traced back to many of the greatest silent films made anywhere: The City as Plaything. In such touchstones as LES VAMPIRES; PARIS QUI DORT (THE CRAZY RAY); BERLIN, SYMPHONY OF A CITY; THE MAN WITH THE MOVIE CAMERA; THE CROWD; SUNRISE; LONESOME; PARIS BELONGS TO US; ALPHAVILLE; PLAYTIME; FOUR NIGHTS OF A DREAMER; OUT 1; and CELINE AND JULIE GO BOATING—not to mention DIVA, NIGHT AND DAY, and (to take a less obvious example, where "city" becomes over 400,000 young people camped out on a farm pasture) WOODSTOCK—the city is posited as a gigantic whirling and humming toy, mysterious and luminous. In many of these examples, it seems to exist mainly for the amusement of children, lovers, and other small conspiratorial groups harboring their own special codes and secrets.

What is it that makes Paris a city uniquely suited for stimulating and rewarding such fantasies? Speaking as one fortunate enough to have lived in that city for five years—only a couple of blocks away from the Pont-Neuf, in fact, which represents the magical, spectatorial vantage point in both FOUR NIGHTS OF A DREAMER and PONT-NEUF—I would say that the very *mise en scène* and *mise en place* of the city's appointments encourages one's imagination to drift in such dreamy directions. The night lighting of buildings, streets, bridges, and statues—not to mention river boats—is quintessentially theatrical, and anyone who has ever sat at a Parisian café table facing a street during the day *or* night has had an experience somewhat akin to a theatergoer sitting in an orchestra seat before an ongoing spectacle. Paris is the only city I know where everyone is encouraged to stare in public situations, and certainly a city where there's always plenty to stare at.

There's also something specifically Cartesian about the French sense of fantasy in relation to the life of the mind, a conceit implying that anything you can think has to be real on some level. (This has negative as well as positive consequences in Carax's work. In BAD BLOOD, for example, having certain attitudes toward various action genres—heist movies and thrillers, for instance—is viewed as if this were the equivalent of *making* a heist movie and thriller, a common form of false syllogism in French filmmaking.) When we clamor for verisimilitude in Anglo-American movies, what we generally mean by "real" is some form of ideological construction that we'd just as soon not have to think about directly. By contrast, when a missing person poster for Michelle (Juliette Binoche) suddenly turns up all over Paris in PONT-NEUF—a poster so "unbelievably" widespread and endlessly reproduced that one is made to feel briefly that no other poster exists in the city—the outlandishness is poetically apt, because it corresponds to the paranoid sense of threat that Alex feels about the world impinging on his love, an overwhelming emotional reality that is no less valid than the more mundane physical reality an American director would be more likely to honor. (Far more American—even Hawksian—is a speech by Hans about how women, with their vulnerability to rape and beatings, their periods and whatnot, don't belong on Pont-Neuf, which he and Alex have cordoned off as their own preserve while this bridge is under repair. The fact that this all turns out to be because Michelle reminds Hans of his long-lost wife is more Hawksian still.) Perhaps even more striking, given the grand scale of the movie's Pont-Neuf set (built in the south of France) and the overall monumentality of its view of Paris, is the fact that it's essentially only a three-character story, with the spectacular made to feel private and intimate at every turn.

Fantasy of this Cartesian kind is common enough in French movies (though check out the neglected and very great 1933 musical HALLELUJAH I'M A BUM for the nearest Hollywood equivalent). What seems less common is Carax's insistence on placing such a fantasy within the same overall continuum as a documentary depiction of the homeless in Paris. More specifically, the film virtually begins with a sequence showing Alex, after the car runs over his leg, being taken by the police to a shelter for the homeless along with others who are clearly real homeless people and not actors. For American tastes, such neorealism about the homeless doesn't mix with heady fantasies about three fictional homeless characters that dominate the remainder of the movie—fantasies that include the capacity to sneak into the Louvre one night to peer at a Rembrandt canvas by candlelight and then make love on the museum floor. Yet surely if quasi-documentaries about the homeless spring from the same sources as fantasies about them, they should be allowed to coexist on the screen as well.

Indeed, part of what makes Carax's poetry subversive in relation to American sensibilities is its refusal of certain boundary lines that we establish in relation to fantasy and poetry. In THE LOVERS OF PONT-NEUF these boundary lines relate to the homeless; in BAD BLOOD, more daringly, they relate to AIDS. According to the quasi-fantasy plot of BAD BLOOD, Alex, a petty criminal and card sharp, is asked to replace his recently deceased father in a planned theft from a drug company of a virus that offers the only known cure for the deadly disease STBO—a disease "transmitted by caresses" that is said to develop from "love without love" ("the younger you are, the higher the risk") and to infect both partners "even if only one partner makes love without love."

I suppose this poetic conceit could be called insensitive, and perhaps even tasteless, toward people who have AIDS and ARC. But to call it "homophobic," as some critics have, seems a clear case of political correctness running amok (or at least awry), particularly if one considers that no gay sex figures in the plot. There *is* a certain amount of homoeroticism in scenes that show Alex with Marc (Michel Piccoli) and Hans (Hans Meyer), the two older crooks, when all three are going around shirtless in the summer heat, conjuring up an ambience of closet homosexuality that evokes the American-style macho thrillers of Jean-Pierre Melville—a style, one might add, in which homophobia sometimes appears to be barely a kiss away. But to equate Carax's AIDS-inspired fantasy with homophobia simply because he *isn't* gay is to fall into a dubious kind of contemporary tribalism whereby AIDS becomes the exclusive intellectual and artistic "property" of people who practice homosexual sex and those who appoint themselves to speak for them—an attack roughly equivalent to charges made against William Styron, a non-Jew, for positing a non-Jew as the tragic heroine of a novel about the Holocaust in *Sophie's Choice.* ("How dare he write a novel about *my/their* Holocaust!" seems the unconscious subtext of such a complaint, which doesn't necessarily come from concentration camp survivors.) And in the case of Carax and BAD BLOOD, it might be argued that the specter of dangerous sex is so central to the emotional cast of the whole movie that however one judges Carax's articulation of it, the theme can't be written off as a frivolous adjunct to what the movie is about; it even accounts for why Alex and Marc's girlfriend Anna (Binoche) never have sex during their long vigil together, the most vibrant stretch of the movie.

■

> ... (see again Laughton's extraordinary THE NIGHT OF THE HUNTER if you want to grasp what the *film orphan* is: the spectator's identification can't go any deeper than with the character of the orphan, the child alone in the darkness).
>
> —*from Carax's review of* PARADISE ALLEY

Still in his teens (he was born in Suresnes, France, to a French father and an American mother in 1960), Carax made half a dozen critical contributions to *Cahiers du cinéma* in 1979–80, shortly after starting to make his first short (which was never completed). He began with a passionate defense of PARADISE ALLEY, Sylvester Stallone's first film as a writer-director, then went on to publish one film festival report (Hyères, including a celebration of a Robert Kramer retrospective), a brief *reportage* on the shooting of Godard's SAUVE

QUI PEUT (LA VIE), an article about a program of new and old Polish films at the Cinémathèque (Zanussi, Skolimowski . . .), a terse put-down of the French feature C'EST ENCORE LOIN L'AMÉRIQUE, and a brief review of Stallone's ROCKY II. A year and a half after the last of these, Olivier Assayas reviewed Carax's short film STRANGULATION BLUES at Hyères. Since then, the most significant Carax texts in *Cahiers* have been an extended dialogue with Philippe Garrel in no. 365 (November 1984), an interview about MAUVAIS SANG in no. 390 (December 1986), and a special issue of the magazine devoted to LES AMANTS DU PONT-NEUF, published as a supplement to no. 448 (October 1991)—edited by Carax himself, and consisting mainly of illustrations. (He has also appeared as Edmund in Godard's KING LEAR [1987] and as himself in Garrel's LES MINISTÈRES DE L'ART [1988].)

The most significant of Carax's critical pieces is undoubtedly the first. Fascinated with both the pessimism and the nightmarishness of Stallone's 1978 feature (no doubt assisted by the film's French title, LA TAVERNE DE L'ENFER)—a grim wrestling story about three grown orphan brothers in Hell's Kitchen in 1946—Carax writes about both the plot and the film's texture as if he's recounting an orphan's nightmare, clearly responding to both the physicality and the bleak finality of Stallone's vision in spite of the movie's humor and its happy ending: "The characters struggle to arrive at the end of each sequence and Stallone's camera doesn't come to their assistance—quite the contrary. . . . In Stallone's cinema, each shot triumphs or loses." Checking out the movie for the first time recently on video, I found it easy enough to see the infernal singularity Carax was writing about; after all, this is an expressionist, doom-ridden movie in which an impoverished black wrestler drowns himself on Christmas Eve *because he's happy* and where the climactic, $9,000 wrestling match in Paradise Alley, a sleazy nightclub, gets carried out in a driving rain because the establishment has serious leaks in its roof.

One can't say that Carax was the only critic to have responded to Stallone's style (see, for instance, Richard Combs's perceptive review in the March 1979 *Monthly Film Bulletin*), but the nature of his response as a teenage critic in relation to both the physicality and *nostalgie de la boue* (taste for lowlife; literally, "yearning for the mud") of his subsequent movies is still worthy of notice. In BOY MEETS GIRL—the first and perhaps the least of his features, certainly the most morose and unrelievedly nocturnal, shot in high-contrast black and white—the same sort of suicidal depression, no doubt influenced in particular by the youthful despair in Bresson's THE DEVIL, PROBABLY (1977), seems everywhere apparent.

Perhaps the most striking things about MAUVAIS SANG and LES AMANTS DU PONT-NEUF are how they were made. Both had a shooting schedule of about thirty weeks. (In the case of PONT-NEUF, thanks to various technical and financial problems, the thirty weeks came in three separate stages, beginning in August 1988 and ending in March 1990.) Both were mainly shot in makeshift studios constructed specifically for these films. And both are quite clearly movies that are not generated by strictly filming preexisting scripts; they entail a kind of ongoing improvisation with actors, sets, and day-to-day inspirations that seems to have more in common with the sources of certain early silent pictures than with those of most movies being made today. Without this freedom, one doubts that the more remarkable qualities of the actors could flourish: Lavant's emulations of Peter Lorre (a Carax favorite) and his spastic-expressionist body language; Binoche's ability to suggest early Anna Karina in BAD BLOOD or her awesome capacity to look like a different person in almost every shot of PONT-NEUF.

This is perhaps the most pertinent attribute distinguishing Carax from the two other "punkish" French filmmakers with which he's most often (and often unfairly) linked—the much older Jean-Jacques Beineix (DIVA, BETTY BLUE) and the much callower Luc Besson (SUBWAY, LA FEMME NIKITA), both of whose links to earlier cinema seem principally an acquaintance with various Hollywood tropes, not the poetics of a Jean Epstein or a Jean Grémillon (whose LA PETITE LISE is evoked more than once, and briefly glimpsed, in BAD BLOOD). At best, Beineix and Besson are notable for the ways they fulfill certain scenarios, not for their wild journeys into the unknown; it's hard to believe that either would ever think of repeating a shot precisely or momentarily cutting off the sound track to achieve their poetic effects, as Carax does in BAD BLOOD and PONT-NEUF, respectively.

■

> The cinema is an anti-universe where reality is born out of a sum of unrealities.
>
> —*Jean Epstein*

What is it about expressionism and surrealism, at least in their original European forms, that apparently make them anathema to the American mainstream? When German expressionism first encountered Hollywood technology in 1927, it yielded one of the greatest of all silent pictures, F. W. Murnau's SUNRISE (1927)—a masterpiece that is recalled more than once in THE LOVERS OF PONT-NEUF—but a movie that also flopped at the box office, no matter how much it impressed and influenced directors like John Ford and Howard Hawks in their own work. Since then, it's questionable whether other instances of Hollywood expressionism have ever rung many cash registers outside of those in Disney animated features like SNOW WHITE AND THE SEVEN DWARFS and PINOCCHIO. Some, like CITIZEN KANE, THE 5000 FINGERS OF DR. T, ERASER-HEAD, OR BRAZIL (to cite four rather unequal and dissimilar examples), have racked up extensive critical and/or cult reputations, but the mass public has generally been scared away. (I'm not counting the comic-book reductions and dilutions of this style, as in Tim Burton's movies.) And when it comes to surrealism, the record is not much better. Shorn of most or all of its antibour-geois political program, it makes certain inroads in the lighthearted fantasies of René Clair's 40s Hollywood comedies, the lurid imaginings of Sternberg's THE SHANGHAI GESTURE, the giddy dreamlike rhythms and spatial continuities of Albert Zugsmith's overlooked CONFESSIONS OF AN OPIUM EATER/SOULS FOR SALE, and the pornographic thrillers of David Lynch, among other places, but it rarely becomes both commercial *and* permissible in its more dangerous forms.

Carax's poetics depend mightily on memories of both of these European styles, especially in THE LOVERS OF PONT-NEUF. When Alex and Michelle get drunk together for the first time, the giant liquor bottles that we glimpse lying beside them on the pavement seem to partake of both traditions, suggesting both a surrealist fantasy à la Magritte and a drunken expressionist vision à la James Ensor or Franz Marc. When Alex sets fire to dozens of posters with Michelle's face that flank both sides of a métro passageway, the conceit recalls the disembodied hands clutching candelabras in the hallway in Cocteau's BEAUTY AND THE BEAST. More generally, PONT-NEUF might be said to recall every studio-built Paris from AN AMERICAN IN PARIS to FUNNY FACE to "Le Dernier Réveillon" (the first episode of LE PETIT THÉÂTRE DE JEAN RENOIR, about a romantic couple of starving beggars) to the lovely Alexandre Trauner sets in ROUND MIDNIGHT; but at their most hyperbolic, Carax's aesthetics seem to owe even more to paintings.

What they seem to owe to the silent American cinema, above all, is their raw sense of physicality. The exhilarating athleticism of the parachuting se-quence in BAD BLOOD and the waterskiing sequence in PONT-NEUF, with the actors plainly doing their own stunt work in spectacular surroundings, evoke Douglas Fairbanks and Buster Keaton, but these are only the most blatant examples of a cinema of untrammeled gestures and acrobatic exertions. When Marc and Charlie (Serge Reggiani), an old crony who runs a parachuting club, greet one another at an airplane hangar in BAD BLOOD, this becomes the occa-sion for a brief, wild interlude of barks and mimed violent threats between the two men in silhouette—a kind of drunken Punch and Judy show that suddenly unfolds between blackouts. When Alex, in the same film, is trying to get Anna (Binoche) to stop crying, he proceeds to enact a kind of circus vaudeville that begins with ventriloquism (a trick he resorts to elsewhere in the film), pro-ceeds with goofy pantomime and fire-eating (a trick he reprises at length in PONT-NEUF), and concludes with tossing up apples that eventually become transformed into a torrential rain of vegetables crashing down on him. Most dazzling of all, to the strains of David Bowie's "Modern Romance" on a radio, Alex walks outside the butcher shop where he and Anna are hanging out, and, accelerating his movements and contorted postures to the music, he walks, limps, runs, jumps, turns, spins, and does cartwheels for what seems like sev-eral city blocks, the camera dizzily following him all the while.

A similar choreography transpires on the Pont-Neuf with Alex and Michelle during the bicentennial July 14th fireworks display while a transistor radio blares out everything from Arabian pop music to a Strauss waltz. It's an ecstatic expressionistic moment that, for me, evokes not only the Luna Park fireworks in SUNRISE, but another one of that picture's ecstatic moments that occurs shortly afterward. Janet Gaynor and George O'Brien, the rural hero and heroine, happily reunited after a crisis in their marriage, return from the city at night in a makeshift sailboat, and briefly pass a raft on which other country folk dance wildly around an open fire. As Gaynor giddily rocks her head back and forth to the Gypsy-like music, which momentarily overlaps with the slower romantic theme in Hugo Riesenfeld's multilayered score, creating a brief cacophonous overload, this superb externalizing of the couple's sexual bliss in a passing narrative detail—both seen at once in separate portions of the frame as they drift off in opposite directions—has the same kind of wanton, lyrical abandon that Carax reaches for and often achieves in his own movies. Though the American public mainly didn't buy such poetry back in 1927, and the lack of hygienic glamour in Alex and Michelle may scare off *Entertainment Tonight*'s style consultant today, the sublimity of such moments describes precisely what we aren't getting right now in stateside movies, Miramaxed and otherwise, and what we sorely need. But no need for despair: PONT-NEUF closes with a promise from Carax, and a threat: "Let Paris rot!" As a barge carrying Alex and Michelle leaves the capital of pain for Le Havre and the Atlantic, the overall implication is not merely a reminder of Vigo's L'ATALANTE but also a suggestion that Carax may be making the United States his next cinematic port of call. If so, let's hope he doesn't get held up indefinitely in customs.

—*Film Comment*, May–June 1994

For sharing their observations, their erudition, and in some cases their issues of *Cahiers du cinéma* or their videos, the author wishes to thank Michael Almereyda, Cecilia Burokas, Nataša Durovicŏvá, David Ehrenstein, Bill Krohn, Lorenzo Mans, Richard Peña, and Alan Williams.

No Stars, a Must-See
(THE PLOT AGAINST HARRY)

I hate stars. There's a part of our culture that devotes itself ceaselessly to producing, promoting, and consuming them, and a lot of people would have you believe that they rule our consciousness—our politics, our fantasies, our ideas, our conversation, our art and entertainment. But one of our best-kept and most precious secrets is that a great deal goes on in our culture and in our lives that has nothing, absolutely nothing, to do with stars and everything to do with ordinary people.

Insofar as we can distinguish between illusion and reality—and the popularity of someone like Reagan suggests that we neither can nor want to very much—ordinary people, not stars, form the fabric of our daily existence; and most movies, simply by virtue of the fact that they have stars, ignore, deny, and impugn that fabric. An inordinate amount of energy in our society is devoted to proving that stars (Reagan or Bush, Cruise or Streep, Madonna or Jagger, Trump or Warhol, Spielberg or Sontag) are ordinary people just like you and me, when it might be more useful to prove that ordinary people—the people we live with—are the stars that actually belong in our constellations.

"Ordinary people" sounds like a pejorative term, a put-down, but in fact it's a category of individuals that is infinitely wider and more varied than a category like "stars," which is narrow to the point of tedium. Yet we act as though stars are as wide as the galaxy (when they're usually no bigger than TV screens) whereas we consider ourselves small, earthbound, and insignificant—we who can make stars appear or disappear at will, simply by buying tickets or flicking switches or turning our heads.

■

Part of what's great about THE PLOT AGAINST HARRY, a low-budget black-and-white picture made between 1966 and 1968 and released only this year [1990], is that it has absolutely nothing to do with stars. A star didn't write it or direct it, and no one resembling a star appears in it. The writer-director, Michael Roemer, a German Jewish refugee, made his first feature at Harvard in 1947, A TOUCH OF THE TIMES—conceivably the first independent feature ever made at an American university, but you won't find it listed in any film histories, and no one I know has ever seen it. Most of the remainder of his career has been spent in comparable (if occasionally prestigious) anonymity: on numerous documentary crews, as producer and/or director of countless films for public television, as occasional film critic, and, since the early 70s, as professor of film and American studies at Yale. Except for THE PLOT AGAINST HARRY, the only film of his that I've seen is NOTHING BUT A MAN, a fiction film about southern blacks that attracted a fair amount of attention in 1964 but hasn't been revived too often since then.

Roemer criticizes NOTHING BUT A MAN today as narrow and somewhat sentimental, and so it is; but a quarter of a century later, it still towers over the other films of that period (with the exception of Cassavetes's SHADOWS) by white men about black life: TAKE A GIANT STEP; ONE POTATO, TWO POTATO; BLACK LIKE ME; HURRY SUNDOWN—the list is mainly terrible. NOTHING BUT A MAN, featuring Ivan Dixon and Abbey Lincoln, may not be enough—its approach to its subject is relatively genteel and circumspect—but it's a long way from terrible.

After the success of NOTHING BUT A MAN, Roemer had a chance to become a star—he was offered several scripts by major studios, most of them about blacks—but he and his longtime collaborator, Robert M. Young (who cowrote, coproduced, and shot NOTHING BUT A MAN), decided to remain independent. Then, in 1966, the Seattle-based conglomerate King Broadcasting offered Roemer complete freedom to make an independent feature of his own choosing and to have final cut on it, and Roemer embarked on the project that became THE PLOT AGAINST HARRY—a comedy influenced by the relatively straight, realistic style of Chicago's Second City about a not-quite-successful, second-generation Jewish American.

After making a PBS documentary that he and Young were already committed to (FACES OF ISRAEL), Roemer spent a year of research on HARRY that included working as a caterer's assistant at bar mitzvahs and Jewish weddings on Long Island, following an attorney around Manhattan law courts, investigating the New York numbers racket, interviewing a call girl, and visiting a lingerie showroom. Most of another year was devoted to writing a script (with Roemer and Young regularly and concurrently taking on other jobs to pay the rent), followed by extensive casting carried out by Roemer himself. Martin Priest, a professional who played a small part as a southern bigot in NOTHING BUT A MAN, was cast early on in the lead part of numbers racketeer Harry Plotnick (and a comparison of the two radically different performances reveals that Priest is a consummate pro). But for many of the other parts, Roemer went looking for non- and semiprofessionals, and came up with some remarkable finds, all of them decidedly unstarlike.

For the role of Harry's former brother-in-law, Leo Perlmutter, who runs a kosher catering business, Roemer found Ben Lang, an auditor for the New York State Department of Labor who had studied acting in the early 50s; many members of the cast are wonderful, but along with Priest, Perlmutter is my personal favorite. For the part of Jack Pomerance, the treasurer of a temple and president of its catering committee, he found a businessman who ran a maid service and acted in his spare time. A songwriter, entertainer, and occasional collaborator with Duke Ellington named Henry Nemo wound up in the part of Harry's flunky, Max (and it is Nemo's own song, "Holding On to a Love," that's sung on a tacky set by someone behind the wheel of a fake car in the climactic telethon sequence). Harry's ex-wife, Kay, was played by a psychoanalyst (Maxine Woods), his son-in-law, Mel, was played by a Brooks Brothers salesman (Ronald Coralian), his daughter, Millie, was played by a housewife (Margo Solin); Millie's fiancé was a cabdriver, Harry's granddaughter was Roemer's own daughter, and one of the call girls was played by an actress, Hollis Culver, who is today known as Holly Solomon, owner of the famous Holly Solomon Gallery in Manhattan. Other parts were taken by lawyers, publicists, and various professional actors (Sally Kirkland is an extra in the telethon sequence, and Zack Norman does a walk-on), including Yiddish stage veterans recruited from an old folks' home.

After shooting the film in locations all over New York (and in a hotel lobby in New Haven), Roemer edited the film and then screened it a few times for the cast, crew, and friends. No one laughed, many found it hard to follow, and some actively disliked it, so King Broadcasting, with the resigned consent of Roemer—believing he had made a failure—shelved the picture and wrote it off as a tax loss.

About twenty years later, while putting together a complete set of his films on video to give to his children, Roemer was surprised to find the technician in charge of the video transfer laughing uproariously. Belatedly concluding that the film might not be a failure after all, Roemer remixed the sound track, struck a new 35-millimeter print, and halfheartedly submitted the film to both the New York and Toronto film festivals. Both accepted it within the same week.

∎

Part of the grace and beauty of THE PLOT AGAINST HARRY stems from the fact that although it has at least three dozen characters and a complicated plot, it glides past the viewer with the greatest of ease. The movie covers what happens over the few days after Harry Plotnick emerges from nine months in prison. The basic tone is comic and satiric, but the comedy and satire almost never take the form of outright gags; they come across as affectionate rather than scathing or malicious—though a wealth of social criticism is implied throughout.

Harry, who is worth about $130,000, finds that he's getting phased out of the numbers racket by competition, a turn of events spurred by the defection of one of his main operators. As he struggles in vain to regain his foothold, he gets chastised by his parole officer and passes out in the lobby of his hotel; taken to a hospital, he's told that he has an enlarged heart.

Harry decides to go legit and wants to buy the kosher catering business where his former brother-in-law, Leo, works. The business services a temple and Harry needs to secure the rabbi's approval of the purchase, so Leo arranges for Harry to be inducted into his lodge, the Mystic Knights of the Sojourners (after Harry donates $2,000 to their children's hospital), and to appear on a call-in radio show as a reformed racketeer. Then Harry discovers that his books are being audited and that Max, his flunky, has recorded all the payoffs to cops over the past twelve years; Max sets fire to the books and is arrested for arson. Harry collapses a second time in a TV studio during a telethon and, believing that he's dying, takes the rap for the arson and donates $20,000 to the telethon. Taken to another hospital, he's told that contrary to his earlier diagnosis he doesn't have an enlarged heart but an acute case of constipation. About to return to prison for a year, he asks his ex-wife whether she'll visit him on Sundays, and she shakes her head.

Family gatherings and family-related activities comprise much of the film's action, as do Harry's repeated and largely unsuccessful efforts to ingratiate himself with his family—including his older sister, Mae (Ellen Herbert), his former wife, Kay, and his daughters, Margie (Sandra Kazan) and Millie. Implicit throughout most of this is the sense that the respectable society that Harry wants to rejoin is every bit as corrupt and as venal as the rackets, but the film is so intimately acquainted with its chosen milieu that this point never has to be underscored or spelled out in any detail; it's simply there to be recognized—or not, if the spectator chooses to overlook it. Perhaps the closest the film ever comes to making an ironic commentary (apart from the grotesqueries of the lodge induction, the telethon, and a dog obedience school) is a scene at the home of Margie and Mel, where Harry is being unjustly accused of the arson in the foreground while in the background, on the floor, his granddaughter is looking through a series of nude photos that her father has taken of her mother. Roemer cuts briefly to a closer shot of the granddaughter, but even here there's nothing strident or obtrusive about the point that's being made: Roemer simply cuts to a closer shot so we don't miss what the other characters in the scene are ignoring.

Harry is basically a sad, sweet character, a classic fall guy, but Roemer doesn't try to sentimentalize him or steer away from his more callous traits; we see him at one point trying to convince a member of a Mafia family to rough up the defector from his organization, and near the end of the film, when he discovers that he's not about to die, he's all too willing to take back his telethon donation if he can figure out how to get away with it. For most of the movie, he's a figure of unbounded generosity, bestowing gifts and favors and money at every turn, but Roemer allows us to see this as both a reflex of Jewish guilt and as a pathetic attempt to win back the affection of his estranged family and associates.

The nonjudgmental tone of the film is part of what makes its wry comedy so special and appealing; it is part and parcel of the richness of the world that Roemer depicts, a richness that he refuses to short-change by scoring off easy points against the characters or the milieu. It would be meaningless to call Roemer's vantage point "objective"—he obviously cares about Harry, for instance—but his skills as a documentarist are everywhere apparent, and they give a kind of depth to his fictional world that makes this movie much closer to the better (and mainly earlier) fiction of Saul Bellow, Philip Roth, and Bernard Malamud than to the star-oriented worlds of Hollywood movies.

■

In the course of attempting to explain why Roemer's movie took twenty years to reach us, Stuart Klawans theorizes in the *Village Voice* that Roemer's elliptical storytelling and his "unwillingness to manipulate the audience . . . merely baffled people who were expecting a comedy," and adds, "THE PLOT AGAINST HARRY reminds us of a time when Americans had greater material and moral expectations, and less willingness to think their way through a film."

It's a nice try, but I think he's wrong. What "clicks" or doesn't click with an audience is the result of so many different factors—historical, social, economic, aesthetic, promotional, emotional, intellectual, and simply circumstantial—that I would be reluctant to leap to any conclusions about why THE PLOT AGAINST HARRY didn't make it into theaters in 1968, or why it did in 1990. Filmmakers, producers, and distributors always depend on a desperate form of guesswork to decide what audiences will like, and who's to say that Roemer's movie wouldn't have been appreciated if it had been released in its own time, in spite of a few bewildered preview audiences? It's true enough that the passage of time changes our perspective on much of what we see, and the appeal of the movie as a time capsule is not wholly irrelevant to some of the pleasures it affords us today.

But though it may be correct that Americans "had greater material and moral expectations" in 1968, it's hard to believe that they "had less willingness to think their way through a film." Some of the films that American audiences thought their way through in 1968 include ACCATONE; BELLE DE JOUR; LES CARABINERS; CHARLIE BUBBLES; CHINA IS NEAR; LA CHINOISE; FACES; LOVE AFFAIR, OR THE CASE OF THE MISSING SWITCHBOARD OPERATOR; PETULIA; TARGETS; 2001: A SPACE ODYSSEY; and WEEKEND. It would be dotty to claim that THE PLOT AGAINST HARRY would have presented intellectual, stylistic, or conceptual challenges that were any more arduous than those posed by the dozen movies listed above; on the contrary, one can argue that on certain levels it was and is an easier film to follow and enjoy than any of these others. What *is* different today, in fact, is that if most of the foreign-language pictures in this list were made last year, they would not have been distributed in the United States at all—distributors would deem them too difficult and esoteric for stateside consumption.

So there's no particular cause for self-congratulation in the fact that Roemer's film can reach audiences today. (One shudders to think of how many good films are being kept off the market in 1990.) If there's a lesson to be learned from this particular case, it's that being able to see what is right in front of us is seldom a simple matter.

■

Seeing what's right in front of us is made more difficult by a number of factors in movies, and the usual presence of stars is arguably one of them. Stars tend to command and dominate the spaces they occupy, whether these spaces are made up of other people or settings or props or other objects, and this often means that stars divert our attention from people and things that are equally (or, in some cases, more) worthy of our interest. The absence of stars in THE PLOT AGAINST HARRY allows a vast social universe to take shape before our eyes; if someone like Dustin Hoffman were playing Harry rather than Martin Priest, it's highly questionable whether we'd be able to see as much of this universe. The issue isn't whether Hoffman would be "as good" or "better" than Priest but whether his stardom would prevent him from doing anything quite as life-sized—or prevent us from noticing other people and things in the same frames. The sheer existence of movie stars implies that movies are and should be bigger than life, and therefore bigger than us; the absence of stars in THE PLOT AGAINST HARRY makes things more democratic and equitable, closer to our day-to-day existence.

—Chicago *Reader,* March 9, 1990;
revised October 1995

The Rattle of Armor, the Softness of Flesh

Bresson's LANCELOT DU LAC

LANCELOT DU LAC embodies the perfection of a language that has been in the process of development and refinement for over thirty years. If it stuns and overwhelms one's sense of the possibilities of that language—in a way, perhaps, that no predecessor has done, at least since AU HASARD BALTHAZAR—this is not because it represents a significant departure or deviation from the path Robert Bresson has consistently followed. The source of amazement lies in the film's clarity and simplicity, a precise and irreducible arrangement of sounds and images that is so wholly functional that nothing is permitted to detract from the overall narrative complex, and everything present is *used*. It is a film where the rattle of armor and the neighing of horses are as essential as the faces and bodies of the characters, where indeed each of these elements serves to isolate and define the importance and impact of the others.

The sheer rawness of what is there disconcerts, but it shouldn't lead one to focus unduly on what isn't there, or track down some elusive clue to the Bressonian mystery. To a certain extent, Bresson's films are *about* mystery, but their manner of arriving there is always quite concrete, just as the fictions of Kafka and Beckett are carefully constructed around certain principles of omission. Filling in these omissions is an act that every spectator/reader has to perform on some level, but anyone wishing to describe a Bresson film—as opposed to the experience of one—is obliged to leave these "white spaces" intact rather than attempt to fill them in, for otherwise he runs the risk of merely taking his own pulse. The evidence, one can argue, is clearly intelligible to the eyes and ears, if only one can look and listen. For this reason, it seems useful to speak here of Bresson's art as one of immanence, not one of transcendence, and one where the inside is always revealed by remaining on the outside. "There is a nice quote from Leonardo da Vinci," Bresson has remarked, "which goes something like this: 'Think about the surface of the work. Above all think about the surface.' "

■

Another relevant quote: "Le cinéma n'est pas un spectacle, c'est une écriture." Following a Bressonian law of contrast, it is only with the most "spectacular" of his subjects that the implications of this distinction become most cogently demonstrated. Apparently Bresson first made this statement at a Cannes press conference in 1957, shortly after UN CONDAMNÉ À MORT S'EST ECHAPPÉ (A MAN ESCAPED) was shown; even then, LANCELOT was already something more than just a twinkle in his eye. It is a project he has nurtured over twenty years—periodically announced as his next film, and periodically postponed because of the problems of financing it.

One indication of the sustaining power of his dream—a blend of chance and predestination oddly echoing the metaphysics of his fictional world—can be seen in his selection of Laura Duke Condominas to play Guenièvre, a decision initially reached when he came across a photograph of her, with no prior information about who she was. It was only afterward that he discovered she was the daughter of Niki de St. Phalle, codirector (with Peter Whitehead) of the recent film DADDY—and his original choice for Guenièvre some two decades ago.

The shooting, which lasted nearly four months, took place in the Vendée region (including the Ile de Noirmoutier) last summer; the sound mixing alone took three and a half weeks. To my knowledge, there are only two facets of Bresson's dream that remain unrealized. He was unable to shoot the film in separate English and French versions, a desire he spoke of in an interview with Godard eight years ago. (As I write, an English-dubbed version is being prepared.) And as a concession to the producer, he has agreed to call the film LANCELOT DU LAC rather than LE GRAAL, the title given to his shooting script.

■

In all his previous films since LES DAMES DU BOIS DE BOULOGNE, Bresson's procedure has been either to work closely with a preexisting text (Bernanos's in LE JOURNAL D'UN CURÉ DE CAMPAGNE and MOUCHETTE, Dostoevsky's in PICKPOCKET, UNE FEMME DOUCE and QUATRE NUITS D'UN RÊVEUR, André De-vigny's in UN CONDAMNÉ À MORT, historical records in PROCÈS DE JEANNE

D'ARC) or to invent a completely original narrative (BALTHAZAR). In LANCE-
LOT, he has used the background and characters of Arthurian legend as the
basis for an original story, systematically eliminating all the fantastic elements. The magic of Merlin and the Lady of the Lake are totally absent, and
all we see of the Grail is an image that appears behind an early title that
sketches the story's background—an emblem that briefly recalls the cross appearing at the end of LE JOURNAL D'UN CURÉ DE CAMPAGNE.

The remainder of the legend has been tailored to suit Bresson's purposes.
As in the final section of the thirteenth-century *Vulgate Cycle,** the central
focus is on the adulterous affair between Lancelot and Guenièvre, seen within
the wider context of the unsuccessful Grail quest (virtually over before the
film begins) and the dissolution of Artus's kingdom. Many of the same incidents are included: Mordred's plot to expose the adultery to the king, Lancelot's appearance at a jousting tournament in disguise, his recovery from his
jousting wound in Escalot, his subsequent rescue of Guenièvre, and, after the
siege of the castle of the Joyeuse Garde, his decision to return her to Artus.
On the other hand, it appears that all of Bresson's characters are considerably
younger (although the girl who falls in love with Lancelot in Escalot is more
or less "replaced" by an old peasant woman who shelters and cares for him);
Lancelot dies not in a hermitage but on a battlefield; and an enormous amount
of the plot is simply stripped away.

For that matter, according to Michel Estève,[†] neither the tents nor the
Round Table nor the chess game nor the wooden tub in which Guenièvre
bathes belongs to the period, all of them constituting conscious anachronisms
on Bresson's part. This is a distinctly modern LANCELOT, in striking contrast
to the relatively "medieval" atmosphere of Bresson's last two films, both set
in contemporary Paris, where the gentle creature in UNE FEMME DOUCE often
suggested a lonely maiden in a tower waiting to be rescued, and the dreamer
in FOUR NIGHTS OF A DREAMER resembled a wandering knight in search of a
pure love that was equally hopeless. The sense of elongated durations and
passing seasons that we associate with the romances of Chrétien de Troyes is
more evident in BALTHAZAR, or even in John Ford's THE SEARCHERS, than in
the tightly compressed episodes of LANCELOT, where action and event is all.

The comparison with Ford is hardly gratuitous: LANCELOT is surely the
closest thing we can ever hope to get to a Bressonian Western or adventure
film, although it also achieves a tapestrylike stillness in certain scenes that
plays against the livelier movements. The use of simply repeated motifs—like
Guenièvre's lighted window, the sound of a crow punctuating her brief moments with Lancelot in a hayloft, or separate shots of a riderless horse and
a bird in the closing sequences—recall the methods of a twentieth-century

---

*Available in English translation as *The Death of King Arthur,* translated by James Cable
(New York: Penguin Books, 1971).

† *Robert Bresson,* rev. ed. (Paris: Seghers, 1974).

"medieval" poem like e. e. cummings's "All in green went my love riding," where certain words (red, deer) are reiterated to create an overall tableau effect, as in the following lines:

> Four lean hounds crouched low and smiling
> the merry deer ran before.
>
> Fleeter be they than dappled dreams
> the swift sweet deer
> the red rare deer.
>
> Four red roebuck at a white water
> the cruel bugle sang before.

Most modern of all, perhaps, are the characters of Guenièvre and Lancelot, although the specific signs of their modernity are not at all easy to pinpoint. The scenes between them seem to adhere rather closely to the courtly tradition, and the spiritual malaise affecting Lancelot—torn between his love for Guenièvre, his vow to God to end their adultery, and his loyalty to Artus—contains no discernible elements that are added to the legend. And yet the absence of any psychology, the elliptical exposition of their feelings, and the degree to which Bresson isolates them from their environments and defines them in relation to each other, all serve to give them unmistakable contemporary reverberations. And the anonymous scenes of war and carnage that enclose their story register with an effect that is even more timely, exposing a dark terrain where blood is being spilled today.

■

(1) In a dark forest, two broadswords meet and clash. The camera pans back and forth, following the clanking movements of the unidentifiable armored figures as they continue to fight. One sword is raised, and in one fell swoop the other figure is decapitated. A stream of blood rushes from the stump, spilling on the ground.

(2) In a dark forest, an unidentified armored knight and his horse are wounded. Close-up: an arrow has pierced the horse's skull over one eye. Cut to a bright shot of a dark bird diving in an empty white sky. The knight slowly rises to his feet, sword in hand, and leans against a tree. Cut to a riderless horse galloping through the forest. The knight utters a single word, "Guenièvre": we recognize the voice as Lancelot's. He drops his sword and collapses with a heavy rattle on a pile of armored bodies. Cut to another shot of the bird in the sky. Lancelot's head drops with a metallic shudder and his body becomes still.

The appalling violence that opens and closes LANCELOT presents us with war as anonymous and indifferent slaughter, with faceless phantoms in the darkness battling and perishing beneath heavy armor that instantly turns into scrap metal as soon as the bodies become mute. The gush of blood from the decapitated knight and the last word of Lancelot are the only concrete signs that we are witnessing men and not machines, death and not an abstraction of death.

■

Bresson has always been unusually lucid about his working methods. In various statements over the years, he has repeatedly outlined the following strategies: (1) Use individuals without any previous acting experience and instruct them to recite their lines as tonelessly as possible, without expression. (2) Shoot always in natural locations. (3) Replace an image with a sound whenever possible. (4) Structure visual "syntax" not around single images but around the relationships between images—a process partially arrived at by favoring images that are relatively flat and nonexpressive, neutral and uniform.* (5) More generally, pare away everything that is "unnecessary," that is, inorganic.

The rigor of Bresson's economy is beautifully apparent in the first lines of dialogue that we hear in the film, spoken by the old woman of Escalot as she binds together bundles of sticks with the help of a little girl: "He whose footsteps one hears before seeing him will die within the year." "Even if it's his horse's footsteps?" asks the girl. "Even if it's his horse's footsteps."

In this brief exchange, we are introduced to the idea of predestination, thematically as well as concretely; the last words are immediately followed by the sound of a knight approaching on his horse, whom we subsequently see. We are also presented with the notion of sound preceding image—which becomes the central editing principle of the tournament sequence, and is much in use elsewhere. Finally, there is a forecast of the explicit ways in which the destinies of the horses are bound to those of the men who ride them: Lancelot's return to Camaalot is intercut with shots of his horse responding to his fellow creatures in a nearby stall (evoking Balthazar's encounter with the circus animals); the death of Lancelot's horse in the final sequence immediately precedes his own; and throughout the film, much of the dialogue is punctuated by the sounds of horses, so that their presence or proximity is frequently felt even when they aren't seen.

Bresson's manner of infusing naturalistic detail with formal significance is particularly masterful in the marvelous use he makes of armor; in his hands, it serves as practical extensions of all but the second of the working strategies cited above. It functions as an additional layer of nonexpressiveness, increasing neutrality and uniformity in separate images and cloaking identities in

* "The flatter an image is, the less it expresses, the more easily it is transformed in contact with other images." "It is necessary for the images to have something in common, to participate in a kind of union."

many crucial scenes—the tournament as well as the forest battles. (Indeed, apart from the old woman and little girl, no positive identification of any of the characters becomes possible until Lancelot arrives in Camaalot, and lifts his visor to greet Gauvain.) When Gauvain is defending Lancelot to Artus against Mordred's charges while the three are on horseback, each line of dialogue is preceded by the character lifting his visor to speak: again, a naturalistic detail, but one that heightens the antitheatrical basis of Bresson's style precisely by *playing* on a "theatrical" device—each lifted visor serving as the equivalent of a raised curtain, which reveals only another blank surface.

The concentration on hands and feet that is a constant in Bresson's work becomes all the more affecting here when it is set against the shiny surfaces of metal in other shots. Or consider the overall effect of contrast achieved between the suits of armor and the image of Guenièvre standing in her bath, which makes flesh seem at once more rarefied and vulnerable, more soft and graceful, more palpable and precious. The on- and offscreen rattle of the armor throughout the film reinforces this impression, at the same time that it isolates the more lifelike sounds coming from horses and men, and emphasizes their (minimal) expressiveness—thus investing Lancelot's last word with a sensual impact it wouldn't otherwise have.

■

Bresson has described himself both as a painter and as a *metteur-en-ordre.* Combining these notions, he establishes and mixes his sounds like colors on a palette and then places them "in order," establishing relationships that are purely aural as well as visual-aural. The spare use of drum and bagpipe, the armor, horses' footsteps, sounds of blood and water (including a rainstorm, glimpsed in one extraordinary fixed shot), a door rattling, birds calling, flags waving in the wind, a flurry of arrows whizzing through the air, and the crack of lances hitting shields are only a few of the essential ingredients. It is said that while working on the sound track, Bresson wanted to include at one point the sound of a horse chewing on his bit; having no recorded examples that were satisfactory, he wound up manufacturing the noise with his own teeth. It is a story that irresistibly brings to mind the methods of Tati—perhaps the only contemporary of Bresson who composes and organizes his sound tracks on a comparable level.

The extreme darkness of many of the forest scenes—in itself a source of great beauty—often helps to accentuate the function of sounds in guiding our attention, but the frequent expositional use of sound in brighter locations is equally striking. In the cottage of the old woman of Escalot, we first discover the presence of a fire burning in the hearth through the sound of its crackle. And in the astonishing tournament sequence, sound becomes the primary narrative force: the crowd is heard but remains virtually unseen, and we hear the collision of lances with armor in the first two encounters before we are permitted to see the outcomes.

Many critics have spoken of Bresson's style as one that ideally eliminates the possibility of suspense—usually citing the title UN CONDAMNÉ À MORT S'EST ECHAPPÉ, which gives away the outcome of the plot, as crucial evidence. But as Hitchcock reminds us in his interview book with Truffaut, knowing the outcome of an event can often *intensify* suspense, and surely UN CONDAMNÉ À MORT frequently plays on our expectations to generate tension, even if the form of this tension is severely disciplined. And in the jousting tournament of LANCELOT, whether we know (through some acquaintance with the legend) the outcomes or not, we are being "directed" as rigorously as in any Hitchcock showpiece: there are few other action sequences in all cinema that create as much anticipation and excitement.

Finally, of course, there are the voices—neutral and uniform in their apparent lack of expressiveness, but presences charged with meaning and effect in relation to the overall complex of sound and silence, where the lack of overt emotion becomes a sounding brass against which the words themselves are able to resound. "Tu es vivant, et tu es là," says Guenièvre to Lancelot, back from the Grail quest. "Rien, plus jamais, ne t'écartera de moi!" In the system of meanings established by Bresson, presence defines absence, life ("Tu es vivant") defines death ("Guenièvre!"), a dark earth defines a bright sky, and love defines the renunciation of love—armor and flesh, sound and image, Lancelot and Guenièvre composing one another through diverse channels to form an indissoluble surface that speaks.

—*Sight and Sound,* Summer 1974

The Functions of a Disease (SAFE)

I know that Americans are supposed to hate whatever they can't understand, and certainly current Hollywood filmmaking is predicated to the point of tedium on this truism. But part of what makes Todd Haynes's SAFE the most provocative American art film of the year so far—fascinating, troubling, scary, indelible—is that it can't be entirely understood. The mystery and ambiguity missing from mainstream movies are all the more precious, magical, even sexy here, in a 35-millimeter feature employing professional actors set partly in the plusher suburban reaches of the San Fernando Valley.

By chance the star of SAFE, Julianne Moore, also plays the female lead of the least mysterious Hollywood feature of the moment, the unspeakable NINE MONTHS—a movie that essentially celebrates the world that SAFE attacks. This makes Haynes's film even more dangerous: seeing both films might be like combining chemicals that produce lethal explosives. One suspects that anyone who sees both in swift succession will be flirting with social or political revolution or some sort of madness. And given what the two films have to offer, revolution or madness may not be inappropriate responses.

My first encounter with SAFE was two months ago, at Cannes; and though I had certain misgivings about it, the movie stayed with me in a way and to a degree that Haynes's other films—SUPERSTAR: THE KAREN CARPENTER STORY,

POISON, and DOTTIE GETS SPANKED—have not. Yet I can't claim that seeing the film a second time yielded substantially more treasures. What you see and hear is what you get. In fact the movie is distinctive in part because of its poetics of absence—the clearest sign of its indebtedness to Michelangelo Antonioni and Chantal Akerman, who are both notable for their layered uses of both sounds and images.

Haynes's own layered constructions of sounds and images have a way of defamiliarizing—"making strange," as the Russian formalists put it—the characters and settings. But having set this unhinging process in motion, Haynes seems as helpless as his spectators in controlling the fallout, and as a result there isn't much agreement about the meanings expressed. Unlike some of my colleagues I would argue that this movie's emotions are much clearer than its ideas, but certainly the degree to which satire figures in the film is not crystal clear. Attitude outstrips analysis in this movie by a ratio of about three to one, and one of the confusions fostered by this imbalance is the idea that Haynes's hatred for his characters and their milieus and his precise grasp of their speech patterns ("All right, hands up, who wants decaf?"), their appearance, and their homes necessarily add up to a careful analysis of who they are and what makes them tick.

Such analysis is hardly essential to what Haynes is doing formally, but it becomes necessary once one considers how much this movie is saying as satire. As much as I may applaud Haynes's skewering of the world of conspicuous consumption and privilege—the world for which this society is so bent on giving up things like art and education—I'm not entirely persuaded that he doesn't belong to that world himself. Part of his movie, for instance, seems devoted to smirking at twelve-step programs, yet such programs do get some people off addictions. Haynes's critique, like his depiction of the "designer" prison in POISON, offers a classbound view of class struggle.

■

Perhaps the biggest single area of confusion regarding SAFE is the question of what the movie's actually about. I would argue that Haynes's hatred for most of what he's showing is his real subject, and a perfectly legitimate one. But the movie's press materials and most reviewers disagree: according to them, the movie's subject is "environmental illness," a buzzword that if I'm not mistaken first became widespread in 1987, the year in which the film is set. This "allergy to the twentieth century," whose victims develop extreme reactions to everyday chemicals, is richly suggestive of our unhappiness with the world we've created. But approaching it as a suggestive allegory isn't at all the same as treating it seriously as a subject. Some critics have accused Haynes of making SAFE a replica (ironic or otherwise) of a disease-of-the-week TV movie, but a much likelier source of inspiration is TV journalism—arguably even more dubious as a source of enlightenment. Such journalism has the power to obfuscate the world we're living in by giving names and illusory shapes to things that we know little about—things that may not even exist.

I'm not in a position to say whether "environmental illness" exists or not, and neither is Haynes. But I can cite my own experience: in my early teens, when I was both socially alienated and afflicted with numerous allergies, I was given a scratch test and proved to be allergic to practically everything in it, even Alabama's state flower. Later most of these allergies were reduced or eliminated by homeopathic injection. But the key issue, I would argue, is not whether environmental illness exists or whether that was what I had but whether the formulation of such a concept is of any use to doctors and patients in the process of healing.

The role that environmental illness plays in SAFE is above all dramatic; it organizes the plot. An obviously alienated wealthy housewife named Carol White (Moore) who always seems to be apologizing for her very existence develops physical symptoms related to her environment. Her doctor insists that nothing is wrong with her, but once the term "environmental illness" is introduced, the movie and the character gain narrative direction.

Moore's portrayal of Carol, at times suggesting a squeaky mouse, is brutally effective but perhaps not entirely plausible. ("Nobody is *that* empty," a filmmaker friend who champions the film has argued. But disagreements over plausibility in the film may be in part generational—after all, Haynes's posthumanist, post-TV relation to his characters turned the Carpenter family into Barbie dolls in SUPERSTAR.) Carol's first line is "It's freezing in here," said to her husband Greg (Xander Berkeley) in their garage as they get out of their car. Next we see them having sex in the missionary position, Carol going through the motions, clearly not enjoying it, as Greg grunts his way to a climax. Then we see her picking flowers in her garden, saying good-bye to Greg as he leaves for work, and informing some movers where a sofa should go in her living room. After her aerobics class, Carol hears another woman say that the twelve-step program is just another form of addiction—a remark that anticipates the second half of the movie and apparently has Haynes's full approval. Carol's companions also note that she doesn't sweat.

In the scenes that follow, everyday events seem to take the place of any plot, and all the interior and exterior spaces are made to seem massive, with Carol lost in their reaches like a loose cog; both her overstuffed living room and her garden are made to seem as vast and as hollow as city railway terminals. Even more impressive than Haynes's visual sense is his sound track, which in these sections creates an eerie s-f atmosphere and a feeling of displacement through a number of subtly alienating strategies. These immense, opulent suburban settings are inflected by our sense of their emptiness, not to mention Carol's.

Carol returns home, leaves to visit a friend, comes home again after a visit to the cleaners, speaks to her mother on the phone, and is suddenly appalled when she discovers that a black rather than a teal sofa has been delivered. The next day, she wakes to find her house busy with painters and Latino servants already at work, returns to the cleaners, complains about the black sofa at Nelson's customer service in Sherman Oaks, explaining that it doesn't go with anything else she has. Then, while listening to an apocalyptic Christian fundamentalist on her car radio, she starts to cough from exhaust fumes, finally pulling into an empty parking garage, stopping her car, and doubling over as she wheezes.

From this point on, whether Carol's watching a TV feature about "deep ecology" that looks and sounds like a commercial, falling asleep on the despised black sofa, or deciding with her friend to go on a fruit diet, the idea has been planted that illness is not so much an affliction for her as a much-needed validation, a form of identity. It's a name for her nameless distress, which the film has been at pains to illustrate in numerous ways. Initially her "illness" takes the form of not responding to a dirty joke at a fancy restaurant with Greg and another couple; she apologizes to her husband on the way out, and he suggests she see her doctor. Predictably, the doctor tells her nothing is wrong and takes her off the fruit diet.

But after the movie has guided us through a few more episodes of the genteel nothingness comprising Carol's creepy existence, more symptoms appear—a nosebleed at the beauty parlor, a recurring headache when Greg wants to have sex, and vomiting when she tries to make up with him the next day. These symptoms give us a certain relief as well as distress: for the first time, the movie has a recognizable plot, shape, and direction—Carol's disease. Prior to that, there's been nothing to respond to—just the so-called American dream of wealth, space, and comfort and a concomitant sense of void, alienation, and boredom (which the ads leave out). Then along comes disease, and with it come focus, meaning, and purpose; and even if this meaning becomes a horror of a sort, at least it has a name, "environmental illness."

Carol eventually goes to the Wrenwood Center, a New Age country retreat where the remainder of the movie is set. Here she's assigned her own cabin, walks around with her own oxygen supply, and willingly submits to the center's regimented lifestyle: sexually segregated meals, carefully directed group therapy sessions, and the ideology of self-love as a form of healing. Greg and her stepson come to visit her at one point toward the end of the film, but whether she's on the road to recovery strikes me as a moot point. (Her "recovery" is about as meaningful as Vera Miles's at the very end of Alfred Hitchcock's THE WRONG MAN, a film of comparable negativity.) Carol has just moved into a bubble-shaped bunker on the center's grounds that's even more of a retreat from the world than her cabin; her only companions are her oxygen tank and her mirror. The fact that she loves herself, or thinks she does, may represent some marginal improvement in her condition, but considering the zero Haynes has chosen to make of her, it's hard to know what her "self" consists of.

The *Village Voice*'s Georgia Brown and the *New York Free Press*'s Godfrey

Cheshire, both intelligent critics, have accepted this ending as somehow hopeful rather than the final nail in Carol's coffin (my own interpretation). Brown has even chastised me in print for having called Haynes "heartless" (in fact I called SUPERSTAR heartless), arguing that he is brimming over with compassion for Carol, the Carpenter family, and I suppose Barbie dolls, too. (After all, in more ways than one SAFE is a remake of both SUPERSTAR and the disease-horror segment of POISON.)

Without wishing to put the man or his movies on trial, I beg to differ. Haynes may not dislike Carol as much as he does Greg or the fatuously cheerful founder of the Wrenwood Center (Peter Friedman), and he may sympathize with her acute alienation, but I don't think he's treating her as any sort of role model. In an interview with Alison Maclean in the summer issue of *Bomb* magazine, Haynes confirms this impression, noting that "basically, SAFE is on the side of the disease and not the cure. It's the disease that completely opens Carol's eyes and the cure that returns her to [a] sealed-off existence." He also remarks that SAFE was partly inspired by his anger at a book by Louise Hay about AIDS published in the mid-80s, saying that it "literally states that if we loved ourselves more we wouldn't get sick with this illness. . . . That's scary."

Brown and Cheshire are both southerners by birth and haven't lived in the Los Angeles area, so maybe Haynes's southern Californian posthumanism—no doubt inflected by one's distance from other people on the freeway and in Sherman Oaks living rooms—is relatively unfamiliar. But neither succumbs to the nearsighted view that SAFE has something important to say about environmental illness—unlike the authors of a press release I received headlined, "New Movie Misses Mark on Chemical Sensitivities." It begins,

> Sony Pictures' soon-to-be-released movie SAFE pioneers thoughtful exposition of the devastating impact of multiple chemical sensitivity (MCS) on the estimated 2% to 10% of Americans who suffer from this painful, debilitating, and isolating illness. But, according to a nationwide support group of about 3,000 MCS patients, the film's message is compromised by the vague ending which fails to address one of the most fundamental issues about this hideous disease [that its origin is physical, not psychological]. The public's welfare is better served by knowing all the facts, say recognized health care professionals.

Apparently, knowing anything about art—such as Haynes's own admission that he's on the side of the disease, not the cure—is of lesser importance.

—Chicago *Reader,* July 28, 1995

England on the Inside

The Films of Mike Leigh

Among the buzzwords Marshall McLuhan coined in the 60s, "global village" has always seemed one of the more dubious.* The naive notion that TV brings the whole world to our doorsteps—and presumably our doorsteps to the rest of the world—seems founded on a series of half-truths that don't bear close scrutiny. What do we mean by "the world," for instance? And what do we mean by TV? TV may afford us some touristic glimpses of elsewhere, with all the ideological baggage that tourists bring with them, but when it comes to closer and better understandings of foreign cultures, I suspect TV may do more harm than good by fostering complacent illusions of knowledge: images wrapped in tidy American sound bites for easy consumption, postage-stamp peeks into worlds that are often defined in part by what we don't know about them.

What TV seldom offers us—unless we understand other languages and possess satellite dishes—is the rare privilege of overhearing other cultures talk to themselves, experiencing them from within rather than on our own terms. To be on the inside looking out offers a different kind of knowledge,

*Perhaps the term can be salvaged if one adopts the meaning suggested by the late Serge Daney in one of his last interviews: placing the emphasis on "village" rather than on "global" and acknowledging that "TV culture" is in some ways similar to "village culture." [1995]

attained more by osmosis, intuition, and direct experience than by simplification, translation, or exegesis. Late last year I had the good fortune to visit Asia for the first time, not as a tourist but as a member of a film festival jury in Taiwan. I spent most of my time with the six other jurors—four from Taipei, one from Hong Kong, and one from New Delhi—and though our deliberations were carried out in English, many of the other conversations were in Mandarin Chinese, which everyone but the Indian juror and myself spoke. Obviously I missed a lot as a result, but I'm sure I would have missed even more if everyone had spoken only English—because most of the life of Taipei is lived in Mandarin. Similarly, I quickly discovered that the labels I had at my disposal for various forms of government—"capitalism," "socialism," "democracy" — were far from adequate to describe a society as different from ours as Taiwan's, where many of the capitalist industries are state-run and where recent democratic reforms have to be weighed against a long and lingering history of martial law and censorship. (Even the issue of whether Taiwan is a country or a Chinese province is a subject of much debate there.)

When I returned from Taiwan I started looking at the TV films of English director Mike Leigh, and began to wonder why it's taken so long for someone as gifted as Leigh to become known in the United States. His first theatrical feature, the 1971 BLEAK MOMENTS, won prizes at both the Chicago and Locarno film festivals before receiving limited stateside release. His second theatrical feature, HIGH HOPES, released seventeen years later, did much better; two years after that came LIFE IS SWEET, which is still running at the Music Box and just won prizes from the National Society of Film Critics for best picture, best actor, and best supporting actress. In between BLEAK MOMENTS and HIGH HOPES, Leigh was far from inactive; in addition to writing and directing nine or ten plays in England between 1971 and 1988, he wrote and directed a dozen features and several shorts for BBC TV and England's Channel 4. English friends of mine would periodically speak of Leigh with a kind of reverence and affection that suggested he was a kind of national treasure, but no evidence of this was available over here.

Starting this weekend, the Film Center is offering a comprehensive (if not quite exhaustive) Leigh retrospective that will run for most of the rest of this month, including BLEAK MOMENTS, HIGH HOPES, nine TV features, and six shorts. I've been able to see or sample most of the lot, and it's a remarkable body of work that offers perhaps the most in-depth portrait of English life in the 70s and 80s to be found in movies.

Last fall I saw Famous Door Theatre's first-rate (if ill-attended) Chicago production of Leigh's recent play *Smelling a Rat*—apparently the only American production his stage work has received. I'm now reading a 1979 play, *Ecstasy;* some sense of Leigh's attention to local detail can be gleaned from a short note he's appended to it: "Jean and Dawn are natives of Birmingham. Mick is from County Cork, Len is from rural Lincolnshire, and Roy and Val are from inner North London, where the play is set. The dialogue, language, and usage in *Ecstasy* are extremely precise, and in the author's view the play should only be performed in the correct accents." It might be argued that work of this kind isn't meant for export. (The Ulster accents in FOUR DAYS IN JULY are especially difficult.) But still, what I see and hear in his work is closer to my own experience of England than what I've seen or heard in any other work; and if Leigh's filmic oeuvre were subtitled in American English, I think the results would be more muddled than illuminating.

■

When I met Mike Leigh during the last Chicago Film Festival he gave me some information about his unorthodox working methods, which have led him to prefer the credit "devised and directed by . . ." to "written and directed by . . ." Although he does produce a script and expects his actors to adhere to it, what comes first is a lengthy period of rehearsals, improvisation, and what he calls "research" with the actors—a working method that seems to have some relation to Stanislavsky's.

He prepared for LIFE IS SWEET not only by delving into the backgrounds of the four leading characters—a mother (Alison Steadman), a father (Jim Broadbent), and their twenty-one-year-old twin daughters (Jane Horrocks and Claire Skinner)—but also by working out in some detail what happened on all their family trips. Since none of these trips seems to play a role in the film, one might suppose that there's something quasi-mystical about this approach. Not at all: Leigh insists that what finally counts is what appears on the stage or screen, and that the elaborate preparations are basically carried out to pin-point the characters. In jazz terms, one might say that this process merely establishes the chord changes on which the script improvises.

This approach helps to account for the extraordinary density and reality—and frequent mystery—of many of Leigh's characters, who always seem to have lives that extend beyond the borders of the work. But conceptual elements also figure in his construction of characters. In LIFE IS SWEET, Aubrey (Timothy Spall)—an oddly mannered friend of the family who opens a preposterous "gourmet" bistro called the Regret Rien—seems more a caricature than a character, but a caricature who points to something quite real in contemporary English life. Leigh told me that his principal instruction to Spall, which Spall found extremely difficult to implement, was to play someone who had no personality of his own—the implication being that Aubrey was rather like his ludicrous restaurant, a postmodernist composite of character traits borrowed willy-nilly from elsewhere.

American critics looking for non-English equivalents to Leigh's style have often mentioned John Cassavetes, but though I've done it myself it's a comparison that has limited usefulness, especially since Cassavetes doesn't seem to have had much influence on Leigh. (In terms of working methods, a closer parallel would be Jacques Rivette's thirteen-hour 1971 serial OUT 1, a work with which Leigh is unacquainted.) Leigh's films do often resemble Cassavetes's in one important respect: they frequently seem plotless, and at any given moment it is often impossible to tell where they're going. Frequently the subject emerges when the "invisible" dramatic situation reaches a crisis—a quarrel, a burst of hysteria, even a death—and thereby becomes visible. This suggests that Leigh's apparent artlessness is only apparent, and a closer look at his works bears this out. One discovers, for instance, that he's a master of camera placement, but not the sort of master who calls attention to his craft.

■

Born in Salford, Lancashire, in 1943, Leigh has been "devising" and directing works since 1965—at last count twenty-one stage plays, one radio play, eighteen works for British TV, and three feature films. One of them, BLEAK MOMENTS, started out as a play, and one of his best-known TV works, ABIGAIL'S PARTY, is simply the videotaping of a stage production done earlier the same year. But otherwise, as far as I can tell, there's no recycling in Leigh's work, and judging from the dozen works that I've seen or sampled, their range—at least in terms of settings and characters—is impressively wide.

Class bias often seems to play an active role in Leigh's work: the higher up the economic ladder his characters are, the more odious they usually appear. The stylistic layering in HIGH HOPES reinforces this bias, with a concomitant increase in caricatural effect. The English writer Gilbert Adair has suggested that the moral accuracy of this bias can be more valuable than the accuracy of circumstantial details: "From Alan Bridges to Piers Haggard, and from Charles Sturridge to the man who directs the Hovis ads, the British cinema is positively crawling with filmmakers who have 'got' the ruling classes down to the last gaiter button, as they used to say, and I find it endearing and wholly to Leigh's credit that he has pitched his tent far from that particular mainstream."

Although some actors appear in more than one Leigh film, they're always in different sorts of parts—most noticeably his talented wife, Alison Steadman, whose only common trait in such works as HARD LABOUR, ABIGAIL'S PARTY, THE SHORT AND CURLIES, and LIFE IS SWEET is the highlighting of different kinds of nervous tics. Leigh doesn't have what we would ordinarily call a repertory company. He might be said to have a workshop, which many gifted actors have passed through—including Ben Kingsley as the owner of a small taxi company in HARD LABOUR, Brenda Blethyn as a busybody spinster in GROWN-UPS, and Tim Roth and Gary Oldman as lowlifes in MEANTIME.

■

Looking at Leigh's films chronologically, it becomes apparent that his social and political vision—which is fully apparent in his masterpiece HIGH HOPES—

took shape only gradually. Broadly speaking, his 70s work focuses on couples' failed relationships, whereas his 80s work is more concerned with dysfunctional families.

BLEAK MOMENTS (1971) may have been a remarkable film debut, especially made as it was at the tail end of the "swinging London" era, but watching it is often agonizing—as painful in its way as the out-of-tune piano played at the film's beginning and end. (Music is often used aggressively in Leigh's work: cheerful melodies are frequently employed for ironic or sarcastic effect.) BLEAK MOMENTS was made for 17,000 pounds—about $41,000 at the exchange rate of that period—and runs for almost two and a half hours. It chronicles the painfully awkward and embarrassed silences, usually broken only by halfhearted non sequiturs, between several South London suburbanites: a lonely accountant's clerk living with her retarded sister; another woman working in the same office who dotes on the disabled sister; a hippie drifter and folk guitarist living in the clerk's garage; and a stuffy, uptight schoolteacher. The clerk's only romantic possibilities appear to be the hippie and the schoolteacher, and the interactions charted are basically missed connections. (Schoolteacher, after pedantically citing Marshall McLuhan: "Which do you find easier, watching television or radio?" Clerk: "I find it easier watching the radio.") Besides this, nothing much happens, and any sense of a society beyond these characters is at best perfunctory.

This is not the case with HARD LABOUR (1973), Leigh's first TV film, but here the society he seems to have in mind could be plotted on a chart. Basically a work of bitter and remorseless socialist realism, HARD LABOUR follows the exploitation and suffering of a middle-aged maid (Liz Smith) at the hands of her employers, her grown children, her husband, and finally her indifferent priest, to whom she pours out her miseries before he returns diffidently to his newspaper.

The 1977 ABIGAIL'S PARTY (which might be described as Leigh's *Who's Afraid of Virginia Woolf?*) is comparably schematic, although the class and dramatic situations are quite different, and this time the bitterness is played out as black comedy. A vulgar middle-class housewife (Steadman) married to a repressed husband (Tim Stern) who works in real estate "entertains" her neighbors: a younger disgruntled couple consisting of a nurse (Janine Duvitch) and her monosyllabic husband (John Salthouse), and a polite divorcée (Harriet Reynolds) whose teenage daughter Abigail is throwing a party downstairs. The two wives keep stoking the divorcée's anxiety about the party, which we never see. The tensions are constant and palpable: the repressed husband wants to put on classical music and show off his leather-bound set of Shakespeare, his wife insists on playing rock and barks various orders and reproaches at him, and the nurse repeatedly describes her own husband's inadequacies to the older wife. The film becomes a kind of encyclopedia of the ways that people can make one another uncomfortable while pretending to relax, building toward a cataclysmic climax. Less strictly "realistic" than Leigh's other works—perhaps in part because this is a taping of a stage play, but also because Leigh's approach is so consistently and ruthlessly satirical—ABIGAIL'S PARTY is decidedly more effective as drama than either BLEAK MOMENTS or HARD LABOUR.

So is THE KISS OF DEATH, which was made the same year. But here Leigh's subject is much more subtle and muted, at times to the point of obscurity: a young coroner's assistant (David Threlfall) who giggles compulsively in most social situations. There's clearly some relationship between the hero's proximity to death and his dysfunctional social behavior—behavior that often suggests Method acting and reaches a sort of climax in his highly tentative courtship of a girl who works at a shoe store. But though Leigh supplies a few stray clues, such as the fact that the young man is reading *Dracula,* he does very little to spell this relationship out, leaving most conclusions to the viewer.

By the time of GROWN-UPS (1980) and MEANTIME (1983), Leigh's style and his grasp of social context are both fully achieved. We might consider these the first two parts of a masterful trilogy about Thatcher's England that culminates in HIGH HOPES (1988). GROWN-UPS plants a young working-class couple (Philip Davis and Lesley Manville) in a council house in Canterbury next door to an older middle-class couple (Sam Kelly and Lindsay Duncan). The older man proves to have been the former religious instructor of the younger couple, but for quite some time this is the only "plot" that emerges from the comic contrasts and the brief, brittle interactions between the two couples, who barely know one another. The catalyst proves to be the younger woman's sister Gloria (Blethyn), a spinster and frequent visitor whose life seems so threadbare that she can live only vicariously through her relatives. When her loutish layabout brother-in-law finally gets so sick of Gloria's intrusiveness that he throws her out of the house, she runs hysterically next door and locks herself in the bathroom. The extended scene of screaming emotional chaos that follows, involving all five characters, is an astonishing piece of virtuoso acting and directing, a scene that clarifies and amplifies all the issues that have been lurking beneath the surface of the plotless narrative. In one fell swoop the climax brings to the fore all the factors that keep these characters together as well as drive them apart—a quintessential Thatcherite mix having to do with property, class differences, sex, self-definition, social conscience, and patriarchy—and the epiphany is simultaneously comic and tragic, a characteristic Leigh effect.

In MEANTIME, set in London's East End, Leigh looks at what produces a skinhead, and the development is comparably logical though at first it appears indirect to the point of opacity. Basically what we see and mull over is a family living on welfare in a council high-rise, and the events consist mainly of the older brother (Phil Daniels) berating and undermining the desperately unhappy and nearly catatonic younger brother (Roth), calling him "Kermit" (as in Kermit the Frog) and sabotaging the job set up for him by their Aunt Barbara by turning up at her flat ahead of him. . . .

In fact, it's almost impossible to do justice to a Leigh plot because behavior and milieu are almost everything. Like a pointillist painter, Leigh builds his films with minuscule brush strokes—behavioral and environmental details often so tiny that they can't be perceived by the naked eye (or ear) until they start to accumulate and form patterns. Only when the painting is complete can we stand back and say what it is we've been looking at. This may help to explain why so many of his characters, who often seem awful, become endlessly fascinating and even endearing the longer we look at them. (The sweet post-60s hippie couple at the center of HIGH HOPES are the only Leigh characters I can think of who are thoroughly lovable from the beginning.) Leigh's method may also account for the fact that the English lives he depicts—so depressed and drab and hopeless—eventually signify something clear and powerful, not only where they're coming from but perhaps even where they're going.

—Chicago *Reader,* January 10, 1992

Political Subjects

The Significance of Sniggering

Zwigoff's CRUMB

Considering how conventional most of it looks as filmmaking, Terry Zwigoff's CRUMB has a remarkable fluidity and density as thought; it may look like a documentary—unobtrusively shot by Maryse Alberti, gracefully edited by Victor Livingston—but it unfurls like a passionate personal essay. The subject is Robert Crumb, America's greatest underground comic book artist—unknown to most people born much before or after 1943, the year of his birth, because he usually shuns the mainstream as a money-grubbing swamp. Zwigoff, an old friend, shot the movie over six years and edited it over three, and the sheer cumulative mass of this two-hour movie seems partly a function of the extended amount of time he's had to mull over his subject.

A member of Crumb's former band, the Cheap Suit Serenaders, and a fellow collector of rare 20s and 30s blues and jazz records, Zwigoff has previously made documentaries only on musical subjects—blues artist Howard Armstrong in LOUIE BLUIE, a history of Hawaiian music in A FAMILY NAMED MOE. In one of his interviews, he notes that he was in psychotherapy while shooting CRUMB, and this has surely made its mark on the material. Clearly he's out to tackle Crumb as an artist, not merely as a comic book artist, and his layered approach to advancing on his biographical terrain—crosscutting effortlessly between Crumb with each of his brothers on opposite coasts and

223

Crumb himself ruminating over his work at home; leapfrogging between his first wife, son, two former lovers, and various colleagues and commentators—has all the elegance of three-dimensional chess. The subject matter is thorny and depressing as well as fascinating, and the approach is unusually serious and methodical: just about everything that's said about Crumb in the film is intelligent, and seems to have been included because Zwigoff agrees with it on some level.

But despite the film's clear and purposeful editing, the issues raised and explored keep dovetailing into countless disparate yet interrelated questions, big questions that torment the mind and heart. What does it mean, finally, to be an American artist? What are the key differences between satire and pornography, confession and entertainment, art and obsession, sanity and schizophrenia? What does it mean to have and be a brother, especially growing up in a brutally dysfunctional Catholic family—ruled by a violent father who busted Robert's collarbone when he was five and a mother addicted to amphetamines, a family whose three brothers slept together in the same bed until their teens? (Crumb's two sisters declined to appear in the film, and it isn't too hard to figure out why.) Even the movie's title begins to seem metaphorical: one thinks of a crumb in the all-American cake, a slender morsel of American pie in the sky. The vexing questions keep coming.

Questions, for instance, like what the true legacy of 60s counterculture is. And has there been a decline in the overall quality of American life since the 20s, as Crumb sorrowfully claims when we see him moving to France in 1993? How innocent are most artists, including confessional ones, about the meaning and impact of their own work? To what extent can art-making function as a possible bulwark against madness? What are the crucial differences between personal art and impersonal business franchises, especially in a society that so plainly values the latter over the former? And finally, what is the significance of sniggering in relation to certain sexual obsessions?

Let's start with that sniggering, which we hear whenever we see Robert get together with his older brother, Charles (still living with their mother and unemployed since 1969), or his younger brother, Maxon (living alone in a San Francisco flophouse, meditating two hours daily on a bed of nails). Both of his brothers are also exceptionally gifted and self-aware artists, but unlike Robert they're misfits who never climbed out of obscurity and often wound up institutionalized, on medication, or both. Just about everything that's most memorable about CRUMB can be referred back to these brothers; by the time the film is over, one is fully persuaded that if Robert weren't drawing constantly and compulsively he'd be every bit as doomed as they are. (It pains me to refer to these real people as if they were fictional characters, but the film's careful strategies in establishing their personalities make it hard to do otherwise; whether Zwigoff intends this or not, they *become* characters within the context of the film.)

That terrible yet familiar laughter shared by Robert with each brother reveals a kind of tortured complicity with sexual obsession—the fact that Robert as a five- or six-year-old kid was sexually drawn to Bugs Bunny, that Charles as an older kid became secretly preoccupied with Hollywood boy actor Bobby Driscoll, and that Max, in his late teens, the most sexually repressed of all, already subject to epileptic fits, became a molester of women, fully capable of stalking a woman on the streets of San Francisco and pulling down her shorts, an event he describes to Robert with a curious mixture of horror and relish. The fact that each brother is fully aware of his illness and even lucid about it only seems to heighten their shared, contorted amusement, which unnervingly sounds like ordinary locker room repartee, infatuated with its own gross-out dementia.

On some level, every American male knows the sound of that nervous tittering, and the world of Robert Crumb's comics is not only suffused with it (his own adult sexual obsession is amazonian, big-assed, thick-legged women) but also encircled by it. I can't think of any other movie that's dealt with this kind of laughter so directly. Cassavetes's FACES probably came the closest, but there it was simply backslapping businessmen dealing with everyday sexual embarrassment. CRUMB cuts deeper, letting us see the potential madness lurking beyond the simple nervousness of sexual panic—a madness disquietingly made to seem as American and almost as ordinary as that pie in the sky. This is one creepy movie, and it should come as no surprise that David Lynch, who helped to get it released, is mentioned at the top of the credits.

■

There are few artists as compulsively and relentlessly confessional as Robert Crumb, and in some respects CRUMB functions simply as exegesis of and critical commentary on three and a half decades of published work. Since I first encountered Zwigoff's haunting masterpiece last summer I've been reacquainting myself with Crumb's work and catching up with things I'd missed, and it's remarkable how consistent most of it is. (For a provocative overview, I'd recommend *R. Crumb's America.*) Of the ten published volumes of *The Complete Crumb Comics* (which don't include several sketchbooks and collections like *R. Crumb's America,* though all include biographical or autobiographical introductions), perhaps the first three qualify as apprentice work. But after that Crumb's graphic style and view of the world are fully formed. Apart from the occasional collaboration and commissions, what mainly changes in his work is the degree of explicit self-reference—the extent to which Crumb himself supplants his characters. And the movie, by providing a detailed context, helps to unpack many references that previously seemed hermetic.

Case in point: The first time I read *XYZ Comics,* back in 1972, I didn't even notice that an obscure and unfunny story called "Nut Factory Blues" was signed "C. & R. Crumb"—coauthored by Charles and Robert in a variation of their joint childhood efforts, with each brother drawing and writing the text for his own character. Clearly all the drawing in "Nut Factory Blues" is by Robert, but as he explains in his introduction to volume 9 of *The Complete Crumb Comics,* much of the dialogue derives from a conversation with Charles at a mental institution in Philadelphia in 1972, and the characters standing in for the brothers—Fuzzy the Bunny and Donnie Dog—were Charles's childhood inventions. (The story's title derives from a 1931 blues record.)

In recent years Crumb has separated himself even farther from the mainstream. His collaborations have been with his wife, cartoonist Aline Kominsky. Their daughter, Sophie, was born in 1981, and in 1993 he traded six of his sketchbooks for a house in the south of France and moved there with his family, an event chronicled in detail at the end of CRUMB. Earlier this year *Self-Loathing Comics* appeared, in which each spouse recounts the banal daily routines of their life in France, with the two stories fusing in a single panel on the comic book's center pages. The April 24 issue of *The New Yorker* carried a two-page story in which the couple recounted their responses to seeing CRUMB on video, each drawing her or his own character and furnishing the appropriate dialogue within shared panels. (Aline: "I just read in *Newsweek* that the Academy Awards judges turned off CRUMB after 25 minutes." Bob: "Yeah? Good! If they'd loved it can you imagine the hell our lives would become?")

The healthy contempt for callow merchandising that suffuses such productions—echoing Crumb's spiteful decision to kill off Fritz the Cat after he became the star of two animated features (against Crumb's will and without his control) and his anger about related misappropriations—points to an artisanal pride and a desire to control his work that stand in direct opposition to the ambitions he's expected to have in a culture that equates quality with quantity. At the same time, his shrinking subject matter and expatriate status suggest that he's backed himself into a corner; without America or his old flaky cast of characters to keep his comics going, he's seemingly had to milk his own persona dry. Yet part of what CRUMB shows us is that a move so potentially debilitating may have been psychically necessary.

■

I've never met Robert Crumb, but he served as my guide the first time I took LSD, in 1968, when we were both twenty-five. Significantly, that encounter involved fraternal complicity as well as fraternal betrayal, a subject that's at the center of Zwigoff's movie. Both Robert and Max at times can barely suppress their rage toward Charles, nor can Charles suppress his toward Robert; this movie is as much about fraternal resentment as the influence of Charles on both Robert and Max. Though the movie doesn't spell out all the family dynamics, it still offers plenty to mull over: an "amazonian" mother who takes amphetamines to lose weight in order to please her exacting husband, a trio of sons who invent a world of their own to escape the same tyrant.

My younger brother, Michael, who'd already dropped acid several times and was supposed to be my guide, failed to turn up at my Greenwich Village flat. We'd dropped our matching tabs while speaking on the phone that afternoon, then he boarded the downtown subway to my apartment. But he got lost, and I didn't see him until the next day. Fearful of being alone, I turned to R. Crumb's *Head Comix*—the first mainstream Crumb collection, which I'd just bought—for company, guidance, and edification. Considering that Crumb ascribes much of the freedom of his work (in relation to narrative as well as subject matter) to his first taste of acid in 1965, a visionary experience that unleashed most of the characters and visual concepts he's known for today, he wasn't a bad choice. I'm sure I could have done much worse—indeed, *did* do much worse when I ventured out a few hours later to see BARBARELLA, a much more corrupt, strictly mercantile package of 60s zeitgeist.

The point is, even a screwball like Crumb had more workaday wisdom to get me through the night than most of what the rest of the culture was offering—or still has to offer, for that matter. Crumb may have been nuts, but he wasn't a fool: he fully understood at what points his own preoccupations coincided with those of the counterculture. And there was something oddly sane about his overall vision of the freakout period we were both living through; as CRUMB shows, he was always somewhat detached from it, as he is from humanity in general. My brother might well have made my trip easier, but Crumb made it a lot funnier.

His art saved me from a bad trip, no small accomplishment. Beginning with an introductory page that presented Crumb himself as a mad scientist, *Head Comix* featured numerous free-form trips to instruct and bounce off my own. The cast of characters included Fritz the Cat, the dancing dudes of "Keep on Truckin'," Schuman the Human ("Better known as 'Baldy' he goes forth with his fine mind to find God!" reads the opening caption. "And believe me, he took along a lunch!"), Mr. Natural (most likely based on Max, today a Hindu), Flakey Foont, Whiteman (a portrait of Robert's uptight father, as we learn from CRUMB), Western Man (alias President Lyndon B. Johnson), The Old Pooperoo, Kitchen Kut-Outs (including Clever Mr. Ketchup, Sammy Saucer, and Beatrice Bread Slice, the latter named after Crumb's mother), and finally Angelfood McSpade, a naked African woman Crumb hadn't yet gotten around to naming at that stage in his career.

Then as now his grossly stereotypical images revealed the underside of a world I already knew, a nostalgic world that grew in part out of old ads, animated cartoons, and furniture store displays—an archetypal past America, strictly working-class, urban, and comfortably squalid, populated by a community of goofy amblers and dim-witted, wiseass layabouts. (Crumb's huge collection of 78s, his old-fashioned hats and bow ties, and the Cheap Suit Serenaders are only some of the more obvious manifestations of this world outside his comic books.) Superimposed on this quaint, idyllic world—and oddly coexisting with it—were enormous quantities of lust, cruelty, violence, fear, resentment, loneliness, anxiety, spiritual desperation, and the sniggering laughter already alluded to. A warm and wistful view of the 20s, 30s, 40s, and 50s superimposed on a surreal and highly satirical view of the present, it conjured up a jostling street life of adolescent epithets, infantile games, and diverse adult endeavors that fully justifies art critic Robert Hughes's description of Crumb (in CRUMB) as "the Brueghel of the last half of the 20th century" who offers us "lusting, suffering, crazed humanity in all sorts of bizarre, gargoyle-like allegorical forms." Hughes adds that "there wasn't a Brueghel of the first half," yet ironically the first half of this century is the source of most of Crumb's scenic backgrounds.

■

The Brueghelesque Crumb is an ironic observer and social chronicler, and if that's all his art consisted of, CRUMB wouldn't be nearly so disturbing. But then there's Crumb the asocial narcissist and devoted nose picker, tireless explorer and exploiter of his own inner demons—closer to Hieronymus Bosch than to Pieter Brueghel—fueled by self-absorbed pornographic fantasies, bent on creating images for masturbation, and getting some of his rocks off by celebrating gratuitous violence, much of it against women. (One feels sure that Crumb himself can't always tell whether his panels critique or celebrate violence, and wonders how much acid he actually took back in the 60s and 70s.) His wife defends this work, however, as an expression of pure id that has nothing to do with what her husband is really like ("He gets it out in his artwork").

Crumb himself is plainly ambivalent: he doesn't like to censor himself, but he's not always persuaded that what he does is socially defensible, and often he's as befuddled as we are about the meaning of the work. If one could only separate the social Crumb from the asocial Crumb, the task of assessing his work would be a lot easier. But in fact these two sides of him overlap and blur in a manner that seems quintessentially American; his art breaks down the same barriers between self and society, between fantasy and reality, that hallucinogenic drugs like LSD were intended to remove. And an unreconstructed rebel like Crumb never bothered to reinstate those barriers. His art, which combines the caricature of Hogarth with the lyrical self-diddling of Genet, is a volatile, dangerous mixture that ultimately eludes a precise moral agenda and any prescribed social use.

Two 1993 items included in *R. Crumb's America,* "When the Niggers Take Over America" and "When the Goddam Jews Take Over America," both clearly meant to ridicule racist paranoia, have reportedly been appropriated by neo-Nazi skinheads in the United States and Europe, all of whom are presumably too stupid to realize that they're the intended targets. It would be comforting to report that these items are hilarious and dead-on; in fact they're plodding, obvious, and unfunny. But even if one rejects these two strips as misfires, there are plenty of others in the Crumb canon that rest uneasily between self-indulgent fantasies and grim commentaries on the ideology they purport to criticize. (In CRUMB, Crumb himself expounds on and guides us through "A Bitchin' Bod," a morbid story he started about a headless women presented by Mr. Natural to Flakey Foont as a literal sex toy. He threw the strip away, he explains, until his wife persuaded him to complete it despite his reservations. It hardly qualifies as uninflected pornography, but it's still an open question whether such a sicko fantasy overwhelms any commentary that might be offered about it, by Crumb or anyone else.)

Crumb recounts a story in the introduction to volume 9 of *The Complete Crumb Comics* that starkly illustrates the conflict between his artistic and ethical reflexes. Zwigoff, horrified by a visit to a slaughterhouse, decided to publish a comic book inveighing against cruelty to animals and convinced various artists, including Crumb, to contribute stories. Crumb's major offering in the 1972 *Funny Animals* is the two-part "What a World"—and as Crumb freely admits, it was "one of the sickest, most violent, bloody, nihilistic as well as sadistic, misogynist things I'd ever drawn." Crumb's story and some of the others submitted led Zwigoff to disassociate himself completely from the comic book before it appeared. Obviously his friendship with Crumb survived this rift—and *Crumb* makes no allusion to the incident—but it's also notable that even given a cause that he himself deemed "noble," Crumb still indulged the demonic side of his art.

Much of CRUMB's soul and intelligence derives from the determination to confront problems of this sort and own up to their complex ramifications, not to let either Crumb's work or its detractors off the hook. The movie's refusal to settle for one Crumb or the other as a substitute for the whole artist is really a decision to take art seriously rather than regard it as an adjunct to other enterprises, as usually happens in this culture. Ultimately, one feels that Crumb's work is being defended rather than attacked. But the film also leaves the impression that art—like life, and unlike entertainment—isn't a picnic in the park.

On one level the movie is an inspirational story about how a sensitive, nerdy individual with a traumatic childhood can turn that misery into some form of art. But then there's the story of Charles, the older and originally more gifted brother—the bullying guru who got Robert and Max started as artists. Zwigoff gives us an opportunity to look over Charles's shoulder into an abyss. We learn that before he stopped producing his homemade comics in 1961, he got more and more into dialogue and less and less into drawing. We see the evolving results as Robert flips through the pages of Charles's work—words crowding out pictures, then pages and pages of just words followed by even more pages, seemingly hundreds of pages, covered with tortured, intricate scratches that are no longer words, that are no longer anything but scratches. It's the most terrifying image in any movie I've seen this year, a steady, mocking bass line throbbing behind everything positive and exalting this film has to say about the power of art to transform suffering.

—Chicago *Reader,* June 2, 1995

"The day I stop suffering, I'll have become someone else." "There's no such thing as chance." "To speak with the words of others—that's what I'd like. That's what freedom must be." From the Café aux Deux Magots to the adjacent Flore, from the streets and sidewalks of a grayish Paris to other people's flats, for the better part of 219 minutes, Alexandre (Jean-Pierre Léaud) continues to hold forth. "In May '68 a whole café was crying. It was beautiful. A tear-gas bomb had exploded . . . a crack in reality opened up." Charmingly, narcissistically, elaborately, endlessly: "I don't do anything; I let time do it." "Abortionists are the new Robin Hoods . . . the scalpel replaces the sword." "The world will be saved by children, soldiers" (pregnant pause) "and fools."

Much less talkative is his beloved Gilberte (Isabelle Weingarten—a Bresson discovery back for another nonperformance), who forsakes him to get married, and Marie (Bernadette Lafont), the older woman he lives with, casually exploits, and is clothed and fed by. But a verbal match of sorts is offered by the doleful and doelike Veronika (Françoise Lebrun, in an extraordinary, glowing debut), a promiscuous nurse he picks up one afternoon. Next to Alexandre's, her words come across as blunt and unvarnished. "I can fuck anyone." "Watch out—you'll push in my Tampax." "I've screwed a maximum of Arabs and Jews." While serving Nescafé: "I like the feel of a prick against my ass, even if it's soft. One sugar or two?" And in a long drunken soliloquy tainted with death and despair, tears and mascara streaking down her cheeks: "There are no whores. . . . Love is nothing if you don't want a baby together."

Central to the feel and method of Jean Eustache's THE MOTHER AND THE WHORE is its obsessive confessional tone, much closer to Pialat than to Rohmer; its slavish fidelity—apart from some time abridgements—to repetitious verisimilitude; its sense of private ghosts being desperately laid to rest. (The ghostly fades between sequences conjure up spectral memories of Murnau as much as the beautiful scene at the Gare de Lyon restaurant, where Alexandre compares the setting to a Murnau film, a locus of transitions.)

In barest outline, boy meets whore, courts her—a crucial shift of operations from Deux Magots to Flore, with each successive date set at an earlier hour—and eventually beds her in Marie's flat while the latter is away in London. Marie returns, he introduces Veronika, and abortive attempts at a three-way sleeping arrangement culminate in Marie's attempted suicide, Alexandre's reduction to self-loathing and manic helplessness (retreating to the bathroom in the midst of an emotional crisis to spray himself with cologne), and Veronika's convulsive lament for the emptiness of her many sexual exploits. She insists on going home and Alexandre accompanies her, listens to more drunken abuse ("You disgust me. I may be pregnant by you. I love you"), leaves, and then hurries back to propose marriage. She accepts, vomits offscreen into a basin, and we end with the camera fixed on Léaud, stunned and slumped on the floor against her refrigerator. It is less a resolution of conflict than a depletion—an exhaustion of the will that seems (like the characters) more prone to regurgitate sickness than reflect on it.

Yet obstinately and paradoxically, this monumental epic of psychic imprisonment sticks in one's craw. Refusing to see beyond the characters and their limitations, the film repeatedly pushes us back into their snarled and messy lives. Encased in the retrospective black-and-white ambience of Nouvelle Vague—when Léaud was Antoine Doinel, or MASCULIN-FÉMININ's Paul, or the provincial hero of Eustache's earlier LE PÈRE NOËL A LES YEUX BLEUS—the film turns these youthful dreams into bitter ashes. Formally the antithesis of Rivette's OUT 1 in its exclusively written dialogue and old-fashioned narrative linkage, it carries a bleak mood that is equally redolent of post-1968 disillusionment, and similarly suggestive of vicious concentric circles.

Over the plot's relentlessly even progression, Alexandre's nonstop aphorisms cumulatively take on the appearance of habitual camouflaging gestures. (Eustache wrote the part expressly for Léaud, and it is clearly a character that both of them understand down to their bones.) And the mounting impact of Veronika's obscenity and sarcasm—evaluating her body parts like a used car salesman—ultimately turns, for all its leveling effect, into another kind of cant and cliché, offering no promise of release.

Static medium shots of people talking: a zero point of cinematic style, perhaps, but Eustache holds to it with such precision that the slightest pan—Veronika's reproachful greeting of Alexandre defining a quick trajectory across a room—carries an unusual weight. Elsewhere, it defines a neutral surface on which faces, voices, and words (the latter two rendered in direct sound) are made to register as epiphanies, regardless of what they say or do.

"The film begins in the first person," Eustache has noted, "in order to end in several first persons." Specifically, a strict adherence to the hero's field of vision is veered from only twice. The last time we see Marie, after the others' departure, she is listening to a scratchy Edith Piaf record—the static camera recording her own virtual stasis for the song's duration. As much of a climax as the tirade by Veronika that immediately precedes it, this shot similarly composes a definitive "still-life," with the ironic lilt of Piaf's song ("Les Amants de Paris") serving as a mock epitaph. Soon afterward, we glimpse Veronika changing into her bathrobe before Alexandre enters her room to propose—a more academic and less striking demonstration of the same principle, that Alexandre's glib overview and control of events has been irrevocably broken.

And what has replaced it? Taking apart a social-ethical system to show us its bleeding entrails, Eustache makes no effort to sew it up again. The female roles indicated in the film's title have been invested with enough ambiguity to suggest a reversal—Veronika becoming the expectant mother, Marie the abandoned whore—but not enough to suggest that any alternative roles might exist. Freedom collapses—helped along by a few shallow cracks Alexandre makes about Sartre, sitting at a nearby café table—and life reverts to Catholic bourgeois "necessity," which is implicitly treated as biological truth. Nouvelle Vague dies an ignominious death, and the spirits (if not the minds) of Claudes Berri, Sautet, and Lelouch lurch to the fore.

Perhaps this is overstating the case; but as a view of cinema as well as a view of life, LA MAMAN ET LA PUTAIN seems to me profoundly reactionary. This is already hinted at in the jokey treatment of Alexandre's idle friend, whose cluttered room with stolen wheelchair and Nazi memorabilia suggests a fascist playpen; or in the nostalgic use throughout of old records, reflections of yearnings for the presumed certainties and absolutes of the past. And yet, like LONG DAY'S JOURNEY INTO NIGHT, like the better parts of ICE or FACES, the film's compulsive picking at wounds reveals a genuine impasse, a tragic lack in ourselves that cinema seldom admits, much less describes—a cry of animal defeat lending Eustache's essentially destructive masterpiece a scarred authenticity that sears the mind and persistently haunts the emotions.

—*Sight and Sound,* Winter 1974–1975

Film Writing Degree Zero

The Marketplace and the University

> Perhaps it is time to study discourse not only according to
> its expressive values, or in its formal transformations, but
> also according to its modes of existence: the modes of
> circulation, attribution and appropriation of discourse vary
> with each culture. . . . [T]he effect on social relationships
> can be more directly seen, it seems to me, in the interplay
> of authorship and its modifications than in the themes or
> concepts contained in the works.
>
> —*Michel Foucault, "What Is an Author?"*

It seems likely that *Hollywood Directors 1914–1940* and *Movies and Methods** are the two most interesting anthologies of writing about film recently published in English. Each marks a substantial foray beyond the standard recycling operations of most anthologies, making available a wealth of helpful material that is otherwise hard to come by. An easy enough assessment, on the face of it, yet one that conceals a nagging question: what do we mean by "interesting" and "helpful"? In what way can both books be considered deserving of the same ambiguous adjectives? How far do they allow themselves to be considered within the same universe of discourse?

First, a few basic distinctions. All fifty of the selections in Koszarski's collection were written between 1914 and 1939 by "Hollywood directors"—stretching that term to include such figures as Alice Guy-Blaché, Paul Fejos, Robert Flaherty, and Maurice Tourneur. Nearly all the articles originally appeared in mass circulation newspapers, magazines, trade journals, or previous collections: *Breaking into the Movies, Careers for Women, Ladies' Home Journal, Motion Picture Director, Moving Picture World, Photoplay*

**Hollywood Directors 1914–1940*, edited by Richard Koszarski (Oxford: Oxford University Press, 1976); *Movies and Methods,* edited by Bill Nichols (Berkeley: University of California Press, 1976).

Magazine, Popular Mechanics, Shadowland, Theatre Magazine, Travel, and so on.

Thus the form of these pieces is popular journalism, and Koszarski concedes in his introduction that some of them might have been ghostwritten: "Often the obsessions voiced under these bylines are so characteristic as to label their authors unmistakably. But if at times a 'written to order' piece has slipped in, the worst we can say is that it was issued as an authorised statement, and now exists as a puzzle for interested historians." It is worth adding that Hollywood generally dictates the total view of cinema that the book projects. When, for instance, the editor reflects that "perhaps only Hitchcock approached the degree of pre-planning practised by Lubitsch," one is clearly not being encouraged to think of Eisenstein or Ozu. As in Andrew Sarris's *The American Cinema*—which Koszarski occasionally reflects in his discerning thumbnail sketches of Edmund Goulding's visual style and the differences between Sennett and Roach comedies—the cross-references tend to be *sui generis.*

On the other hand, excepting only reviews by Osip Brik and Viktor Shklovsky from the late 20s, nothing in *Movies and Methods* was written earlier than 1948, and very few of the fifty-two pieces predate the 60s. And in further contrast, the articles chiefly come from magazines and books devoted to criticism: *Cinéaste, Film Comment, Film Quarterly, The Film Till Now, Movie, New York Review of Books, Screen, Sight and Sound, Velvet Light Trap, Women & Film,* and so on. The mode of popular instruction about how to launch and sustain a film career is as conspicuously absent here as the mode of criticism is from the Koszarski collection; concern with film budgets is replaced by concern with intellectual and academic investments, and the issue of authorship is addressed quite differently. As Nichols remarks in his preface to the final section: "Most of these writers have little or no interest in preserving the Romantic fiction of the solitary and creative genius. . . . This project of 'decentering' critical study away from the individual, the author or point of origin, and towards processes and systems which in many ways can be said to 'speak the subject' is one shared by structuralism and semiology alike."

Both books, one could note, explicitly alter the original purpose of their contents. Koszarski's collection is chronologically ordered and put together with a kind of scholarly care that seeks to convert his findings into material that is *historically* useful: an aspiring movie actress today is not likely to read Marshall Nielan's thoughts in 1922 on "Acting for the Screen: the six great essentials" for concrete advice. Nichols arranges his own selections under three main headings (Contextual Criticism, Formal Criticism, Theory) and various subheadings (Political Criticism, Feminist Criticism, *Auteur* Criticism, etc.) to illustrate different critical methodologies—contriving, in a more indirect fashion, to suggest a history and development of another sort.

Each anthology, then, is presented as a disciplined academic endeavor that seeks to affect existing film discourse, not merely duplicate or pay homage to it. Yet an almost immeasurable gulf seems to stretch between the books and their separate points of focus. They confront us with two different kinds of discourse that one might choose to identify, respectively, with the Marketplace and the University.

■

> The mass-culture maker . . . is essentially a reflector of myths, and lacks concrete experiences to communicate. To him man is an object seen from the outside . . . To the professional of mass culture, knowledge is the knowledge of what is going on in other people; he trades his own experience for an experience of experience.
>
> —*Harold Rosenberg, "The Herd of Independent Minds"*

Read in bulk, many of the pieces in *Hollywood Directors* tend to slide off the mind. Like much popular journalism, they seem designed to be read in a state of semiattentiveness, a benign sort of stupor in which nice-sounding platitudes drum on the consciousness with all the dulling comfort of rain on a roof. A halfway house between talking and writing, they often fail to satisfy as either because the tone comes across as artificial and strained. Indeed, much of the material registers as slightly harried, impatient answers to eager, dimwitted questions that are not reproduced but are easily enough imagined:

Tell me, Mr. Borzage, what are the main qualities you think a director should have? "A Director should have some of the qualities of a leader, the ability to make decisions that are right most of the time, and the quality which inspires confidence in those about him." *Mr. Langdon, in your considered opinion, what is it that makes people laugh?* "The four greatest stimuli to laughter are rigidity, automatism, absentmindedness, and unsociability." *What is the American film industry doing to fight fascism overseas, Mr. Tuttle?* "A group of young cartoonists from Hollywood's animated cartoon studios are preparing plans for cartoons to knife the dictators right in their Mickey Mice." *How do you go about directing a picture?* "It is no more possible to dogmatize about the methods of work of a film director than it would be to lay down laws about how an author should write his books. In both cases generalization can go no further than the primary and superficial details of routine."

The sensible response of George Cukor to this last hypothetical query—which virtually invalidates the thrust of most of these declarations—merely reminds one that most of these articles are necessarily treading water, trying helplessly to come up with certainties in a context where *lack* of secure authorship often characterizes the form and subject alike of their statements. Inevitably, all these efforts inhabit a Marketplace terrain where knowledge, in Harold Rosenberg's words, "is the knowledge of what is going on in other people," and this knowledge itself continually threatens to supplant the director's own powers of expression—whether on the screen or on the page; the ostensible subject is movies, but the specter of money hovers in the background, virtually calling many of the shots. Thus "knowledge" in this framework often resembles the triumph of the ape cited by Vladimir Nabokov, who "after months of coaxing by a scientist, produced the first drawing ever charcoaled by an animal: this sketch showed the bars of the poor creature's cage."

When this knowledge is sufficiently provocative, the results can be entertaining and/or instructive: Maurice Tourneur adroitly running through a catalog of movie clichés in 1920 and bemoaning his failure to get his films shown when he tried to move beyond them; Keaton explaining in detail why an expensive rubber-fish gag in THE NAVIGATOR failed to draw laughs; William Cameron Menzies recalling how he had to scrap a replica of the Campanile of Toledo for a Mary Pickford vehicle after audiences asked what Madison Square Garden (which copied this campanile) was doing in a Spanish setting; Cecil B. DeMille solemnly noting that in film, unlike theater, "I have found that what is called acting will count for nothing beyond fifteen feet." Perhaps most rewarding is Mack Sennett recounting rules of decorum as dictated by the tastes of his audience circa 1918—a list that conveniently matches some of the insights a "structuralist" critic might glean from a Sennett comedy fifty years later:

> The copper is fair game for pies, likewise any fat man. Fat faces and pies seem to have a peculiar affinity. On the other hand . . . Shetland ponies and pretty girls are immune. It is an axiom of screen comedy that a Shetland pony must never be put in an undignified position. . . . You might as well show Santa Claus being mistreated. The immunity of pretty girls doesn't go quite as far as the immunity of the Shetland pony, however. You can put a pretty girl in a comedy shower bath. You can have her fall into mud puddles. They will laugh at that. But the spectacle of a girl dripping with pie is displeasing.

All such concrete observations get down to the brass tacks of a commercial director's trade. It is in the more nebulous realm of theory that these spokesmen (or their mouthpieces) tend to lose credibility. And one might even quarrel with the precise accuracy of F. W. Murnau's description of his own work in 1928:

> They say that I have a passion for "camera angles." . . . To me the camera represents the eye of a person, through whose mind one is watching the events on the screen. It must follow characters at times into difficult places, as it crashed through the reeds and pools in SUNRISE at the heels of the Boy, rushing to keep his tryst with the Woman of the City. It must whirl and peep and move from place to place as swiftly as thought itself, when it is necessary to exaggerate for the audience the idea or emotion that is uppermost in the mind of the

character. I think the films of the future will use more and more of these "camera angles," or as I prefer to call them these "dramatic angles." They help to photograph thought.

As evocation and explanation of what happens in the celebrated journey across the marshes near the beginning of SUNRISE, this is certainly up to the standard of what most reviewers were writing about the film at the time; in certain respects, it no doubt tells us more. Yet read today, it borders on the ingenuous. Thought indeed may be the substance that is photographed when the camera noses after George O'Brien and then darts suddenly *past* him, through a dense network of branches, before coming to a halt in front of Margaret Livingston, waiting for him in a clearing under the moon. But it is not clear whether the thought that is uppermost is the character's or Murnau's. Arriving at the clearing well ahead of the hero, and by a somewhat different route, the camera imposes a dreamlike fatality on O'Brien's destination, as if he were being reeled in like a fish—a pawn not only of the City Woman but also of the director/spectator/voyeur who first perceives her. And it is the voluptuous *experience* of thought, one might add, that is being filmed, not its implied intellectual or emotional content—a thought that might include the Boy's obsessions in its trajectory, but still moves independently of them.

From the vantage point of the Marketplace, such qualifications might seem like nit-picking. But Murnau's method of description is certainly foreign to the way that Hitchcock would spell out the specifics of such a sequence today. Does the increased value of exactitude imply that Hitchcock knows more than Murnau did, or only that Hitchcock, unlike Murnau, has an audience that is interested in such fine distinctions?

■

In Hollywood, "knowledge of what is going on in other people" usually means a sharp eye for changing fashions, and a further point of interest in this collection is the degree to which other arts are valued in relation to film—an approach that probably would be less fashionable in comparable circles today.*
"Slowly but surely," writes Rex Ingram or his scribe in 1922, "the cinema is coming into its own, taking its place, if not beside sculpture and painting as an art, most certainly ahead of the spoken drama." For Slavko Vorkapich in 1930, "A perfect motion picture would be comparable to a symphony." Significantly, Paul Fejos's own reference in 1929 is to fairy tales, pointing toward the construction of LONESOME and his still to be made MARIE, LÉGENDE HONGROISE, both of which belie Koszarski's claim that "Fejos' sense of narrative was weak." And William DeMille—older brother of Cecil, and director of the neglected CONRAD IN QUEST OF HIS YOUTH—draws persuasively on *Don Qui-*

---

*It might be said that the social and physical sciences currently play an equivalent role for most directors and critics: Marx, Pavlov, and Laing rather than Rembrandt, Brueghel, and Doré.

xote in a side-splitting treatment in 1935 of Mickey Mouse as New Dealer and Popeye as Fascist, with "good old Pluto fulfilling the duties of Sancho Panza."

Seen as a scrapbook, *Hollywood Directors* becomes itself a quixotic gesture in its noble efforts to preserve romantic fragments from a rapidly vanishing past. The disappearance or virtual unavailability of films directed by Maurice Tourneur, William DeMille, Ingram, Fejos, Murnau, and countless others makes Koszarski's resurrections of their "authorized statements" doubly poignant. And these scattered ramblings, however limited in their range of detail and nuance, may ultimately have to serve as substitutes for works that the Marketplace has already absent-mindedly burned, buried, lost, or squandered.

■

> The spreading influence of political and social facts into the literary field of consciousness has produced a new kind of scriptor, halfway between the party member and the writer, deriving from the former an ideal image of committed man, and from the latter the notion that a written work is an act. Thus while the intellectual supersedes the writer, there appears in periodicals and in essays a militant mode of writing entirely freed from stylistic considerations, and which is, so to speak, a professional language signifying "presence."
>
> —*Roland Barthes,* Writing Degree Zero

Retrieval work of another kind is to be found in *Movies and Methods,* a critical anthology that has the uncommon virtue of concentrating mainly on pieces that haven't inundated other "textbook" collections. While an ideal anthology would go further and commission its own translations of important and unavailable texts—and correct those it reprints more carefully, so that Jean-Louis Comolli isn't rechristened Jean-Luc and Straub isn't credited with imaginary titles like THE DIARY OF ANNA MAGDALENA BACH—the least that can be said of Bill Nichols's mammoth assemblage is that it spreads its nets far and wide, and the language on display here is accordingly varied.

Polemically speaking, however, the editorial notes and most of the final section on Theory point this anthology in an unmistakable direction—and one that largely coincides with Barthes's description of "typical" writing in *Esprit* and *Les Temps Modernes* in the early 50s. This is apparent from the first page of the introduction, where the simple use of a feminine pronoun ("methodologies intervene between the writer and her subject") already announces a style ostensibly formed by political and intellectual allegiances, and is no less evident on the last page of text, the conclusion of a glossary explaining everything from "Analog/Digital" to "Textual System(s)."

This anonymous, collective style resembles that of *Hollywood Directors*, insofar as neither book can be read straight through without some mental calcification setting in; but the implications of authorial absence are quite different. In Koszarski's book, it is characteristically a sign of the director's defeat in letting his or her voice be heard—a problem reflected in many of the same directors' films, and cruelly parodied when their various complaints, hopes, and axioms about this difficulty begin to sound more and more like each other's. In *Movies and Methods,* conversely, it becomes a sign of apparent triumph: facelessness here is more prone to be a badge of authenticity, commitment, membership in a burgeoning community of common aspirations.

Within such a framework, language is taken to be a necessary evil more than a methodology of its own, and any notion of *performance* (as opposed to demonstration), which might include writers as dissimilar as Barthes, Manny Farber, and Jonas Mekas, is effectively rendered obsolete. Sontag barely scrapes in, and only after an editorial warning that her "vantage point is that of the solitary intellectual beholden to nothing so impersonal as a methodology." Safety in numbers is the evident watchword; and much as an institution like the Academy Awards partially serves to offset the more cutthroat aspects of an industry by promoting an image of social cohesion, the "community of scholars" is a not entirely false myth that helps to ensure the preservation of a corporate image.

The solitary reader drifts through the thickets of this discourse in something like the way that spectators/tourists get about in Tativille—on a kind of conveyor belt that guarantees distance, carefully chosen sights (and sites), and alternate options of attention. But if one should choose to depart from the planned itinerary and move about at will, one quickly enters a chaotic Babel; and if the tourist/reader occasionally slams into a glass door, the comedy isn't always intentional.

> Lincoln's mediation also forces the film to crack open revealing the ideological function of his role. For example, Lincoln's seemingly benevolent representation of the Law actually originates in a terrible, castrated, castrating operation which produces Law "as a pure prohibition of violence whose result is only a permanent indictment of the castrating effects of its discourse," and which effectively restrains him from a full self-realisation of the qualities he mediates (he is wholly other). Lincoln himself cannot be "had," possessed, known. He frames the context.

This is Nichols himself, discussing the justly celebrated *Cahiers du cinéma* analysis of YOUNG MR. LINCOLN. Stumbled into haphazardly, as an isolated patch of prose, it is likely to inflict bruises; approached more circumspectly and contextually, through the filters provided by other discourses, it becomes relatively lucid. For squatters in the Semiology-Structuralism settlement who have already set up shop, it is nothing more than the continuation of a discussion that has been long in progress. If you've stuck around and dutifully made the acquaintance of the *Cahiers* collective—who, in turn, might have helped introduce you to the local barber, Althusser, and funny Doc Lacan who lives across the way—you can listen to Nichols and find that he's just talking horse sense.

Given the proper orientation, one can also make one's own alignments among the warring factions in residence. This lends additional suspense to the confrontations as Rothman has it out with Dayan on "The System of the Suture," Abramson beats Wollen to the draw while protecting Pasolini's ranch, and Nichols himself—in a showdown finale destined to forge a legend, after nearly a hundred pages of contextual preparation—picks off Wollen, the *Cahiers* gang, Metz, and Eco, thereby establishing more space in town so that Bateson and Wilden might stake their own claims.

■

The metaphor is a deliberately vulgar and excessive one for an activity that might also, with justice, be called collective work. Yet the spirit of competition and potential usurpment is no more absent from much of this prose—particularly the portion coming from American sectors—than from the Western town in MY DARLING CLEMENTINE, another privileged site in many of these debates. Even if the status of the individual author ("the Romantic fiction of the solitary and creative genius") is partially undermined by the University discourse, the mood of contest within a forum of ideas remains very much in evidence. And the consequences of this attitude are worth considering.

Part of this is reflected in the treatment of history promulgated by this anthology's categories and selections, which the section Formal Criticism makes especially evident. As Nichols admits elsewhere, "Many of the articles included here employ more than one method, and an element of arbitrariness enters into their classification." Retrospectively, this can help to account for the fact that "Political Criticism" and "Feminist Criticism" occupy separate subdivisions of "Contextual Criticism," that Russian formalist reviews are used to lead off the Political (and not the Formal) section, and that "Formal Criticism" is subdivided into "*Auteur* Criticism" and "*Mise-en-Scène* Criticism" (the latter of which includes a study of the abstract work of Paul Sharits).

But is all this as arbitrary as it might first appear? "*Auteur*" and "*mise-en-scène*" are both somewhat bastardized terms harking back to a specific historical juncture—the point at which they were culled from the pages of *Cahiers* (and, in the case of the latter, decked out with gratuitous hyphens that were never used in French) and then pressed into different functions, chiefly through the work of Andrew Sarris in the early 60s. An essential part of this juncture was the privileged status accorded to Hollywood, coupled with an almost systematic avoidance of the formal branches of filmmaking that lay outside the studio systems.

Coming at a time in Anglo-American criticism when such figures as Fuller, Hawks, and Sirk were being denied recognition as artists, these terms (however imprecise) proved effective as polemical calling cards. And, by and large, the major aims of the battle were won—to the extent that when Nichols in his introduction refers to Fuller and Nicholas Ray as "neglected" directors, one wonders what he could possibly mean by that adjective. But the fact that history is usually written by the victors can make recent events seem disproportionately important, while earlier happenings of arguably greater significance are all but obliterated from memory. It is apparently within these conditions that the seminal sources of formal film study (Munsterberg, Arnheim, the Russian formalists, Eisenstein, Epstein, Balázs, etc.) can be either ignored or displaced—and contemporary inheritors of this tradition, such as Burch and Michelson, essentially bypassed—for a definition of formal criticism that begins with Truffaut and Sarris.

Other shortcuts are visible in the isolation of the YOUNG MR. LINCOLN analysis from any account of *Cahiers du cinéma*'s history, and subsequent uses of certain terms in that essay. When "classic cinema" was provisionally defined there, the authors sensibly noted that "obviously in the course of these studies we will have to examine, and perhaps even challenge it, in order finally to construct its theory." Now that the term has become a standard fixture in University prose, the necessity for such an interrogation has seemingly vanished, leaving the term free to reap ideological havoc as it continues to validate an object that has not yet even achieved theoretical status. This leads to such thrilling nonstatements as Daniel Dayan's rallying cry—"The system of the suture is to classical cinema what verbal language is to literature"—and implies elsewhere an unspoken collective agreement which, like the hyphenated *mise-en-scène,* has grown overnight from a momentary expedient to an ill-defined dwelling unit where scores of professors can promptly take out leases.

The academic debates made possible by this kind of fungus growth, ranging from the purposeful to the pedestrian, are of course a very recent development; and, ironically, it is the strenuous desire to remain *au courant* that dates these texts most decisively. Many of Nichols's most recent selections are already a mite rickety because of the contextual chains of reference anchoring them in particular stages of various debates. This is anticipated in a note explaining that most selections were made in 1972–1973, and a remark elsewhere that "this anthology is concerned with a process, a struggle for knowledge, *not* the enshrinement of certain approaches as timeless truth"—a form of openness that is clearly one of the book's strong points.

This means, however, that the conscientious student who buckles down to "master" a 1971 lecture by Christian Metz in hopes of keeping abreast of the latest semiological developments, is bound to be in for some galling frustration when she discovers that Metz's positions have since undergone substantial revision, making the focus of her mastery hopelessly *dépassé*. A useful clarification of this sort of problem comes in David Bordwell's 1975 autocritique of a 1971 study of CITIZEN KANE, testifying to the methodological advances that criticism has made over a very short period.

In the course of this development, the calculated efforts of the University to shun the tactics and consequences of Marketplace criticism have been both a boon and a deception—welcome in the stance of scholarly disinterest and theoretical rigor, myopic in the apparent belief that such a pure division is possible. Who's to say, after all, that *Movies and Methods* won't affect the classroom rentals of YOUNG MR. LINCOLN? And in many selections devoted to other topics—the populist films of Capra, Borzage's DISPUTED PASSAGE, CRIES AND WHISPERS, GODFATHER II—one can feel the tension of University methods vying with Marketplace superlatives, language that oscillates uneasily between the rigors of academic demonstration and the looseness of informal speech.

■

Stepping back from the specter of Marketplace and University prose, one begins to wonder whether other options are open to film writing. If, according to Pasolini, there is something called a cinema of poetry, can't one also conceive of a poetics of criticism? The oblique critical content of *Hollywood Directors* often suggests that film aesthetics resemble mail-order recipes; the incomparably greater precision of most pieces in *Movies and Methods* seldom indicates that criticism can or should be anything but a sluggish, plodding process tracing methodical steps up theoretical ladders. Yet Eisenstein, Epstein, Barthes, and others offer substantial proof that critical writing need not be crippled by subservience to either faction. Most Russian formalist criticism remains to be translated, but a few of the tantalizing samples that have already appeared suggest that literature and criticism, art and science, lyricism and precision, rigor and imagination don't have to be nearly as incompatible as these two categories imply.

—Sight and Sound, Autumn 1977

In terms of craft, originality, and intelligence, there are few young international filmmakers around today to match Atom Egoyan—a Canadian writer-director with a bee in his bonnet about video, photography, voyeurism, sexual obsession, troubled families, and personal identity (not necessarily in that order). But of his half-dozen features to date, the only one I'm comfortable calling a flat-out masterpiece is his fifth, CALENDAR—in many ways the least premeditated or worked over of the bunch.

There are various ways of categorizing Egoyan's six features, but perhaps the most useful involves distinguishing between the relatively low-budget ones, which tend to be my favorites—NEXT OF KIN (1984), FAMILY VIEWING (1987), CALENDAR (1993)—and the more expensive ones: SPEAKING PARTS (1989), THE ADJUSTER (1991), EXOTICA (1994).* Though all these movies have similar preoccupations and many have similar formal structures, a few distinctions are worth noting. Egoyan is an assimilated Armenian who was born and raised and continues to live in Toronto, and all his features include

---

*This review appeared about half a year before the U.S. release of EXOTICA, Egoyan's first commercial hit—a feature whose uncommon mixture of pornography and warmth gave it a mainstream appeal broader than that of his previous films, and a film that I may well have underrated here. [1995]

performances by his wife, Arsinee Khanjian, an Armenian actress who was born and grew up in Beirut's Armenian community. But the only Egoyan movies that can be said to directly address his Armenian roots, as well as his ambivalence toward them, are NEXT OF KIN and CALENDAR. The other four, by contrast, tend to place their focus more on elements of Canadian culture, especially those bound up with repression in Ontario and with sexual aberration, including incest. (It's worth mentioning that Egoyan is far from the only Canadian who associates incest with puritanism and repression; check out David Cronenberg in DEAD RINGERS and Guy Maddin in CAREFUL, for instance.)

What has always seemed problematic about Egoyan's slicker (and, to my mind, more pretentious) productions, for all their virtues, is that they exploit various sexual hang-ups more than they try to understand them. In contrast to his low-budget films, which at least on the surface are more naturalistic, SPEAKING PARTS, THE ADJUSTER, and EXOTICA all have the shape and feel of allegorical fantasies, but closed, claustrophobic ones, without road maps or commentaries. This isn't to say that they're simply pornographic, or that analysis is entirely absent from them. What bothers me is that they use ideas *about* both pornography and analysis as come-ons to the audience, but the painful and difficult material we're drawn into ultimately loops back on itself without leading to any new understanding.

In other words, these films are structured like the obsessions they deal with. Because of that, narrative progression in the usual sense is generally kept to a minimum; at most one sees the gradual exposition of an already existing situation, or variations on a theme, but no real character development or the advancement of any didactic argument. (In all of Egoyan's movies, internalized emotional states count for much more than plot points.) These films are often alluring, at least initially, insofar as they're hypnotic and mysterious. Yet they never quite explain enough to entirely dissolve the mysteries or break the hypnosis; at best the denouements merely round out the descriptions of the obsessions involved. As political statements about human potential they qualify as defeatist, and it's not all that easy to separate diagnosis from disease. They're spiritual stripteases that never quite reveal a naked soul; at some point, it seems, the equivalent to a fig leaf in Egoyan's imagination steps in, a spiritual counterpart to the Ontario censor board.

To be fair, CALENDAR has virtually no narrative progression either, and there's no denouement to the mysteries it sets up. But because the tone is more comic here, and the sexual tension less guilt-ridden, one doesn't emerge from this picture feeling cheated. It also helps a lot that the protagonist is played by Egoyan himself. Implicating himself more directly in his own material, he becomes at once more modest and more relaxed; his touch is lighter and funnier and his directorial hand is surer. But the biggest difference between this and Egoyan's previous manner is the subject matter itself.

■

Egoyan has said, "In conceiving CALENDAR, I wanted to find a story that would deal with three levels of Armenian consciousness: Nationalist, Diasporan, and Assimilationist." The film has two basic time frames, intercut and interwoven in a number of inventive ways. The first involves a trip to Armenia taken by a North American photographer and his wife (Egoyan and Khanjian, respectively the assimilationist and diasporan). He is taking photographs of ancient rural churches for a calendar, and their guide and driver (Ashot Adamian, the nationalist) speaks in a language only the wife can understand. (None of their conversations is subtitled, so unless we speak Armenian we have to depend, like the husband, exclusively on her for translations of what's being said.) In this time frame just about all we see are the wife and guide, from the vantage point of both a video camera and a still camera operated by the husband. But as we see and hear their conversations in front of various churches, we also *hear* the husband, alienated by the growing rapport between the other two, speaking petulantly to his wife.

The other time frame is later, after the husband has returned home and the wife has remained in Armenia. It's marked by the twelve successive pages of the finished calendar, which is located beside a water cooler in his apartment; on top of the water cooler is a telephone and answering machine. We see a series of scenes of the husband sitting in the adjacent room with various young women—one per month—pouring wine and making small talk, music playing in the background, until each woman asks to use the phone. Each then retreats into the room with the phone and the calendar, where she speaks seductively to someone in a foreign language. (Each woman speaks in a different language on the phone, but all of them speak English with the husband.) Around this time, Egoyan's character usually takes out his notebook and starts writing in it, and we hear his reflections offscreen, in the form of an ongoing letter to his wife about the cause of their separation. (Whether the separation is temporary or permanent is one of the many issues the film leaves open; we hear the wife calling from Armenia on the answering machine twice, but the husband refuses to pick up the phone either time, and his overall behavior often suggests he's paranoid about the exchanges his wife had with the guide.)

The repetitions in both time frames may make the film seem at times like a minimalist exercise, but in fact the constant and varied interweaving between the two blocks of material—which often includes sound from one time frame overlapping the other—is dense and intricate, and some of the visual compositions in both settings are breathtaking. (Egoyan is especially canny in the way he varies the placement of the wife and guide in relation to the various churches.) Some of the video footage is played in fast-forward or in reverse, alerting us to the fact that the husband/photographer is playing back this footage alone in his apartment; at one point, we even see him masturbating to his wife's image on his TV screen. And there are numerous visual rhymes between the photographs of churches in the calendar and the scenes between husband, wife, and guide on the different sites where the photographs are being taken—rhymes whereby the husband's own art becomes the mocking residue (as well as the initial cause) of his marital discord.

The precise nature of the husband's nearly identical sessions with the various women is never spelled out. At first they appear to be dates, but subsequent clues suggest they're auditions; either way, they're always laden with erotic possibilities that are then disrupted each time the women begin speaking to someone else in a foreign language, thereby reproducing some version of the husband's Armenian trauma. (We hear a couple of messages on the answering machine from someone named Julia describing some of the women coming over and the various languages they can or can't speak, which establishes that these scenes are preplanned rather than coincidental; one of the many comic repetitions is that each time the husband pours wine for himself and his companion, it's just before she leaves the room to make her call, and each time he finishes off the bottle.)

Like the hapless protagonists in SPEAKING PARTS, THE ADJUSTER, and EXOTICA, Egoyan is clearly involved in a repetition compulsion, an obsessive loop. Yet while the repetitions in the apartment are ritualized, much as they are in the other films, those in Armenia (the conversations between wife and guide and between wife and husband) are much more off-the-cuff. (I've been told by one of Egoyan's principal producers that this film, unlike his others, was made virtually without a script.) And the constant juxtapositions of chance and control, acts and reenactments, on-screen and offscreen voices, dialogue and music, English and non-English, country and city, exteriors and interiors, events and their visual traces in photographs and on video, create lush formal patterns that are both hilarious and evocative, painfully recognizable as well as pleasurable.

Most important of all, they mean something. The themes of voyeurism and sexual obsession, family discord and isolation, media and identity, are for once wedded to something more universal than the relatively abstract social commentary and mannerist charades that tend to dominate Egoyan's other features. This time these themes and formal procedures all dovetail into the issue of tribalism, and it's hard to think of another subject in the world at the moment that has more immediate relevance or resonance. The process by which ethnic sites become calendar illustrations—and ethnicity and history become a commodity—entails a chain of communication that passes from nationalist to diasporan to assimilationist, bringing the first two closer together and moving the second two farther apart, a chain all of us are involved in nowadays on multiple levels, in relation to both our own families and ethnic roots and those of others. (What this movie says about monolingual North Americans abroad, with their cameras poised as shields, speaks volumes, but it's far from the whole story.) It's part of a larger process that's tearing the world apart, and it seems ironic that a tossed-off, 16-millimeter lark like CAL-ENDAR, an Armenian-German-Canadian coproduction, should go to the heart of such a subject while Egoyan's more studied and costlier movies seem relatively provincial and classbound, more a matter of art house esoterica for the carriage trade. The difference between this film and his others isn't at all that between Canada and Armenia; it's between closeted obsessions and the world we all live in, and the fact that Egoyan has stepped to the other side is much cause for rejoicing.

—Chicago *Reader,* August 19, 1994

Us and Them (BLOOD IN THE FACE)

If memory serves, it was around my junior year in college, during the mid-60s, when a conservative friend and classmate brought my brother and me to a John Birch Society meeting in Hyde Park, New York, held inside a trailer in a trailer camp. The friend advised us to conceal our identities as liberal Jews (he was half-Jewish himself) and try to blend in with the surroundings, which we did.

It was a sparsely attended meeting. Beforehand we made small talk with the handful of other people present, including the couple who owned the trailer and a young man who identified himself as the son of communists and who cheerfully explained that the society had deliberately adopted the structure of the Communist party, complete with cell meetings like this one and vows of secrecy. He and everyone else in the room seemed friendly, normal, everyday folks, until the film projector blew a fuse just as they began to screen a movie.

Then the paranoid speculations began: they made extensive flashlight searches of the yard around the trailer, looking for spies and saboteurs. After the fuse was replaced and the projector was started up again, the power failed a second time. Someone asked who was in charge of the local public utilities. "It's not him," another volunteered. "I know him pretty well, and he's a conservative." The meeting ended prematurely, with assurances that a thorough investigation would be made into the matter of who had sabotaged the projector.

On the ride back to campus our conservative friend—who went on to write for the *National Review* and teach at Harvard—was clearly delighted by their lunatic suspicions. When I met him years later in Paris, he took a similar Mencken-like pleasure in reading aloud lengthy extracts from the *Playboy* interview with John Wayne, which contained such nuggets as, "I've directed two pictures and I gave the blacks their proper position. I had a black slave in THE ALAMO, and I had a correct number of blacks in THE GREEN BERETS" and "Our so-called stealing of this country from [the Indians] was just a matter of survival. There were great numbers of people who needed new land, and the Indians were selfishly trying to keep it for themselves."

■

I haven't seen this friend in twenty years, but I'll bet he'd get an enormous laugh out of BLOOD IN THE FACE, a documentary about members of the American Nazi party, the Ku Klux Klan, and the Aryan Nation. I found the film compulsively watchable myself, though probably not for the same reasons he would. The paranoid lunacy captured here by filmmakers Anne Bohlen, Kevin Rafferty, and James Ridgeway is light-years beyond the idle fancies of the Birchers I met or the dim complacencies of John Wayne. These are people who believe that Jerry Falwell is a Jew (existentially if not racially), that Ronald Reagan is a dupe of the Jewish conspiracy, that not one single Jew was gassed during World War II, and that Russian tanks are currently lined up across the Mexican border waiting to make their move. But the impulse to find these people hilarious, as my onetime friend might, or simply terrifying, as many others might, was not what kept me fascinated.

Laughing at these groups, I think, dismisses them too easily, whereas recoiling in terror gives them too much credence. (Paranoia, we must remember, is even more contagious than sexually transmitted diseases.) Caught between these extremes, I found myself agape at how much like the rest of us these people are, only more so. What they say may boggle our minds, but it's clear that what we say boggles *their* minds—and considering that our statements have a much wider circulation, at least in the mass media, that's a lot of mind boggling to reckon with. And since they appear to be every bit as confident in their beliefs as we are in ours, the alienation that we automatically feel from them registers at odd moments as the mirror image of the alienation they must feel from us.

Us and them: it's the division felt in most war movies, horror movies, action movies, westerns. What's interesting about BLOOD IN THE FACE is that this division is all that's being talked about on the screen, but we never see it even once in the contemporary footage that makes up most of the film. All that we see there is harmony and heterogeneity: like-minded individuals agreeing with one another and enjoying each other's company, unchallenged by the semivisible and semiaudible filmmakers who are basically content to record what they see and hear.

Since the filmmakers intercut quite freely between at least three distinct groups—American Nazis, Ku Klux Klan members, and Aryan Nation support-ers—I couldn't tell whether the apparent agreements between these constitu-encies were real or fictions partly created by (or for) this film. I also resented seeing some of the speeches and comments reduced to sound bites rather than more sustained presentations. Isn't lumping all these malcontents together into a composite stew of xenophobic bile, crackpot theorizing, and apocalyptic fervor a little bit similar to the way these groups view everyone else?

I hoped that many of the questions raised by this film would be answered by James Ridgeway's book of the same title, published last year, which I looked at only after I saw the movie. The most important clarification comes in the middle of a discussion of Robert Miles, a onetime George Wallace supporter and former Grand Dragon of the Michigan Ku Klux Klan who's currently a Michigan pastor and leader of the racist right and is featured prom-inently in the film:

> During the 1980s Miles's Cohoctah farm, not far from Flint, Michigan, be-came a meeting place for different factions of the far right, among which Miles sought to promote unity. At one three-day meeting in April 1986, for example, perhaps 200 people showed up. They included such leaders as Glenn Miller of the White Patriot Party from North Carolina; Thom Robb, the Christian Identity preacher who was also national chaplain for the KKK; Debbie Mathews, widow of the martyred Order leader Bob Mathews; William Pierce, author of the *Turner Diaries*; and Don Black, the Alabama Klansman who had been imprisoned for conspiracy to invade the Caribbean island of Domenica, and was then running for the U.S. Senate in his state's Republican primary. Representatives from Can-ada's racist organizations, including John Ross Taylor, head of the fascist West-ern Guard, also made speeches.
>
> Participants at this gathering listened to talks on the history of the movement, tedious harangues against Jews, blacks, and other "mud people," and even a report on Satanic ritual murders. Events culminated in a cross burning on the back lot of the farm. Garbed in a Scottish kilt Miles held forth, acting as master of ceremonies and officiating as minister at a Klan marriage conducted by flash-light under the smoldering cross. He was also an indomitable advocate of an out-trek to the Pacific Northwest, where Aryans could set up an all-white home-land. Throughout, Miles did his best to broker competition among different groups, sternly advising everyone not to carry firearms, and warning the gather-ing to take care that their cars weren't pockmarked by the fire from the cross burning, and to beware of the press.*

***Blood in the Face* (New York: Thunder's Mouth Press, 1990), 85, 87.

Apparently not all of the press: barring only a few details (among them those contained in the final sentence), these two paragraphs effectively summarize BLOOD IN THE FACE: clearly all or virtually all of the film's contemporary footage comes from the three-day gathering in 1986. That's an important fact, and I can't understand why the filmmakers chose to omit it—or at least obscure it by giving no date or any other clear indication of setting (except for one early title, "Cohacio, Michigan"). I can understand their decision to exclude voice-overs and to minimize explanatory titles, but surely some knowledge about the context of the event—including a clear understanding that it *was* a single event—is essential if we want to read the film as anything more than a parade of exotic zoo animals. (There are some archival clips interspersed with the contemporary footage. These mainly show George Lincoln Rockwell, founder of the American Nazi party; a woman who witnessed his assassination; German Nazis; familiar shots of concentration camp corpses being dumped into graves; the aforementioned Bob Mathews; the murdered radio talk show host Alan Berg; and David Duke campaigning in Louisiana in 1989.) We get one hint of how the film came to be made toward the end, when Miles addresses the filmmakers: "We invited you here so that we could use you just the same way that you were using us."

Theoretically two antithetical charges can be made against the film—and I've heard that both of them *were* made when BLOOD IN THE FACE was shown earlier this year at the Blacklight film festival. One, it provides a forum to a lot of dangerous people, and two, it's been edited in such a way that the groups' least intelligent and informed speakers monopolize the proceedings.

I have no way of judging the accuracy of the second charge, though it is true that the filmmakers occasionally resort to glib comic editing (in the manner of ROGER & ME's Michael Moore, who receives an acknowledgment in the final credits) in order to undercut what someone is saying. After a woman argues that racial separatism is virtually the same thing as trying to save whales and seals, adding that "animals stay to their own species," there's a cut to two dogs of separate breeds sexually frolicking.

Undoubtedly Ridgeway's book has its own uses, but it seems to share with the movie a debilitating breeziness. (The book includes some information about the John Birch Society, for instance, but not a clue about its current status. One chart shows the society continuing into the present, but all discussion of it is in the past tense.) One reason why the film's reticence about overall context is so damaging is that this makes it almost impossible to gauge how heterogeneous these separate hate groups are. After all, they've been brought together for an event specifically designed to unify them—an event, in other words, partially conceived for purposes of propaganda. People who describe Leni Riefenstahl's TRIUMPH OF THE WILL as an "objective" documentary of a Nazi rally, including Riefenstahl herself, are conveniently eliding the fact that the rally was convened so that a film could be made of it. I'm not trying to suggest that BLOOD IN THE FACE is at quite this level of premeditation, but I wish that Miles's agenda and the filmmakers' agenda—including information about how the film came to be made—were more precisely spelled out.

Certain details definitely throw the supposed heterogeneity of the groups into question. The film opens with the camera drifting past many people standing casually on a lawn outside a meeting hall, eventually identified by an impromptu sign as Hall of the Giants. ("Giant" is Klanspeak for "head of a province.") But giants aren't exactly what we see. We notice two men in Scottish kilts, one in army fatigues, many with Nazi armbands, some in suits, and some in jeans. We hear the voices of a few kids, but the only woman we see is walking away from the gathering; when we cut to the beginning of the meeting inside, however, a few more women are visible. Next we get snippets from seven separate talks, then the discourse continues in casual statements made over lunch at a picnic table outside, and here the lack of heterogeneity is striking: though all of these people seem to be working class—a fact underlined immediately afterward, first by Miles and then by five uniformed American Nazis, one of them female—it's equally striking that one speaks with a pronounced European accent and that none, with the possible exception of the uniformed woman, conforms to the Nordic specimens we associate with Hitler's Nazi rallies. They're merely unglamorous Americans who feel disenfranchised, just like most of the rest of us.

■

"Can it be that *everybody* is looking for a way to fit in?" Harold Rosenberg asked in his book *The Tradition of the New.* "If so, doesn't that imply that nobody fits?

"Perhaps it is not possible to fit into American life," he continued. "American Life is a billboard; individual life in the U.S. includes something nameless that takes place in the weeds behind it."

The hatred and paranoia we witness in BLOOD IN THE FACE are certainly disquieting, but they're also familiar, and far from exclusive to members of so-called hate groups. I have to admit that I've occasionally felt these things myself, some of it directed against people like the people in this film. (Why else did I sneak into that John Birch Society meeting, and why else did they perceive that spies might be in their midst?)

In a curious way, feelings of this sort are a substantial part of what people in this country hold in common, but because the targets are different, they lead to warring tribes, as well as to coalitions of the sort in this film. Sometimes I wonder which of the two is worse—the coalitions that make wars possible, or the wars that make coalitions necessary. During the recent confirmation hearings of Clarence Thomas, the whole country seemed to be going through a fresh version of this tortured factionalism (or "fractionalism"), which repeatedly splits us apart. Whether one believed Thomas or Anita Hill, the anxiety and despair were the same.

I can recall once hearing a radio interview with George Lincoln Rockwell, probably when I was in my teens. The interviewer was the late Joe Pyne—an early example of the hate-filled talk show host who's become so much of a symbol of our era (see TALK RADIO and THE FISHER KING)—and he was so vicious and rude throughout the program that I found myself, perversely, sympathizing more with Rockwell. In the final analysis they were both monsters, but the fact that Pyne could elicit this response from me has made me wonder ever since whether expressions of hatred can obliterate moral distinctions of any kind.

The title BLOOD IN THE FACE comes from one of the racist statements made in the film, that you can't trust anyone you can't see blushing. Before I realized what the source of the title was, I'd assumed a more violent meaning, as in "blood *on* the face," and I wouldn't be surprised to hear that many others have made the same assumption. That suggests that the violence we automatically bring to this material—emotional as well as polemical—is fully commensurate with the violence directed back at us.

—Chicago *Reader,* December 6, 1991

Other Cinemas

Feudal Attraction (JU DOU)

Like most people reading this, I know next to nothing about the history of China, which is thousands of years older than the United States, and has a population over four times as large. In high school I was required to take courses in Alabama and American history; world history was an elective, but if that course had anything to do with China, I no longer recall any details. I also managed to get through seven years of college and graduate school without further edification on the subject.

I suspect that most people in China are comparably uninformed about the United States. When my youngest brother was in Kenya in the late 60s, he spent time conversing with some Red Guard members who were stationed there, and used to have friendly arguments with them about where Coca-Cola, which they liked, came from. It was difficult for them to accept that anything they liked came from the United States, just as it's difficult for many of us to accept that anything we like about China (e.g., the 1989 student protests in Tiananmen Square—routinely and misleadingly labeled prodemocracy in the American press) isn't American in origin.

Given this tradition of shared ignorance, I think it's less than useful to describe JU DOU—a beautiful and disturbing new film from the People's Republic of China—by comparing it to THE POSTMAN ALWAYS RINGS TWICE, as a good many American reviewers have done. Some of them have even had the brass to criticize the film for not living up to this comparison; "the postman barely rings once," quips a blurb writer in *The New Yorker*, who goes on to criticize the stylization of one of the characters for recalling—and not living up to—a British s-f programmer called CHILDREN OF THE DAMNED (1964). The implication is clear: it's the business of Chinese filmmakers to study, emulate, and adhere to the standards and aesthetic principles set by Anglo-American pulp writers and hacks so that they can rise to the same cultural level as James M. Cain and directors Tay Garnett and Anton Leader.

For the sake of argument, let's concede for the moment that there are a few loose and superficial correspondences between Cain's novel, CHILDREN OF THE DAMNED, and JU DOU. Cain's novel was written and set in 1934, JU DOU is set in the 20s—not the same decade, but we're talking ballpark figures. Both stories center on a passionate adulterous affair between the wife and an employee of a loutish boss in a rural area. But this is about as far as the comparison can go, and the only possible connection to CHILDREN OF THE DAMNED is the presence of a silent, threatening, and destructive child.

The problem with such comparisons is that they obscure considerably more than they clarify, by boiling down a story into what we already know and discarding or minimizing the rest. To give some idea of what is being discarded and minimized, a fairly detailed synopsis of JU DOU is necessary (readers who'd prefer to see the film before hearing the whole story are invited to take their leave at any point). Considering the fact that the film was recently nominated for an Academy Award (the first time a Chinese-language film has ever been nominated) and that the Chinese government, which has prevented the film from showing publicly in China, also tried unsuccessfully to have the nomination withdrawn, it's important to try to understand not only what it means to us but also what it means to—and for—China.

■

The beautiful Ju Dou (Gong Li) is the third wife of the owner of a dye factory named Yang Jinshan (Li Wei), a cruel, impotent tyrant who purchases her for the express purpose of fathering an heir; when he discovers that he's incapable of impregnating her, he beats and tortures her. If we assume that such barbaric practices belong only to China's past, the film's director, Zhang Yimou, insists we're wrong. "In remote rural areas among the peasantry," he said in a recent interview, "you will still find far more serious cases of oppression than Ju Dou's. Even today, you can buy a woman at the price of RMB 2,000 to 3,000 [approximately $400]. There's no way the government can stop this. Sometimes the women escape, but if they are caught, they are chained, humiliated, and beaten in a very inhuman way."

The employee in JU DOU (Li Baotian) is an adopted nephew of Yang Jinshan named Yang Tianqing—unlike Ju Dou, he bears the family name of his uncle—who has been working for Jinshan for a long time before Ju Dou turns up. His affair with Ju Dou begins at her instigation and only after a certain amount of prodding; he was content to peek at her bathing herself through a hole in the wall. When she discovers that he's been spying on her, her first response is to stuff the peephole with straw. Later, after Jinshan leaves on an overnight trip, she goes to Tianqing's room and finds the door bolted. Only on the following day, after she confronts him ("Why are you afraid? . . . Do you think I'm a wolf? . . . I've kept my body for you") and embraces him, do they finally make love.

Some time afterward, a doctor declares that Ju Dou is pregnant. Jinshan, believing that the child is his own, offers a grateful prayer to his ancestors, but Ju Dou whispers to Tianqing that the child is his. When the child is born, the elders in the village meet and one of them selects his name, Yang Tianbai (played by Zhang Yi as a child and Zheng Jian when he grows older). The affair between Ju Dou and Tianqing continues in secret during the baby's infancy whenever Jinshan is away; she even offers Tianqing some of her breast milk. But when Jinshan's donkey returns alone to the dye factory, Tianqing dutifully goes out looking for his boss; finding him unconscious, Tianqing carries him home on his back.

After the doctor announces that Jinshan is paralyzed from the waist down, Ju Dou and Tianqing become more open with him about their relationship, though the social front all three characters present to the village remains the same. After Ju Dou angrily tells Jinshan that Tianqing is the baby's father, Jinshan tries to kill Tianbai. Another crucial difference between Tianqing and his counterpart in THE POSTMAN ALWAYS RINGS TWICE is then revealed: he is unwilling to murder his boss and uncle, despite Ju Dou's expressed desire that he do so; the most he can do is threaten, "If you touch my son again, you'll see what happens."

Jinshan responds to this crisis by trying to burn the dye factory down, but Tianqing and Ju Dou manage to extinguish the fire and then punish him by keeping him trapped in a bucket on wheels that they periodically hoist into the air with ropes, which causes him to pray to his ancestors for revenge. Some time later Tianbai plays with a cart while his parents sit on a hillside expressing concern about his failure to speak. "Anyway, he *is* your son," Ju Dou says to Tianqing. "We'll tell him when he's older." She goes on to say that her period is late and that she may be pregnant again. When Tianbai runs back home alone to the dye factory to dunk reeds he has gathered in a vat of dye, Jinshan moves behind him to drown him. But at a crucial moment the boy turns around and utters his first word to him: "Daddy." Overjoyed, Jinshan embraces Tianbai. When Ju Dou and Tianqing return, he introduces them as "Mother" and "Brother."

At a village gathering where Tianbai is toasted by the elders, Tianqing bursts into tears, and the locals comment that he's drunk.

After Ju Dou painfully tries to abort a second child with chili powder and vinegar, and proposes fleeing the village with Tianbai, Tianqing replies, "If they knew, they'd kill us." When she proposes poisoning Jinshan with arsenic, he takes umbrage: "How dare you—after all, he's my uncle." "And what am I to you?" she yells back. The doctor gives her medicine after she passes out, and we discover that her abortion was a success, though the doctor expresses some suspicion about how she became pregnant again.

One day, while playing in the dye factory, Tianbai accidentally causes Jinshan to fall into a vat of red dye and drown; he laughs as the old man goes under. When Tianqing returns, he accuses Ju Dou of murdering her husband. When she sarcastically calls him a respectful nephew, he slaps her. "You're beating me too?" she says. "Revive the old man and you can both beat me!"

Tianbai—who, it is clear by now, despises both his parents—is declared Jinshan's sole heir by the village elders. There is gossip by now about the adulterous relationship, and the elders rule that Tianqing move out of the house and that Ju Dou be forbidden to remarry. The disgraced Ju Dou and Tianqing stand apart from the villagers during the funeral procession (whether this is because of their infidelity or traditional is not clear), though both of them make public displays of grief and even lie under the coffin as it's being carried. Tianbai sits on top of it.

Seven or eight years pass. Tianqing visits Ju Dou and Tianbai with gifts for both of them, but the boy refuses to speak to him and rejects the gift. Ju Dou still wants to tell Tianbai that Tianqing is his father, and after Tianbai overhears some of the male villagers gossiping about Ju Dou and Tianqing, he rushes after one of them with a meat cleaver. Finally giving up the chase, but having bloodied his own hand with the cleaver, he returns to the dye factory, beats up Tianqing, and proceeds to wreck part of the factory. Ju Dou tells Tianbai that Tianqing is his father, but he only responds by locking him out of the factory.

Ju Dou and Tianqing meet again and go down to a cavelike cellar to make love; the lack of air in the chamber means they will eventually suffocate, and they implicitly agree to a suicide pact. But Tianbai appears in the cellar, rescues Ju Dou, and murders Tianqing in the same vat of red dye in which Jinshan drowned. Grief stricken, Ju Dou takes a torch and burns the factory to the ground.

∎

Perhaps the most curious aspect of JU DOU, at least to a Western viewer, is the fact that all of the major adult characters are depicted realistically and Tianbai is not. When I asked a Chinese acquaintance about this after seeing the film for the first time, at the Toronto film festival last fall, he replied that the film was essentially about the inability of China to break away fully from its feudal past, and that Tianbai was the embodiment of this feudalism.

I've given such a detailed synopsis to establish the links of the major characters with the village, which most American reviewers I've read—as well as the synopsis provided by the distributor—have overlooked. Without this context, the comparison with THE POSTMAN ALWAYS RINGS TWICE might seem at least halfway viable; with it, such a comparison no longer seems relevant. Feudalism is a key concept in the history of China, but in an American context it has virtually no meaning at all. When Zhang Yimou remarks that Ju Dou's relative slowness to rebel against her condition, as well as Tianqing's sense of abasement and fidelity toward his uncle, "is the result of thousands of years of Confucian education" and a "lack of confidence in relation to one's ego," he's alluding to a history and a social meaning that simply can't be translated into American equivalents. Jinshan's feudal ownership of Ju Dou and Tianqing and the dye factory, which is eventually inherited by his legal son, is accorded a social sanction that effectively makes any escape impossible. Even the fact that Tianbai is responsible for Jinshan's death can't break the chain of tradition that winds up crippling everyone, including Tianbai; his social and historical birthright ultimately overrides even his biological birthright, and the passion that produces him ultimately consumes him. The accidental death of his false father leads inexorably to the murder of his real father, just as Jinshan's attempt to destroy the factory by fire is ultimately fulfilled by Ju Dou, the character who hates him and what he stands for the most.

The first film I ever saw from the People's Republic of China was Li Wen-Hua's BREAKING WITH OLD IDEAS (1975), a film about the building of a college for rural workers, made during the last years of the Cultural Revolution. It can be rented on video here, but to the best of my knowledge it is no longer being shown in China. Indefatigably cheerful about creating a new social order that integrally involves the peasants, strictly realistic in style, and both frontal and symmetrical in framing, this film seems a world apart from the "fifth generation" films from China that emerged in the 80s—films such as Tian Zhuangzhuang's THE HORSE THIEF, Huang Jianxin's THE BLACK CANNON INCIDENT, Zhang Junzhao's ONE AND EIGHT, Wu Tianming's OLD WELL, Chen Kaige's YELLOW EARTH, and Zhang Yimou's first feature, RED SORGHUM.

The directors of these films were in their teens during the Cultural Revolution, and when they enrolled in the Beijing Film Academy—the only film school in China—they were all adults with a decade of postrevolutionary experience behind them. They were also the first contemporary generation of Chinese filmmakers exposed to Western films, and the films they directed show traces of this exposure in a way that BREAKING WITH OLD IDEAS clearly doesn't. They remain our major pipeline into contemporary Chinese cinema, but it's important to bear in mind that some of their best-known films in the West are not necessarily well known in China. (THE HORSE THIEF, for example, got very limited domestic exposure; JU DOU has had no mass exposure at all and has been seen only at a few private screenings and on unofficially circulated video copies.)

The Western influences on these films shouldn't mislead us into taking these films as would-be Western artifacts. It's even questionable whether the Western practice (and auteurist implication) of assigning a possessive credit to directors, which I've followed here, is fully appropriate; none of these directors is credited with his own script, for instance. Zhang Yimou may well be the most versatile member of the group—he was the cinematographer on ONE AND EIGHT, YELLOW EARTH, and OLD WELL, in which he also acted—but on JU DOU he is credited with a codirector, Yang Fengliang, and the script of the film, though it was apparently written under Zhang's supervision, is by Liu Heng, the author of the contemporary novella *Fu-Xi, Fu-Xi,* which JU DOU is based on. Moreover, from the little that I know about the novella, the film is far from a simple, straightforward adaptation. The action of *Fu-Xi, Fu-Xi* takes place between the 20s and the 70s (according to Zhang, keeping all of the film's action in the 20s made it easier to get the script approved), and the adulterous couple in the original are a brother and sister.

Some commentators have suggested that JU DOU is being suppressed in China because of its erotic content, and I must admit that the film is more sexually explicit than any other films from the People's Republic I've seen. But its pessimism about the feudal past may be an even more relevant factor. The film—which was financed by the Japanese production company Tokuma and used Japanese equipment, but was made with an all-Chinese crew—went into preproduction before the Tiananmen Square crackdown. When the crew was reorganized two months later, the budget had been reduced by a third. Certainly the government crackdown can be interpreted as a feudal throwback of sorts, so it seems possible that the story could be interpreted along similar lines: insofar as Tianbai represents "the return of the repressed," his brutality and lack of forgiveness can easily be associated with the Chinese government's punitive responses.

Visually stunning, with ravishing uses of color and beautifully modulated lap dissolves, JU DOU may not be the most formally striking Chinese film I've seen—I still prefer THE HORSE THIEF,* which I'm happy to say has recently become available on video—but it certainly is the most effective and dramatic in terms of commercial moviemaking, both as spectacle and as storytelling. The film is organized around recurrences and rhyme schemes involving both colors (of fabrics and dye vats) and architecture (with the wooden steps lead-

---

*See my detailed review in *Foreign Affairs,* edited by Kathy Schulz Huffhines (San Francisco: Mercury House, 1991), 369–373.

ing from the factory up to Jinshan's bedchamber serving as a pivotal site). The buildings used date back to the Ming dynasty (1368–1644), and probably for this reason suggest the feudal period even more than the characters and village customs do. A passionate tragedy with a contemporary social message, JU DOU can only be understood if we step beyond the confines of our own historical context and think about a culture where even the contemporary spans centuries.

—Chicago *Reader,* April 19, 1991

Next month Akira Kurosawa will celebrate his 82nd birthday. Having long outlived Kenji Mizoguchi, who died in 1956, and Yasujiro Ozu, who died in 1963, he continues to work in an era that clearly seems remote and alien to him, though his films of the 80s and early 90s have enjoyed much more international currency than those of any of his Japanese near-contemporaries.

I've been somewhat slow to appreciate the mastery of Kurosawa in relation to the works of Mizoguchi and Ozu, perhaps in part because I started off on the wrong foot. The first Kurosawa film I ever saw was RASHOMON (1950), the single movie that was most responsible for introducing the Western world to the Japanese cinema. As it happens, I saw it as a teenager after reading the two short stories by Ryunosuke Akutagawa that it was based on. The more important of these stories, "In a Grove," offers seven conflicting testimonies about a single incident involving rape and murder. Kurosawa's film incorporates four of these testimonies, but frames them in a manner that radically undermines their original implications. Akutagawa's story offers no conclusion, and because none of the testimonies is given precedence, the radical implication of the story—irrational by any conventional standard—is that all of the testimonies are truthful. Kurosawa's much softer and sentimental conclusion, which is made clear in his framing story, is that everybody lies.

My irritation with this change has tended to bias me ever since against the sentimentality of much of Kurosawa's work. It might be argued that, apart from RASHOMON and THE SEVEN SAMURAI, most of this sentimentality is in his films with contemporary settings; his period films, which are much more action oriented, tend to be purer in intent. But if even Kurosawa's greatest contemporary works, such as IKIRU and HIGH AND LOW, have their saccharine elements, it might also be argued that his greatest period film, THRONE OF BLOOD, manages to avoid sentimentality only by running the risk of ruling out humanist emotion altogether.

Given the awesome size of Kurosawa's achievement over half a century, I fully admit that this bias is more than a little churlish. Indeed, now that his latest feature, RHAPSODY IN AUGUST, is being castigated across the globe for its sentimentality and irrelevance, it seems like a good time to come to Kurosawa's defense—especially since I find this film more affecting and accomplished than any of his movies since KAGEMUSHA (1980).

As Kurosawa's last film, DREAMS, made clear, he's more than a little horrified by the modern world—a sentiment I happen to share. He places all of his trust in the elderly and in children, while chiding the adults in between—a sentiment I can readily understand but am somewhat more skeptical about, if only because it smacks of expedient simplification. This sentiment lies at the heart of RHAPSODY IN AUGUST, and the movie would be inconceivable without it. But I don't believe that the value of the film, which is tied in part to its transgressiveness, can be reduced to this premise. We recently commemorated the 50th anniversary of the Japanese attack on Pearl Harbor. Kurosawa's film commemorates the atomic bomb dropped on Nagasaki four years before the 50th anniversary of *that* event. It seems to me that the discomfort many people have felt watching this movie has much more to do with the bombing than with the film's partiality toward the old and the young.

■

Before getting to the particulars of RHAPSODY IN AUGUST, it seems worth pointing out that this isn't Kurosawa's first film about the atomic bomb. I haven't seen the other one, I LIVE IN FEAR (also known as RECORD OF A LIVING BEING), which was made in 1955, ten years after the atomic bombs were dropped on Hiroshima and Nagasaki. One reason I haven't is that it's probably the biggest commercial and critical flop in Kurosawa's career to date (though some notable critics, including Georges Sadoul and Noël Burch, have argued strongly on its behalf).* The plot features Toshiro Mifune as a seventy-year-old who is so shaken by information about radioactive fallout (after the Bikini test explosions) and the possibility of further nuclear holocausts that he wants

---

* Having just caught up with the film [December 1995], I find it a troubling commentary on the Japanese family and state (and the relation between the two) and the everyday truces made by both in relation to the intolerable—clearly one of Kurosawa's most provocative features.

to force his entire family to emigrate to Brazil. Declared incompetent by members of his family who bring him to court, he winds up confined to a mental hospital.

It seems significant that the cool international reception accorded to I LIVE IN FEAR has been virtually duplicated with RHAPSODY IN AUGUST. (Faces were made every time I mentioned the film to Asian critics in Taiwan late last year.) Clearly less satirical or ironic in intent than the earlier film, RHAPSODY IN AUGUST, based on Kiyoko Murata's novel *Nabe-No-Naka*, centers on Kane (Sachiko Murase), an elderly woman who survived the Nagasaki explosion and still lives in the nearby countryside. While her son Tadao (Hisashi Igawa) and his wife are off in Hawaii for most of the summer visiting his uncle, a very successful pineapple grower who's now dying, her four grandchildren are staying with her in the country, trying to persuade her to visit her brother herself and take them along. ("Going from Nagasaki to Hawaii is the same as going from Nagasaki to Tokyo," one of them argues.) She eventually agrees, and writes to the Hawaiian relatives that she will come, but only after she attends a memorial service for her husband, who was killed by the bomb. After visiting the schoolyard where their grandfather died, now a small memorial, the grandchildren begin to learn more about the past, beginning with the names of Kane's many other siblings. They visit places in the countryside associated with them (and with the nuclear explosion), such as a cedar grove in the mountains and a waterfall basin.

Then the children's parents arrive. Tadeo speaks about the jobs being offered by Clark (Richard Gere), the Japanese-American son of Kane's dying brother. Tadao also admits that he never told the Hawaiian relatives that his father was killed by the bomb. Kane is offended by his and his wife's mercenary interests, and the grandchildren are equally offended by their parents' cynical decision to conceal how Kane's husband died.

Kane has already spilled the beans about her husband in her letter to Hawaii, and Clark, deeply moved by the news and eager to learn more, soon arrives to visit. After attending the memorial ceremony commemorating the death of his uncle and other victims of the Nagasaki holocaust, he receives word that his own father has died and takes the next plane back to Hawaii. The family plans to follow him, but Kane, grief stricken by her failure to see her brother before he died, begins to reexperience the past. (As one of the grandchildren puts it, "The clock in her head is running backwards.") Waking during a thunderstorm, she rushes out of the house into the rain, believing that the bomb is falling, and in slow motion the members of her family chase after her, never catching up.

■

At no point in RHAPSODY IN AUGUST is any historical or political explanation for the Nagasaki explosion offered, much less refuted, apart from "war." It's been argued that this omission coincides with the gaping omissions in school textbooks in Japan—deletions that I suspect are worse but not radically different from those found in U.S. textbooks. But I think it can also be argued that historical finger-pointing about the bomb is irrelevant to Kurosawa's purposes. When the grandchildren visit monuments to the Nagasaki holocaust contributed by countries from all over the world, and we're presented with a montage of these monuments, each one identified by country to strains of Vivaldi, one of the kids remarks, "I don't see one from America," and is simply told, "America dropped the bomb." This isn't finger-pointing but simple factual information. It might be added that, if anything, the mythical treatment accorded to Richard Gere in the film when he turns up speaking Japanese—presented as if he were a visiting prince, though Gere, bearable for once, plays the part with some humility—makes it perfectly clear that American-bashing isn't even remotely part of Kurosawa's agenda. It would be more accurate to say that his emotional loyalties are exclusively with the perceptions of Kane and her grandchildren, and with Clark insofar as he shares them—perceptions that war itself is a crime committed by rulers and sustained by conformist adults (represented here by the parents) against "the people," without reference to nationality or politics.

What might be regarded as the narrowness or naïveté of Kurosawa's vision of the bomb's meaning is actually a passionate form of commitment to the people who experienced it directly and those whose still-uncorrupted innocence allows them to discover the truth of that experience in strictly personal terms. This is far from being a fashionable way of approaching the subject, but it is equally far from espousing the nationalistic or other ideological alibis that might serve to "explain" the bomb while ignoring or dismissing those personal experiences.

In fact, the major stylistic influence in evidence in RHAPSODY IN AUGUST is late John Ford, DONOVAN'S REEF in particular. This relationship can be seen and felt in many particulars: in the rapport and complicity between the very old and the very young, in the mythical treatment of Hawaii as a utopia (particularly as a site of cross-cultural synthesis and intermarriage), in one of the grandchildren's comments about Clark ("He's as tall as John Wayne!"), in the pastoral celebrations of nature, and even in the eventual repair of an old-time organ to accompany a festive communal singalong (in DONOVAN'S REEF, something similar happens with a broken slot machine). It could be claimed, for that matter, that the regal treatment accorded to Clark/Gere in the movie isn't merely a matter of kowtowing to a Hollywood star, but a function of seeing this character as an emissary from utopia because he's a Japanese-American raised in Hawaii.

The film's poetry isn't merely a matter of this overall pastoral ambience, some of which could also be found in DREAMS; it's also one of illustration and inflection, visible in both the framing and the editing. We learn that one of

Kane's long-dead brothers, who lost all his hair after the bomb fell, spent most of his time afterward drawing eyes; one of the grandchildren draws a similar eye on a blackboard, and Kurosawa briefly and effectively cuts back to this eye at later points. When Kane recalls the flash of the explosion itself as a giant eye, the film promptly illustrates this surreal vision—a gigantic eye opening between the sky and the mountains. And when two of the grandchildren return home one day from the cedar grove, they learn that an old lady, another survivor of the explosion, is visiting Kane without either of the old women saying a word; beautifully violating a standard rule of editing, the film cuts directly from a shot of the two framed through an open window to a closer shot from the same angle inside the room, with the women situated at opposite ends of the frame.

Some narrative details are homey and touching: the grandchildren complain to Kane about her cooking, saying she makes the food too soft because it's easier for her to eat with her dentures; later, after an older sister takes over the cooking, Kane turns up to serve the children slices of watermelon. Other details are mysterious and beautiful: Kane and her grandchildren seated on a bench watching the moon; an entire sequence during the memorial service in which Clark and one of the boys observe in wonder a parade of ants.

"It's the forbidden, forgotten image, the vision of the conquered that Akira Kurosawa offers us, which television—the Gulf war proves it again—is incapable of producing." Writing in *Cahiers du cinéma* last May, Frédéric Sabouraud put his finger on the moral choice exercised by Kurosawa in dealing with the impossible subject of nuclear holocaust. What Kurosawa seems to be saying in his final, powerful images is that no matter how much we care and how fast we run, we still can't catch up with the truth of those who actually experienced the atomic bomb in Nagasaki.

—Chicago *Reader*, February 21, 1992

Let's start with three central and related facts, the first about Taiwan, the second about Taiwanese cinema, and the third about us.

(1) Until six years ago, Taiwan spent this whole century under martial law, and over three previous centuries it suffered from nearly continuous occupation—by the Dutch in the seventeenth century and the Manchus in the seventeenth, eighteenth, and nineteenth centuries. In 1895 it was ceded to Japan as one of the spoils of the Sino-Japanese War, and it remained a Japanese colony for the next half century, until the Japanese surrender at the end of World War II. At this point mainland China took control; but four years later, when the communists seized the mainland, the deposed Kuomintang, led by Chang Kai-shek, shifted their base to Taiwan—claiming that their rule was only temporary, until they could wrest the mainland back from the communists. But as it turned out they remained in power until 1987, when Taiwan finally became a democracy. Economically flourishing today, with a population of over twenty million, Taiwan is a country with a very strong sense of the future but, as a result of its fractured history, a confused and fragmented sense of its past.

(2) Until four years ago, every Taiwanese movie without exception had postsynchronized Mandarin dialogue. (It's cheaper to shoot without sound, and this standard practice makes it easier to dub Taiwanese pictures into

Cantonese and other regional Chinese dialects; for the same reason, virtually all Taiwanese films are subtitled in Chinese so that the dialects won't restrict understanding by other regions.) But director Hou Hsiao-hsien eliminated this practice in CITY OF SADNESS because he wanted to preserve the idiosyncratic delivery and Taiwanese dialect of one of the actors, Li Tien-lu, an eighty-year-old puppet master and former stage performer who had already played the parts of grandfathers in two of Hou's features, DUST IN THE WIND (1986) and DAUGHTER OF THE NILE (1987). Although Taiwanese accents had previously been heard in Taiwanese films, critic Ted Shen informs me that they were mainly used for comic purposes (as southern accents sometimes are in American films). But Hou employed the regional accent of Hualien, the city in southern Taiwan where he grew up, straightforwardly in his autobiographical A TIME TO LIVE AND A TIME TO DIE (1985). Thus he has not only introduced the realism of direct sound recording to Taiwanese cinema but also made Taiwanese accents more prominent and important in Taiwanese filmmaking.

(3) No film by Hou Hsiao-hsien, the greatest of all Taiwanese filmmakers, has ever had a U.S. distributor.

■

Talking about Hou Hsiao-hsien's films isn't easy in a country as cheerfully indifferent to the rest of the world as ours—a country so shamelessly ethnocentric that the worst, most compromised, and least interesting film of John Woo gets fifty times more press coverage than his others simply because it was made here and not in Hong Kong, and a country so juvenile that a director like Woo, who makes fantasies for eleven-year-old boys about masses of people getting sprayed with bullets, receives fifty times more attention, even in publications for grown-ups, than a director like Hou, who makes realistic movies for grown-ups about the way people live. (It may also be relevant that the United States hasn't recognized Taiwan diplomatically since 1979, when it began recognizing mainland China; according to the existing diplomatic rules, it can't recognize both.)

I can't count myself entirely blameless in this process of neglect. The last time the Film Center's Barbara Scharres brought a new Hou film to town was in June 1990, when CITY OF SADNESS was shown twice. It's probably Hou's most difficult film, and though I made it a Critic's Choice the week it was shown and the number-two movie on my ten-best list that year (after Jane Campion's SWEETIE), I was too intimidated by it and too fearful of misdescribing it to write about it at any length.

In some ways I like Hou's remarkable and exquisitely beautiful THE PUPPET MASTER, about the life of Li Tien-lu, even more—certainly more than Campion's immensely popular THE PIANO, an exciting and beautiful enough fantasy in its own right. A philosophical look at identity and the nature of freedom, it comprises the second part of a projected trilogy by Hou called

"The Three Tragedies," about Taiwan in the twentieth century, and covers thirty-six years, from the birth of Li Tien-lu in 1909, fourteen years after the Japanese takeover, to the end of World War II. CITY OF SADNESS, the first part completed, covers the four years between the end of World War II and the retreat of the Kuomintang to Taiwan in 1949, when Taipei was declared the "temporary" capital of the Republic of China. Still to be made is A MAN NAMED PUTAO TAILANG,* which will cover forty-some additional more years of Taiwanese history, from the 50s to the present.

■

It has often been said that American identity is something of an existential problem because of our melting-pot origins; and being American often means not only reflecting your origins but also, to a great extent, *not* reflecting your origins. But as a country with an existential identity crisis, Taiwan has ours beat in spades.

Significantly, all the statements I have read by Hou about this film relate to Chinese identity, not Taiwanese identity. (Example: "THE PUPPET MASTER perhaps represents the Chinese people's attitude towards life. It is in fact Li Tien-lu's attitude towards life, and it is also mine.") If you write a letter to someone in Taiwan, you address it "Taiwan, Republic of China." And even if you manage to separate Taiwanese art and culture from Chinese art and culture (no easy matter), it's still necessary to address the influence of Japanese art and culture: the streets of Taipei are full of examples of Japanese architecture, and the older residents of the island, like Li Tien-lu, still speak Japanese as well as Chinese.

The degree to which Chinese and Japanese forces and influences affect what "Taiwanese" means on every level, at every moment, is only one of the film's thematic strands, but it's a central one. That concern also relates to the meaning and importance of Taiwanese accents, especially in light of the fact that, after 1949, the Kuomintang outlawed Taiwanese dialects in such institutional settings as schools and the government. By the same token, Taiwanese history is a relatively new subject—prior to 1987, it was effectively a forbidden subject—and Hou's ambitious undertaking to uncover, even create that history has the force of a psychic necessity: "If you don't understand your home," he has said, "you can't love it."

■

Much as Taiwanese language, culture, and history have been outlawed in the past, the art of Li Tien-lu was subject to repression, coercion, and alteration. In 1937, when another Sino-Japanese war broke out and the Japanese banned

---

* Completed in 1995, this wound up being called GOOD MEN, GOOD WOMEN, and proved to be entirely worthy of its predecessors, though also undistributed in the United States.

all performances of traditional Chinese theater, he found work as a traveling actor; four years later he was obliged to join the Japanese Puppet Propaganda Group. (One of the most fascinating puppet performances in the film is wartime agitprop, complete with villainous American and English soldiers.) As in FAREWELL MY CONCUBINE, the way political upheavals shape, and often limit, individual destinies is clearly important. Yet here this is not simply a message to be delivered, as it sometimes is in Chen Kaige's relatively bombastic epic, but rather a zone of thought Hou enters, contemplates, queries, tests, and endlessly explores.

This inquiry may have had some bearing on the film's title. As a puppet master who learned his craft from his father, began working as a stage assistant at nine, and gave his first puppet performance at fourteen, Li figures in some ways as an artist-god; yet in other respects he's often a puppet himself— a fact that his own narration clearly acknowledges. Another part of this inquiry has to do with the relation between the family and the state, but no sooner is this question broached in THE PUPPET MASTER than it becomes vexing, almost impenetrable: given the history of Taiwan and the ambiguities of Taiwanese identity, one can only ask, What is a Taiwanese family, then or now? And what is—or could be—a Taiwanese state?

■

Eschewing close-ups, THE PUPPET MASTER consists exclusively of medium and long shots—most of them extended takes from fixed camera positions— and adopts three forms of storytelling: re-creating scenes from the childhood, adolescence, and early adult life of Li Tien-lu, with Li himself occasionally narrating the events offscreen; showing Li today in many of the same locations, recounting his past directly to the camera; and showing us extended scenes from the kinds of theater in which Li worked, both as puppet master and as live performer in Chinese opera and vaudeville.

The most immediately accessible parts of the film are usually the shots showing Li himself—largely because he talks about his past with enormous charm and directness, but also because he nearly always appears at a particular location shortly after it has been introduced dramatically. The sudden switch of gears between "fictional" and "nonfictional," and between past and present, with Li meanwhile shifting from offscreen to on-screen narration, is usually accompanied by some narrative clarification that provides an illuminating change in our perspective. The only rough parallel I can think of in Hollywood filmmaking is the use of real-life "witnesses" in Warren Beatty's REDS; but here it's as if John Reed himself, not people remembering him, suddenly appeared on-screen.

Emotions are rarely absent from these scenes with Li, though they're sometimes delayed because his exposition reveals the story gradually. A characteristic example occurs quite late in the film and involves the death of Li's youngest son, when he and his family were living in a "coffin shop" in a small village to which they'd been evacuated. We move from a shot of Li's wife crying in her bedroom (we don't know why) to a long take in which we hear and observe from a distance some hammering in a courtyard, accompanied by Li's offscreen narration; only after we cut to Li in the same setting, continuing to talk, do we learn of his son's death, its tragic circumstances, and the fact that Li had to nail the coffin together himself—which suddenly accounts for the hammering we've been hearing and seeing.

By contrast, the long stretches of theater and puppet theater performance are usually more abstract and intellectual in effect, in part because we can't always understand the action. But the performances themselves are invariably mesmerizing and beautiful. I especially love the rapid waving of a blue and white flag during puppet performances to signify a lake or a river.

■

Understandably, given the film's endlessly searching questions about freedom and identity, Hou's choices in this elliptical narrative are often both unexpected and telling. As Godfrey Cheshire points out in an extended article about Hou in the November–December [1993] *Film Comment,* we see much more and learn much more of Lei-tzu, a prostitute Li becomes involved with during the war, than we do of his wife.

What we learn about Lei-tzu is also highly selective: one of Li's lengthiest on-screen narratives—describing his first impressions of Lei-tzu when he was an opera performer doubling as an usher—focuses on the expensive cigarettes she was smoking when she entered the theater, one of which she offered to him, in a package decorated with storks. (Later we observe her elaborate method of offering him cigarettes and then lighting them in the brothel where she works, shown as a special kind of love play.) Images also play an important role when Lei-tzu gets some professional photographs taken of herself, and Li (Lin Chung) examines them all, tearing them up one by one until he arrives at the one he likes, which he kisses. Li's feelings for Lei-tzu seem to follow from his capacity to make free choices about her: deciding to follow her when she leaves the Happy Show Theater, deciding which photograph of her he prefers.

The question of Li's sexual fidelity to Lei-tzu—which she tests when she pretends to go see her sick grandmother and has another prostitute offer to sleep with him while she's "away"—is never matched by any discussion of his fidelity to his wife. Similarly, we get a detailed account from Li about how he cured a serious lip sore Lei-tzu had, using a grotesque folk remedy involving frogs, but hardly a word about the fate of his wife when she contracted malaria in the coffin shop.

I suspect that Hou's emphasis on Li's relationship with Lei-tzu comes from the complex weave of choices Li made and obligations he undertook during childhood and adolescence, including an arranged marriage. As the film shows, his mother died of TB when he was only eight (about the time World War I ended), and his father remarried a former prostitute the following year; it was mainly the stepmother's bullying that drove Li to puppetry, though the payment for his performances went to his father. Much later, when his grandmother couldn't get along with his stepmother, he was allowed for the first time to keep the money he made in exchange for housing and taking care of his grandmother—though his duty to her was compromised when a Japanese police chief required him to perform on the emperor's birthday and she died during his absence.

■

Just as the theaters in which Li worked were Chinese and Japanese, Hou clearly draws on the artistic traditions of both these cultures. Because Li did much of his work in remote mountain areas, THE PUPPET MASTER is the first Hou film I've seen in which landscapes, as opposed to exterior settings, play a substantial role. Traditional Chinese landscape paintings from at least the sixth century onward appear to have exerted a strong influence (though one extraordinarily lit, astonishingly beautiful shot of the sea and clouds suggests Turner), particularly in the minuscule role the human presence has in these towering vistas: one often has to examine the compositions closely before people, roads, paths, and buildings become visible at all. In storytelling terms, some of these shots are confusing because we can't always tell precisely what the characters are doing. But on a broader level this is surely the point: the specific activities of a few individuals are trifling next to the larger, more enduring shapes and formations.

In terms of cinematic influences, Hou has most often been linked to Yasujiro Ozu, despite the fact that he developed his long-take, stationary-camera style long before he saw his first Ozu picture. In the case of THE PUPPET MASTER, I think almost as apt a comparison can be made with another Japanese master, Kenji Mizoguchi—at least if one overlooks Mizoguchi's camera movements and concentrates on his repetition of the same basic camera angles in the same settings in scenes separated by many years, a formal device that figures powerfully in his TALE OF THE LATE CHRYSANTHEMUMS (1939). In one of the earliest scenes in THE PUPPET MASTER we see Li as a boy being beaten by his mother for stealing calligraphy manuals: he kneels on the floor, then briefly moves out of the frame in an effort to escape her blows; the scene is shot through a doorway at the right, and a wall or room divider fills most of the left side of the screen. (The relative darkness caused by natural lighting here and elsewhere, as well as the camera's distance from the action, makes the details as indistinct as they are in some of the landscape shots—though I hasten to add that nothing essential is ever kept from our attention.) On later occasions and in other circumstances Hou returns to the same camera angle, and each time there's a kind of emotional rhyme, a sense in which our memory of the first scene complicates and inflects whatever's happening. Thus part of Hou's art is compositional and pictorial—an invitation to look long and hard at certain carefully selected, exquisitely framed scenes and settings—and another part is temporal and musical, an invitation to recall, compare, and synthesize shots widely separated in time.

■

An anecdotal aside: In the early 80s Li Tien-lu toured Arkansas, and at the invitation of its governor performed at the state capital's fine arts museum. He met Bill Clinton afterward for dinner, and as a token of good luck presented him with a puppet of Sun Wukong, the monkey king from the classic Chinese novel *Journey to the West*. Roughly a decade later Clinton was elected president during the Chinese Year of the Monkey.

■

Even if Hou's films eventually acquire a U.S. distributor, I don't expect them to achieve the kind of audiences, attention, and acclaim accorded to the pictures of John Woo—or those of Jane Campion, for that matter. They don't serve their meanings up to you on a platter, and they're too philosophical to ram you in the gut the way most movies (and their publicity campaigns) are currently expected to. But if a more awesome and affecting new picture than THE PUPPET MASTER has turned up in Chicago this year—a movie more relevant to the future of cinema and the twenty-first century—I haven't seen it.

—Chicago *Reader,* December 3, 1993

Inner Space (Tarkovsky's SOLARIS)

> We take off into the cosmos, ready for anything: for
> solitude, for hardship, for exhaustion, death. Modesty
> forbids us to say so, but there are times when we think
> pretty well of ourselves. And yet, if we examine it more
> closely, our enthusiasm turns out to be all sham. We don't
> want to conquer the cosmos, we simply want to extend
> the boundaries of Earth to the frontiers of the cosmos.
> For us, such and such a planet is as arid as the Sahara,
> another as frozen as the North Pole, yet another as lush
> as the Amazon basin. We are humanitarian and
> chivalrous; we don't want to enslave other races, we
> simply want to bequeath them our values and take over
> their heritage in exchange. We think of ourselves as the
> Knights of the Holy Contact. This is another lie. We are
> only seeking Man. We have no need of other worlds. We
> need mirrors. We don't know what to do with other
> worlds. A single world, our own, suffices us;
> but we can't accept it for what it is.
>
> —*scientist in Stanislaw Lem's* Solaris *(1961)*

It's taken nearly two decades for SOLARIS (1972), Andrei Tarkovosky's mind-boggling Soviet "reply" to 2001: A SPACE ODYSSEY, to open in this country in its original form; but whatever doubts one might have about this beautiful film, I don't think that anyone could accuse it of being dated. Speculative technology plays such a minimal role in Tarkovsky's cosmology that state-of-the-art hardware is virtually irrelevant to his vision. (One quaint example of the former is the videotapes employed in the film; they all have the shape and size of audiocassettes, but the images they project are in black and white and in 'Scope, and the video screens are correspondingly rectangular.) A handsome wide-screen spectacle set in a remote galaxy, the movie expresses plenty of awe and terror about imponderables, but what's fundamentally at issue is the state of man's soul, not the physical state of the universe.

Having seen SOLARIS four times over the past eighteen years, but only in its complete, 167-minute form, I can't detail the differences between this version and its mutilated predecessors that have been circulating in the United States since 1976. I know that the original U.S. distributor hacked away thirty-five minutes without consulting Tarkovsky and that subsequent prints making the repertory theater rounds—partially dubbed and partially subtitled, cobbled together out of separate versions—were even shorter. Given the film's difficulties in its complete subtitled version, I have no doubt that SOLARIS in its truncated forms must have been pretty incomprehensible.

Based on a Polish science fiction novel of the same title by Stanislaw Lem, Tarkovsky's provocative head-scratcher can't really be "explained" to anyone's satisfaction by using the original source material as guide. A staunch nonbeliever in film genres ("I do not believe that the cinema has genres—the cinema is *itself* a genre," he noted in a 1981 interview), Tarkovsky ironically regarded SOLARIS as the least successful of his films for probably the same reason that most people want to see it—because of its associations with science fiction. "Unfortunately the science fiction element in SOLARIS was too prominent and became a distraction," he wrote in his fascinating (if maddening) book *Sculpting in Time.* "The rockets and space stations—required by Lem's novel—were interesting to construct; but it seems to me now that the idea of the film would have stood out more vividly and boldly had we managed to dispense with these things altogether."

■

Although portions of Tarkovsky's film defy synopsis, it is certainly possible to describe the main outlines of the plot, such as it is, with a minimal amount of surmise to fill in the gaps.

The film opens at the idyllic, rural childhood home of Kris Kelvin (Donatas Banionis), a psychologist, who is back to visit his aging father and the latter's second wife before leaving on a space mission. He arrives with his little girl, who will apparently stay in the country during his absence, and there is a hint that Kevin is hoping to resolve a conflict of some sort with his father before he leaves—a hope that is unfulfilled. There have been unexplained occurrences on the planet Solaris, where a permanently orbiting space station was established many decades ago; Kelvin has been asked to travel there alone to investigate, with the idea of closing down the space station after subjecting the planet's oceanic surface to a final, exploratory burst of radiation.

Before Kelvin leaves, he is visited by Burton (Vladislav Dvorzhetsky), one of the original Solaris crew members, who arrives with his little boy. Burton had been sent to explore the planet's misty, swirling surface some twenty years before in search of Fechner, an astronaut who disappeared and was never found. With Burton, his father, and his stepmother, Kelvin watches a videotape of Burton's report on the mission to a scientific committee in which he describes sighting a thirteen-foot-high naked male child in a garden on the planet's surface. At this point in the report, Burton shows his own film of what he saw; all that is visible is cloud formations, and the committee dismisses his account as a hallucination brought about by strain. After the visit, however, on his way back to the city with his son, Burton calls back to the country house on a videophone to report that twenty years ago, following the committee meeting, he went to visit Fechner's family: Fechner's son, whom he saw for the first time, was the spitting image of the child he had glimpsed on Solaris.

When Kelvin arrives at the ramshackle Solaris space station, he finds it nearly deserted. The two remaining scientists, Snouth (Yuri Jarvet) and Sartorius (Anatoly Solonitsin), mainly stay cooped up in their laboratories and are unresponsive to most of Kelvin's questions; a third scientist, Gibarian (Sos Sarkissian), has committed suicide and left behind an enigmatic videotape addressed to Kelvin, which Kelvin plays back. (Much of this portion of the film seems steeped in a haunted house atmosphere: the squeaks and other offscreen sounds and barely perceptible movements at the edges of the frame, along with the slow and suspenseful camera movements, all conjure up a sense of the uncanny without spelling it out.)

Eventually Kelvin discovers that the amorphous surface of Solaris is a living entity, but not one that communicates directly. Rather, it materializes human figures drawn from the guilt-ridden memories and fantasies of the astronauts on the space station, so that each of them is literally accompanied by his own demon—a process that began after the astronauts first exposed the planet's surface to radiation. The various demons are glimpsed so elliptically that we know next to nothing about them: Sartorius is accompanied in his own lab by a male dwarf in pajamas; Gibarian on his videotape is seen briefly with a little girl (who is occasionally seen wandering about the space station, although Gibarian's corpse is now in cold storage); Snouth's demon appears at times to be an adult figure, although we perceive this figure so obliquely that we can't even be sure of that.

Kelvin's own demon appears in his cabin while he sleeps. We see a great deal of her; it is his dead wife, Hari (Natalya Bondarchuk), who committed suicide on Earth after the failure of their marriage. Initially he is so horrified by her reappearance that he sends her off in a rocket, but she materializes before him again. Later she attempts suicide again by drinking liquid oxygen, but within moments she comes back to life in a series of spastic jerks. These and other resurrections of Hari occupy most of the remainder of the film. During this time, it becomes clear that her double is beginning to have an independent existence and feelings of her own, and Kelvin, who is now determined to remain on the space station indefinitely, struggles to make amends for his former lack of commitment to her. Finally, however, while he sleeps, she succeeds in destroying herself for Kelvin's sake, leaving behind a letter for him which she gives to Snouth.

Kelvin begins to think again about returning to Earth, and Snouth notes that islands are beginning to form on Solaris's oceanic surface. On one of these, we see Kelvin back beside the pond near his country house. Greeted by his dog, he approaches the house and peers through the window, making eye contact with his elderly father; rain is inexplicably falling inside the house, splattering books and teacups—a scene that clearly rhymes with a sudden rainfall outside the house in the film's opening sequence—and mist rises from his father as the water falls. Kelvin meets his father at the back door of the house, kneels at his feet, and embraces him. The camera cranes upward, higher and higher, until we see the house on an island in the middle of Solaris's vast ocean.

■

The fact that we see so much of Hari on the space station and so little of the demons associated with the other astronauts can probably be traced back to the fact that Lem's novel is a first-person narrative. In keeping with this subjective emphasis, the entire film focuses on Kelvin's conscience and consciousness, and the objective side of the plot—everything that might be said to constitute the ingredients of a science fiction adventure—gradually comes to seem like nothing but a pretext for telling Kelvin's individual story. In the final analysis, whether we interpret the final scene as a dream sequence is irrelevant; by this time the objective and subjective plots have become indistinguishable. The same ambiguity applies to certain previous sequences (omitted in my synopsis) in which the living room of Kelvin's country house merges with various parts of the space station to form an indissoluble whole.

Bearing this ambiguity in mind, one might argue that Tarkovsky's SOLARIS, unlike the Lem novel, qualifies more as anti-science fiction than as science fiction. In this respect it bears a certain resemblance to stories in Ray Bradbury's *The Martian Chronicles* in which explorers on Mars hallucinate scenes and characters from their long-lost childhoods. A less obvious yet equally pertinent comparison can be made between Tarkovsky's vision and a book I consider the greatest of all science fiction novels, Olaf Stapleton's *Star Maker* (1937)—a book that, significantly, has been cited with admiration by both Lem and Jorge Luis Borges, although it has never received much sustained attention in hardcore s-f circles.

A speculative account of the entire history and breadth of the cosmos, *Star Maker* has a canvas so vast that the two-billion-year span of mankind, the focus of Stapleton's previous *Last and First Men* (1930), figures here in the space of less than a paragraph—a mere drop in the bucket. The crucial paradox underlying the book's awesome sweep is that the entire plot is framed by the mundane marital discord experienced by the human narrator. A rustic Englishman leaves his home in the midst of a quarrel to stand on a nearby hillside and gaze at the stars; here he experiences the entire narrative of the book in the form of a vision, before returning to the modesty and mundaneness of his individual life and problems.

Just as important, Stapleton's modest and humdrum prose becomes the vehicle for his staggering sense of the cosmic. While the contradictory conceit of most science fiction writers trafficking in related subjects is that man can somehow think beyond the limitations of man's consciousness in imagining the cosmos, Stapleton's point of departure is precisely the reverse. Accepting the frailty and inadequacy of his vantage point at the outset, Stapleton proceeds to scale the heights like no other s-f writer before or since, precisely because he knows how to use his limitations as an integral part of his descriptive technique.

Stapleton had a pronounced influence on Arthur C. Clarke, as one can detect in both Clarke's novel *Childhood's End* and the Clarke/Stanley Kubrick film 2001: A SPACE ODYSSEY. But 2001, which utilizes its resources to imagine an intelligence greater than man's, ultimately loses sight of the everyday underpinnings essential to Stapleton's vision. Tarkovsky's view—which is ultimately a good deal more conservative and pessimistic than either Clarke's or Stapleton's—uses the everyday not as a springboard into the cosmic but as a sign of man's inability to attain such reaches.

The fact that the only universe man can truly explore exists inside his own head is a key to Stapleton's technique (which Clarke and Kubrick learned from), but not to his vision. In the case of Tarkovsky, it becomes the irreducible message. So it is perfectly logical that Tarkovsky came to regret the science fiction furnishings of SOLARIS, as provided by Lem, as a vehicle for his vision. We should note that Lem's novel is set exclusively on the space station; the action of the film is principally (if misleadingly) set there only so that Tarkovsky can ponder the significance of Kelvin's country house and family.

Consequently, in place of interstellar space travel, we get very slow pans past underwater plants swaying to drifting currents in the pond near this country house, and a lengthy hypnotic sequence that follows a car speeding along a freeway, through several long tunnels, and into a city as night falls. (The city is sufficiently anonymous that it could be almost anywhere—Los Angeles, Moscow, Tokyo, Berlin; no fully legible street signs are visible on the freeway.) Later, inside the space station the camera drifts endlessly across various details in a reproduction of Brueghel's *Hunters in the Snow* that is hanging, along with four other Brueghels, in a stateroom.

None of these meditative moments is motivated conventionally in narrative terms, although the first two are linked to narrative moments: Kris Kelvin brooding by the pond in which the underwater plants sway, and Burton returning from the country to the city with Kelvin's son in a driverless car. (The selective survey of the Brueghel painting is "placed" retrospectively by a shot that occurs at the end, from a home movie that apparently shows Kelvin as a child in the snow.) To say that these moments effectively "replace" interstellar travel in the film is to suggest that they provide poetic rather than narrative substitutes—moments of seemingly endless drift that temporarily suspend the film's narrative flow. All of these camera movements mystically imply a continuous movement toward revelation that never actually arrives at one—a kind of spiritual tease. As in STALKER—probably Tarkovsky's greatest film, another work adapted from a science fiction novel that uses the genre's come-on, the notion and the promise of infinity, only to frustrate this expectation with an insistence on man's finitude and the poverty of the human imagination—the external journey of the plot, which we see, proves to be secondary to the inner journey of the characters, which we don't see. Bits of electronic music figure effectively in Eduard Artemev's score, but the essential theme is Bach's F Minor Choral Prelude.

Another level of ambiguity is introduced by periodic shifts between color and black and white. As in most of the director's other features (apart from ANDREI ROUBLEV, which shifts to color only in its epilogue), few of these switches can be accounted for by any consistent thematic, formal, or atmospheric strategy. A joke used to circulate in Russia that Tarkovsky shifted from color to black and white whenever he ran out of money, and other Russian directors have, by their own admission, occasionally shifted to black and white in midfilm when they ran out of color stock. In the case of SOLARIS, some of these transitions occur in the *middle* of individual shots, which rules out any economic motivation. Whether the reasons behind them are conceptual or arbitrary, the shifts have the overall effect of intensifying the private and esoteric aspects of Tarkovsky's style—aspects that are clearly related to his spirituality.

■

To me, at least, the notion of spirituality in film art has always had something more than a little suspect about it. Filmmakers as diverse as Robert Bresson, Carl Dreyer, Leo McCarey, Kenji Mizoguchi, Yasujiro Ozu, Jean Renoir, Roberto Rossellini, and Michael Snow are frequently praised for their allegedly "transcendental" styles when it seems more appropriate to value them for qualities that suggest the opposites of spirituality and transcendence: the brute materiality of the worlds of Mizoguchi and Renoir, the physicality of McCarey and Ozu, the carnal sense of flesh in Bresson and Dreyer, the skepticism of Rossellini, the relentless mechanisms of Snow. If "pure" transcendence is what one is after, I'm afraid that even the more bogus spirituality of Disney, DeMille, and Spielberg may come closer to the mark.

I'm not trying to argue that a filmmaker's religious beliefs are irrelevant to his or her art. But it does seem to me that none of the best filmmakers requires religious beliefs in order to be understood or appreciated. Bresson's Jansenism may play some role in the selection and shaping of his plots, but divine providence is evident in neither the sounds nor the images of AU HASARD BALTHAZAR, and both LANCELOT DU LAC and L'ARGENT can easily be read as atheistic. Conversely, Dreyer's ORDET and Rossellini's VIAGGIO IN ITALIA (STRANGERS) may both conclude with religious miracles, but this doesn't mean that Dreyer or Rossellini necessarily believes in them *as* religious miracles; both filmmakers, in fact, have made statements that suggest the contrary (and Dreyer, as we now know from Maurice Drouzy's biography and other evidence, was not especially religious). John Huston's remarkably precise film adaptation of Flannery O'Connor's novel *Wise Blood* is the work of a believer "translated" by a nonbeliever, and there is nothing in the film that suggests any obvious sort of betrayal.

But when we come to a spiritual filmmaker like Tarkovsky, the question of acceptance or rejection becomes more complicated. I have to confess that, as a thinker about spiritual and holy matters, Tarkovsky often strikes me as pretentious, egocentric, and downright offensive; his sexual politics (especially in NOSTALGHIA and THE SACRIFICE) are Neanderthal, and his view of piety is generally neither attractive nor inspiring. Yet as a passionate, critical thinker about the world we live in, and as a poetic filmmaker whose images and sounds have the ring of truth, I find it impossible to dismiss him. Even when his films irritate or infuriate me, they teach me something in spite of my objections.

Several years ago, in *American Film,* J. Hoberman offered an intriguing three-way comparison of Tarkovsky, Stan Brakhage, and Hans-Jürgen Syberberg as conservative avant-gardists: "All are seers who see their art—and all of Art—as a quasi-religious calling; all three tend toward the solipsistic, invoking their parents, mates, and offspring as talismatic elements in their films. All three are natural surrealists, seemingly innocent of official surrealism's radical social program. All three privilege childhood innocence . . . and all three are militantly provincial. Tarkovsky is as hopelessly Russian as Syberberg is terminally German and Brakhage totally American."

Hoberman's comparison is instructive, but I'd like to suggest another parallel figure for consideration whose formal originality and problematic ideology are equally relevant: David Lynch. This is not to suggest that the ideologies of Lynch and Tarkovsky are in any way equivalent: if SOLARIS can be considered as a "humanistic" response to 2001, there is certainly nothing humanistic in the same way or to the same degree about ERASERHEAD, DUNE, BLUE VELVET, TWIN PEAKS, or even THE ELEPHANT MAN. Yet virtually all of the attributes assigned by Hoberman to his trio—to which one might add the equally salient trait of male chauvinism—apply to Lynch as well.

I'm not claiming that Tarkovsky's films "transcend" their sexism or their arrogance; these qualities remain, along with the films' beauties and genuine profundities, and no theory can shake them loose. But they are serious in a way and to a degree that is rare in contemporary movies, and their shortcomings are never a matter of aesthetic compromise or philosophical floundering—both of which can be found in some of Lynch's commercial efforts.

It might be added that misogyny plays a less pronounced role in SOLARIS than in some of Tarkovsky's other features, in part because of the strength and impact of Natalya Bondarchuk's remarkably nuanced performance as Hari. Kelvin's conscience may be the film's subject, but it is Hari's character that provides the film with its own conscience. Next to her, all the male astronauts register as so many blocks of wood—even (or, perhaps, especially) when they are engaged in heated philosophical discussions, which is often.

Like HAL, the computer in 2001, Hari doesn't qualify as "human" to the same degree as the other characters. But this doesn't prevent her repeated deaths and resurrections from being highly affecting—tragic, disturbing, appalling—much as HAL's death in 2001 winds up moving one more than any of the human deaths in that film. Hari may be, like HAL, nothing more than a human projection that has gained a certain lonely autonomy. But like HAL she winds up providing us with a powerful lesson about what it means to be human, and what it means to die.

—Chicago *Reader,* January 12, 1990;
revised Spring 1990

Tribal Scars (Sembène's BLACK GIRL)

If you trace African film back to its first fiction feature, it is only thirty years old. Yet far from being underdeveloped, it begins on a more sophisticated level than any other cinema in the world. By some accounts Ousmane Sembène's hour-long BLACK GIRL was made in 1965, by others 1966, a characteristic ambiguity when it comes to African movies. Do you date them according to when they were made or when they were first shown? And given the scant and largely unreliable print sources that we have to check, how can we be sure about either date?

One reason for the sophistication of BLACK GIRL is that by the time Sembène made it he was already in his early forties and had published four novels and a collection of stories (including the story BLACK GIRL is based on), studied filmmaking with Mark Donskoi at the Gorki studio in Moscow, and made three short films back in Africa (L'EMPIRE SONHRAI, BOROM SARRET, and NI-AYE, all from the early 60s). By his own account, his main reason for becoming a filmmaker was that his stories could reach more Africans, especially those unable to read. (Illiteracy plays a key role in the plot of BLACK GIRL.)

The story BLACK GIRL is based on has the same French title as the film, "La noire de . . . ," which translates as "the black woman [or girl] of [or from, or belonging to] . . . ," conveying a good many additional connotations. The English translation of the story, included in the collection *Tribal Scars*, is called "The Promised Land," and though the central plot of the story and the film are similar, the overall form and many of the details are not. In both, an illiterate Senegalese woman from Dakar named Diouana, who's hired as a servant by a white French couple living there with their young children, is thrilled when the wife proposes taking her with them to the French Riviera. But Diouana soon feels trapped, exploited, completely isolated, and depressed, and finally winds up slitting her own throat—an incident that's recounted briefly on one of the back pages of a local newspaper. (Sembène's story was reportedly inspired by just such an item in *Nice-Matin*.)

"The Promised Land" begins with the arrival of the police at the villa in Antibes where the suicide takes place, then flashes back to Dakar, freely shifting the narrative viewpoint between Diouana and her white mistress as it proceeds chronologically to the suicide. The story concludes with a poem, "Longing," addressed to "Diouana, / Our sister," in which the narrative voice becomes explicitly and exclusively African.

The film begins with Diouana's arrival in France—where the family is staying in an ugly high-rise rather than a villa—and gives us two separate flashbacks recounting her life in Dakar, before and after she's hired by the French family. The narrative viewpoint is exclusively hers—she narrates much of the action, speaking petulantly to herself—up to the point of her suicide. Then, in a powerful coda, we see the French husband back in Dakar returning Diouana's belongings to her mother—a sequence that can be described as both poetic and explicitly African in its thrust without duplicating anything in the original story's poem. Other important differences between the story and film include Diouana's age—close to thirty in the story, clearly much younger (though not explicitly stated) in the film—and the drunken old sailor in the story who tries to warn Diouana about France being more or less replaced in the film by a politically conscious young boyfriend, who has a picture of nationalist hero Patrice Lumumba on his wall and forebodings of his own. It's worth noting that Senegal achieved full independence only in 1960; both Diouana's glamorous dreams and her incapacities seem fully bound up in this fact.

Considering Sembène's passionate anticolonialism, it seems highly significant that BLACK GIRL was made not because of but in spite of the Film Bureau created by the de Gaulle government's Ministry of Cooperation in 1963—an organization created to provide technical and financial resources to African filmmakers that began by assisting Sembène on BOROM SARRET. In theory the Film Bureau couldn't dictate the choice of subject matter by filmmakers it helped. Nevertheless, it rejected Sembène's script for BLACK GIRL, because, as film historian Manthia Diawara puts it, "Sembène equated the way French Assistance Technique used cheap African labor to a new form of slavery." (The sequence in which the heroine gets selected by the French wife from a pool of African women on the street plainly evokes a slave market.) In other words, the story of Diouana's disenchantment with her patrons had obvious bearing on the Film Bureau's own patronage and patronizing attitudes. (Sembène's hatred of charity and foreign aid as a form of postcolonial paternalism runs through his oeuvre; it forms an essential part of GUELWAAR.)

To make his first feature Sembène ultimately had to turn to André Zwobada, an old friend and colleague of Jean Renoir's who, back in the 30s, helped to write Renoir's Communist documentary LA VIE EST À NOUS and was assistant director on THE RULES OF THE GAME. In the 60s, Zwobada was the main editor for the French government's newsreel service Actualités Françaises; sharing Sembène's contempt for the paternalism of the Film Bureau, he wound up producing BLACK GIRL and arranging for its postproduction to be done at the Actualités Françaises facilities in France. (Thanks to this arrangement, many of the film's actors—all of them wonderfully precise and believable nonprofessionals—are dubbed by others; Sembène himself appears briefly in a couple of scenes as a schoolteacher, smoking his pipe.)

Ironically, the Film Bureau wound up purchasing the noncommercial distribution rights to BLACK GIRL after it was made—seeking to control its distribution after failing to stifle its production. Broadly speaking, it sounds like the African/French version of Sundance and Miramax: buy up, promote, and thereby contain the independents, especially the feistier ones who spit in your face. This is also the implication of Lizbeth Malkmus and Roy Armes's tentative suggestion, in their recent book *Arab & African Film Making,* that the sixty-minute running time of BLACK GIRL may be the consequence of some requirement of the original distributors; the film apparently once had a color sequence detailing Diouana's "first reactions to France."

My own gut instinct would be to assume that if the film ever did have a color sequence, it would likely have had more to do with Diouana's fanciful notions about France—based on such things as the photos she and her boyfriend see in an issue of *Elle*—than with what she actually finds there.[*] For the extraordinary thing about the film's black-and-white cinematography is how essential Sembène makes it—formally, thematically, and even semantically—to the story he has to tell. As another critic, Lieve Spass, writing in the magazine *Jump Cut,* has pointed out, "Diouana wears a white dress with black dots; her suitcase is black; the apartment seems entirely in a black/white color scheme; the food prepared falls into the same categories—black coffee, sterilized milk, white rice; even the whisky consumed generously by the Frenchman bears the label 'Black and White' "—an opposition "enacted most dramatically when the camera focuses on Diouana's inert black body in the white bathtub," and one that is matched by the movie's no less striking juxtaposi-

---

[*] I was wrong about this. A friend and former critic, James Staller, recently wrote to me saying that he saw a print in New York that opens with a color sequence. [November 1996]

tions of French music (barrelhouse piano evoking SHOOT THE PIANO PLAYER) and African music (instrumental as well as vocal) on the sound track.

Indeed, both the black-and-white cinematography and the music display an almost brutal concentration and economy that are basic to the film's style and meaning; they uncannily get us to share the naive consciousness of Diouana as it blooms or withers in different spaces—buoyant and freewheeling in the streets of Dakar when she learns she's going to France, aggrieved and constricted in the Antibes apartment that encompasses nearly all of the France she sees. Though critics like Diawara, Malkmus, and Armes habitually describe Sembène as a social realist, it's hard to think of any other artist pegged with that moldy label who's so intimately and poetically concerned with what freedom and oppression actually *feel* like, not simply what they consist of. And if Sembène is in fact a social realist, he must be a pretty weird one to strip his plot to such emotional and poetic basics that we can't walk away from this movie with the usual basic data. We don't even know where the French family's home base is, and we know next to nothing about Diouana's past and family—it's not even clear whether the little boy associated with her in Dakar is a friend, acquaintance, or brother. But we're not persuaded that any of this information matters in the slightest. By the same token, I'm fully convinced that nothing in this movie can be weakened or spoiled by knowing the story in advance, which is why I'm not showing any hesitation about revealing it. For Sembène, the event is mere raw material; articulation is everything.

In fact, the intense capturing of everyday experience through a minimalist "newsreel" palette of New Wave shooting (natural lighting, handheld camera movements) and postsynced sound is precisely what lifts this movie well beyond the limits of a simple tract. We share Diouana's giddy pleasure as she endlessly circles her neighbors telling them the news of her job ("J'ai du travail chez les blancs!") and as she, to the grim disapproval of her boyfriend, skips barefoot over a colonialist war memorial in downtown Dakar labeled "For Our Dead, A Grateful Nation"—just as we share her subsequent humiliation in Antibes when her first letter from her mother, consisting mainly of reprimands, is read aloud to her by the French husband, who then proceeds to compose her "reply" in his own words when she fails to provide him with any. In all three cases Diouana's naïveté and ignorance are central to the scene's meaning, but Sembène refuses to allow any smug feelings of superiority—on our part or his. He also manages to work in plenty of irony regarding her boyfriend's seriousness about the war memorial and her employers' insensitivity about her illiteracy—without simply indicting them either. Everyone is criticized, but no one is stereotyped. When the French wife objects to Diouana wearing high heels in the apartment and Diouana responds by dropping them off in the center of the living room carpet, the silliness and sadness of both characters register with equal intensity. There's a similar pathos in the husband's efforts to assuage Diouana's misery with wads of money. For all the simplicity of the materials and the fablelike aspects of the story, a complex and passionate intelligence is shaping the meaning in every scene.

I'm an amateur when it comes to African aesthetics—in large part because I have the disadvantage of knowing them mainly secondhand through such outsiders as Jean Rouch and John Coltrane. Yet it seems to me that they may have something to do with a certain freedom from conceptual rigidity. It is this that allows Sembène to shift in "The Promised Land" between the viewpoints of mistress and servant and between the forms of prose and poetry and in BLACK GIRL to get us to share the consciousness of a single alienated character and then to create his most awesome emotional impact and summary statement after her death, when that consciousness is no longer present. He achieves this through one of the most basic artifacts and symbols in African aesthetics, a mask—a key object, I should add, that plays no part at all in "The Promised Land."

Shortly after Diouana gets hired by the French family in Dakar, she buys the mask from the little boy to present to them as a gift; they already have two or three others, so it's merely an addition to their collection (as she is). We encounter the mask again at the tail end of the second flashback, after we see her in bed with her boyfriend—a detail that retroactively places this scene *before* the presentation of the gift in the first flashback (another example of Sembène's freedom from conceptual rigidity). When Diouana is in the depths of her depression in Antibes and starts to pack her suitcase she angrily takes the mask back, occasioning a fight with the wife for possession of it that the husband settles in Diouana's favor.

Finally, the husband brings both Diouana's suitcase and the mask back to her mother in Dakar and attempts to ply her with francs; the mother simply walks away from him, refusing his guilt-ridden moral bribery. But the boy silently reclaims the mask, and putting it on, tracks the husband back to his car, provoking his paranoia all the way. After the husband drives away, the boy, facing the camera, removes the mask, and the movie ends. There are few endings in all of cinema as powerful and rich as this—brimming with tragic wisdom and latent meaning, with finality and promise, with humor and pain. Diouana and Africa and the mask and the boy have finally become one, an indissoluble and unbearable human fact staring us all in the face. It's at this point that African cinema begins.

—Chicago Reader, April 21, 1995

Alternate Histories

> I wanted to make a work in the spirit of Dickens, with
> characters so dense that they appear as archetypes. . . .
> I thought it could have made a very popular film,
> a commercial film that everyone would have liked. In
> place of that . . . I'm afraid to see it! It's terrible,
> what they did to me on that. The film was snatched from
> my hands more brutally than one has ever snatched a
> film from anyone . . . it's as if they'd kidnapped
> my child! They brought in another cutter who
> pretended to have "saved" the film!
>
> —*Orson Welles in* l'Avant-scène du cinéma,
> *no. 291–292 (1–15 July 1982) (my translation)*

It's generally known that, for a variety of reasons, some of the films of Orson Welles survive today in two or more versions. James Naremore has told me he once saw a print of THE LADY FROM SHANGHAI in Germany that included alternate takes of certain scenes and somewhat different editing, plus a few shots he hadn't seen before or since. (This sounds roughly comparable to the "Italian" version of Stroheim's FOOLISH WIVES, apparently sent overseas before the domestic version was completed.) Better known are Welles's two separate versions of MACBETH, running 107 minutes and 86 minutes. (The second was prepared after Welles was asked to cut two reels and redub the "Scots" dialogue; it contains offscreen narration missing from the long version but *doesn't* contain the single take lasting an entire reel which preceded Hitchcock's ROPE by a year.) Still better known are the two editions of TOUCH OF EVIL—the 93-minute version originally released and the 108-minute version discovered in the mid-70s that has virtually supplanted it. Since Welles was barred from the final stages of editing, neither can be considered definitive; indeed, it's impossible to speak of a definitive TOUCH OF EVIL.

The same is true of MR. ARKADIN (1955). But in this case the consequences are much more confusing because of the number of ARKADINS we have to choose from—plus the fact that the version best known in this country is very far from the best.

Here, in simplified form, is more or less how the story line goes.

In Naples, a man, Bracco (Grégoire Aslan), mysteriously knifed in the back, whispers two names while dying: "Gregory Arkadin" and "Sophie." The only people to hear are Guy Van Stratten (Robert Arden), an American smuggler, and his girlfriend, Mily (Patricia Medina). Hoping to snare a fortune via blackmail with these names, Guy tracks the fabulously wealthy Arkadin (Welles) to a castle in Spain and, against the man's wishes, woos his sheltered and beloved daughter Raina (Paola Mori). Unexpectedly, Arkadin, who claims to suffer from amnesia, hires Guy to prepare a confidential report on his activities prior to 1927. Guy conducts interviews all over Europe and in Mexico, basically tracking down former members of a gang of white slavers to which Arkadin belonged. These include Oskar (Frederick O'Brady) and Sophie (Katina Paxinou) in Mexico and Jakob Zouk (Akim Tamiroff) in Munich; Mily helps out by speaking with a black marketeer (Peter van Eyck) in Tangiers and with Arkadin himself on his yacht. As Guy uncovers Arkadin's past, he gradually discovers that his employer, afraid Raina will learn who and what he once was, is having his old associates murdered, as well as Mily. Fearing for his own life, Guy flies to Raina in Barcelona ahead of Arkadin, who is following in a private plane. Guy convinces Raina to tell her father, over the plane's radio, that she now knows everything, at which point Arkadin kills himself by leaping from the plane. Raina leaves Guy in disgust.

■

In 1958 the editorial board of *Cahiers du cinéma* collectively decided that MR. ARKADIN—more precisely, CONFIDENTIAL REPORT, as they knew it—was Welles's greatest film, the one that belonged on their list of the twelve greatest films ever made. At the time, not long after the film's appearance in Europe, there was no public awareness that Welles had lost editorial control over it; the director had lent his presence at the Paris premiere, and apparently made no public statements about his creative difficulties until some time later. Even now we have less information about the making and the editorial reworking of ARKADIN than we have about any of the other Welles narrative features released during his lifetime.

What we *do* have is a tantalizing panoply of texts—for the purposes of this discussion, seven—in a variety of media. They range from the stylistically conventional to the stylistically radical, from the tossed-off to the aesthetically intricate. The *Cahiers* editors' odd preference notwithstanding, I don't consider ARKADIN a masterpiece in any of its versions or incarnations. But I find most of it fascinating and much of it beautiful and exciting—"it" in this case being a conflation of ARKADINS nos. 3, 6, and 7 (in descending order of importance) among the exhibits I propose to submit for consideration.

What's offered below isn't so much a map of a "definitive" ARKADIN as an exploration of a few of the processes that the story and film went through. It is, if you will, a a kind of detective story without a denouement, but with plenty of clues. The mode is tentative historical inquiry, selective and suggestive in intention rather than exhaustive, with a few critical remarks appended.

In pursuit of my own confidential report, I have greatly benefited from three invaluable sources in addition to the primary texts: an afternoon spent with a good many loose pieces of the producer's workprint materials—examined on a moviola with two other Welles scholars, Ciro Giorgini and Bernard Eisenschitz—thanks to the exceptional generosity of Fred Junck and Marco Müller; a phone interview graciously granted me by Patricia Medina; and *This Is Orson Welles* by Orson Welles and Peter Bogdanovich, a book I have been editing for HarperCollins. I'd also like to thank Geoff Andrew, Tag Gallagher, James Pepper, Bill Reed, and Bret Wood for furnishing me with some of the primary materials.

Pre-Texts

1: "Greek Meets Greek"—half-hour episode of the London-based radio series *The Adventures of Harry Lime,* a spin-off of the Welles character in the 1949 Carol Reed/Graham Greene film THE THIRD MAN. Written by and starring Welles, directed by Tig Roe, and probably recorded in 1951, the segment is quite unremarkable except as the source for ARKADIN's skeletal plot and key themes.

2: *Masquerade*—early version of Welles's script for ARKADIN, dated March 23, 1953, the year before shooting commenced. *Masquerade* differs from most or all of the later versions in the following ways:

(a) The opening quotation is not an aphorism about a king and a poet and a fatal secret, but a quotation from Emerson:

> Commit a crime, and the earth is made of glass. Commit a crime and it seems as if a coat of snow fell on the ground, such as reveals in the woods the track of every partridge and fox and squirrel and mole. You cannot recall the spoken word, you cannot wipe out the foot-track, you cannot draw up the ladder, so as to leave no inlet or clew.

This also appears in the French and Italian editions of the novel, but apparently none of those in English. As Richard T. Jameson has pointed out to me, the same quotation is recited by Edward G. Robinson in Welles's THE STRANGER (1946).

(b) Apart from the precredits sequence of the riderless plane—which exists in every version of the film but not the novel—there are no flashbacks and no offscreen narration. The plot progression is strictly chronological.

(c) The investigator is called "Guy Dumesnil" and is described as "young and attractive" and "an Americanized European" (not an American called Guy Van Stratten). The Jakob Zouk character (played by Akim Tamiroff in the film) is called "Jakob Nathansen."

(d) Most of the major scenes in the script are in the film, although some are set in different countries. Arkadin's masked ball is in Venice, not Spain ("This is clearly an attempt on Arkadin's part to out-do the famous Bestigui Ball, and is in fact, in many ways, a duplication of it. . . . The canals are filled with illuminated gondolas carrying Arkadin's guests, all in costumes of the Venetian 18th century. . . ."). Similarly, the pawn and junk shop of Burgomil Trebitsch (Michael Redgrave) is located in Marseille, not Copenhagen. A few scenes in the film, such as the one featuring the flea circus director (Mischa Auer), are not in the script.

(e) Perhaps the most extended material available here but missing from all the other versions of ARKADIN (except for the novel, where it figures in a somewhat different form) involves Van Stratten's adventures when he first arrives in Mexico, before he questions Oskar and Sophie. He attends the funeral of Sophie's elderly toy poodle Ki-Ki, * and tracks down Oskar in a "kosher café" run by Sophie, where he plays the accordion for tips. Van Stratten lures Oskar onto a rented boat by offering him a high fee to entertain guests on an alleged pleasure cruise, at which point he begins to torture him for information by depriving him of heroin. Only a brief version of this boat scene survives in the film.

(f) In the film, there is a confrontation between Van Stratten, Arkadin, and Raina in Guy's hotel room in Paris; the script sets the scene in Van Stratten's flat, and Arkadin appears only belatedly. (In the workprint, Welles conducts a rehearsal for part of this scene and, in instructing Mori how to deliver some of her lines, gives the setting as New York.)

■

Films and Filming:
"a phenomenon of an age of dissolution and chaos"

I was developing the rushes of ARKADIN in a French lab. Can you imagine that I had to have a special authorization for every piece of film, even if only 20 yards long, that arrived from Spain? The film had to go through the hands of the customs officials, who wasted their time (and ours) by stamping the beginning and end of each and every roll of film or of magnetic sound tape. The operation required two whole days, and the film was in danger of being spoiled by the hot weather we were then having.

*Oddly enough, Welles had a beloved small dog of that name in Hollywood at the end of his life.

The same difficulties cropped up when it came to obtaining work permits. My film unit was international: I had a French cameraman, an Italian editor, an English sound engineer, an Irish script girl, a Spanish assistant. Whenever we had to travel anywhere, each of them had to waste an unconscionable amount of time getting special permissions to stay to work. . . . Similar complications arose when, for example, we had to get a French camera into Spain. . . .

The true culprits are the producers. They prefer the security of a limited but certain profit from a national or regional market to the infinitely wider possibilities of a world market, which would of course entail, at the outset, certain supplementary expenses. (Orson Welles, "For a Universal Cinema," *Film Culture* 1. no. 1 [January 1955])

A few words about the making of MR. ARKADIN. Louis Dolivet, the French producer, who died not long ago, was a good friend and political mentor to Welles in the United States during the mid-40s. (See Barbara Leaming's biography *Orson Welles* [New York: Viking Penguin, 1985], for particulars.) Dolivet never produced a feature prior to ARKADIN and, to the best of my knowledge, never produced another afterward. The little evidence we have suggests that ARKADIN's production was an exacerbating experience for him and Welles alike and that their friendship ultimately proved to be one of its casualties. To make matters worse, Paola Mori—the professional name of the Countess di Girfalco, who later became Welles's third and last wife—was criticized so harshly for her performance by Dolivet and others that she gave up acting, appearing again only in cameos in THE TRIAL and the unfinished DON QUIXOTE. (Again, the workprint rehearsal footage is suggestive: Mori's musically accented voice is distinct from the English-accented voice we hear in the released films, raising the possibility that "Raina" 's voice was subsequently dubbed by another actress.*)

It appears that most of the film was shot in Spain—much of it in a studio in Madrid—with a certain amount in Munich and Paris locations and probably a few pickup shots elsewhere in Western Europe. (One can't take seriously any of those accounts claiming that part of the shooting was done in Mexico.) On the basis of my interview with Patricia Medina and the slates visible in certain outtakes, we know that many scenes were shot, wholly or partially, in or near Madrid. These encompass such fictional settings as a hotel in Mexico City, the docks in Naples, Arkadin's yacht, the interior and environs of his Spanish castle, a café in Tangiers, a nightclub on the Riviera, and the inside of a Munich cathedral!

Patricia Medina has never seen ARKADIN, so all her memories are tied exclusively to her own participation in the film. She was under contract to Columbia at the time, and when Welles phoned her in London to ask her to play Mily, she had very little time to shoot because she was due back in the states

---

*I've subsequently learned that the young Billie Whitelaw did the dubbing.

to act in something else (probably MIAMI EXPOSÉ). Welles replied jokingly, "Then we'll have to kill you off." (Mily's murder, alluded to offscreen in the film, was never shot in any form.) Medina flew to Madrid and all her scenes were shot there, most of them in a studio, over about ten days.

Overall, she remembers the shoot as a happy event. The first scene she did was on the yacht with Arkadin. The night before shooting, Welles showed her the set, asking scornfully, "Doesn't it look just like the Staten Island Ferry?" The yacht set was up in the air; one had to climb up into it. After Medina returned to her hotel, Welles phoned to ask her if there was anything in her hotel that "belonged in a yacht." She looked around and found very little. When she arrived for filming the next morning, she discovered that Welles had been up all night redressing the set with furniture temporarily swiped from the lobby of the Madrid Hilton, where he himself was staying. He announced that they had time for only two takes because the furniture had to be returned before it was missed. (One detail in this scene was improvised: when Mily says "Shut up!" to a screeching bird in a cage, neither the screech nor her line was in the script.)

Medina's participation in the scene featuring the procession of penitentes near Arkadin's castle was all done in a studio. Interestingly, although Paola Mori appears in the same sequence, Medina never met her during the shooting. If one examines this scene closely, it becomes clear that Mily and the procession never appear in the same shot; the illusion of proximity is supplied and intensified by the shadows—ostensibly of the penitentes—flickering across Mily and Guy.

When she left for the States, Welles asked her to send a still of herself that could be blown up for a poster advertising Mily as a bubble dancer. She neglected to do so. When she arrived in Paris sometime later to do the dubbing with Welles, she was appalled by the still that he had found and used on his own. (When Van Stratten learns of Mily's death later in the film, this picture recurs in some versions, identified in the dialogue as "the only available photo taken before death.") And that marked the end of her involvement, save that much later she was contacted by Dolivet to act in some additional scenes; learning that Welles wouldn't be directing them, she refused.

But back to The Seven ARKADINS. . .

■

3: MR. ARKADIN, the film—that is to say, the version of the film closest to Welles's conception. This became available in the United States through Corinth Films; we owe the original existence of this version in the United States to Peter Bogdanovich, who discovered it in Hollywood in 1961, and to Dan Talbot of New Yorker Films, who acquired it for the belated U.S. premiere and release of ARKADIN the following year.

According to the film's editor, Renzo Lucidi (recently interviewed by Ciro

Giorgini), the first four sequences of this version correspond precisely to Welles's intentions. It opens with Van Stratten visiting Jakob Zouk in Munich, then continues as a series of flashbacks narrated offscreen by Van Stratten, periodically returning to Zouk's attic flat.*

Welles spent four months editing, averaging (according to Lucidi) two minutes of finished film per week. He was barred from the cutting after failing to meet Dolivet's Christmas 1954 deadline, but continued to communicate his intentions to Lucidi. Once Lucidi had finished editing this version, however, Dolivet apparently asked for the film to be reedited without most of the flashbacks—in chronological order after the opening sequence—and this was the principal version released in Europe as CONFIDENTIAL REPORT. (See no. 6, below.)

In *This Is Orson Welles,* Welles maintains that at least two important scenes of his were eliminated from all the released versions of ARKADIN. This would seem to be corroborated by Frank Brady's citation, in his Welles biography, of an undated *New York Herald Tribune* story in which Welles complained that fourteen minutes were removed from his version. To Bogdanovich, Welles cited another party scene and an additional scene between Arkadin and Van Stratten, both of which showed Arkadin "as a sentimental, rather maudlin Russian drunk"; Arkadin's character, he added, was inspired to some extent by Stalin.

Given Welles's relative unfamiliarity with the release versions of his film—which he clearly found painful to watch—these remarks *may* have alluded to further material in Arkadin's masked ball, or at the Christmas party in Munich (where we do see Arkadin drunk). Alternately, they may refer to two complete scenes of which we no longer have any record in any of the seven ARKADINS. Since Welles had a penchant for revising his scripts while shooting—and even, on occasion, revising dialogue while postdubbing and editing—both hypotheses are plausible.

Apparently one of the reasons why ARKADIN was so late—seven years!—in opening in the United States was a $780,000 legal suit filed by the European production company Filmorsa against Welles in New York, claiming that Welles's behavior was responsible for the film's ultimate commercial failure. This action was launched on April 7, 1958, but papers weren't filed until September 28, 1961; on the following day brief news stories were run in the New York papers, citing "drinking excessively on and off the set" as the principal charge. In the *Times,* Welles called the charges "blunderbuss, catch-all phraseology, naked generalizations, unsupported inferences and patent irrele-

---

* Welles's own testimony to Bogdanovich (*This Is Orson Welles* [New York: HarperCollins, 1992], 237) contradicts Lucidi to the extent that Welles recollects his version beginning "with a shot of an enormous empty beach and a naked girl [Mily] being washed in by the sea"—a brief shot that appears in no. 6 immediately after the yacht scene, is missing from nos. 2, 3, and 7, and doesn't begin any of the existing versions that I'm aware of.

vancies," while one of his lawyers maintained that it was Filmorsa rather than Welles that had broken the contract. The charges, in any case, were eventually dropped.

∎

4: *Mr. Arkadin,* the novel, signed by Welles but not written by him—although the version available in English is an anonymous translation of a French novel ghostwritten by Maurice Bessy that was based, in turn, on a version of Welles's film script, in English, that was written at some point after no. 2. The novel was originally composed for newspaper serialization in France, and first appeared in book form there at the time of CONFIDENTIAL REPORT's French release.

The novel is divided into three sections, entitled "Bracco," "Sophie," and "The Ogre." Narrated in the first person by Van Stratten, it most closely resembles no. 7 in its overall form. The most significant material missing from all other versions relates to Van Stratten's mother, a professional gambler who, at the time of the novel, is occupying "a tiny two-room flat at Beausoleil with Myrtle," an English gambling companion, and appears briefly, along with Myrtle, in the second chapter.

Although Lucidi has recently maintained that Welles wrote the novel, all the other available evidence—including a conversation I had with Welles in 1972—refutes this. A comparison of the novel's dialogue with the film's suggests in virtually every case that the former is a retranslation back into English of French dialogue adapted from an English script; the meanings of lines are generally the same, but the words and phrasings are almost always different.

∎

5: The Spanish version of the film. If the current "Spanish version" is identical to the one that opened in Madrid in March 1955, then this is probably the first version that premiered anywhere. I've been able to see only a few parts of this version—presumably the most significant parts—in Ciro Giorgini's invaluable TUTTA LA VERITA' SU MR. ARKADIN, a 1991 TV documentary for Italy's RAI.

The Spanish version was apparently shot simultaneously with the principal production. It features different actresses playing the parts of Sophie and Baroness Nagel (and perhaps other Spanish actors as well), as part of the arrangement made for a Spanish coproduction. A different editor is also credited, Antonio Martinez. In the precredits sequence, the pilotless plane is said more vaguely to have been sighted somewhere in Europe rather than "off the coast of Barcelona"; in the glimpses of the actors shown in the credits, we see Amparo Rivelles instead of Suzanne Flon as the Baroness Nagel, Irene Lopez Heredia instead of Katina Paxinou as Sophie; Robert Arden is inexplicably identified as "Bob Harden." As for the scenes involving Rivelles and Lopez Heredia, the first of these alternates shots of Welles (dubbed by someone else) with reverse angles of Rivelles in what appears to be a crude approximation of the same set (a fancy Paris restaurant); it seems highly unlikely that Welles directed these reverse angles. But in the scene with Lopez Heredia and "Harden," the set appears to be the same one used in the English-speaking versions, and the lighting and mise en scène, while not quite identical, are sufficiently Wellesian to suggest that Welles himself might have directed this alternate version of the scene.*

6: CONFIDENTIAL REPORT—the version of the film that opened in London in August 1955 and apparently the main version that was and is shown elsewhere in Europe, including France.

It seems quite possible that an early draft of Welles's script was used as a guide in reediting this version, a detailed description of which is available in French in the issue of *l'Avant-Scène du Cinéma* cited at the beginning of this article. (This description includes annotations about materials found in the workprint). As Giorgini shows in his documentary through a split-screen technique, the differences between this version and no. 3 are more than just a matter of chronological sequence; they involve variations in editing and dialogue and/or narration within scenes, and in a few instances may even involve different takes.

There are at least two brief scenes in CONFIDENTIAL REPORT that are missing from both no. 3 and no. 7—a scene in which Van Stratten speaks to a black American pianist in a bar on the Riviera while looking for Mily and Arkadin's "Georgian toast" near the end of his masked ball, in which he recounts a curious dream set in a cemetery. This also happens to be the only version containing shots of hanging papier-mâché sculptures representing bats in the opening credits sequence. (As to what they refer to in the film, they could be either objects in Trebitsch's junk shop or part of the decor at Arkadin's masked ball; when queried about these bats by Bogdanovich, Welles had no recollection of them.)

Another major difference between CONFIDENTIAL REPORT and all other versions is a block of offscreen narration by Van Stratten, quoted below, that accompanies four shots of him approaching a rundown house in the snow (shots visible in all the versions). I haven't been able to determine whether Welles wrote or recorded this exposition; if he did, it seems probable that this was later superseded by the different sort of exposition he employed in no. 3. The end of this narration certainly blunts the power of the film's most beautiful camera movement, a backward retreat down a dark tunnel of a hallway:

Here I am at the end of the road. Naples, France, Spain, Mexico, and now Munich. Sebastianplatz 16. In the attic of this house lives Jakob Zouk, a petty

---

*Apparently he didn't. See the invaluable companion volumes Esteve Riambau's *Orson Welles: Una España inmortal* and Juan Cobos's *Orson Welles: España como obsesion* (Valencia: Ediciones Filmoteca, Filmoteca Espanola, 1993). [1995]

racketeer, a jailbird, and the last man alive besides me who knows the whole truth about Gregory Arkadin. My confidential report is complete now. My original fee for this job was $15,000, and it looks like a little bonus will be tossed in—like a knife in my back. But Zouk will get his first unless I can save him. And then me—the world's prize sucker.

7: The principal public domain version that circulates in this country on video; it may also still be available on film. With the probable exception of the Spanish version, no. 5, and the possible exception of the radio show, no. 1, and the novel, no. 4, it is the least satisfactory version of ARKADIN that we have. But because of its wide availability on video and its frequent showings on TV, it is more than likely the ARKADIN that most Americans know.

For the most part, this qualifies as a clumsily truncated version of no. 6, with many of the significant losses occurring at or near the beginning. Characteristically, the offscreen narration that begins after the credits starts in the middle of a sentence, with Van Stratten on the docks in Naples (which is where no. 4 begins as well).

■

A Tentative Conclusion: "Give the gentleman his goose liver"

In his preface to the English translation of André Bazin's *Orson Welles,* François Truffaut divides all of Welles's films into those made with his right hand and those made with his left hand, adding, "In the right-handed films there is always snow, and in the left-handed ones there are always gunshots; but all constitute what Cocteau called the 'poetry of cinematography.' " AR-KADIN is the only Welles film with both snow and gunshots, but I think Truffaut is probably correct in considering it one of the left-handed films. Its moments of poetry are intense and indelible, but the feeling of chaos that it imparts, while fundamental to this poetry, is at times less than adequate to the more prosaic needs of the narrative. Eric Rohmer was right to classify the film as a tale or fable rather than a realistic story or a thriller, and it might be argued that the relative hospitality of French criticism toward unrealistic narrative helps to account for the relative favor ARKADIN has found in French criticism.

Anglo-American critics have generally been put off by the same elements. Dwight Macdonald characteristically complained about the lack of attention paid to Arkadin's business dealings and the visible artifice in Welles's makeup for the part; others have seized on the superficial plot resemblances to CITIZEN KANE to berate the film for its incoherence, its performances, and/or its production values.

I share some of these biases, although a few seem misplaced. For all the film's lack of realism, it still has some validity and interest as a cold war allegory, as James Naremore has suggested. Naremore notes Robert Arden's "uncanny resemblance to a young, athletic Richard Nixon," and if one connects this with Arkadin's resemblance to Stalin—a resemblance underlined by Arkadin's habit of killing off former associates and witnesses—the struggle of the two over Raina, who might be said to represent Western Europe in the mid-50s, is full of suggestive and subversive possibilities. The fact that Arkadin and Van Stratten are presented as moral equivalents—older and younger versions of the same unscrupulous lout—is central to this reading.

Arden's performance as Van Stratten is commonly singled out for abuse, even by most of Welles's defenders, but after repeated viewings it seems to me that it's the unsavoriness and obnoxiousness of the character rather than the performance itself that is responsible for most of this attitude. A comparable syndrome applies to Tim Holt's George Minafer in THE MAGNIFICENT AMBERSONS: because both characters occupy the space normally reserved for charismatic heroes, we feel we're supposed to like and/or sympathize with them, and when their respective films make this impossible, we wind up blaming either the actors or Welles's casting rather than accept the premise that we're meant to have a difficult time with these people.

This is not to suggest that the performances in ARKADIN are above criticism. I agree that the film has one debilitating performance, but this is given by neither Arden nor Paola Mori (who may be relatively unskilled but still seems quite adequate to the demands the script makes of her). I'm afraid it is given by Welles himself. The falseness of his makeup and the variability of his Russian accent can't be rationalized by the elusiveness of Arkadin's character, because no norm is ever established for these traits to deviate from. One can accept the film's premise of presenting us with a gallery of grotesques, but not a title ogre whose face is little more than a Halloween mask. At separate junctures, Arkadin is linked to Neptune and Santa Claus, and at his own ball he hides behind a mask; most of the plot is devoted to uncovering his original identity as a lowlife named Akim Athabadze. But even this latter phantom, glimpsed in a faded photograph belonging to Sophie, lives more in our minds than Gregory Arkadin does on screen. (Mainly this is because of Sophie herself; she and Zouk wind up providing most of whatever soul the movie has, thanks in large measure to Paxinou and Tamiroff.) Welles appears to have conceived of Arkadin as a tissue of paradoxes, but his own performance, even if it contains some lovely line readings, doesn't bridge or embrace those paradoxes. At best it only alludes to them.

The character's silliest moment comes when he informs Van Stratten in a Munich cathedral, "I no longer think of you at all." Considering the fact that he has already trailed Van Stratten across the Atlantic and back, and followed him not only to and around Munich but even to this very spot, it would be an understatement to call this remark disingenuous. Maybe the missing scenes alluded to by Welles would have provided more of a context for such anomalies; or maybe not. Either way, it's worth noting the degree to which stubborn irrationality plays a major role in Welles's work, from Kane and George Minafer to Iago and Othello, from most of the characters in THE LADY FROM SHANGHAI and TOUCH OF EVIL to all of the characters in THE TRIAL.

Perhaps the most underrated feature of ARKADIN is Paul Misraki's wonderfully evocative and rhythmic score, which sometimes plays even more of a shaping role in the film than the plot, dialogue, or mise en scène. Nostalgia for a lost innocence plays as important a role in ARKADIN as it does in KANE, AMBERSONS, and CHIMES AT MIDNIGHT (where it is also tied to snow), although the site of this innocence is less localized than the nineteenth century or the Middle Ages is in those films (not to mention Tanya's bordello in TOUCH OF EVIL). Like Arkadin himself, it's anywhere and everywhere, sometimes where we least expect it. It's Christmas and goose liver and the last time someone said "Come to bed" to Jakob Zouk. It's the youths and romantic yearnings of the Baroness Nagel and Sophie, and a scruffy little Salvation Army band in the street. More mysteriously and disturbingly, it's the sudden, irrational, backward retreat of the camera down a dank tenement corridor, into a dark womb of oblivion.

—*Film Comment,* January–February 1992

TIH-MINH, OUT 1

On the Nonreception of Two French Serials

1. On the Issue of Nonreception

What connections can be found between two French serials made almost half a century apart? Aside from the fact that both of them appear on my most recent "top ten" list,[1] I'm equally concerned with the issue of why such pleasurable, evocative, enduring, multifaceted, and incontestably beautiful works should remain so resolutely marginal—unseen, unavailable, and virtually written out of most film histories except for occasional guest appearances as the vaguest of reference points. The problem isn't simply an American or an academic one; although no print of either serial exists in the United States, it can't be said that either film has received much attention in France either.[2] Yet both are major testaments to the joys of spontaneous filmmaking and the complex adventures these entail, for their viewers as well as for their makers.

Louis Feuillade's seven-hour, twelve-episode TIH-MINH, shot on the Côte d'Azur in 1918, released in early 1919; first seen by me at the Museum of Modern Art in April 1969. Jacques Rivette's nearly thirteen-hour, eight-episode OUT 1, shot mainly in Paris in spring 1970, rejected by French state television, shown publicly only once (September 9–10, 1971, Le Havre) as a workprint. First seen by me (in a finished print) at the Rotterdam Film Festival in February 1989; finally shown as a serial on the Paris Première cable channel in the early 90s, and recently released in France on video. (It's available on four SÉCAM videocassettes from Mily, 8 rue Pradier, 75019 Paris; phone 42-00-02-30.)

Properly speaking, I've never seen either serial in its integral form *or* as a serial, which already suggests part of the problem in keeping such works alive and discussed: their implied mode of reception is no longer ours, and the same applies to their original status as texts. The seven-hour TIH-MINH that I saw in 1969, a version held by the Brussels Cinémathèque, is (or was) missing most or all of the film's intertitles, but it runs about an hour longer than the (mainly) intertitled version held by the Paris Cinémathèque, shown at the New York Film Festival in 1980 and seen by me more recently on video. When I saw OUT 1 in 1989, about forty minutes of the sound track in the sixth episode were still unlocated; these have subsequently been found and restored, but prior to most or all of its post-Rotterdam showings, Rivette did further editing on the serial, altering the order of certain scenes and making a few deletions, which makes the final running time 750 minutes instead of 760—a shorter version that I've also had access to on video.[3]

Complicating the textual status of OUT 1 still further is the 255-minute OUT 1 SPECTRE (1972), which Rivette spent the better part of a year editing out of the original material—not so much a digest of the longer film as a different work with a substantially different structure and tone. Part of the fascinating difference between the two films can be seen in the ways that identical footage can often carry disparate meanings and perform radically different dramatic and narrative functions according to its separate placement in each film. (The opening shot of SPECTRE, for instance, occurs almost three hours into the serial. And one of the more striking differences in the long version is that Michel Lonsdale, the director of one of the film's two theater groups, emerges as the central character—not only because of his role in guiding his group's improvisations and psychic self-explorations but also because his ambiguous role as a rather infantile patriarch becomes pivotal to the overall movement of the plot.) The only English subtitled print of SPECTRE, no longer complete, has received scattered screenings in the United States since 1974, though it remains undistributed; the longer OUT 1 has never been subtitled or shown here at all.

Within the institution of mainstream criticism, the absence of any commentary about these films is of course wholly unremarkable and unlikely to change even if either or both serials should acquire U.S. distribution. But the sustained passivity and silence of U.S. film academics about making Feuillade more available—apart from one episode of FANTOMAS, nothing of his is distributed—seems harder to explain, even though it clearly belongs to a characteristic vicious circle of neglect and inertia in which any revision of the standard canon becomes unlikely. Still, if one wants this situation to change, one has to start somewhere, and this article is motivated by the assumption that even a rudimentary account of both serials is preferable to continuing neglect and indifference. After all, as David Thomson has pointed out, Feuillade is "the first director for whom no historical allowances need to be made." Come to think of it, he may be one of the last as well. And one would hate to think that the possibility of a English subtitled version of OUT 1 on video is an outlandish utopian dream.

What follows are a few suggestions about certain common points of interest—as well as some equally important divergences—between these two major, epochal works. By necessity, these remarks will be somewhat tentative and sketchy—notes toward more comprehensive work that might be undertaken by myself or by others if these films become more readily available.

2. A Few Correspondences

> When I have occasion to look through the camera lens, my instinct is to move further and further back, because when I see the face, I want to see the hands, and when I see the hands I want to see the body. Yes, I think I always want to see the body as a whole, then the body in relation to the décor, then the people in relation to whom the body interacts, reacts, moves, submits. . . . It's simply because I haven't the temperament, taste, or talent to make a montage cinema; it's a cinema that on the contrary functions more on the continuity of events, dealt with in a global way.
>
> —Rivette to Serge Daney, 1990[4]

Setting aside the issue of intentionality, which obviously has different ramifications in the cases of Feuillade and Rivette, one of the key sources of interest to be found in both serials rests in their poignancy and suggestiveness as historical documents—TIH-MINH as a bourgeois reflection of the aftermath of World War I, OUT 1 as a bohemian reflection of the aftermath of May 1968. The colonialist trappings of TIH-MINH, the anti-German and anti-Bolshevik sentiments (many of which suggestively coalesce around a German spy named Marx), the preoccupations with espionage, surveillance, disguise, and diverse forms of mind and memory control are redolent of the late teens not merely as waking dreams but as everyday hypotheses, and much of the magic of this serial resides in the continual and often subtle crossovers that occur between these two registers. Similarly, virtually all of OUT 1 can be read as an epic meditation on the dialectic between collective endeavors (theater rehearsals, conspiracies, diverse countercultural activities, manifestos) and activities and situations growing out of solitude and alienation (puzzle-solving, plot-spinning, ultimately madness)—the options, to some extent, of the French left during the late 60s.

Formally, both serials could be called Bazinian in their preference for the long take and for mise en scène in depth over montage as a purveyor of meaning, a characteristic highlighted in the above remarks made by Rivette to the late Serge Daney. (In this respect especially, the aggressively edited, splintered, and Langian SPECTRE forms a striking dialectic with the long version of OUT 1, although both films share with TIH-MINH a preference for actors seen in full figure.) But in Rivette's case, the adherence to this approach ultimately leads to a kind of parodic summation of Bazin's notions about realism—a Rouch-like pseudodocumentary mired in fantasy—that might be said to undermine Bazinian theories more than simply illustrate them. In Feuillade's case, where it becomes difficult to speak of any conscious theoretical impulse, one is nonetheless persuaded to agree with Francis Lacassin, Alain Resnais, and others when they suggest that Feuillade combines the realism of Lumiere with the fantasy of Méliès into a mixture all his own.

In the first episode of OUT 1, one watches what appears to be a "cinéma direct" documentary of theater exercises performed by two separate groups and the lonely trajectories of two marginal outsiders—an apparent deaf-mute with a harmonica named Colin (Jean-Pierre Léaud) begging for money in cafés and a flirtatious, working-class hustler named Frédérique (Juliet Berto) finding various ways of extracting money from people. Then, very gradually, as in a vast novelistic fresco, these four seemingly disconnected subjects begin to link up, and various crisscrossing plots start to take shape. The disparate performance styles of various actors similarly proceed to blend and coalesce, as if bringing a core of covert meanings to the surface.

For reasons that are never explained, Colin receives a few cryptic, handwritten messages—all of them incidentally composed by Rivette himself—containing allusions to Balzac's *Histoire des treize* and Carroll's *The Hunting of the Snark* that he sets about decoding. Eventually this leads in another episode to a visit with a Balzac scholar (Eric Rohmer) who explains Balzac's concept, touched on in three novellas, of a secret alliance between thirteen Parisians of diverse professions who seek to rule all of society. Still later, it leads to Colin's discovery of the possible existence of a real-life counterpart to this alliance that formed prior to 1968, including a few members of both theater groups and some of their friends. (The action is all set during the spring of 1970, the time of the film's shooting.)

Meanwhile, Frédérique steals a letter alluding to the same alliance that she tries to parlay into a basis for blackmail. Many of the characters, indeed, wind up revealing various secrets—even Colin starts talking a blue streak in one of the intermediate episodes, losing his deaf-mute pose for several hours—and the conspiracies grow thicker at the same time that both groups start to dissolve. Even though certain scenes toward the end defy explanation or decoding—in a dialogue between Colin and Sarah (Bernadette Lafont), some of their lines are played backward on the sound track, and Frédérique is killed in an obscure intrigue on a rooftop—the overall design and meaning of OUT 1 become increasingly lucid as the serial unfolds. By the end, the paranoid fiction that the actors have generated has almost completely subsumed the documentary, even though the implied conspiracy continues to elude their grasp as well as ours. The successive building and shattering of utopian dreams—the idealistic legacy of May '68—are thus reproduced in the rising and declining fortunes of all the characters, outlining both the preoccupations and the shape of the work as a whole.

Collectivity and solitude, the two great Rivettian subjects, become intertwined like themes in a grand fugue, and in the overall sweep of the narrative, they become epic, mesmerizing subjects, especially in relation to the social and political issues of the period. In both this film and SPECTRE, the solitary act of decoding and the collective struggle of actors toward representation—both within the fiction and without—proceed neck in neck, then become intimately intertwined, and finally become untangled again.

Given the improvisational aspects of both serials—no doubt more programmatic as well as more dispersed in OUT 1, where each actor was invited to invent his or her own character and dialogue, but surely operative as well with Feuillade, who was known to create much of his story lines in the midst of shooting—the resemblance of each to a kind of automatic writing only enhances a capacity to enter the dreams of its respective period. (One peak in this regard is surely the 45-minute take of a single theater exercise that occurs somewhere in the middle of the Rivette serial—a shot that became possible in 16 millimeter during this period only because of the size of the camera's film magazines.) Certainly Rivette was aware of Feuillade's serials when he made OUT 1, even if the precedent he has cited more often in interviews is the original rough cuts of certain Jean Rouch films such as PETIT À PETIT.[5] Feuillade is even recalled explicitly in the final episode, in the fatal rooftop shootout between Frédérique, cloaked in a black mask and wielding a very old-fashioned revolver, and her lover, Renaud (Alain Libolt)—just as Rivette would later link the same actress and Dominique Labourier in CÉLINE ET JULIE VONT EN BATEAU (1974) to Irma Vep (Musidora) and her gang in LES VAMPIRES, by briefly dressing both of them in black tights.

Both films have accrued legends of a sort. In Gilbert Adair's recent *Flickers: An Illustrated Celebration of 100 Years of Cinema*,[6] a centennial array of 100 annotated stills representing 100 films and 100 years, TIH-MINH, the twenty-fourth film selected, is declared "the greatest, which is to say, the weirdest, most uncanny, most dreamlike" of the Feuillade serials, though LES VAMPIRES is understandably deemed the "most celebrated." Significantly, however, Adair's discussion of the serial is restricted exclusively to the remarkable still that he selects, which reveals eleven of the kidnapped society women sequestered in the Villa Circe—a still image that Adair treats exclusively as an *objet trouvé*, a surrealist discovery, rather than as part of a narrative that he recognizes or identifies. In other words, Adair chooses to regard the film itself as if he were an amnesiac unable to recall anything about it apart from this single enigmatic image:

> What, we wonder, as we gawp at it, what on earth led to this delirious tableau? That it makes for an arresting picture, granted—but we mustn't forget, meanwhile, that it also forms part of a narrative, of a story. So where, we ask ourselves, could it possibly have started from in order to arrive *there*? And what in heaven's name is going to happen next? (Is the recumbent woman on the extreme left about to *suckle* her companion?) If a splendid Rousseauesque lion were suddenly to wander through the drawing-room, we would scarcely bat an eyelid.[7]

The alternative to Adair's amnesia is, of course, to try to make sense of these sequestered ladies in the plot, but given the truncated state of most copies of TIH-MINH, this becomes difficult. (What are we to make, for instance, of the various references to them as the Villa Circe's "living dead"?) Thus the temptation to view them as poetic conceits that are somehow detachable from the remainder of the serial is irresistible. (I can still recall the appreciative laughter and associative reference of David Ehrenstein, a fellow cinephile, at the Museum of Modern Art in 1969 when these women ran amok in a garden like so many butterflies set loose: "SHOCK CORRIDOR!" he said.)

OUT 1 has long had the reputation of being "Rivette's twelve-hour film" or "Rivette's thirteen-hour film," a mythical object like the uncut GREED whose status as a touchstone rests almost exclusively on its unavailability. Sad to say, if the so-called uncut GREED[8] were to materialize tomorrow, it is doubtful whether many contemporary cinéphiles would be interested in seeing it. This was certainly the case when the uncut OUT 1 was screened in Rotterdam in 1989, and only a handful of spectators showed any interest in viewing it, either in its entirety or piecemeal.

3. Characters and Actors as Double Agents

One of the most remarkable sequences in TIH-MINH is the very first, a prologue preceding the narrative proper, simultaneously presenting nine of the serial's major characters and the actors playing them. Most of these figures appear against a bare black backdrop, in a characteristic pose and costume, often with a few simple props: Dr. Davesnes (Émile André), left hand in pocket, is smoking a cigarette and looking around; Jeanne d'Athys (Lugane [the pseudonym of Georgette Lagneau, who would become Feuillade's second wife in 1921]), the hero's sister, sniffs and arranges flowers in a tall vase;

[Dr.] Gilson (M. G. [Gaston] Michel), the first of the three major villains, also known as Marx, picks up a phone receiver and listens; Rosette ([Jane] Rolette), the maid, appears bashfully, hiding her face in her apron. Next come the two other villains: "the Asiatic Kistna" (Louis Leubas), a bearded Hindu in a turban, rubs his fingers together over a smoking urn; the Marquise Dolorès (Georgette Faraboni), hovering over an ornate white pedestal, holds a flower between her teeth. Placide (Biscot [the pseudonym of Georges Bouzac]), the other servant, blocks his own face with an upright feather duster, then lowers it to reveal a goofy grin and bulging eyes. Last but not least come the romantic leads—Tih-Minh (Mary Harald), appearing twice in succession, as an Asian woman dissolving into a Western woman, both seated in the same lush domestic setting; and "the explorer" Jacques d'Athys (René Cresté), dressed in both tie and bathrobe, holding a book and standing beside a small Buddha-like statue—a dandyish consumer-hero who half a century later would irresistibly evoke Hugh Hefner in his Playboy Mansion. (One is reminded of LES VAMPIRES, where again the villains prey only on the rich and where the putative hero comes across as a pampered nincompoop who, until he belatedly collects his wits and defeats the Vampire gang in the last episode, has to depend on his mother, family friends, and a team of other helpers to work out most of the clues and effect most of the rescues. Even when this hero triumphs at the end, it is his new bride who polishes off the sexy Irma Vep.)

Several points about this lineup are worthy of note. This succession of characters/actors generally takes on more scenic detail as it develops, implying a gradual enlargement of the fictional world. Heroes and villains are freely interspersed, as are masters and servants. (Not long afterward, in the story proper, a division is established between the Lucile Villa, where Jacques, his mother, his sister, Tih-Minh, Placide, and Rosette reside, and the Circe Villa, where Gilson/Marx, Kistna, and Dolorès hang out and plot their own strategies.) The most significant characters missing here are Sir Francis Grey, played by Édouard Mathé, and Tih-Minh's French father, Laurençon—raising the possibility that both figures, who make their first appearances relatively late in the serial, weren't prefigured at the outset.

A whole essay could be written speculating on the varying relationships each character has with both the camera and his or her immediate surroundings. The two servants, for instance, display an acute awareness of the spectator's gaze combined with an unbridled mugging that is unshared by the others. (These same characteristics are evident in the no less comic characters of Mazamette [Marcel Levesque] and Eustache [Bout de Zan] in LES VAMPIRES—pointing to the same premodernist tendency to superimpose the euphoria of the filmmaking process over the fictional action that we more commonly associate with later directors such as Renoir, Rivette, Cassavetes, and Altman.) And the degree to which other characters in TIH-MINH—Davesnes, Dolorès, Jacques—command and survey their immediate surroundings (in contrast to

Gilson, whose surveillance is both auditory and "long distance," via telephone, and to Kistna, Jeanne, and Tih-Minh, whose attentions are restricted
to their immediate props) tells us a great deal about how we are supposed to
regard them.

The two successive views we're offered of the title heroine, played by an
English actress—an Annamite orphan and refugee "saved" from Indochina by
Jacques and brought by him to France in the serial's opening scene, just after
this introduction—gives us an encapsulated account of colonialization in the
space of a single dissolve. Our first, "Asian" view of her shows her seated on
a sofa in lotus position, holding a fan; our second, "Western" view shows her
feet down, a kitten in her lap; both present her as a creature *and* object of
luxury.

The coexistence of characters' and actors' names within the same shots is
of course a staple of silent film, yet it carries a significant surplus of meaning
here. Like the two-part presentation of Tih-Minh, it points up a facet of this
serial as a whole that is shared by OUT 1—that no one is merely who he or
she initially appears to be but a palimpsest of separate guises and identities,
a series of improvisations that makes each character essentially a "work-in-
progress," a text undergoing successive and almost continuous revisions. Part
of this comes about in OUT 1 through the specter of "the 13" that runs through
Rivette's serial as both a puzzle and a grand utopian theme—never entirely
elucidated or resolved but never entirely dissipated either. (It's tempting to
read "the 13" as a coded allusion to *Cahiers du cinéma*'s Conseil des dix
or, more specifically, to the critics within that group determined to become
filmmakers, and utopian in some of their linked aspriations: Rivette, Godard,
Truffaut, Rohmer, Chabrol, Moullet et al. By the same token, the title shrine
in Truffaut's underrated THE GREEN ROOM can be partially viewed as a morbid
reflection on *la politique des auteurs*.) Part of it comes from the work of many
of the characters as participants in two experimental theater groups; and still
another part derives from the various fictions proffered, imagined, or uncov-
ered by Colin and Frédérique, each of whom stumbles on traces of "the 13"
and then tries to profit from this discovery. (Colin, posing as deaf-mute or
journalist, seeks only intellectual profit, the solution of various riddles offered
by coded messages that he intercepts; Frédérique, seeking to trick individuals
out of money, adopts the various poses of a con artist and blackmailer.) All
these conditions establish the characters as performers and/or pretenders, people with something to hide as well as something to show.

A major difference between the serials—accounting for their vast difference in popular appeal, at least to the audiences of their respective periods—
rests in the notion of a fixed text beneath or behind all the revisions. In TIH-
MINH, a supreme confidence in the fixed generic identities of heroes and villains and in the fixed social identities of masters and servants makes all the
"revisions" of these characters and the improvised spirit of their enactments a
form of play that never threatens their root functions and identities as narrative

figures. In OUT 1, the absence of this social and artistic confidence—a veritable agnosticism about society and fiction alike that seems to spring from both the skepticism of the late 60s and the burden placed on all the actors to improvise—gives the narrative a very different status, entailing a frequent slippage from character to actor and from fiction to nonfiction. Because none of the masks seems entirely secure, the fiction-making process itself—its pleasures, its dangers, even its traps, dead ends, and lapses—becomes part of the overall subject and interest. Here there is no fixed text beneath the various proliferating fictions that might guarantee their social and generic functions; what one finds instead is a series of references and allusions—Balzac and Renoir, Aeschylus and Lang, Rouch and Godard, Hitchcock and Feuillade—that can provide only theoretical pretexts or momentary, unsustainable models, as well as an overall spirit of play.[9]

4. Other Prologues

Beginning as a documentary that is progressively overtaken by fiction, OUT 1 as a whole has no prologue, merely a rudimentary itinerary set down in five successive intertitles—"Stéphane Tchalgadjieff presente/OUT 1/Premier Episode/de Lili à Thomas/Le 13 avril 1970"—followed by an opening shot of five actors in a bare rehearsal space performing elaborate physical exercises together to the sound of percussion. Minus the date, the same pattern of intertitles launches every other episode, each of which is labeled as a further relay between two characters, beginning in each case with the second character named in the previous segment.

All seven of the remaining episodes have prologues, each of which is structured identically: 26 black-and-white shots drawn from the color footage of the preceding episode—the first 24 static, silent stills accompanied by the same percussion heard in the first shot of the first episode, each still held for the same duration, the last two shots in motion and carrying their original direct sound. Thus the notion of precise links in a chain—between one episode and the next, between one character and the next—is maintained throughout as a strictly practical principle as well as a formal one. Each black-and-white prologue provides both a ghostly abstraction of the preceding segment as an aide-mémoire and a version of the "13" (2 x 13 = 26) as a compulsive rearrangement of existing data that might provide certain clues about what is to come. Similarly, each relay-title posits a beginning and an end to the trajectory of characters within each episode while establishing that each new beginning was formerly an end and each new end will form a new beginning—another form of abstraction-as-synopsis that retraces the action as if it were a kind of puzzle that might yield hidden meanings. (In SPECTRE, these titles vanish, but the black-and-white stills are reformulated at various junctures to provide cryptic extensions to as well as recollective summaries of the action, accompanied by a droning hum rather than percussion. As Rivette described this sound and function in a 1974 interview, "What we have is just a meaningless frequency, as if produced by a machine, which interrupts the fiction—sometimes sending messages to it, sometimes in relation to what we've already seen or are going to see, and sometimes with no relation at all. Because there are stills from scenes, especially toward the end [of SPECTRE], which don't appear in the body of the film and are frankly quite incomprehensible.")[10]

5. Messages, Documents, Origins, Calling Cards

The narrative underpinnings of both TIH-MINH and OUT I are largely traceable back to secret messages and documents that can be read as both gratuitous and arbitrary, though why they can be read this way differs in each serial. In TIH-MINH, this state of affairs is a material consequence of intertitles that are either missing (in the Belgian Cinémathèque version seen by me in 1969) or, in many other key instances, illegible (in the video copy of the French Cinémathèque version seen by me more recently), and probably has most bearing on the contents of a Hindu document leading to the death of Tih-Minh's father in Tonkin in 1911—in the longest and most important flashback in the serial, as well as the only sequence actually set in Indochina.

This tale is recounted by the villainess Dolorès after she's captured in the Lucile Villa by the heroes, thus restoring to Tih-Minh part of the lost memory imposed by the villains' potion of forgetfulness made from opium that renders her an amnesiac for most of the serial. (Near the end of the flashback, Tih-Minh's memory has been restored, and she narrates the closing portions herself.) Rather Sternbergian in setting and lighting, this interpolated story is set in and around the house of the heroine's father, Laurençon—a French functionary with a French family back in France who fathered Tih-Minh with an unseen Indo-Chinese woman in Tonkin. (Presumably the mother died in childbirth, though there's no explanation of her absence in the print I've seen recently.) Without being a wicked man, we're told in an intertitle, Laurençon hadn't much time to spend with his daughter (who briefly sits in his lap, but seems to spend most of her time outside picking flowers). A suspicious-looking German named Marx, disliked by Laurençon, settles in the neighborhood, periodically visits the house, and is present one day when an old Hindu on the verge of death who has fled from his own country asks to see a French official and produces a document—indecipherable in the version of the serial I've seen recently—that he wishes to will to France before he dies. (According to Richard Abel's description of the serial in *French Cinema: The First Wave, 1915–1929,* this is "a secret document that will lead . . . to an immense war treasure.") Marx sneaks a look at the document while Laurençon is giving the old man some money and a "hospital ticket," and the Frenchman, observing this indiscretion, orders him to leave, just before Tih-Minh returns from outside with her bouquet of flowers. The next night, Marx sneaks back into the house to steal the document, strangling a coolie servant and shooting Laurençon dead in the process. Symbolically, the vase of flowers previously gathered by Tih-Minh gets overturned, and Tih-Minh, waking from her hammock, struggles with Marx and scratches his face before he makes his getaway. After we see Tih-Minh in grieving close-up with her dying father, she concludes, in the present, "Then I left, brought by my mothers' parents to the other end of Tonkin. . . . It must have been there, Jacques, that you met me." Back on the Côte d'Azur, the repeated kidnappings of Tih-Minh by the villains are motivated by their belief that she can direct them toward the war treasure.

The substitution of Jacques for Laurençon—French fiancé for French father—seems transparent, as does the implicit substitution of Tih-Minh herself, as colonial booty, for the much-sought-after war treasure, and the substitution of England for France during the final episodes. (The serial's concluding intertitle: "Henceforth, the English government could pursue its civilizing mission in the Orient without interference.") But it's also worth speculating whether a substitution of Hindu for Indo-Chinese is equally operative in the film's colonial mythology. The old Hindu in the flashback is clearly a "good" character, but Marx's subsequent confederate, "the Asiatic Kistna," is just as clearly a villain (and TIH-MINH's U.S. title, one should note, was IN THE CLUTCHES OF THE HINDOO). It's uncertain whether the precise contents of the old Hindu's document would clarify this issue, but without this basic information, it seems useless to speculate.

One should add that the absence of the original intertitles in most or all of the Feuillade serials revived in France and the United States during the 60s and 70s was an important aspect of their rereading, enhancing and encouraging a formal perception of their narrative mechanisms stripped of certain narrative particulars. Consider, for instance, Annette Michelson's highly suggestive and evocative remarks about LES VAMPIRES, written during the 60s, which zeros in on the visiting cards whose identifying close-ups were precisely among the messages elided from the prints seen during that decade:

> Haussmann's pre-1914 Paris, the city of massive stone structures, of quiet avenues and squares, is suddenly revealed as everywhere dangerous, the scene and subject of secret designs. The trap-door, secret compartment, false tunnel, false bottom, false ceiling, form an architectural complex with the architectural structure of a middle-class culture. The perpetually recurring ritual of identification and self-justification is the presentation of the visiting card; it is, as well, the signal, the formal prelude to the fateful encounter, the swindle, hold-up, abduction or murder.[11]

Only during subsequent decades, when LES VAMPIRES was fully restored—intertitles, inserts, and all—would contemporary viewings of the serial more nearly approximate those of 1915 audiences.

In OUT 1, on the other hand, the coded messages received and then elaborately decoded by Colin—in an obsessive quest that implicitly parodies the spectator's own efforts to find a totalizing meaning in the film's crisscrossing narratives—are gratuitous and arbitrary *by design*. Indeed, one of the most telling differences between the serial and SPECTRE is that the messages received by Colin are different in each work, even though Colin's responses to these messages and their overall narrative functions are precisely the same.

6. Amnesia and Surveillance

These two themes, equally important in certain respects in both serials, point to the placement of the spectator as well as the placement of the characters. Regarding amnesia, the spectator's need to "forget" the plot of each serial between episodes, for a week's duration, and then to recall it again is duplicated by the situation of certain characters, deflected from their own paths and desires by memory loss until put back in touch again with their pasts (and their presents). In TIH-MINH, the title heroine's amnesia—keeping her in a troubled fog for most of the serial—is the most obvious instance of this. And I have already alluded to the willed amnesia of Gilbert Adair regarding the serial's narrative as prompted by an individual still. In OUT 1, amnesia is less literal, but the repression of memories about the 13 by various potential members and the periodic suspension of various guises and roles associated with Colin and Frédérique (such as his status as a deaf-mute and her status as a blackmailer) function rather similarly; for long stretches, characters become other than who they customarily are (or formerly were), assuming other identities and roles in the action.

Regarding surveillance, one also finds a certain congruence between the privileged position of the spectator in relation to all the characters and the placement of the potentially all-knowing characters in relation to the action. What we mean by "all-knowing" in the two serials is of course quite different. In TIH-MINH, it can mean all-hearing as often as all-seeing because of the concealed microphones hidden by the villains in the garden at the Lucile Villa, but it can also mean Jacques and Placide peering through a basement window of the Circe Villa at night and finding, to their astonishment, a whole flock of kidnapped society women dressed in white—or climbing a trellis to the second floor, and spying on Kistna preparing his forgetfulness potion in his laboratory. In OUT 1, "all-knowing" generally comes in two forms—inside the action proper, where it generally relates to theater work, and outside the action, where it becomes either a form of abstract knowledge gained by Colin in decoding messages or the rather banal and concrete information intercepted by Frédérique in reading stolen letters.[12]

7. Notions of Actuality

Apart from the flashback in Indochina, there are very few deaths in TIH-MINH—people who fall to the ground usually get up again—and, if memory serves, despite the fact that both theater groups in OUT 1 are putatively preparing to perform plays by Aeschylus, *Seven Against Thebes* and *Prometheus Bound,* there are no deaths at all in the Rivette serial apart from that of Frédérique, and apparently none whatsoever in SPECTRE. (One can't be entirely sure about the messenger played by producer Stéphane Tchalgadjieff—brained by Bulle Ogier with a bottle in the basement of the hippie boutique where she works, for no apparent reason, and never seen again.)

Despite this apparent tameness, and for all their extended comedy, both serials vibrate with a pronounced and prolonged feeling of danger and menace. In TIH-MINH, this is largely a matter of certain spectacular, death-defying stunts—most of them undertaken by Placide, the resourceful butler of the Lucile Villa, whose courage and energy often imply, by way of contrast, a certain decadence in the relative resources of his main employer, the "official" explorer/adventurer Jacques d'Athys. (Many of these stunts involve Placide hiding in a trunk or a basket that gets carried along a precipitous mountain road.) . . . In OUT 1 as in Rivette's 1968 L'AMOUR FOU, one feels that the dangers being skirted mainly have to do with sanity rather than physical well-being, but they are no less suspenseful and perturbing for all that. (See note 3.)

8. Topics for Further Cross-Referencing

TIH-MINH: Feuillade, Our Contemporary. Opulence and Terror, The Villa as Prison and as Refuge (cf. LAST YEAR AT MARIENBAD and THE EXTERMINATING ANGEL). Servants Outclassing Their Masters (cf. THE SERVANT). Expressionism Comes to the Third World, and Vice Versa (cf. Orson Welles's HEART OF DARKNESS, APOCALYPSE NOW, BLADE RUNNER . . .).

OUT 1: Rivette, Our Historian. Paranoia versus Antiparanoia (cf. Lang's Mabuse films and SPIONE, MURIEL, NOT RECONCILED, Pynchon's *Gravity's Rainbow* . . .). The Lure of Nineteenth-Century Masterplots (Balzac, Hugo, Carroll, etc.) in Twentieth-Century Mythology. Improvisation and the Fear of Acting in Relation to Existentialism. Duration and Lived Experience.

Both films: if memory serves (a dangerous postulate when it comes to works of this duration), World War I goes unmentioned, or virtually unmentioned, in TIH-MINH, whereas the Vietnam War goes unmentioned or virtually unmentioned in OUT 1—two structuring absences. Yet given the importance of Vietnam in TIH-MINH, would it be possible to imagine that each serial "knows" the lost reference—indeed, what one might call the Lost Continent— that the other serial is trying to uncover, that a fruitful conversation between these two works is theoretically possible? Such, at any rate, is the assumption of many of the preceding remarks.

To be continued . . .

Notes

1. *Sight and Sound* (December 1992): 24. Annette Michelson also included TIH-MINH in her own list in the same poll, p. 22.

2. A few exceptions: On TIH-MINH, see Francis Lacassin's *Louis Feuillade* (Paris: Éditions Seghers, 1964), 83–85, 185, and *Maître des Lions et des Vampires: Louis Feuillade* (Gretz: Pierre Bordas & fils, 1995), 232–235, 237, 247–252; Claude Ollier's *Souvenirs écrans* (Paris: Cahiers du cinéma Gallimard, 1981), 244–256; and the special Feuillade issue of *Les Cahiers de la Cinémathèque* (no. 48, 1987)—in particular, "Louis Feuillade francmaçon?" by Marcel Oms, pp. 39–40, and "L'Orient de Louis Feuillade" by François de la Breteque, p. 68, as well as Jean-André Fiéschi's "Feuillade l'homme aimante" in *Cahiers du cinéma*, no. 160 (November 1964): 30–39, and a paragraph by Richard Abel in *French Cinema: The First Wave, 1915–1929* (Princeton: Princeton University Press, 1984), 77–78. On OUT 1, see my long out-of-print collection, *Rivette: Texts & Interviews* (London: British Film Institute, 1978), 4, 39–53, 95–96; and François Thomas's article in *Positif*, no. 367 (September 1991): 10–16. Although most of the texts in *Rivette: Texts & Interviews* have been reprinted in the *Cahiers du Cinéma* collections published by Harvard University Press, the lengthy interview with Rivette on both versions of OUT 1, originally published in *La Nouvelle Critique*, no. 63 (144) (April 1973), is not available elsewhere in English. A detailed synopsis of SPECTRE is included in my essay "Work and Play in the House of Fiction" (*in Placing Movies: The Practice of Film Criticism* [Berkeley: University of California Press, 1995], 144–146).

3. By far the most important of Rivette's deletions—one of the most powerful scenes in the entire serial—is a lengthy *plan-séquence* featuring Jean-Pierre Léaud in the final episode, which occurred originally just after a comparably lengthy scene between Bulle Ogier and Bernadette Lafont. (In fact, the final episode in its original, 90-minute form showed all four of the major characters—Ogier, Léaud, Juliet Berto, and Michel Lonsdale—going to pieces in a separate extended sequence; no trace of any of these four sequences remains in SPECTRE. Lonsdale's scene is placed last, and his reduction to a mass of blubbering jelly during a crying jag on a beach seems to bring the serial full circle from the wordless hysteria of his group's first exercise.)

I haven't had an opportunity to query Rivette about his deletion of Léaud's climactic scene but suspect that this hair-raising sequence, which shows (or showed) Léaud's character alone in his room, in a state of hysteria oscillating between despair and (more briefly) exuberance, carried too many suggestions of Léaud's subsequent real-life emotional difficulties for Rivette to feel comfortable about retaining it. Based on my notes taken at the Rotterdam screening, the sequence, punctuated by a few patches of black leader, shows him crying, screaming, howling like an animal, banging his head against the wall, busting a closet door, writhing on the floor, then calming down and picking up his harmonica. After throwing away all three of the secret messages he has been trying for most of the serial to decode, he starts playing his harmonica ecstatically, throws his clothes and other belongings out into the hall, dances about maniacally, and then plays the harmonica some more. Dramatically and structurally, this raw piece of psychodrama suggested certain parallels with the sequence relentlessly recording Jean-Pierre Kalfon's self-lacerations with a razor in Rivette's L'AMOUR FOU (1967)—a disturbing piece of self-exposure in which the fictional postulates of the character seem to crumble into genuine pain and distress, representing in both films a dangerous crossing of certain boundaries into what can only be perceived as madness.

4. From an interview filmed as part of Claire Denis's JACQUES RIVETTE, LE VEILLEUR, a 150-minute documentary made for the French television series *Cinéma de notre temps*. The text of this interview is included in French and Italian in *Jacques Rivette: La règle du jeu* (Torino: Museo Nazionale del Cinema di Torino, 1992); the English translation here is my own.

5. See, for instance, the interview by Carlos Clarens and Edgardo Cozarinsky in *Sight and Sound* (Autumn 1972): 196, in which Rivette briefly discusses the eight-hour, four-hour, and 90-minute versions of PETIT À PETIT edited by Rouch.

6. London and Boston: Faber and Faber, 1995.

7. Adair, *Flickers*, 48–49.

8. See my monograph on GREED in the BFI Film Classics series (1993, distributed in the United States by Indiana University Press) for a detailed account of why the so-called uncut GREED refers not to one but to several possible and successive versions of the film approved by Stroheim, scarcely a single object. For reasons explored elsewhere in this essay, much the same ambiguity applies to the "uncut" OUT 1: does this refer to the "complete" film shown in Le Havre only as a workprint, the "complete" version shown in Rotterdam with part of the sound missing, or the subsequently cut (and recut) version shown theatrically in various Rivette retrospectives and on European television?

9. The issue at stake isn't so much the skill of Rivette's actors—which varies enormously—as the perfunctory nature of many of the fictions that they embody. And though OUT 1 is arguably the most accessible *and* entertaining of all Rivette's films, its recent resurrection has unfortunately occurred during a period when most audiences are far from being receptive toward self-consciously synthetic narrative.

10. "Phantom Interviewers Over Rivette," by Jonathan Rosenbaum, Lauren Sedofsky, and Gilbert Adair, *Film Comment* (September–October 1974): 23.

11. Quoted by Richard Roud in his "Feuillade" entry in *Cinema: A Critical Dictionary*, vol. 1 (London: Secker & Warburg, 1980), 354.

12. Ironically, the only point in OUT 1 in which Colin and Frédérique appear in the same shot occurs at a hippie boutique called l'Angle du hasard, where they briefly cross paths. In OUT 1: SPECTRE, this moment, which formally represents a climactic tying together of all the plot strands, takes place immediately before the film's intermission, halfway through the film, when the spectator is being (falsely) persuaded that he or she is finally being led out of narrative chaos; in the serial it occurs during the fifth episode.

—adapted from an article written for *The Velvet Light Trap*, vol. 37 (Spring 1996)

If you want to be "up to the minute" about cinema, there's no reason to be concerned that it's taken four years for Jean-Luc Godard's ambitious video series to reach Chicago. After all, James Joyce's *Finnegans Wake*, the artwork to which HISTOIRE(S) DU CINEMA seems most comparable, written between 1922 and 1939, was first published in 1939, but if you started to read it for the first time this week, you'd still be way ahead of most people in keeping up with literature. For just as *Finnegans Wake* figuratively situates itself at some theoretical stage after the end of the English language as we know it— from a vantage point where, inside Joyce's richly multilingual, pun-filled babble, one can look back at the twentieth century and ask oneself, "What *was* the English language?"—Godard's babbling video similarly projects itself into the future in order to ask, "What *was* cinema?" Indeed, the fact that it's a video and not a film already tells you a great deal about its point of view.

Joyce's province was the history of mankind as perceived through language and vice versa, both experienced and recapitulated through a single, ordinary night of sleep. Only superficially more modest, Godard's province is the twentieth century as perceived through cinema and vice versa—the title can be translated loosely as "Film (Hi)story/Film (Hi)stories"—both experienced and recapitulated though technology. Clips and sound tracks are examined and juxtaposed—partly through the ordinary operations of a video watcher (fast-forward, slow motion, freeze-frame, muting, and programming) and partly through more sophisticated techniques like editing, sound mixing, captioning, and superimposition.

As "unwatchable" and as "unlistenable" in many respects as *Finnegans Wake* is "unreadable," the first two parts of Godard's HISTOIRE(S)—entitled respectively ALL THE HI(STORIES) and ONE (HI)STORY ALONE—are also almost as hard to translate as the Joyce book, though the English subtitles affixed to the version showing here do help somewhat. (The video contains some stretches in English and a few in untranslated Russian.) The subtitler, Orna Kustow, sensibly hasn't tried to do justice to all the wordplay, though a valuable service is carried out by identifying many of the film titles by their English equivalents rather than their literal translations. J'AI LA DROIT DE VIVRE, for instance, is subtitled YOU ONLY LIVE ONCE, the original title of Fritz Lang's film, rather than "I Have the Right to Live," and LA LOI DE SILENCE is rightly identified as Hitchcock's I CONFESS rather than rendered as "The Vow of Silence." But even so, the original French titles contribute to Godard's meanings, so bilingual viewers have an advantage. (When TEMPETE SUR LE CINEMA is subtitled "Tempest Over the Cinema," for instance, this elides the reference to Pudovkin's STORM OVER ASIA, known in French as TEMPETE SUR L'ASIE.)

This isn't to suggest that having a perfect grasp of French—which I don't, by the way—would make this video crystal clear. A poet who proceeds largely through intuitive metaphors and pithy slogans suggesting playful, dialectical paradoxes, Godard has never been easy to take "straight"—not even when he was writing criticism for *Cahiers du cinéma* in the 50s. Alone among his critical colleagues who became filmmakers, he insisted from the beginning that his writing and filmmaking were essentially alternate vehicles for the same discourse; his early movies functioned as film criticism the same way his reviews anticipated much of his filmmaking. (Significantly, the first part of the video essentially begins with two technological sounds/images/rhythms: film turning on an editing table and Godard tapping typewriter keys—the first legato, the second staccato.) ALPHAVILLE, for instance, can be read in part as a detailed critique of German expressionist cinema,* and WEEKEND as a series of annotations on American movies interrelating murder and capitalism, such as MONSIEUR VERDOUX, JOHNNY GUITAR, and PSYCHO.

■

To suggest some of the complexity and richness of Godard's HISTOIRE(S), let me attempt to describe everything we see and hear over a two-minute stretch near the beginning. This section comes shortly after we hear Godard say, "All

---

* See my article "Theory and Practice: The Criticism of Jean-Luc Godard," in *Placing Movies: The Practice of Film Criticism* (Berkeley: University of California Press, 1995), 21–22, for a specific illustration of this premise.

the histories that have been, that might have been," and its ingredients include a quote from André Bazin ("Cinema substitutes for our gaze a world corresponding to our desires") parsed out into five phrases, a dozen film clips, a passage from the adagio of Beethoven's Tenth Quartet, and segments from the sound tracks of two separate films. The first clip, and the most subliminal, consists of successively larger color close-ups, connected by jump cuts, of a woman whose eyes seem to be painted blue; if I'm not mistaken, this woman appears in the film-within-the-film in Godard's own feature CONTEMPT, which uses the Bazin quote as its epigraph. Then, behind "Cinema substitutes" are intercut alternating clips from Murnau's FAUST (Mephistophocles greeting Faust at a crossroads) and Minnelli's THE BAND WAGON (Cyd Charisse dancing around Fred Astaire in a production number) while we hear both the string quartet and part of the narration and dialogue from Resnais's LAST YEAR AT MARIENBAD, both of which continue through most of the segment. Behind "for our gaze" are intercut alternating clips from Renoir's THE RULES OF THE GAME (servants beating sticks against trees, rousing rabbits out of hiding for wealthy guests to shoot) and Mizoguchi's CHIKAMATSU MONOGATARI (a woman stumbling through a forest and fighting off a man who approaches her). Behind "a world" are intercut alternating clips from two films I don't recognize, though the first appears to be French: in one, a man stands in the ocean holding a nymphet and teaching her how to swim, and in the other a group of wealthy couples enter a nightclub and start to dance. Behind "corresponding," Lillian Gish limping exhaustedly across a street in Griffith's BROKEN BLOSSOMS is intercut with a raucous race involving dance hall women (including Marlene Dietrich) riding cowboys piggyback from Lang's RANCHO NOTORIOUS, and at this point the sound track of the Lang film, in sync with the images, briefly takes the place of the MARIENBAD narration. Finally, behind "to our desires," three intercut clips alternate: Gish continues to cross the street and catches her breath on the other side, masked soldiers on horseback in Eisenstein's ALEXANDER NEVSKY attack with lances, and a lush period ball scene is glimpsed from Visconti's THE LEOPARD; by this time, dialogue from an earlier section of MARIENBAD has supplanted the narration.

Here are a few thematic connections that I suspect Godard has in mind: FAUST, THE BAND WAGON, and MARIENBAD represent three very different versions (or "substitutions") of the Faust theme: the production number in THE BAND WAGON comes from a musical based on *Faust,* and Charisse dancing around Astaire in a gangster setting is explicitly linked in the editing to Mephistophocles tipping his hat to greet Faust, while the narration from MARIENBAD (beginning, "You haven't changed—you still have the same remote eyes, the same smile, the same sudden laugh . . .") constitutes a comparable seduction of the film's heroine by the hero. In short, three forms of hypnotic persuasion into a world of fantasy fulfillment are presented together.

Similarly, one might surmise that Renoir's rabbits and Mizoguchi's fleeing woman are linked as the victims of predators, that Gish (fleeing from her father's abuse) and Dietrich are accorded contrasting means of locomotion in relation to men, and that the three final images define three forms of cinema "corresponding to our desires"—feminine fragility, war/violence, and production values. As for the string quartet, your guess is as good as mine.

Some of the subsequent juxtapositions include a witch burning from Dreyer's DAY OF WRATH with Rita Hayworth singing "Put the Blame on Mame" in GILDA, the wicked witch from Disney's SNOW WHITE AND THE SEVEN DWARFS with Bernard Herrmann's PSYCHO score, Renoir's ELENA ET LES HOMMES with "The Night They Invented Champagne" from GIGI, a shot from BONJOUR TRISTESSE with a Monet landscape, and successive evocations of Lang's THE INDIAN TOMB, Cukor's BHOWANI JUNCTION, and Duras's INDIA SONG. But I don't want to suggest that you have to be able to identify Godard's specific references in order to appreciate his video; at best it can help one to enjoy certain inflections. When one block of material announces, "1940, Geneva, Max Ophüls. He falls upon Madeleine Ozeray's ass just as the German army takes the French army from behind," it may help to know that Godard is alluding to Ophüls's unfinished filming of a stage performance in Geneva of Molière's *École des femmes,* but that isn't really the principal point of this rude simile. Much more significant is the simultaneity of what's happening in cinema and what's happening in the world outside—a point made equally when Godard uses a guest at a masked ball in a skeleton suit in THE RULES OF THE GAME (1939) to allude to concentration camp victims. (Actually, a similar cast of mind can be seen in a mocking juxtaposition eliminated by the French censors from Godard's first feature, BREATHLESS—a cut from Charles de Gaulle's car following Dwight D. Eisenhower's car in a procession down the Champs-Elysées to Jean-Paul Belmondo following Jean Seberg down the sidewalk.)

In terms of the video's overall myth, cinema and the twentieth century—almost interchangeable in Godard's terms—are contextualized by two key countries (France and the United States), two emblematic producers (Irving Thalberg, Howard Hughes), and two emblematic world leaders (Lenin, Hitler); two decisive falls from cinematic innocence (the end of silent film that came with talkies and the end of talkies that came with video); and two decisive falls from worldly innocence (World War I and World War II). A good many of the epigrams and glosses might be said to emanate directly from these reference points: "But if myths start with Fantomas, they end with Christ," "World War I would let Americans ruin French cinema," "(Hi)stories with an 's' . . . with an 'SS,' " Thalberg as "the only man who conjured up 52 films a day," Hughes as an aviator identified with ONLY ANGELS HAVE WINGS.

■

Once I played a record of Cyril Cusack reading aloud from *Finnegans Wake* at a friend's house, and it provoked sustained giggles of delight from her two grammar school children; I wouldn't be surprised if Godard's audiovisual babble had a comparable effect. Adults, more prone to worry over what they can't immediately decode—and therefore less likely to see the forest for the trees—may have some problems with it, just as they might with Joyce. Godard's work should be approached in a spirit of innocence. When asking big questions, it usually helps if you keep them simple, and despite some appearances to the contrary this is what I believe Godard has done. As he puts it at one point, "Cinema, like Christianity, is not founded on history. It tells a story and says, 'Believe it.' " And at another: "It's not a just image. It's just an image."

—Chicago *Reader,* July 16, 1993

Pages from the Endfield File

Many things have stood in the way of Cy Endfield becoming better known. A blacklisted filmmaker who moved to England in 1951 in order to continue working, he had to hide for years behind a hired front (Charles De Lautour)—to whom he had to pay typically half his fees—and various pseudonyms even there due to threats by the U.S. projectionists' union to block American distribution of English films on which blacklisted personnel worked. His auteurist profile is disrupted by a two-part filmography (seven features in the United Sates, 14 abroad) consisting mainly of genre films that aren't easy to come by today. Better known among professional magicians than among film buffs, he is usually unknown in both groups for his remarkable inventions—the Microwriter, a computerized, pocket-sized, four-key typewriter (1978), and the Agenda, a computerized pocket organizer (circa 1982)—or his designed chess sets like the Spasky-Fischer Commemorative, used in the 1972 world tournament, and Chesslandia.

Fortunately, Endfield's two best films by most accounts, including his own and mine—THE SOUND OF FURY (1951) and ZULU (1964)—are readily available, the first on video as TRY AND GET ME, the second on both video and letterboxed laserdisc, and it isn't hard to find THE UNDERWORLD STORY (1950),

MYSTERIOUS ISLAND (1961), and SANDS OF THE KALAHARI (1965). Over the
past few years, a gratifying surge of interest in his work has led to tributes at
Chicago's Film Center, in Rotterdam and Telluride, and on the BBC; an inter-
view for National Public Radio, a column by Todd McCarthy in *Daily Variety*
(September 11, 1992), a few pages in Brian Neve's *Film and Politics in
America* (Routledge); and some preliminary forays of my own. A few basic
misunderstandings in reference books have been cleared up: contrary to James
Monaco, Endfield died not in 1983 but on April 16, 1995, and contrary to
Ephraim Katz, he was born in Scranton, Pennsylvania, not South Africa, and
never revoked his U.S. citizenship.*

In early 1993, after many phone conversations and exchanged audiocassettes (a substitute for letters because of Endfield's failing eyesight), I was
privileged to spend a little over a day with Endfield and his gracious wife,
Maureen, at their home in rural England. Part of what follows derives from
that meeting as well as generous help from Thom Andersen, Tom Luddy,
Howie Movshovitz, Pierre Rissient, Mehrnaz Saeed-Vafa, Barbara Scharres,
Habie Schwarz, and Bart Whaley.

> *Jonathan Rosenbaum:* There are references to magic in most of your films, but
> the first examples that come to mind are all negative: magic as dehuman-
> ized nightclub entertainment in THE SOUND OF FURY, as a means of deceiv-
> ing gullible Africans in TARZAN'S SAVAGE FURY, and as the regular work of
> a blackmailer in THE LIMPING MAN. Negativity remains a powerful and
> meaningful constant in your work, but I'm curious why magic elicits that
> particular response from you.
>
> *Cy Endfield:* It seems to me now that from the very beginning of my interest in
> magic, in the performance of tricks, I knew that there was a spurious as-
> pect. For the price of a dime or a quarter, one could buy a knickknack that
> had some hidden little mechanism in it and at that moment outwit Ein-
> stein—at that moment humiliate Einstein by puzzling him, and congratu-
> late oneself that one knew something Einstein didn't. I trace in my memory
> this understanding that magic has an aggressive component in it, that it
> derides the intelligence of its audience by obscure and underhanded
> devices.
>
> When did this all begin? I think when I was 12 or 13 years old, I was
> sent to a boys camp by my parents. A counselor was assigned to my tent—
> a college youth who was a magician. Later on he accrued some identity for
> himself as Roger Barkin, the poetic magician; he did all his patter in poetry.
> In any event, the element that attracted me was the dexterity aspect of it. I

---

* See Endfield's own letter in the March–April 1992 *Film Comment*, p. 79, written in response
to my "Guilty by Omission"—an essay reprinted (with corrections) in *Placing Movies: The Practice of Film Criticism* (Berkeley: University of California Press, 1995), 281–294.

became early on a card expert; I designed my own tricks, and achieved some identity in the fraternity of magicians, because I submitted articles to magic magazines that described tricks.* I carried around this hobby and used it to help identify myself and take command in certain situations. In due course I was being classified as one of the bright youngsters who could do things that others couldn't do.

By this time I had gone to Yale and had come to New York in pursuit of a career in theater. I think the fact that I did tricks, sometimes being paid for them, gave me a sense of professional identity in connection with theater, and my general interest, which led me to hitchhike to New York and take up residence there, was motivated by my interest in magic. The connection retained its force and affected my whole life—and whatever work emanated from that life.

"I made a sort of Hitchcockian effort to put tricks into most of my pictures," Endfield told me somewhat later, citing as one example a variation of the "egg and cup" trick done by actor James Booth with a bullet in the hospital in ZULU.

Born November 10, 1914, Endfield was in his early twenties when he moved to New York after graduating from Yale. (He was a year late in starting there due to the collapse of his father's business in Scranton.) His interest in theater, which led to him acting in a college production of *Waiting for Lefty*, brought him in New York to the New Theater League, "the center of activity that grew out of the work of Clifford Odets and the Group Theater, under the direction of men like Elia Kazan and Lee Strasberg." Endfield dates his discovery of his directorial vocation back to the experience of preparing a scene from Molière's *The Fabulous Invalid*, a lengthy dialogue between two ladies, for a class demonstration. (Later on, he also taught at the New Theater League, and Shelley Winters and Martin Balsam were among his students.)

> I made my living at the time by organizing a small entertainment group who worked in social satire, very much in the spirit of *Beyond the Fringe*, and we worked in nightclubs, at weddings and bar mitzvahs and workers' social events. Eventually I was offered a position to run an amateur theater—as a salaried professional—in Montreal. I went away for a year, where I directed plays by Ibsen and others, original musicals, and so on. This work took me into the mountains, the Catskills—the herring farms, as they were called, the adult camps and hotels—and there I did direction of plays and musicals and other forms of entertainment. I considered myself qualified as a director, and

---

* See also Endfield's article "I Lobby My Hobby" in the January 1943 *Esquire* and Lewis Ganson's three-volume *Cy Endfield's Entertaining Card Magic*, published in London in the mid-50s.

eventually joined three or four others in an automobile ride across the United States, all of us en route to Los Angeles to take over the movie business. I arrived there in September 1940, and by the end of '41 I had made very little progress.

As a magician, Endfield sometimes hung out at the Hollywood Magic Shop on Hollywood Boulevard. It was there one day that he met and impressed his idol, Orson Welles, with his card tricks—a meeting that eventually led to him being hired by Welles's manager, Jack Moss, as an apprentice on the Mercury unit at RKO while Welles was away in Brazil.* (During the same period, Endfield and his first wife—whom he'd met in Montreal, and who worked in Los Angeles with Elsa Lanchester at the Turnabout Theater—were dinner guests at Lanchester and Charles Laughton's home along with Jean Renoir the same night Pearl Harbor was bombed. As Endfield dryly recalled, both Laughton and Renoir interpreted this event as the onset of a worldwide communist revolution and were mainly concerned about the consequent fate of free artistic expression.)

Endfield's first consequential Hollywood job was at M-G-M during the summer of 1942, where his first assignment was directing (and largely writing) INFLATION, a two-reel propaganda short requested by the Office of War Information to back up a recent speech by FDR. After it was favorably reviewed in the trade press, and seven hundred copies (many times the usual print orders) were struck, Endfield had every expectation of being assigned to direct a feature next. But just before the film was scheduled to open, a telegram from Nicholas M. Schenck, president of Loew's, Inc., M-G-M's parent company, ordered M-G-M to pull all prints. Later it emerged that the Chamber of Commerce's national office requested the suppression, apparently afraid that manufacturers would object to some of the inflationary scams described in the film. Endfield quickly went from being "a white hopeful" at M-G-M to "a very black sheep indeed." The film's next public screening, at Telluride, would have to wait another half a century.

INFLATION offers us two patriarchal sages seated behind desks, each of whom intones a documentary-footage voice-over when he isn't seen addressing the camera or talking into a telephone receiver. One of them—literally the Devil (Edward Arnold)—commands much more space and attention; on the other end of his phone receiver is Adolf Hitler, his pal, whom we faintly hear shrieking in frenetic German. The other one, Franklin Roosevelt, is heard speaking over the radio and sometimes seen addressing the camera.

---

* For a detailed account of this episode, see the original version of this article in *Film Comment* (November–December 1993): 50–52.

We first find the Devil cackling over shots of lightning bolts and documentary evidence of wartime devastation. Then we see him seated behind the glass desk in his futurist tycoon's office, chortling to his sullen, sultry mistress, who is periodically seen smoking long cigarettes or pouring long drinks of dry ice: "Wonderful, wonderful! The best season I ever had!" A signed photo of Hitler rests on his desk and a black raven is perched directly over it.

Clearly there's nothing subtle about INFLATION, nor was there meant to be. The Chamber of Commerce may have been perturbed by this punchy expressionist short because Endfield carried out his assigned task—attacking various forms of capitalist greed and selfishness leading to inflation—all too well. It seems relevant that the Devil and a couple of wholesome housewives are both glimpsed at unsettling low angles—the Devil from beneath the surface of his glass desk, the housewives almost from knee level, chatting on a suburban doorstep—and it's difficult to decide which of these two angles seems more sinister. At the age of twenty-seven, Endfield's singular flair for portraying brutish self-interest in a wholly believable and lucid (if sardonic) manner is already firmly in place.

The capitalist selfishness the Devil gleefully encourages begins with the buying binge of factory worker Joe Smith (Horace McNally), who goes with his wife (Esther Williams in her preswimming phase) on a shopping spree as soon as he collects his paycheck. "You look wonderful," he says late in the trip when she tries on a fur wrap, to which she replies, "Gee, honey, it took four dresses and a new coat for you to say so." When the clerk suggests that Joe can buy even more for his wife and himself on credit, there's a cut to the Devil on the phone beaming, "Well, it's started, Adolf—a blitz without bullets," explaining that with few goods around, price bidding is bound to start soon. Laden with packages, Joe and his wife wind up listening to FDR on a radio in a shop speak at length about all that should be done: "stabilize prices . . . ration scarce commodities . . . invest in war bonds . . . discourage installment buying," and so on.

"Look at me—Joe Sap!" a chastened Joe declares at the end of this speech, and his wife agrees that they've been "overdoing it." But all the other citizens we meet in this short remain, more plausibly, unenlightened, whether it's a chorus girl buying nylons on the black market, a tailor being taught by the Devil how to switch labels on a garment and thereby cheat on price fixing, housewives expounding on the virtues of hoarding and stockpiling, or a fellow in a restaurant being convinced by the Devil to cash in his war bonds and buy an expensive car to improve his image.

"Would you like to join us?" the Devil asks the camera at the end, extolling the virtues of racial superiority before urging us all to buy, "squawk," be greedy, hoard, and so on. "Do these things and oblige my friend"—he points to the phone receiver, affectionately adding "Sieg heil!"—"*and* your most humble servant." He cackles some more, and the lightning bolts return, welcoming us all to the impending apocalypse.

■

With his career abruptly short-circuited, Endfield received only the most routine assignments at M-G-M.* After exploring the possibility of directing features at Columbia, he lost his draft deferment and wound up at a Signal Corps training center in Missouri. A year later, on maneuvers, he was sent to the hospital, told that he had a chronically spastic colon, and given an honorable discharge. Back in Los Angeles, he discovered that he was legally entitled to eight more months of employment at M-G-M, and got his old position back with minimal assignments on shorts and directing tests. In his spare time, he conversed with Buster Keaton—working in the adjoining office as a gagman on a Red Skelton picture—and listened to *Suspense* on the radio. Finding himself in the same car pool with the latter's producer, William Spier, he proposed writing a script for the show and sold the first four that he wrote; the first of these was called *The Argyle Album* and starred Robert Taylor. (Welles also hired him to rewrite a radio script for his wartime show *Hello Americans,* though he wound up using very little of Endfield's draft.)

After getting a freelance job to rewrite the script for the first "Joe Palooka" feature being produced at Monogram, JOE PALOOKA, CHAMP (1946)—the first in a series based on the popular comic strip—Endfield got to direct as well as write the second, GENTLEMAN JOE PALOOKA (1946), and later directed and cowrote JOE PALOOKA IN THE BIG FIGHT (1949) as well. While working on the latter, Endfield got a call from songwriter Allan Roberts who, in collaboration with Lester Lee, had just written the songs for GILDA and wanted him to write the book for a Broadway musical they were preparing, *Dear Sears Roebuck*— a show that never saw the light of day. While working at Roberts and Lee's cottage office at Columbia, he met the studio actress Marilyn Monroe, and tried unsuccessfully to get his producer at Monogram, Hal Chester, to cast her as Palooka's sweetheart. But shortly afterward, when Endfield and Joe Kirkwood, Jr., the actor playing Palooka, were planning an in-person act to promote the Palooka pictures, Kirkwood himself suggested Monroe as a singer and sketch performer. As a trial run, they performed the act gratis at a few veterans hospitals and men's club benefits, with Endfield serving as writer, emcee, and magician and Monroe assisting in the magic, playing in the comedy sketch, and singing "Diamonds Are a Girl's Best Friend," but the act never went any further.

---

*These consisted of three "Our Gang" comedies (RADIO BUGS, TALE OF A DOG, DANCING ROMEO) and work on a couple of "Passing Parade" shorts about Nostradamus, all in 1944. After his military service, he's credited with three more "Passing Parade" shorts, THE GREAT AMERICAN MUG (1945), MAGIC ON A STICK, and OUR OLD CAR (both 1946).

Most of Endfield's other credits in this period are poverty-row commissions: writing or cowriting two Bowery Boy features in 1946 (MR. HEX and HARD BOILED MAHONEY); writing and directing a comedy with a two-week shooting schedule called STORK BITES MAN in 1947 ("an impossible piece of trash," was all he cared to tell me about it) that received either limited release or no release at all; writing the Chinatown wedding scene in Douglas Sirk's SLEEP MY LOVE in 1948.* But in 1948 he also wrote and directed his third feature, the first that he would later recall with any pride or affection—THE ARGYLE SECRETS, a surprisingly beautiful Z-budget thriller hastily adapted from his first radio script and shot in six days (and the first Endfield film apart from INFLATION that I've seen since early childhood).

If INFLATION is unusually packed and fast-moving, the rarely shown, sixty-three-minute ARGYLE SECRETS is even more so. The cast features well over a dozen fully developed speaking parts, and there are so many interlocking and often paranoid intrigues crammed into one twenty-four-hour story line that even after three viewings I'd defy anyone to come up with a complete synopsis. The sheer darkness of the night scenes only intensifies our occasional perplexity, though it must be added that Endfield and his cinematographer, Mack Stengler, create many remarkable and arresting noir compositions out of this interminable stretch of night, usually with what appear to be minimal light sources. (One of the best utilizes two figures silhouetted behind frosted glass flanking the hero inside a police lieutenant's office; at the end of the scene, when the hero leaves and the police lieutenant picks up the phone to order two cops to shadow him, the "shadows" promptly disappear from behind the glass.) Great quantities of plot and deduction are shoehorned into the dialogue or voice-over narration at various junctures, and Endfield's drastic economy in negotiating this overflow at times produces some startling moments of visual poetry.

If the quest plot carries certain unmistakable echoes of THE MALTESE FALCON, made seven years earlier, the overall brittle, anxious, and doom-ridden mood is even more evocative of KISS ME DEADLY, made seven years later. It seems that the only direct steal in the movie, however, is a shock cut from a character making a belated discovery to a screaming tugboat whistle; Hitchcock in BLACKMAIL gets the same effect from the discovery of a dead body and a train whistle.

The much-sought-after object here is an argyle album containing the records of agreements struck between American and Nazi businessmen during the war, valued as much for blackmail and resale value as for a potential journalistic scoop. As a woman named Marla (Marjorie Lord) explains it, in a

---

*His writing credits after he moved to England, apart from the films he directed, include his script for the 1955 American movie CRASHOUT, an uncredited rewrite on CURSE OF THE DEMON (1957), and ZULU DAWN (1979).

patch of expository dialogue offering a fair sample of Endfield's cadenced prose, "You know, some men weren't so sure we'd win this late and little lamented war. So they made deals, deals with men who should have been their enemies—big money deals so they'd come out all right no matter which side won. The records of those deals were buried deep. What happened? A bomb made a direct hit. A bank vault opened like a spoiled tin can and spilled its rotten secrets. Then came the scavengers, the looters who always follow air raids, and with them Winters, who found among the debris the documents of betrayal. Winters lived in America before, recognized the names inscribed, and knew that he found a fortune—a fortune in blackmail."

This sort of collaboration with the Nazis is a subject that, to the best of my knowledge, no other moviemakers were broaching in the late 40s; but what is most distinctive about THE ARGYLE SECRETS is its view of humanity as inflected by war, a view that seems fully consistent with the one presented in INFLATION five years earlier. Indeed, by the end of the film, even the hero and voice-over narrator—a rather unsavory and callous reporter named Harry Mitchell (William Gargan) who manages to triumph over all the assorted crooks, creeps, and exploiters in the film through his own cleverness—is more than a little tarnished by his own brutality and careerism, despite his claims of being motivated by loyalty to another journalist. (Eleven years earlier Gargan played Father Dolan in Fritz Lang's YOU ONLY LIVE ONCE, which suggests he's a somewhat unconventional casting choice for a hero *or* anti-hero.)

The other journalist is a famous political columnist, Pierce (George Anderson), who builds up interest in his paper for two weeks about the contents of the argyle album, then offers Mitchell an exclusive interview after he enters a hospital, fearing he might not live long enough to tell his tale. Pierce grows faint and dizzy before he can even explain what the album is, though he does show Mitchell a photostat of its cover; and just after Mitchell rushes to the washroom to fetch him some water Pierce dies, an offscreen death memorably signaled by a close-up of the faucet as it ceases to drip (a perfect example of Endfield's surrealist sense of economy). Mitchell determines that Pierce is dead by feeling his pulse, but moments later, when he returns to the room with several others, they find a scalpel planted in Pierce's chest. The police turn up, and after the corpse of Mitchell's photographer is found in the same room only a few moments later, Mitchell flees from the scene and loses himself in traffic, proceeding to Pierce's office, where he promptly (if apologetically) slaps the secretary (Barbara Billingsley) unconscious so he can go through her boss's address book, hoping to track down the album.

Though he's far from a nice guy, Mitchell turns out to be relatively charismatic compared with the war profiteers, hoods, and stupid cops—not to mention a seedy fence and a corrupt doctor—who figure at various points in the plot, a rogue's gallery like the one only sketched in INFLATION. "Relatively" is the operative term here, as it often is in Endfield's moral universe; when Mitchell learns from Marla that she's interested in the album only for its resale value, he remarks, "That's a comparatively decent motive," and she replies, "I'm a comparatively decent person."

Yet despite the jaded view of human impulses on display here, Endfield doesn't really qualify as a misanthrope like Anthony Mann or Stanley Kubrick (two other pessimistic disciples of Orson Welles and the 40s noir tradition). One of the most appealing and unexpected interludes in THE ARGYLE SECRETS occurs when Mitchell, fleeing down a fire escape from war profiteer Winters (John Banner) and his hoods (who have beaten him senseless offscreen, expressionistically depicted in a sequence illustrating his disassociation and delirium), suddenly enters the flat of a working-class Jewish family he knew slightly years before. Much of the ensuing comedy stems from the family's unobservant, trusting attitude toward Mitchell—a boy (Kenneth Greenwald) dutifully carries out his violin practice under the strict orders of his ditsy, anxious mother (Mary Tarcai) and dim-witted but good-natured older brother (Robert Kelland), a rookie cop who suddenly turns up with groceries.

Though Endfield ribs all three of these quaint, myopic characters, he's clearly affectionate rather than caustic. (Jewish himself, he suggested to me that he regarded this scene as something of an in-joke about his early work in the Catskills—a Borscht-circuit background that later led to his highly successful staging of the English production of Neil Simon's first play, *Come Blow Your Horn*.) There's a similar gentleness in his treatment of a stupid police lieutenant (Ralph Byrd), who figures much more prominently in the plot than the Jewish family. And if the "comparatively" decent Marla is still largely a standard-issue noir bitch goddess, the other, more odious types in the story—a southern rascal with a stiletto (Jack Reitzen), a fence whose cover is his job in waterfront salvage (Alex Fraser), and arguably even Winters—offer brief glimpses of humanity. Like the pinpoints of light briefly and strategically illuminating the film's endless reaches of darkness, these small, humanizing breaks in the overall patterns of greed are glancing yet pivotal elements in the overall composition.

"Are you a pessimist?" I asked Endfield when I visited him in England. He replied, "I would prefer realist. But I would add that my realistic appraisal of the condition of man in terms of odds is that the outlook is poor. There *are* options. I think our whole evolution has been founded on two contradictory aspects. One is the survival of yourself as an individual, the other is group survival. So we have two main ideas at cross-purposes, which makes the outlook very bad. And the economic developments of societies have never been stabilized to give the benefits of the creative parts of society, in whose name these parts are invented, to most of our species."

■

Finally graduating to more respectable budgets in THE UNDERWORLD STORY and THE SOUND OF FURY, two more noirs with callous journalists, Endfield revealed himself a consummate action director in the terrifying mob scene that concludes the latter film—a talent he was able to develop only overseas in such films as HELL DRIVERS (1957), SEA FURY (1958), and ZULU. On the other hand, though Endfield's films are usually entertaining, viewers who expect to find the security blankets of charismatic heroes and neat psychological explanations are likely to be perturbed—at times even scared and shaken—by their relative absence in his work. With rare exceptions, these are upsetting movies with values that are often difficult to separate from Endfield's negativity and his capacity to depress us. People who go to movies in order to flee distress—and who no doubt expect their evening news to be cheerful and easily digestible as well—are advised to stay miles away from Endfield's corrosive work.

A social environmentalist, Endfield is interested in how individuals relate to one another and in how groups interact within particular societies and temporary gatherings. He's particularly fascinated by chance encounters on plane flights—THE LIMPING MAN (1953), THE MASTER PLAN (1954), JET STORM (1959), and SANDS OF THE KALAHARI (1965) all begin with people on planes or in airports—and the behavior of a group during a cataclysmic crisis is the focus of the latter two movies as well as THE SOUND OF FURY and ZULU. A keen observer of class differences and (something that's much rarer) class resentments, he's much more interested in the ways that people are socially programmed and in how they function in collective situations than he is in individual psychological profiles, and in this respect he's more a Marxist than a Freudian. (Though avowedly never a card-carrying party member[*]—even when he regarded himself as a Young Communist League worker at Yale, after being introduced to politics by Paul Jarrico—Endfield also developed a grim analysis of human nature early on which informs all his subsequent work.)

Of course this Marxism doesn't make all of Endfield's films procommunist by any means. The eerie plot of THE MASTER PLAN (credited pseudonymously to Hugh Raker for script and direction)—involving a convalescent American major (Wayne Morris) with a head wound, stationed in Germany to plug an intelligence leak, being hypnotized by communists to microfilm secret documents—postulates a cold war universe every bit as hysterical as the parodic version in THE MANCHURIAN CANDIDATE. On the other hand, this remarkable film—which Endfield told me he had practically no memory of making—doesn't leave us with much confidence in the capitalist world, either. Though the invisible communist villains are certainly ruthless, the American major's

---

[*] This fact is disputed by Pierre Rissient, one of Endfield's oldest friends—and probably the individual most responsible for his critical discovery. [November 1996]

superior (Norman Wooland), an English colonel, isn't exactly endearing. When the movie starts we assume that the major's the hero; gradually the colonel assumes this role instead, but so many characters are potential spies that any security defined according to nationality eventually becomes undermined. (The German setting may even make us confuse the communists with Nazis.) When one of the major characters is finally unveiled as a spy, Endfield wastes no time on the person's motivations. Rather he leaves us with a queasy sense that this is a crazed militarized culture in which everyone is a dupe, a spy, a paranoid schizophrenic, or some diseased combination of same.

Indeed, working almost exclusively in thrillers and adventure stories, Endfield shows relatively little patience with certain generic staples widely believed to be obligatory: heroes and villains (at least as they're usually positioned and defined), sympathetic identification figures, and psychological motivations, all three of which tend to be mutually dependent. But all these apparent shortcomings work in his favor as a social analyst by objectifying the social terrains on which his plots unfold.

I'm not trying to idealize his approach. It's likely that his distance from conventional models isn't always intentional and questionable whether his powers as a social critic in the United States ever became fully translated into an English context. THE LIMPING MAN, THE MASTER PLAN, and IMPULSE (1955), three of his earliest English features, all have American protagonists (Lloyd Bridges, Wayne Morris, and Arthur Kennedy, respectively) who drift through complex intrigues rather like sleepwalkers, and CHILD IN THE HOUSE (1956) has its dreamy drifts as well. (It was Endfield's second picture with English child actress Mandy Miller, and its shooting was briefly watched by Charlie Chaplin, who complimented Endfield on his efficient direction of her.) HELL DRIVERS is an effective American-style proletarian thriller (with a few nods to THE WAGES OF FEAR), and was successful enough to lead to a long-term association with Stanley Baker (with whom Endfield formed a production company), but how much it has to say about English life is debatable; and the gravitation of the later work toward "international" social allegory in JET STORM and SANDS OF THE KALAHARI further suggests a loss of specificity that came with exile.

The strained resolutions of THE UNDERWORLD STORY and THE LIMPING MAN are flawed by any standards. In the first, a corrupt journalist (Dan Duryea) undergoes a sudden moral transformation, thereby earning the love of Gale Storm, the belated mantle of a conventional hero, and a formulaic happy ending, all within a matter of minutes. In the second, a mystery plot about a war veteran (Bridges) returning to London is suddenly dissipated for one of those silly "it was all a dream" denouements. But in both cases these flaws contribute to a sense of overall disassociation that bolsters our analytical relation to the events while increasing their power to disturb. Not knowing precisely how we stand in relation to other characters—Howard da Silva's frighteningly cheerful and honest hood in THE UNDERWORLD STORY, or a "serious" Scotland Yard inspector who habitually leers at women in THE LIMPING MAN—we have to fall back uneasily on our own resources.

The absence of any hero in THE SOUND OF FURY proves to be even more purposeful—radically shifting our focus two-thirds of the way through from working-class characters to wealthy characters without losing any thematic or ethical focus. The plot derives from a true incident as filtered through a novel: in 1933, two men were arrested in San Jose, California, for kidnapping and murdering a wealthy man named Brooke Hart; after confessing, they were lynched by the townspeople. This became the basis for Jo Pagano's novel *The Condemned*, which Pagano adapted for THE SOUND OF FURY. Endfield was hired for this independent production as a replacement director, and when he objected to Pagano focusing on an Italian professor as a mouthpiece for his ideas and not placing more emphasis on the working-class victims, Pagano angrily left the project. After Endfield rewrote the first part of the script, producer Robert Stillman convinced Pagano to accept the changes and return to work under Endfield's supervision. Much of the $500,000 picture was shot in Phoenix, Arizona; when several thousand people gathered to watch the lynching being filmed, Endfield improvised ways of using them as extras.

After Endfield made his final cut, Stillman insisted on restoring some of the Italian professor's pontifications. The film opened in December 1950, at the height of the Korean War. (Endfield to Howie Movshovitz: "I started going to cinemas where it was playing, and the manager of one of them told me, 'I never have a performance when I don't get at least two or three people coming around to tell me it's a disgrace to run this kind of anti-American picture.' ") After a private screening that he set up himself, Endfield told me he recalled an upset Joseph Cotten saying to him, " 'Cy, we've both grown up in the same country, but the America *you* know is not the America *I* know.' "

Such wartime sentiments are understandable given the film's potent negativity, but the highly distanced approach taken by Endfield toward all his characters shouldn't be confused with cynicism. Cynicism hardly describes the approach to the jobless veteran (Frank Lovejoy) we're introduced to at the film's beginning, who falls into crime because he can't bear his wife and son having to live without luxuries—and then becomes so guilt-ridden about a kidnapping and murder carried out with his psychopathic partner (Lloyd Bridges) that he blurts out a confession to a hapless manicurist he's dating. Though she may be pathetic and even grotesque, she's hardly bad or selfish either; the dry treatment she's accorded might border on cruelty, but it's far from cynical.

The same could be said of the treatment of both the Zulus and the British soldiers in ZULU—a celebration of courage and nobility on both sides of the conflict—although here, for once, the lack of psychology limits the film's social vision. An epic account of an attack by 4,000 Zulu warriors on a garrison of 104 British soldiers in Natal, South Africa, in 1879 (very persuasively shown and remarkably choreographed, although Endfield never used more than 250 Zulu extras, usually 150), its lack of any explanation for the siege may add to the film's purity as action spectacle, but it also limits our understanding of any historical and social context.*

This isn't to say that these and other Endfield pictures aren't full of cynics and creeps, viewed moreover with a complete lack of sentimentality. Indeed, it might be argued that the world in most Endfield films tends to be divided between victims and predators, though neither category winds up satisfactorily fulfilling the usual parts played by heroes and villains. Society in all of Endfield's best films—and even in a few of his worst (like TARZAN'S SAVAGE FURY)—proves to be so profoundly out of joint that getting rid of a few bad apples scarcely solves a thing. Far from defeatist, his searing social allegories are all about explicitly man-made horrors, which implicitly means they can be unmade or remade.

Take the cynic in SANDS OF THE KALAHARI, whose viewpoint Endfield makes clear is far from his own. This rifle-toting American thug (Stuart Whitman)—an allegorical cold warrior itching to colonize everything in sight—survives a plane crash in the African desert, then devotes himself to shooting baboons and some of his European companions on the theory that they're competitors for food and water who'd do the same thing to him if they had half a chance. By the end he's become Lord of the Baboons, a job for which he seems ideally suited.

A pronounced feeling for abstraction in relation to both physical space (aural as well as visual) and social milieu can be felt throughout Endfield's work. There are haunting scenes in both THE SOUND OF FURY and THE LIMPING MAN in which families are seated in dark living rooms watching TV shows whose violence we perceive only through their staccato sound effects. No less suggestive is the scene in THE SOUND OF FURY when the veteran first meets the manicurist: the emotional distance between these shy strangers is brutally conveyed by the smooching of the other couple they're with, standing directly between them at screen center.

The same visual irony turns up in JET STORM (1959). An explosives expert (Richard Attenborough) driven mad by the hit-and-run death of his little girl boards the same flight as the hit-and-run driver and secretly plants a time bomb somewhere on the plane. After we're treated to a caustic survey of possible human responses to this crisis, and all the adults on board have exhausted their means of persuading the madman to report the bomb's whereabouts, an eight-year-old boy is enlisted to try. At a climactic moment, Endfield frames a loosely hanging phone receiver in the foreground directly be-

---

* To get such an understanding, we have to turn to Endfield's best-selling 1979 novel, *Zulu Dawn* (nearly 250,000 copies sold in England)—a much better realization of his intentions than the eponymous prequel directed by Douglas Hickox, released the same year, which he coscripted.

tween these estranged characters, parodying the very fact of their noncommu-
nication with a symbol of communication that practically dwarfs them both.
It's a representative image of Endfield's blighted, angry, and absurdist but far
from hopeless universe, where the social lucidity of what we see usually becomes the only form of hope and redemption in sight.

■

During the couple of days (February 11–12, 1993) I spent with Endfield—
most of them devoted to conversation and looking at copies on video of CHILD
IN THE HOUSE and SEA FURY—I sensed that he felt some satisfaction in finally
getting some recognition as a director after many years of neglect. (Perhaps
the first sign of this came when an old friend from high school sent him a
clipping that placed UNDERWORLD STORY and TRY AND GET ME at the top of a
list of recent best-selling black-and-white movies on video.) But at the same
time, he was reluctant to claim too much for many of his pictures, half-
implying that I may have overrated some of them, like JET STORM, that he saw
strictly as meat-and-potato operations. He wasn't eager to talk much about the
Joe Palooka pictures (which he barely remembered, and which I haven't seen
myself since early childhood), and, among other films of his I wasn't conver-
sant with, was fairly dismissive about his first English feature, COLONEL
MARCH INVESTIGATES (1953), made up of three pilot episodes for a TV series
with Boris Karloff called *The Department of Queer Complaints,* whose scripts
(by Sidney Buchman) he was initially hired to rewrite, and HIDE AND SEEK
(1963), which he called "just a utility picture." By contrast, he wanted me to
see THE SECRET (his first color film, 1955)* and UNIVERSAL SOLDIER (his last
picture, 1971), a movie about mercenaries in which he appears as an actor
(not a picture that has generally been well received even by his fans), neither
of which I've been able to track down.†

Among those films I *had* seen, he was especially scornful of TARZAN'S
SAVAGE FURY (1952), his last American feature, describing it as a film with
impossible production conditions that his agent had talked him into doing.
Regarding many of his English pictures, his memory often focused on the
actors originally cast for certain parts: Richard Conte in the part played by
Arthur Kennedy in IMPULSE, Robert Ryan in the part played by Jack Hawkins
in ZULU (a character Endfield saw as embodying the worst side of colonial-
ism), Richard Burton and Elizabeth Taylor (at the height of their fame) as the

---

* About a year after THE SECRET was released, Endfield adapted and directed it for the London
stage. The production was not a success—unlike his stage version of *Come Blow Your Horn* in
the early 60s, which ran for two years in the West End.

† Since writing the above, I've been able, thanks to the generosity of film scholar David
Thompson, to see on video UNIVERSAL SOLDIER—a rather dated effort, alas, whose interest mainly
resides in its period flavor and in Endfield's cameo as a landlord with a background identical to
his own. [November 1996]

leads of SANDS OF THE KALAHARI (with Burton eventually replaced by George Peppard, who quit after a day's shooting, to be replaced by Stuart Whitman), Orson Welles for the part in DE SADE (1969) eventually taken by John Huston. (After directing that picture for three or four weeks, including most or all of the film's early scenes, Endfield wound up with a "subclinical virus" that left him immobilized for months in a Berlin hospital; Roger Corman and Gordon Hessler directed the rest.)

What did he take some pride in? What he called his "structuralist" sense of craft in working on scripts: the final sequence of THE SOUND OF FURY (minus the voice-overs); the fact that on MYSTERIOUS ISLAND, he was the first director ever to get special effects wizard Ray Harryhausen to agree to a few changes in his production drawings, and that this "Dynamation" special was the top grosser in England in 1961; the exhaustive, multifaceted research (consuming three quarters of a year) that went into ZULU, leading to Endfield's long-term friendship with Chief Gatsha Buthelezi, the great-grandson of the Zulu king depicted in the film, who played his own great-grandfather in the movie. (The novel *Zulu Dawn* is dedicated to him.) Again on ZULU, Endfield took pride in the fact that he was willing to spend four years shopping his script around until he found all the right conditions for making it the way he wanted to, and the fact that he knew how to compose the shots in the film for 70-millimeter VistaVision.

He didn't want to take much credit for choosing exile over giving names during the blacklist; as he put it to Howie Movshovitz, "I don't feel heroic about it. I didn't have heroic thoughts." But even though he had abandoned his Marxist activism and repudiated Stalinism many years before, it's clear that his social conscience remained intact—not only when he chose exile over betrayal but also when he made THE SOUND OF FURY two years earlier.

Where in American cinema can one go for more succinct expressions of everyday blue-collar despair—the agony of seeing even modest dreams gallop away at high speed—than the successive homecomings of Howard Tyler (Frank Lovejoy) in THE SOUND OF FURY? Each of these supposedly humdrum events is composed as a discrete, concentrated catalog of sensual and emotional facts, from the cacophony of kids scuffling around a wire fence to the pathos of a family radio (perceived in relation to a next-door neighbor's TV) to the slow rhythmic snapping of a window blind in the night breeze across from Tyler's sleeping wife. If the beautiful and disquieting cinema of Cyril Raker Endfield describes a poetry of thwarted ambitions, dark social insights, and awesomely orchestrated spectacle designed to drive us out of our cocoons, this is surely a good place to start.

—Film Comment, November–December
1993; revised December 1995

It seems central rather than incidental to the art and intelligence of Chris Marker that he studiously avoids the credit, "Directed by . . ." A globe-trotting French filmmaker whose only work of pure fiction with actors is a classic s-f short consisting almost exclusively of still photographs (LA JETÉE, 1962), he appears to avoid obvious fiction only in the sense that he finds actuality more than enough grist for the endlessly turning mill of his irony and imagination.

It's tempting to speculate about whom or what he might identify as the "director" of such Marker masterpieces as SANS SOLEIL (1982) or THE LAST BOLSHEVIK (1993). "The twentieth century" seems a likely guess, for part of the meaning in both these alluring works of wisdom is the ambiguity of causes, of agency, of direction itself, in the dreams and nightmares of contemporary history—the issue of who is doing what to whom. Brilliant works of *in*direction, they employ narration written by Marker but spoken by someone else, as if the only route to truth was through intermediaries and filters. (To complicate matters further, in SANS SOLEIL the narration is delivered by a woman, recounting letters sent to her by a man.) In the graceful English versions of these works, the translation provides another form of mediation, as do the various transfers between film and video within each work. SANS SOLEIL is a film and THE LAST BOLSHEVIK is a video, but both make plentiful use of both media. Indeed, the incredibly rich palette of textures, lights, and colors Marker discovers in video in THE LAST BOLSHEVIK (playing this weekend and next at the Film Center) sets new standards for the medium's beauty and expressiveness.

Born Christian François Bouche-Villeneuve in France in 1921, Marker spent his early twenties as a resistance fighter and as a parachutist in the U.S. Army. Prior to making his first film in 1952, he was a published novelist, poet, and journalist, as well as a playwright, though thanks mainly to his studied elusiveness—including his avoidance of photographs and interviews—it's difficult to learn any particulars about this work today. (He has also worked as an editor for the prestigious literary publisher Éditions du Seuil, which brought him in contact with other Left Bank filmmakers who've been his contemporaries, friends, and sometime collaborators, such as Alain Resnais, Agnes Varda, Jacques Demy, and William Klein.)

Surely the most pertinent aspect of this background is that Marker was an accomplished writer before he became a filmmaker—and that he remains a writer in his films. For writer Phillip Lopate, a specialist in the personal essay who also happens to be a movie buff, Marker is "the one great cine-essayist in film history," and it's easy to see why: among other things, Marker "has the essayist's aphoristic gift, which enables him to assert a collective historical persona, a first-person plural, even when the first-person singular is held in abeyance. Finally, he has the essayist's impulse to tell the truth: not always a comfortable attribute for an engagé artist."

There's a wonderful French expression with no easy English equivalent, *ésprit de l'escalier,* and it's profoundly a writer's dilemma: the experience of thinking of something to say after the perfect moment to say it has passed. (The expression translates literally as "staircase wit" or "after wit"—the kind of wit that comes to mind as one is leaving, heading down the stairs.) Marker's artistic persona in his essay films is typically split between his identity as a spontaneous, roving cameraman and his identity as a writer thinking and reflecting much later about what he's shot. His essay films can be seen as waking reveries that finally permit him to join raw initial impressions with studied afterthoughts in an ideal sort of congruence—a marriage made in heaven, so to speak. This utopian control over the flow of time permits all sorts of *mots justes* that would never occur to anyone on the spot. I've never seen SI J'AVAIS QUATRE DROMADAIRES—Marker's 1966 feature consisting of still photographs taken in twenty-six countries over ten years, accompanied by three voices representing the photographer and two of his friends—but it's hard to forget his surreal evocation of a 1959 U.S. exposition in Moscow that figures in the narration: "Abraham Lincoln married Marilyn Monroe and they had lots of little refrigerators." (This comes from *Commentaires,* a two-volume collection of Marker's illustrated film commentaries published by Seuil during the 60s, including commentaries for two imaginary documentaries about the United Sates and Mexico he never got around to making.)

In a tradition of guarded intimacy that seems classically French, the province of writers ranging from Proust to Barthes, Marker develops a relationship with his audience that is at once confessional and secretive: we are made to feel simultaneously that we know him well and that we don't know him at all. Not surprisingly, a similar relationship develops between us and the central figure of THE LAST BOLSHEVIK, the Soviet filmmaker Alexander Medvedkin (1900–1989), whom Marker clearly regards as a friend and mentor. The video, divided into two parts—"A Kingdom of Shadows" and "Shadows of a Kingdom"—takes the form of six letters addressed to Medvedkin posthumously interlaced with Medvedkin himself speaking in interviews. The portrait of the Russian filmmaker that emerges is novelistic in its gaps and ambiguities rather than masked or coy, as Marker's self-representations sometimes appear to be.

A superficial reading of this video—a characteristic example is in the September 1993 issue of *Sight and Sound,* the English film magazine—would be to describe it as a simple documentary about Medvedkin, a neglected figure in the Soviet Union and elsewhere. Certainly it is that, though this doesn't exhaust its ambitions or achievements. More profoundly, it's a contentious essay on the history of Soviet cinema and the Soviet Union itself; beyond that, it's a multifaceted self-portrait and autocritique by Marker of what it has meant to be a committed leftist for most of this century. The subject of THE LAST BOLSHEVIK is what it meant to be a communist—and what it means to think about communism today.

But it isn't enough to say that this video—whose French version is entitled LE TOMBEAU D'ALEXANDRE (Alexander's Tomb)—is about the taste of ashes in Marker's mouth, though that is part of its resonance. On some level, when Marker is asking who Medvedkin was, what happened to him, and how we can judge him today, he is asking the same questions about the left in general and himself in particular. Some of these questions, to be sure, have to be read between the lines. It helps if one knows that when Marker first discovered Medvedkin's work, just before May 1968, a watershed in French utopian thinking, he was part of a French filmmaking collective called SLON, or Societé de Lancement des Oeuvres Nouvelles (Society for Launching New Works), which he founded in 1966 and which subsequently adopted the name Groupe Medvedkine. This appropriation of the name of the one Soviet filmmaker who, as Marker expressed it, put "the camera in the hands of the people," led to SLON distributing Medvedkin's most famous feature, HAPPINESS, in France in 1971 and making a half-hour short, THE TRAIN THAT NEVER STOPS, to introduce it. (Much of this short consists of an interview with Medvedkin, and many excerpts from it are in THE LAST BOLSHEVIK.) Yet significantly, SLON is not mentioned once in the video, and use of first-person plural is kept to an absolute minimum. By implicitly reducing his former collective to "I" much of the time, Marker seems to be dismissing aspects of his own activities, and the dark implications of this dismissal are as disturbing in a way as the doubts he sows about the grotesque, perhaps obligatory compromises of Medvedkin and some of his colleagues during the Stalinist period.

Above all, like SANS SOLEIL, THE LAST BOLSHEVIK is a reflection on what it's like being on this planet at this particular moment—a reflection that's both poetic and practical, passionate and considered. One of the key dilemmas of living in the 90s is the task of trying to distinguish information from advertising in all walks of life, yet that has been a central problem in Soviet art for most of this century, as Marker shows here. Most of what we remember about POTEMKIN and regard as history, from the shooting of sailors under a tarpaulin to the Odessa Steps massacre, is the invention of Sergei Eisenstein, and some of the most famous photographs used to represent and "authenticate" the Russian Revolution prove to be restagings. As George Steiner puts it in the video's opening epigraph, "It is not the literal past that rules us: it is images of the past." In fact, THE LAST BOLSHEVIK is not so much ruled as haunted by images of the past.

■

Early on in the video we see Medvedkin in a 1984 interview saying, "I intend to go on living as long as possible. I don't mean until the twenty-first century, but another five years would be nice." "And five years later you died," the narrator (Michael Pennington) remarks—"the first five-year plan that ever worked."

One five-year plan of my own has been an ongoing effort to persuade the Film Center or Facets Multimedia to book an English subtitled print of Lev Kuleshov's THE GREAT CONSOLER (1933) from the British Film Institute in London—a mind-boggling feature about O. Henry, in prison for embezzlement, writing a story about safecracker Jimmy Valentine that later radicalizes a shop girl. It's long been my suspicion that the most exciting wave in Soviet cinema came not during the 20s, as is generally believed, but in the early 30s, before the Stalinist crackdowns, when most of the major directors were making their early talkies: Vertov (ENTHUSIASM), Dovzhenko (IVAN and AEROGRAD), Pudovkin (DESERTER), Kuleshov (THE GREAT CONSOLER), and others. For a brief period, before the tenets of socialist realism took hold, communist idealism and radically innovative art were allowed to rub shoulders, and in some ways we still haven't begun to deal with the dazzling results (alas, many of the best of these films are still virtually unknown in the West).

Medvedkin's HAPPINESS—which comes at the tail end of this period (1935), the last silent Soviet picture—clearly belongs to this ferment. It's a pity the Film Center isn't showing it in conjunction with THE LAST BOLSHEVIK, but fortunately this wild hour-long comedy, excerpts of which are seen in THE LAST BOLSHEVIK, is available on video from Kino International and a few specialized rental outlets, such as Facets Multimedia. Surrealist satire and slapstick with a hilarious hick hero, it starts off with peasants looking through a knothole in a fence at the easy life of a czar—fruit dumplings leap off a plate and dive into his mouth. Things only get goofier and more outrageous after that: nuns are depicted erotically, priests hysterically wrestle one another for rubles, a tractor runs amok, an entire house creeps like a centipede across a landscape. When the hero, repeatedly foiled in his quest for simple happiness, decides to commit suicide and starts building his own coffin, the cossacks are indignant: "Who permitted you to die on your own? . . . Who authorized you to take death without leave?" Later a woman tries repeatedly to hang herself from a windmill, and the results are even more grotesque.

HAPPINESS gives us a fair sample of Medvedkin's gifts as a director, and Marker gives us clips from many of his other surviving works, including some striking camp extravaganzas that followed HAPPINESS. (Most memorable are NEW MOSCOW—a sound comedy of the Stalinist era with Busby Berkeley-like sets, a magical fireworks display, and at least one creeping skyscraper—and a subsequent rural musical featuring cows in boots.)

But Medvedkin's importance is only marginally connected with the on-screen evidence, which may help to account for why his name is missing from most movie reference books. His most important work—done just before he made HAPPINESS and grounded in burlesque performances he staged as an officer during the Civil War in which actors dressed up as horses to protest the mistreatment of animals—was running an unpublicized revolutionary project known as the "film train." This train—three railway cars that housed a sizable film crew and allowed them to store equipment and process, edit, and screen movies—traveled back and forth across Russia, making silent comedy shorts with various peasant collectives that were designed to address their particular problems. The film train made as many as seventy-two shorts in a single year, none of which was believed to have survived. However, nine of them were recently discovered, and we're treated to samples in THE LAST BOLSHEVIK.

But the important thing about the film train as a concept isn't so much what it yields today in terms of films as what it signified then. As Marker puts it, citing a Chinese parable, "Give a man a fish and you feed him for one day. Teach him how to fish and you feed him for life. . . . You [i.e., Medvedkin] wouldn't give people films, you'd give them cinema."

By the same token, one might say that what Marker gives us is neither a video nor a film, but an exciting new means of expression—the beginning of a dialogue and discussion that flies in the face of the received wisdom that we can now safely put the twentieth century behind us. After the glibness, the dullness, the despair we hear about the death of communism, of utopia, of idealism just about everywhere we turn, in the pages of the *Nation* as well as the *National Review,* Marker reminds us, even in his own disillusionment and bitter irony, that we're much too eager to bury a history and a legacy we never really understood in the first place. Communism is over? Very well then: let's take a good, hard look at what we've decided to dismiss. And weep, as Medvedkin once did when he found he could put two pieces of film together and have it mean something. "Nowadays," Marker reminds us, "television floods the whole world with senseless images and nobody cries."

—Chicago *Reader,* January 21, 1994

Index

NATIONAL UNIVERSITY
LIBRARY SACRAMENTO

Permissions

"Say the Right Thing," "Polanski and the American Experiment," "His Mistress's Voice," "Seen and Unseen Encounters," "Lies of the Mind," "On LATCHO DROM," "Missing the Target," "Spielberg's Gentiles," "A Perversion of the Past," "Vietnam, the Theme Park," "Sexual Discourse," "Hollywood Radical," "ACE VENTURA Reconsidered," "The World According to Harvey and Bob," "Stupidity as Redemption," "Allusion Profusion," "No Stars, a Must-See," "The Functions of a Disease," "England on the Inside," "The Significance of Sniggering," "Tribal Trouble," "Us and Them," "Feudal Attraction," "The Vision of the Conquered," "Searching for Taiwan," "Inner Space," "Tribal Scars," "His Twentieth Century," and "On Second Thoughts" were originally published in the Chicago *Reader.* Copyright © 1988, 1989, 1990, 1991, 1992, 1993, 1994, 1995 by Chicago Reader, Inc.

Parts of "Entertainment as Oppression" were originally published in the Chicago *Reader* and *Sight and Sound* (as "Are You Having Fun?").

Parts of "Pages from the Endfield File" were originally published in the Chicago *Reader* and *Film Comment.*

"Interruption as Style," "The Solitary Pleasures of STAR WARS," "Jack Reed's Christmas Puppy," "Circle of Pain," "The Rattle of Armor, the Softness of Flesh," "Jean Eustache's LA MAMAN ET LA PUTAIN," and "Film Writing Degree Zero" were originally published in *Sight and Sound.*

"Altman and the Spirit of Improvisation" was originally published in *Monthly Film Bulletin* as a review of CALIFORNIA SPLIT.

"Tati's Democracy," "The Problem with Poetry," and "The Seven ARKADINS" were originally published in *Film Comment.* The article "Tati's Democracy" is copyright © 1973 by Film Comment Publishing Corporation. Reprinted by permission of the Film Society of Lincoln Center.

Portions of "Four Books on the Hollywood Musical" originally appeared, in different form, in *Film Quarterly* vol. 35, no. 4, pp. 34–36. Copyright © 1982 by the Regents of the University of California; permission granted.

"TIH MINH, OUT 1: On the Nonreception of Two French Serials" was originally published in *The Velvet Light Trap* volume 37, and is reprinted here, in expanded and revised form, by permission of University of Texas Press.

Compositor:	Maple-Vail Book Manufacturing Group
Text:	10/12 Times Roman
Display:	Runic
Printer and Binder:	Maple-Vail Book Manufacturing Group